Parenting Experts

Parenting Experts

THEIR ADVICE, THE RESEARCH, AND GETTING IT RIGHT

Jane L. Rankin

Westport, Connecticut
London

Library of Congress Cataloging-in-Publication Data

Rankin, Jane L.
   Parenting experts : their advice, the research, and getting it right / Jane L. Rankin.
     p.   cm.
   Includes bibliographical references and index.
   ISBN 0–275–97678–5 (alk. paper)
   1. Parenting. 2. Child rearing. 3. Discipline of children. I. Title.
HQ755.8.R365 2005
649'.1–dc22   2005018638

British Library Cataloguing in Publication Data is available.

Copyright © 2005 by Jane L. Rankin

All rights reserved. No portion of this book may be
reproduced, by any process or technique, without the
express written consent of the publisher.

Library of Congress Catalog Card Number: 2005018638
ISBN: 0–275–97678–5

First published in 2005

Praeger Publishers, 88 Post Road West, Westport, CT 06881
An imprint of Greenwood Publishing Group, Inc.
www.praeger.com

Printed in the United States of America

The paper used in this book complies with the
Permanent Paper Standard issued by the National
Information Standards Organization (Z39.48–1984).

10 9 8 7 6 5 4 3 2 1

Copyright Acknowledgments

The author and publisher gratefully acknowledge permission for the use of the following material:

From CHILDREN FIRST by Penelope Leach, copyright © 1994 by Penelope Leach. Used by permission of Alfred A. Knopf, a division of Random House, Inc.

Material from John Rosemond's Web site: www.rosemond.com used with permission.

From TOUCHPOINTS by T. BERRY BRAZELTON. Copyright © 1994 by T. Berry Brazelton. Reprinted by permission of Perseus Books PLC, a member of Perseus Books, L.L.C.

From TOUCHPOINTS: YOUR CHILD'S EMOTIONAL AND BEHAVIORAL DEVELOPMENT by T. Berry Brazelton (Addison-Wesley 1992, Viking Books 1993, Penguin Books 1995). Copyright © T. Berry Brazelton, 1992. Reproduced by permission of Penguin Books Ltd.

From THE IRREDUCIBLE NEEDS OF CHILDREN by T. Berry Brazelton. Copyright © 2000 by T. Berry Brazelton and Stanley Greenspan. Reprinted by permission of Perseus Books PLC, a member of Perseus Books, L.L.C.

From TO LISTEN TO A CHILD: UNDERSTANDING THE NORMAL PROBLEMS OF GROWING UP by T. Berry Brazelton. Copyright 1984 by T. Berry Brazelton. Reprinted by permission of Perseus Books PLC, a member of Perseus Books, L.L.C.

From TOUCHPOINTS THREE TO SIX: YOUR CHILD'S EMOTIONAL AND BEHAVIORAL DEVELOPMENT by T. Berry Brazelton and J.D. Sparrow. Copyright 2001 by T. Berry Brazelton and J.D. Sparrow. Reprinted by permission of Perseus Books PLC, a member of Perseus Books, L.L.C.

Excerpts from James C. Dobson, *The New Dare to Discipline* (Tyndale, 1992). Reprinted with permission.

Excerpts from James C. Dobson, *Dr. Dobson Answers Your Questions about Raising Children* (Tyndale, 1982). Reprinted with permission.

Excerpts from James C. Dobson, *Preparing for Adolescence* (Tyndale, 1992). Reprinted with permission.

Excerpts from James C. Dobson, *Dare to Discipline* (Tyndale, 1970). Reprinted with permission.

Excerpts from Penelope Leach, *Your Growing Child: From Babyhood through Adolescence* (New York: Alfred A. Knopf, 1989). Reprinted with permission.

Reprinted with the permission of Pocket Books, a division of Simon & Schuster Adult Publishing Group from Dr. Spock's *Baby and Child Care* by Benjamin Spock, M.D., and Stephen J. Parker, M.D. Copyright © 1945, 1946, © 1957, 1968, 1976, 1985, 1992 by Benjamin Spock, M.D. Copyright © renewed 1973, 1974, 1985, 1996 by Benjamin Spock, M.D. Revised and updated material copyright © 1998 by The Benjamin Spock Trust.

Reprinted with the permission of Pocket Books, a division of Simon & Schuster Adult Publishing Group from Dr. Spock's *Baby and Child Care* by Benjamin Spock, M.D., and Michael B. Rothenberg, M.D. Copyright © 1945, 1946, © 1957, 1968, 1976, 1985, 1992 by Benjamin Spock, M.D.

Reprinted with the permission of Simon & Schuster Adult Publishing Group from *A Teenager's Guide to Life and Love* by Benjamin Spock, M.D. Copyright © 1998 by Mary Morgan.

Excerpts from YOUR BABY AND CHILD by Penelope Leach (Dorling Kindersley 2003), text copyright © 2003 Penelope Leach, copyright © 2003, Dorling Kindersley. Pp.: 113, 116, 123, 144, 145, 218, 316, 318, 350, 351, 352, 354, 355, 520, 521, 522, 677, 678. Reproduced by permission of Penguin Books Ltd.

From *A Better World for Our Children* by Benjamin Spock, M.D. Copyright © 1994 by Benjamin M. Spock, M.D. Reprinted with permission of Lescher & Lescher, Ltd. All rights reserved.

Every reasonable effort has been made to trace the owners of copyright materials in this book, but in some instances this has proven impossible. The author and publisher will be glad to receive information leading to more complete acknowledgments in subsequent printings of the book and in the meantime extend their apologies for any omissions.

CONTENTS

PREFACE

A SOCIAL WORKER IS called to the apartment of young parents with a 6-week-old baby. A neighbor has heard the baby crying for hours at a time, interspersed by harsh words between the parents. The mother seems quite depressed and says, "You know, sometimes I just wish that I could put the baby down and close the door to her room and let her cry it out, but this book I read says she'll feel abandoned and that'll make it worse. Is that true? Why doesn't she stop crying?"

A busy pediatrician is confronted by the mother of a 2½-year-old. "My husband and I really think he should be toilet trained by now. He just seems really stubborn about it and we're getting very frustrated with him. The column that I read in the paper says that you should start training at age two and that to wait until three is an insult to a child's intelligence. Can you tell us how to get him trained quickly? I read that it should only take a week, but it's not working, so what am I doing wrong? Is he going to be this slow at everything?"

At parent–teacher conferences, a teacher is asked by parents of an 8-year-old, "What do you think about children watching TV? A book we're reading says that TV makes kids violent, but is that really right? Somebody else we read said that TV reduces kids' creativity. If it reduces creativity, why do you show videos at school and let the kids play computer games like Oregon Trail?"

A high school guidance counselor gets a call from the irate father of a 14-year-old. "I don't know what's going on at your school. My daughter tells me that yesterday they practiced putting a condom on a banana in health class. She's way too young to be thinking about having sex. Aren't you aware that sex education in the schools just increases the chances that kids will start having sex? Is that what you want?"

At a bookstore in the mall, a parent scans the titles in two 8-foot shelves filled floor to ceiling with books and videos on parenting. Who should he trust? Do they really know what they are talking about? Will these people really be able to answer the question he came here for, and will they give good advice?

Parents get information from many sources, including those books and videos that they buy at the mall. Some of it is inaccurate and directly at odds with the training of those professionals who work with them. This book is an analysis for parents, clinicians, teachers, counselors, and other family professionals of the advice that parents get from five of the best-known parenting experts: Benjamin Spock, T. Berry Brazelton, James Dobson, Penelope Leach, and John Rosemond. It compares their advice on key topics with research and published "best practice" standards in those areas. Its aim is to arm parents and practitioners not only with the diverse perspectives of the experts on key topics, but also with information about the appropriateness and accuracy of the advice that the experts provide. As such it is an attempt to bridge the gap between "this magazine article I read" and the immense and largely inaccessible academic literature on child development.

This book is certainly not the last word on what parents should do, but it is my hope that it will help professionals as they help parents meet the daunting responsibilities of raising a family. It also should be a useful resource for parents and grandparents—at least for those who try to make use of the often conflicting advice that is available in the popular media. As a parent, I know that there is a tremendous gulf between reading about parenting and practicing it; the reading is the least of it. As a developmental psychologist, however, I continue to see the value of studying, sharing, and applying the knowledge gained from research and clinical practice to the problems of everyday life. This book is offered in that spirit, and with great respect for the many parents and professionals who work to improve the lives of children.

ACKNOWLEDGMENTS

LIKE PARENTING, WRITING a book is much easier when you have supportive people around you, and I have been blessed with exceptional colleagues who have seen me through the process. Staff at Cowles Library at Drake University went far beyond the standards of good librarianship to assist me. Claudia Frazer, Diane Collett, Mary Beveridge, Teri Koch, Liga Briedis, Bruce Gilbert, and the late Bill Stoppel provided both valuable advice and superb technical assistance. Special thanks to Joan Anderson, staff assistant par excellence, Psychology Department chair Steven Faux, Humanities Center Director Bill Lewis, and former Dean of Arts and Sciences Myron A. Marty, all of Drake University, for their assistance and their personal examples of getting it right. The Drake University Humanities Center was an early supporter of this project.

I am extremely grateful for the support provided by Dean Barbara O'Keefe of the School of Communication at Northwestern University, who made it possible for me to complete the book, and to Northwestern University for welcoming me into its community.

To the thousands of researchers and clinicians whose work I have cited, I extend my appreciation for their dedication to improving the lives of children and their families. I am especially indebted to those who read chapters and thereby substantially improved this book: George Holden, K. Alison Clarke-Stewart, Edward Christophersen, and Robert Larzelere. I take responsibility for any remaining errors and welcome feedback from readers.

My children David and Katie both inspired and endured the book as it spanned the years of their adolescence, and I have appreciated their encouragement, their patience, and their good humor through it all. Finally, I am grateful most of all to Robert Hariman for his unwavering support of this project, his wisdom and generosity, and his sustaining love through all the years. This book is dedicated to him.

CHAPTER 1
INTRODUCTION

A BABY IS BORN. Two individuals become parents, whether or not they are prepared for nurturing the new life in front of them. As they look down on their newborn, full of joy and relief at their child's safe arrival, sooner or later the question creeps into their minds, "Okay, *now* what do we do?" Other questions follow in rapid succession: How important is breast-feeding to my baby's well-being? Should one of us stay home and care for our baby or find someone else to do it, perhaps somewhere else? How should we discipline our child? When and how should a child be toilet trained? How can we teach our child to get along with others and to care, share, and help when needed? How can we promote school achievement? How can we keep our child off drugs and out of trouble? And perhaps the biggest questions of all: What can we do as parents that will lead to the best possible outcome for our child? When can we make a difference? How are we supposed to know what to do before it is too late?

Parents have their own ideas about parenting, of course, yet they cannot help but feel challenged as they adjust to a child whose capabilities expand rapidly and whose future is unknown. The enormous investment of time, energy, money, and emotional resources it takes to be an effective parent helps motivate their search for information. Their own parents serve as models (both positive and negative) and sources of advice (sometimes contradictory), but many of the decisions faced by contemporary parents are not ones that their parents faced—for example, decisions about child care and interactive computer and video games. No wonder that parenting creates a continual need for information, expertise, and reassurance.

Recent decades have seen a burst of media publications related to parenting. As one book editor remarked, "the baby market is huge, and that will always be so. . . . When you're a new mom and you don't know what to do, you don't want to bother your doctor with every one of the hundreds of questions that crosses your mind a day. You can ask your mom, but you're sure things have changed" (Dunnewind, 2003). Sydney Minor, executive editor of Simon & Schuster's trade paperback book titles, notes the increase in the number of parenting books sold: "In the past 20 years this category has grown enormously, as the baby boomers have had kids and are looking for advice" (Frederick, 1998). The percentage of editorial space devoted to child rearing has been increasing in women's magazines, the children and family "beat" is becoming a regular assignment for newspaper reporters, and there has been a boom in parenting magazines. Supermarket giveaway newspapers and magazines on parenting can now be found in most large and midsize cities (Simpson, 1997). New reality TV shows "Supernanny" (ABC) and "Nanny 911" (Fox) provide televised "case histories" with upbeat, common-sense parenting interventions. Newspaper and magazine articles, books, TV segments, and Web sites offer up items related to parenting regularly. A LexisNexis search of U.S. newspapers identified over 8,300 articles, advice columns, and speaker and workshop promotions giving advice on parenting in the 5 years between 2000 and 2005. And that count does not include the burgeoning number of articles and books devoted to single parenting topics, such as toilet training, promoting moral behavior, or dealing with sibling rivalry (K. Holt, 2004).

Media information is immediate, accessible, and obtainable at minimal social cost (no one need know what you read). In addition, increased family mobility, the entry of most childbearing women into the paid workforce, and other social changes tend to diminish neighborhood and community bonds, making mass media ever more important sources of information and advice about private life. Use of public media is widespread and may be more important than informal sources. In a nationally representative survey of parents of children from birth through age 3, 71% reported that they used books, magazines, television shows, or videos to get information about how to raise their children, whereas only 50% reported seeking advice from their mother or mother-in-law (Fuligni & Brooks-Gunn, 2002).

The supply of advice has always kept up with the demand, and that may be part of the problem. Reading randomly among the rows of parenting books in a bookstore, it becomes clear that every author's advice is clear, concise, firm, and supremely confident—and often contrary to what is written by other authors on the shelf. For example, in *The Baby Book* (2003), William and Martha Sears recommend frequent feedings in response to infants' cues, noting the small size of young infants' stomachs. Gary Ezzo and Robert Bucknam, authors of the popular book *On Becoming Babywise* (2001), which boasts that it is used by over 1 million parents, argues that exclusive cue feeding can lead to infant dehydration, low weight gain, and failure to thrive. Both pieces of advice cannot be right, but it is difficult for parents to decide among competing claims. Parents are willing to seek out and follow advice, but which source should parents believe?

Rather than try to sort out the many media sources that offer contradictory advice and whose empirical foundations are usually unclear, parents have turned in recent years to a small number of individuals who have emerged as publicly recognized authorities on parenting. Benjamin Spock, T. Berry Brazelton, James Dobson, Penelope Leach, and John Rosemond are five authors who each have a large following. As individuals they stand out against the background of feature page stories, TV interviews with pediatricians, and Web sites managed by agencies and baby product companies. They attain name recognition as writers and speakers, star in their own TV and radio programs related to parenting, and are mentioned in hundreds of newspaper articles and thousands of times on the World Wide Web. They offer themselves as continuing, reliable, and trustworthy sources of parenting advice. They all provide information, guidance, and reassurance, and most become advocates on public issues about family life. In short, by offering themselves as authoritative and accessible sources of advice, these five writers have acquired enormous stature in a media-intensive society. And their audience is vast. For instance, the first seven editions of *Dr. Spock's Baby and Child Care* have sold a total of 50 million copies in 39 different languages (Spock & Parker, 1998).

But where do their ideas about parenting come from, and just how good is their advice? If parents follow their advice, what likely consequences, intended or not, will ensue for their children? This book examines closely the advice of these five popular authors, the parenting issues they consider and ignore, and how they address the needs of their vast public audience. The experts are compared with each other, and their advice is evaluated by comparing it with findings from hundreds of research studies involving children and families. Implicit in the scientific method is the promise that research can identify factors contributing to children's social, moral, and academic behavior. The choice of procedures and statistical techniques is eclectic and increasingly sophisticated, but the assumption is the same: There are best parenting practices that can be identified. By testing successively refined and improved hypotheses, it is possible to identify practices that will lead to better outcomes for children and for their parents as well. Thousands of systematic observations, interviews, surveys, and experiments address the effects that parents have on their children. But of this rich aggregate of information, only an occasional research report surfaces in a brief article in a newspaper or women's magazine, and then only if it concerns a topic of current public interest—for example, the effects of day care on children. A vast body of research, studies to which tens of thousands of families have contributed their own answers about what works, remains largely inaccessible to the general public.

Research on parenting appears piecemeal in journals, book chapters, and monographs. Publication in professional outlets affords the research project recognition in the academic community, and it is this stamp of quality that leads to positive tenure decisions, grant money, and recognition among professional peers. Few academics venture to write their own parenting books (for some notable exceptions, see S. L. Ramey & C. T. Ramey, 1999a; C. T. Ramey & S. L. Ramey, 1999b; Steinberg, 2004). When research findings relevant to parenting appear in the media, they are likely to be misinterpreted because of enthusiasm and overstatement (Clarke-Stewart, 1998) and oversimplification (W. A. Collins, Maccoby, Steinberg, Hetherington, & Bornstein, 2000). Even in popular publications directed at parents, coverage of parent–child relations more closely reflects broader societal trends than findings of empirical research (Young, 1990). There has been little systematic attempt by most researchers on parenting to ensure that their work is disseminated to and correctly interpreted by those to whom it is most applicable, the parenting public. Nor have there been many attempts by researchers to synthesize findings of parenting research in media widely available to parents, and, as Holden (1997) notes, the variety of approaches to parent–child relationships makes for a disjointed empirical picture. The contrast between the huge amount of information in research reports and the lack of scientifically established knowledge among parents, who are the potential beneficiaries of such information, is even more troubling when it is considered that most large research projects are underwritten at public expense.

A BEST PRACTICE OF PARENTING?

This volume will discuss the work of five experts, each of whom has written several influential books and is known as a media personality. Each of them contributes to contemporary social dialogue about children and families. Yet, as will be seen, their advice is remarkable for its contrasts. If child rearing is just a matter of personal choice in a marketplace of ideas, then conceivably they could all be right and the diversity of their perspectives becomes something to celebrate. But if scientific knowledge can be brought to bear on those points where the media experts disagree, we should be able to identify sources of effective parenting advice that work for the benefit of the child and the family and avoid sources that do not.

Despite the recognition that parenting varies substantially across cultures and classes (McLoyd, 1990; Ogbu, 1981), across children in the same family (Hetherington, Reiss, & Plomin, 1994), and across situations (Holden & Miller, 1999), there have always been efforts to identify parenting practices that promise the best outcomes for children. Much of the empirical research has involved short-term studies of typical families, but for the first time longitudinal studies with extensive assessments (e.g., Caspi, 2000; NICHD Early Child Care Research Network, 2003c; O'Connor, Deater-Deckard, Fulker, Rutter, & Plomin, 1998) can provide data on parenting questions that offer the promise of assessing causal relationships. Clinical studies on the antecedents of referral for academic failure, school suspension, mental illness, substance abuse treatment (e.g., Patterson, 1982; Tremblay, Masse, Pagani, & Vitaro, 1996), and incarceration by juvenile court authorities also provide crucial information on parenting practices associated with bad outcomes. On key questions regarding the classic dilemmas that confront nearly every parent, I will synthesize relevant research findings, drawing heavily on existing research reviews, and compare the results with the media experts' advice.

For comparative purposes, consider the formulation of medical advice. Best practice guidelines for health professionals on many topics appear periodically in major medical journals and Web sites. Typically constructed by teams of professionals known for their expertise on a particular medical topic, "best practice" is a flexible concept, a set of prescriptive guidelines for how practitioners should treat their patients. Findings from randomized clinical trials (Sniderman, 1999) and community effectiveness studies (Wells, 1999) are important components, but empirical research is not the only source for best practice guidelines. A best practice model recognizes that scientific research has to be blended with clinical experience to provide maximally effective guidelines for the art of medicine. Strategies of clinical management proven efficacious in practice are a crucial component, and best practice guidelines are flexible enough to deal with attributes of individual patients and diverse community practices and to be sustainable through time (Information & Knowledge for Optimal Health Project, 2004). Medical guidelines are typically topic specific, however, so that an effective strategy for dealing with attention deficit disorder may not bear much resemblance to an effective strategy for managing diabetic care. Such guidelines rarely can be generalized beyond the specific topic, and in any case they may need to be adjusted in light of more recent research findings or other considerations. Even so, they represent a crucial step in creating uniformly high-quality care.

In the mental health community, the term *evidence-based practice* is similarly used to signify use of the best available research evidence and clinical expertise, along with client values, as a basis for formulating treatment (Barlow, 2004; DeAngelis, 2005). The call for evidence-based practices has come out of national mental health commissions and federal agencies and has been embraced by practitioners as a means to enhance the scientific basis for treatment and to establish its legitimacy to health insurers (DeAngelis, 2005). As good as they are, however, evidence-based and best practice statements from medicine and mental health treatment cover only a few of the topics discussed by the parenting experts in the media. When relevant, I will draw on these documents, most issued as policy statements by the American Academy of Pediatrics, as they can assist in evaluating parenting advice. The National Institutes of Health (2004) have disseminated the findings of many consensus development conferences on medical topics, and there have been calls in the past for similar consensus-building conferences on parenting (e.g., Simpson, 1997). It remains to be seen whether it would be possible to reach similar agreement on many of the questions that challenge parents—that is, for physicians, psychologists, and other professionals to compare their findings and work with parents to construct best practice guidelines. Such guidelines could then be used to assess the media authorities' advice, and this book is one effort toward that end.

Take a topic as seemingly straightforward as day care. One author states his opposition to substitute care for children younger than age 3. Another warns of its risks for all preschoolers. A third rather wistfully notes that it would be preferable if one parent could stay home until the child is 3 months of age. Some provide a justification for their position from empirical research on the issue, and some do not. At the same time, there are a substantial number of data-gathering efforts, capped by the recent National Institute of Child Health and Development study at 10 sites nationwide (NICHD Early Child Care Research Network, 2003b), that provide evidence on the effects of early day care. Surely the results of this study and others and the recent experiences of thousands of families using and avoiding day care should provide answers concerning whether other-than-parent care is a threat to children's emotional connection with their parents or to their cognitive and social development. Yet no comparison has been made between what the experts advise and the research and clinical evidence, drawn from the experiences of thousands of families, that should support or refute them. By drawing on these resources, it should be possible to set out guidelines for parents and others as they struggle with the many difficulties of providing, regulating, and selecting child care.

THE FIVE AUTHORS

The criteria for picking public experts for inclusion in this volume were simple: Included are those who advise primarily on parenting and family issues, who command the largest audiences with their articles and books, and who have established themselves with TV or radio programs or newspaper columns. This excluded general advice columnists, talk show hosts who sometimes address parenting topics, and many highly qualified researchers and clinicians whose advice is not widely known by the public. The question arises of what it takes to become a parenting expert, that is, to be recognized to the extent that these five public figures are recognized. There are 60,000 pediatricians and related professionals who are members of the American Academy of Pediatrics (2004) and an even larger number of psychologists who are members of the American Psychological Association (2004). Why have a few individuals emerged to such prominence when others in their field with comparable professional credentials have not? Many professionals are asked on occasion to provide advice in a public setting, but those occasions are not catapults to celebrity. Some acquire great stature within their professions, but that does not translate to public acclaim. Many are not seeking fame, of course, and those few who have achieved it will have done so by working with and through the media and by honing their communicative skills. One thing certainly is clear: Each of the five experts has mastered the art of writing for and speaking to public audiences. Their columns and books are readable, engaging, and persuasive to a wide range of readers. The question remains, however, whether their advice is accurate.

Perhaps because they are writing for a public rather than a professional audience, the parenting experts draw on much more than expertise. Their advice is the issue of their education but also of their experiences as both children and parents, their religious beliefs and political philosophies, and their encounters with other professionals. In addition, the paths to influence taken by the parenting experts inevitably shape their advice, as does their own sense of their role in public life. These diverse influences may not be evident to those reading them for the first time, but they become apparent once one takes a step back to place them in context. The following biographical sketches are provided to that end. The five experts are introduced in the order of publication of their first book.

Benjamin Spock

Born just after the turn of the last century (1903), Spock was the oldest of six children born to a railroad lawyer and a devoted mother with a distinct streak of New England Puritanism in her child-rearing practices. In the Spock household, moral responsibilities were strongly emphasized, physical affection and praise were rationed, and "progressive" dietary edicts were strictly followed. Physical robustness was encouraged by having the children sleep in an unheated porch during Connecticut winters. Spock believed that his parents' focus on the children of the family accounts for the fact that three of the six siblings became teachers and two went into child psychology (Spock & Morgan, 1989). Educated in private schools, then at Yale, Spock finished his medical education at Columbia, then took medical and pediatric residencies. His interest in giving good answers to parents about such questions as toilet training, thumb sucking, and weaning led him to seek psychiatric training, which eventually led to training in psychoanalysis. He practiced pediatrics in New York City for 10 years, interrupted by service in the Navy during the World War II years, before *The Common Sense Book of Baby and Child Care* first appeared in 1946 (Spock & Morgan, 1989). His personable, supportive writing style and focus on everyday questions that most parents face made the book popular, with 750,000 copies sold in its 1st year. Over the years, the book was repeatedly revised and grew from the 482 pages of the initial paperback edition to the 838 pages of the seventh edition discussed here. Its success led to a new era both in Spock's life and in public acceptance of expert advice on parenting. After its appearance and wide acceptance, Spock worked in faculty and consultative roles at the Mayo Clinic, the University of Pittsburgh, and Case Western Reserve University (Maier, 1998).

In the early 1960s, Spock was drawn into advocacy on behalf of the National Committee for a Sane Nuclear Policy. Aware of his position as the preeminent parenting expert of his era, he became a welfare rights advocate and full-time opponent of the Vietnam war. He spoke on campuses and in public meetings against the war and was tailed by FBI agents (Spock & Morgan, 1989). He led sit-in protests at draft induction centers, attempted to block traffic to the Pentagon, and engaged in other acts of civil disobedience that led to several arrests and eventual indictment and conviction for conspiracy to aid draft resisters. A reversal on appeal saved him from a $5,000 fine and a 2-year jail term (Spock & Morgan, 1989). Widely admired and fiercely criticized, always convinced of the rightness of his positions on topics ranging from nuclear missile testing to the longevity benefits of a macrobiotic diet, Spock's position as a public figure transcended even the considerable success of his writings. Author of 17 books, Spock collaborated on the most recent editions of *Baby and Child Care* with Michael Rothenberg (Spock & Rothenberg, 1992) and Steven J. Parker (Spock & Parker, 1998). Robert Needlman revised *Baby and Child Care* after Spock's death for an eighth edition published in June 2004. Quotations used here are from the seventh edition, the last one that Spock reviewed in final manuscript form. The eighth edition includes Needlman's insights and input from 16 subject matter experts, as well as vintage Spock advice. Much of the book is devoted to the physical care of children, including navel cleansing, allergies, injury prevention, and similar topics; the rest advises parents on behavior and is heavily flavored with applications of psychoanalytic theory to basic problems of parenting, such as thumb sucking and toilet training. In later years Spock wrote monthly columns for *Redbook* and *Parenting* magazines. Spock died in 1998, but his widow and associates maintain a Web site at drspock.com with advice and a line of licensed products.

According to Spock, parents should bring up children "with a feeling that they're in this world not for their own satisfaction, but primarily to serve others" (Spock & Parker, 1998, p. 621). The objective of parenting is to raise children to be "kind, cooperative, feeling people who will give family life a high priority, who will participate in the community, who will enrich their spirits with cultural interests, and who will not let their jobs distort their lives" (Spock & Rothenberg, 1992, p. 780). Parents serve as models for their children:

> Throughout childhood, but particularly before six years of age, children will be watching their parents and trying to pattern themselves after them. That means not that parents have to be perfect, but that they should show respect for each other and their children, let their

spiritual values show, not only in expressing their opinions at the dinner table, but in their attitudes and behavior toward family and friends, toward other groups in the town, the nation and the world. . . . But most important of all is the parent's expression of love for the children, not only in words but in frequent spontaneous hugs. (Spock, 1994, p. 162)

The psychological attribute he particularly despises is self-centeredness. He condemns people who "focus on what they want and what they think they are entitled to, rather than on what they contribute" (Spock, 1994, p. 62). The roots of social malaise are psychological and social in origin: "Our most basic disturbance, I believe, is the intense competitiveness and materialism of our society, which has convinced many people that getting ahead in their work is the most important thing in life and that family happiness, friendships, moral, economic and cultural interests should be sacrificed if necessary" (Spock & Rothenberg, 1992, p. 780). The consequences of these ills are both societal and familial: "Materialism unchecked by idealism leads to oppression of the powerless by the greedy; excessive competitiveness hardens hearts even within families" (Spock, 1994, p. 100).

T. Berry Brazelton

The older son of a family that gained prosperity in the lumber business, Brazelton was born in 1918 in Waco, Texas. His mother was the primary parent: "I felt that my own father allowed his role to be designated by my mother, rather than following his own inclination to be really involved in his children's activities. We ended up as rather uncomfortable pals in my adolescence, trying to talk 'man to man'" (Brazelton, 1992, p. 421). He recounted his earliest experiences baby-sitting children: "I'd take care of eleven at a time when my parents, aunts, and uncles were outside drinking martinis. . . . If you're taking care of that many kids, you have to learn how to get inside them and manage each one individually" ("Brazelton, T. Berry," 1993, p. 89). Brazelton began his education in Waco, graduating from high school at age 15, then went to prep school in Virginia and eventually to Princeton, from which he received his AB in 1940. From there he went on to Columbia, where he completed his MD degree in 1943 (Brazelton Institute, 2004). After medical and pediatric residencies, Brazelton became dissatisfied with the focus on pathophysiology in pediatrics and sought further study in child psychiatry ("Brazelton, T. Berry," 1993).

Brazelton maintained a private practice in pediatrics for over 40 years, but he is best known among professionals for his contributions to practical pediatrics through clinical research. The development of the Brazelton Neonatal Behavioral Assessment Scale permitted earlier adoptions and made the professional community aware of infant abilities, setting the stage for further intervention and research. Among the most honored pediatricians, he has served as president of the Society for Research in Child Development and received numerous awards, including one from the American Academy of Pediatrics for his contributions to the field of child development. Brazelton is presently Professor of Pediatrics Emeritus at Harvard Medical School. He wrote a monthly column for *Family Circle* (circulation 5,002,255) and has written 26 books, including his most recent general parenting books, *Touchpoints: Your Child's Emotional and Behavioral Development* (1992) and *Touchpoints Three to Six* (2001; coauthored with Joshua Sparrow) and specialty paperbacks coauthored with Sparrow (e.g., *Discipline: The Brazelton Way*, 2003). He also starred in two TV series: *What Every Baby Knows* on the Lifetime cable network, and *Brazelton on Parenting* on the Fox Family network, and maintains a Web site at www.brazelton-institute.com/. Brazelton has written over 200 research articles and book chapters on infancy and the early childhood years directed for practitioners and scholars (Brazelton Institute, 2004).

Brazelton's books and magazine columns for parents focus on infants and young children. His descriptions of parents focus on their close involvement with their children: "Parents don't make mistakes because they don't care, but because they care too deeply" (1992, p. xx). He endorses the concept of "anticipatory guidance," telling parents beforehand what predictable developmental crises lie just ahead for their child, so that they correctly interpret and deal with behaviors that may seem problematic but that in fact represent normal developmental changes. "I hope to help parents see their roles more objectively and to make choices about their own behavior which would avoid setting up tension or deepening the guilt that a child may feel about this 'deviant' behavior when it develops" (Brazelton, 1984, p. 2). For example, Brazelton describes thumb sucking as a behavior that all babies will give up in time. Parents who try to intervene to stop it may increase the baby's tension, driving her or him to suck the thumb even more often. Brazelton attaches great importance to individual differences: "Babies' individual temperaments, or styles of interacting with and learning about the world, can influence heavily the way they pay attention and absorb the parents' guiding stimuli. Their temperaments also profoundly influence the parents' reaction to them from the moment of birth. While a child cannot be seen as born with a fixed nature, neither is the environment all-important in shaping a child" (1992, p. xxi).

Brazelton has been active for many years in training pediatricians, and the Child Development Unit he founded at Children's Hospital in Boston has turned out 60 pediatricians who are currently active in research and training (Brazelton Institute, 2004). More recently, his educational efforts have been extended to training a network of trainers, who then teach child development professionals Brazelton's Touchpoints system in 8-hour sessions at sites around the United States. Professionals knowledgeable in Touchpoints can help parents recognize and cope with sudden developmental spurts that cause apparent disorganization in children's behavior and lead to problems (Brazelton, 1992). He has not been reluctant to speak and write on legislation related to children, criticizing then-President Clinton and House and Senate members for "turning the wrong way" on welfare reform and paying insufficient attention to the implications of the Welfare Reform Act for young children (Healy, 1998).

Brazelton also expresses his concerns about the contemporary dilemma of parents, especially mothers of young children who juggle parenting and working outside the home: "Women are suddenly finding: 'I'm split in two, but I can't do either job well, and I'm scared as hell.' The stresses on young parents have logarithmically increased in the past 20 years. I don't think that we've done anybody justice. Developing with their baby is something that they really can't afford to miss" (Kelly, 2000). Brazelton has his own sense of contemporary society as it impacts families. Commenting on a horrific shooting of five at an Arkansas middle school, he remarked that "I just think our country is in deep, deep trouble. This Jonesboro, Arkansas incident was a good example—a tragic example but a good one—of just what our culture is lacking, which is any attention to families early on so they can in turn pay attention to their kids" (Healy, 1998).

James Dobson

Born in Shreveport, Louisiana, in 1936 and raised in a succession of small towns in Oklahoma and Texas, Dobson is the only son of a father who was a Nazarene evangelist and sometime art teacher, and an intense, activist mother "who had a keen understanding of good disciplinary procedures" (Dobson, 1992, p. 23). Dobson recounts that on one occasion when he talked back to his mother, she threw a girdle at him: "The intended blow caught me across the chest, followed by a multitude of straps and buckles, wrapping themselves around my midsection. She gave me an entire thrashing with one blow!" But it was not abusive: "I'm here to tell you that the girdle-blow was an act of love" (Dobson, 1992, p. 24). Dobson attended Pasadena College (a Nazarene institution, now Point Loma University) and received his doctorate in child development from the University of Southern California. He then worked for 3 years as a teacher and school psychologist and joined the faculty of the University of Southern California School of Medicine as a clinical professor of pediatrics.

During these years he developed his sense of being one of the Lord's anointed, most notably around the time of his father's death in 1977. Shortly before his death, his father prayed for sufficient health to continue his ministry, and according to Dobson, the Lord's answer was, "I have heard your prayers, I know that you are concerned about my people and my kingdom. I know your compassion, and I'm going to answer your prayers. In fact, you're going to reach millions of people. But is not going to be through you. It will be through your son" (Stafford, 1988, p. 21). That same year, the younger Dobson founded Focus on the Family in Pomona, California; in 1991, he moved it to Colorado Springs, Colorado. Focus states that it "gathers and disseminates practical information on marriage, parenting, and other subjects related to family life" (Schwartz & Turner, 1994, p. 1431). Focus produces radio programs heard worldwide and operates an evangelical press that develops magazines, tapes, and books by Dobson and other Focus staff and volunteers. An operation with $127 million in total revenue (Focus on the Family, 2004b) and 1,300 employees, Focus receives about 250,000 letters, inquiries, and e-mails a month (Langfitt, 2004). Most are requests for a book or a tape, but about 1 in 10 is a letter seeking advice on a parenting or family issue (Niebuhr, 1995). These are stored in computer files and are responded to with one or more selections from a bank of 1,000 prototype letters approved by Dobson (Steinfels, 1990); difficult cases are referred to 1 of 16 staff therapists (Langfitt, 2004).

But Dobson's political activism has garnered more attention in mainstream news media than his views on parenting. In recent years, he has used his influence with the Focus faithful—2.3 million receive monthly magazines from the organization (Focus on the Family, 2000)—to mobilize them as a lobbying force. Along with other prominent figures in the Christian right, Dobson leaned hard on Republican party leaders in 1998 to take a stand on such conservative social issues as defunding Planned Parenthood, requiring parental consent for abortions, and eliminating the National En-

dowment for the Arts (Gerson, 1998). In 2004, Dobson made clear his preference for George Bush over John Kerry for president and argued for the
Defense of Marriage Act to ban gay marriages (Pratt, 2004). Dobson told
the *New York Times* that he worked for over a year for the November 2004
defeat of Democratic Senator Tom Daschle because Daschle had led the fil-
ibuster to block 10 of President Bush's judicial nominees. In a letter that
aides said was mailed to over a million of his supporters, Dobson warned,
"Let his colleagues beware . . . especially those representing 'red' states.
Many of them will be in the 'bull's-eye' the next time they seek re-election"
(Kirkpatrick, 2005, p. A10). Famous for the folksy, personable warmth pro-
jected in his radio programs, his considerable drive, and his single-minded
devotion to Focus, Dobson is also noted for his stinging memos and tongue
lashings and attempts to control all aspects of Focus operations (Stafford,
1988). His best known book is *Dare to Discipline* (1970), which sold more
than 2 million copies and established Dobson as a national figure. Dobson
has written 21 books on parenting and family counseling (Focus on the
Family, 2004a), has done video and audiotapes, and writes a monthly letter to those who receive Focus publications. The Focus Web site can be accessed at www.family.org/. A revised edition of *Dare* was published in 1992.
He wrote *Children at Risk* (1990) with Gary Bauer, which warns of the dangers of the contemporary American society for children and families.

In Dobson's writing, the goal of parenting is to ensure that children have
respect for authority and that they are God-fearing people. Parents' role is
first and foremost a religious one: "God has given us the assignment of representing Him during the formative years of parenting. That's why it is so
critically important for us to acquaint our kids with God's two predomi-
nant natures. . . . His unfathomable love and His justice" (Dobson, 1992,
p. 19). All psychological concepts must be screened for adherence to the
Bible and some, notably determinism, are not acceptable: "As a Christian
psychologist, I have always filtered man-made theories through the screen
of Scripture, and in this instance, determinism hangs up in the wire. If it
were true, we would be unable to worship and serve God as a voluntary
expression of our love. We would be mere puppets on a string, responding
to the stimuli around us" (Dobson, 1987, p. 25).

Dobson is profoundly disturbed by those mental health professionals
who would advise and counsel families: *"Because in general, behavioral scientists have lacked confidence in the Judeo-Christian ethic and have disregarded the wisdom of this priceless tradition!"* (Dobson, 1982, p. 10). Their failure to curb and
correct human behavior and societal ills is particularly galling for Dobson

because he holds them responsible for causing the problems they would solve: "So where are the experts who promised us utopia a few years ago? Where is the vast army of psychologists, sociologists, physicians, academicians . . . who led us into the abyss? Why haven't they been held accountable for the mess they precipitated?" (Dobson & Bauer, 1990, p. 32). But professionals are clearly not the only ones Dobson blames for the social problems that he describes:

> Indeed, there is an ache deep within my spirit over what we have allowed to happen to our kids. What is it going to take to alarm the mass of humanity that sits on the sidelines watching our kids struggle for survival? It is time for every God-fearing adult to get on our face in repentance before the Almighty. *We* have permitted this mess to occur! *We* allowed immoral television and movie producers to make their fortunes by exploiting our kids. *We* allowed their filth and their horribly violent productions to come into our homes via cable, video, CDs, and network trash. *We* stood by passively while Planned Parenthood taught our teenagers to be sexually promiscuous. *We* allowed them to invade our schools and promote an alien value system that contradicted everything we believed and loved. . . . *We*, as parents, are guilty of abandoning our children to those who would use them for their own purposes. Where in God's name have we been? How bad does it have to get before we say, enough is enough?! (Dobson, 1992, p. 206)

Penelope Leach

Unique as the only woman and the only non-American among the best-known parenting experts in the United States, Leach serves as an important counterpoint to American authors. She is also the only one of them who quit full-time employment to stay home with her children. Born in 1937 in London, the daughter of two writers who divorced early, Leach was not close to her father, who considered children "an expensive bore" and paid her little attention. "But I was extremely close to my mother, always" (Kinkead, 1994). Leach and her sister lived at a boarding school for 2 years before her mother and stepfather married, because it was considered improper for children to live in a household with an unmarried couple. She remembers, "I was always politically involved," because her step-grandmother was the first chairwoman of the Labour party, and her stepfather and mother were involved in a variety of liberal and left causes. She recounts: "I never thought about sex discrimination in my youth because it simply did not exist at home. I also went to an all-girls grammar school so I didn't have to find out for myself in adolescence." Leach earned her BA with honors in history at Cambridge University "When I'd done my degree . . . I knew I wanted to work in child psychology but I was on the wrong side of an arts-science barrier and had to work my way sideways into psychology by starting off with a social work diploma" ("Leach, Penelope," 1994, p. 267). She completed her social science diploma and her PhD in psychology at the London School of Economics. Leach is a fellow in the British Psychological Society and has chaired Britain's Child Development Society. Leach's best known book is *Your Baby and Child* (1989a, 1998). She also wrote *Your Growing Child* (1989b) and an advocacy book entitled *Children First* (1994). Passages from *Your Baby and Child* can be accessed at www.babycentre.co.uk.

Addressing the purpose behind her books, Leach writes: "I believed that the more people knew about children in general, the more fascinating they would find their own child in particular—and I believed that while finding a child fascinating is no substitute for loving her, it could be a most useful support at 4 a.m. when there was not much love around" (1994, p. xii). Her approach also reflects her experience as a parent: "You are going to know this person better than you will ever know anybody else. Nobody else in the world including your partner, however devoted, is ever going to love you as much as your baby will in these first years if you will let him. You are into a relationship which is unique and which can therefore be uniquely rewarding" (Leach, 1989a, p. 13). As for her recommendations for parenting practices: "Some of them came to me directly from my own mother; some of them were learned the hard way on my own children; most of them come to me from the thousands of other parents who let me watch them coping" (Leach, 1989a, p. 15).

Leach's advice includes efforts to maintain the child's self-esteem "Above all, try, when you are irritated or angry, to make clear to the child that you are fed up with his behavior rather with him as a person" (1989b, p. 226). Conformity to parental commands is less important than self-regulation: "Instant and unquestioning obedience might keep life peaceful for some parents for a few years but it cannot produce children who think for themselves and therefore can be trusted to look after themselves from an early age" (Leach, 1989b, p. 217). The goals that she mentions for parenting

seem conventional, but her emphasis on qualities of judgment and feeling
are not:

> Parents want their children to know right from wrong, to do what
> they should and avoid doing what they should not, to be pleasant,
> helpful and polite and to avoid letting them down in public. Those
> are qualities involving not just obedience but ethical judgment and
> choice, not just order but cooperation with a friendly face, not just
> submission but sensitivity to the feelings of others—subtly socialized
> stuff and surely not amenable to shouts and smacks. (Leach, 1994,
> p. 116)

Leach also writes as a social advocate for children and families but rejects
the idea of social decline: "Social debate always relies on statements about
past times and distant places to throw the present into high relief, but most
such statements should start with 'Once upon a time'" (Leach, 1994, p. xi).
Yet current society poses challenges for parents: "I know that most individual parents do everything they can to facilitate the health and happiness, growth and development of their babies; to deliver socialized and
sociable children into society's formal education system and to support
them through it and out into adult life. . . . But our society is inimical to
children and has therefore devalued parents to such an extent that individual good parenting is not only exceedingly difficult, but ultimately, insufficient" (Leach, 1994, pp. xii–xiii).

Noting the affluence and technological advancement of Western societies, she argues that children have not sufficiently benefited:

> The moral imperative for any society, surely, is to do the best it can
> in response to its own unique conditions; doing better than other so-
> cieties that are less well-placed is no good cause for complacency. The
> comparisons that matter, and the ones that anger me, are between
> how things are for our children and how they could be. When we
> make those comparisons the moral high ground crumbles beneath us,
> because our society could do so much better for children than it does.
> (Leach, 1994, p. xvi)

One area in which contemporary culture suffers, according to Leach, is in
support for parents staying at home with children during infancy and early

childhood, and she argues that substitute care, particularly for infants, cannot match the quality of interaction between parent and child (Leach, 1994).

John Rosemond

Born in 1947 and raised in Charleston, South Carolina, and suburban Chicago, Rosemond is the only child of parents who divorced when he was 3 years old. His books, columns, and speeches describe his early years of being cared for by his grandmother while his mother pursued nurse's training. According to Rosemond, his mother left him much to his own devices while she studied, worked, and pursued an active social life (Rosemond, 1989). He attended Western Illinois University and completed bachelor's and master's degrees in psychology, the latter in 1971. After a series of positions in community mental health centers in Illinois and North Carolina, Rosemond practiced psychotherapy from 1980 until 1990. He is licensed as a psychological associate, which entitles a practitioner to practice psychotherapy or counseling with clinical populations only under supervision (North Carolina Psychology Practice Act, 1967, as amended). Rosemond left the American Psychological Association in 1985, about the time the Association denied full membership to those not holding doctoral degrees. He began writing a parenting column in 1976 that currently appears in 200 newspapers and parenting newsletters. The most frequent source of the columns quoted here is the *Charlotte Observer*, Rosemond's hometown newspaper, in the belief that the content is least likely to be edited. From 1985 to 1996, he wrote a monthly column in *Better Homes and Gardens* (circulation 7,613,249). He has over 200 speaking engagements in a typical year (Bolotin, 1999), making him the most active public speaker of the five. Along with his parenting books and columns, he produced a CD released in 1992 entitled *Breakaway Face*, featuring his songs and guitar-playing skills. His best-known book is *Parent Power!* (1990), which was updated and expanded in 2001 (Rosemond, 2001b). Rosemond's Web site (www. Rosemond.com) offers parenting tips, along with his latest column, and markets his books, his monthly magazine, *Affirmative Parenting*, and a calendar with parenting comments for each day of the year. Frequently courting controversy, Rosemond has used his columns to criticize those with whom he disagrees, sometimes by name, as in his attack on T. Berry Brazelton over toilet training (Goode, 1999). He also provoked a reprimand in 1988 from the North Carolina State Board of Examiners of Practicing Psychologists and was the subject of a consent order from the renamed North Carolina Psychology Board that required him to submit his columns for prepublication review for 3 years as a condition of maintaining his license (North Carolina Psychology Board, 1992; Sheehan, 1999).

As Rosemond describes his approach: "It's a low involvement model of parenthood in which children are supervised, given authoritative direction, made responsible for their own behavior and left to solve most of their own problems" (Rosemond, 1993c). He emphasizes the relationship between the wife and husband in parenting: "The secret to raising happy, healthy children is to give more attention to the marriage than you give to the children" (Rosemond, 1989, p. 6). The ideal household is adult-centered: "Children discover who they are by first having it defined for them who *their parents* are, and who they are *not*. They discover their *own* place by first being told where it *cannot* be" (Rosemond, 1990, p. 7). According to Rosemond, the ideal form of family government is a benevolent dictatorship (Rosemond, 1989, p. 48). Good parenting "comes from the heart and the gut. It is not a matter of long, hard thought, but a matter of how intuitively sensitive you are to your needs and the needs of your child and a matter of how firmly grounded you are in the soil of common sense" (Rosemond, 1989, p. 2). Children should be taught to be resourceful, responsible, and to attend to, respect, and obey adults, but ultimately, "the purpose of raising a child is to help him get out of your life" (Rosemond, 1993a).

Rosemond is critical of the current generation of social service professionals: "Some 30 years ago, 'helping professionals' (a term that awards the benefit of the doubt) snatched the child-rearing baton away from the older generation, took a sharp left turn and led America's parents into a blind alley, where we are still piling up, unconscious of going nowhere" (Rosemond, 1994d). These "misguided mental-health professionals—have been trying to make children 'feel good about themselves.' This anti-scriptural, anti-social notion has corrupted American child rearing and is now—as a generation of insufficiently inhibited children is attaining chronological adulthood—beginning to corrupt America" (Rosemond, 1999c, p. 5).

Rosemond is very clear about why current American child-rearing practices are in the disarray he describes:

In fact, it is accurate to say *there is not one single aspect of the rearing and education of children that has not taken on a political dimension,* the result of political scheming. It is also accurate to say that in each case, the instigators of the schemes in question have been liberals. Each scheme promises to expand the powers of government at the expense of civil liberties, and each scheme will create a new client group for the Democratic party. (Rosemond, 1995a, p. 101)

Furthermore, according to Rosemond, the freedom to parent without interference from liberal politicians is at risk as a result of the politicization of parenting: "Ultraliberal elements are clearly attempting to control what takes place within the family, especially how children are reared. . . . Conservatives, meanwhile, are equally determined to defend the sanctity of the traditional family" (Rosemond, 1995a, p. 7). He regards himself as an advocate for the conservative family and political values that he believes prevailed in days gone by. Recently, he has begun describing his writing and speaking as divinely inspired, maintaining that "there is nothing I have ever said that does not have root in His Word. . . . Thank you, Lord, for the many blessings of this most rewarding ministry" (Rosemond, 2001b, p. xiii).

SOURCES OF THEIR ADVICE

If the five media experts' advice were molded by their professional educations and career experiences, a degree of consensus might be expected from being a part of a professional community, but they obviously offer very different philosophies on parenting and family issues. One issue is whether the differences in media experts' advice are idiosyncratic, reflecting individual decisions about particular parenting issues, or systematic, rooted in their life experiences and reflecting their general philosophies, worldviews, and constructions of the social order. As will become evident, most have significantly shifted their positions on one or more key parenting issues during the years that they have been publicly recognized. In light of the experts' extensive influence on parents through the years, attention will be paid to their past and current positions, in part to identify the forces leading to position changes. The media experts' prominence, the disparity of their positions, and their shifts in positions lend credence to the perspective that parenting is culturally embedded and shaped by broader social forces. But from what sources do parenting experts draw for their advice?

Their Childhoods

Spock has written emphatically about his mother's influence on him and on *Baby and Child Care* (Spock & Morgan, 1989), including what he accepted from her (strong moral sensibilities; emphasis on fresh air and early bedtimes) and what he rejected (her Victorian prudishness about sexuality). John Rosemond draws on his seemingly less-than-ideal childhood to make the point that most children turn out all right nevertheless. James Dobson's recounting of the flying girdle story and his own childhood tantrums are used to make the point that parental firmness and physical punishment are not incompatible with affection. Both Brazelton and Leach have written about experiences with their own parents that influence some of the advice they give, but seem to have incorporated less of their own childhood narratives into their writings.

Their Experiences as Parents

All five experts are parents: Spock had two sons; Dobson, Leach, and Rosemond each have a grown son and daughter; and Brazelton is the father of four. But they vary markedly in their use of family anecdotes to illustrate their advice. John Rosemond's public speeches, books, and columns are laced with stories of his successful parenting of his two children. An instance of this: "We assigned nearly all of the day-to-day housework to Eric [then age 9] and his younger sister Amy [then age 7]. Their chores, although considerable, were arranged such that neither child worked more than about one hour a day" (Rosemond, 1994a, p. 3E). The result of this and other parenting interventions (notably getting rid of the television) was that Eric who previously "exhibited every symptom now associated with not only attention deficit disorder (ADD) but also pronounced learning disabilities" 2 years later "was reading above grade level, making all but straight A's, and his behavior—while not completely turned around—was manageable" (Rosemond, 1994a, p. 3E). The other authors disclose less. Spock reports that he used physical punishment only once with his two sons (Spock & Morgan, 1989), similar to the advice he gives against it in recent editions of *Baby and Child Care*. Leach's emphasis on the parent–child relationship includes personal anecdotes; Brazelton draws on his experience as a parent to demonstrate ways to interact with a child who is being difficult; and Dobson uses his own children as examples, particularly regarding disciplinary episodes, to tell how it is done.

Religious Texts

Dobson introduces and justifies his parenting advice as being biblically grounded: "The underlying principles expressed herein are not my own innovative insights which would be forgotten in brief season or two. Instead, they originated with the inspired Biblical writers who gave us the foundation for all relationships in the home" (Dobson, 1982, p. 11). In the last chapter of *The New Dare to Discipline*, he quotes Bible passages on the necessity of father-headed households and the use of corporal punishment. John Rosemond has made occasional biblical references in more recent columns and books. Leach's and Spock's strong moral sensibilities influence their recommendations for parents' actions toward their children, but neither they nor Brazelton mention religious texts to support their parenting positions.

Clinical Practice

Their experiences as pediatricians are particularly prominent in Spock's and Brazelton's writings. It was Spock's need to answer everyday questions from parents in his pediatric practice that first led him to write *Baby and Child Care* (Spock & Morgan, 1989). Brazelton spent even more time in practice (over 40 years) and has written a book for children explaining the procedures in a doctor's examination (Brazelton, 1999). Dobson's experiences as a teacher and psychologist in the public schools (Dobson, 1998a) contribute to his writings on self-esteem, but only a portion of his best-selling *Dare to Discipline* (1970) and his other books are devoted to school issues. Rosemond has a shorter practice history, and Leach's work experience has been primarily as an empirical researcher.

Theory

Spock's training in psychoanalytic theory contributed to his writings on specific parenting topics, such as thumb sucking and toilet training. Leach's conceptualization of parent–child relationships is derived from John Bowlby's attachment theory, which emphasizes their shaping by evolutionary forces. Brazelton's book *The Earliest Relationship* (1990, coauthored by Bertrand G. Cramer) is devoted entirely to theory, research, and clinical studies of the infant–parent relationship and draws explicitly on psychoanalytic theory, Bowlby's attachment theory, and learning theory, incorporating such concepts as imitation, conditioning, and reinforcement. Dobson employs straightforward derivations of learning theory (e.g., rewarding children with stars and pennies for chores completed) in his parenting strategies; Rosemond, with his frequent reliance on punishment to modify behavior, is a less orthodox adherent. But extended theoretical expositions are largely absent from parenting manuals.

Empirical Research

One role that parenting experts play is that of research interpreters who synthesize research findings of individual studies into recommended parenting practices. Brazelton draws on his own research projects on infant assessment, feeding practices, and toilet training. Spock draws on his own study using psychoanalytically oriented therapy with families. Leach worked as a child development researcher for the U.K. Medical Research Council and has written a nearly 400-page review of infant research. Dobson evinces little enthusiasm for the knowledge generated by empirical research, which he faults for its reductionistic tendencies: "I don't believe the scientific community is the best source of information on proper parenting techniques. There have been some worthwhile studies, to be sure. But the subject of parent–child interactions is incredibly complex and subtle. The only way to investigate it scientifically is to reduce the relationship to its simplest common denominators, so it can be examined. But in so doing, the overall tone is missed" (Dobson, 1992, p. 16).

Rosemond uses individual research studies (on the influence of television, on punishment practices) as opening cards for discussion when he considers them worthy of being refuted or if they support his published positions. His basic attitude is one of skepticism: "Social sciences research . . . rarely, if ever, proves anything. It is nearly impossible to establish adequate control of the many variables that affect human behavior. In addition, the research that receives the most hype often depends on who the researcher's buddy is, rather than the quality of the work" (Rosemond, 1993d, p. 2E). The number of research reports has multiplied during the same period that media parenting experts have gained visibility, but there is no indication that public attraction to the experts and reliance on them is due to their use of research or their role as data interpreters.

As this listing makes clear, media parenting experts are not just conduits of information they have accumulated through years of professional experience. They model their readers' process of integrating diverse sources (professional backgrounds, personal experiences, religious beliefs) that they draw on to a greater or lesser extent, providing the basis for wide variation in the advice they disseminate. Empirical research is just one source and sometime makes a surprisingly small contribution to the experts' pronouncements.

RESEARCH STUDIES OF EFFECTIVE PARENTING

Because the focus is on media parenting experts' advice, the reviews of empirical research presented here will not be comprehensive but will rather focus on the issues that concern parents and that are addressed by media parenting experts. The task of reviewing and attempting to synthesize even small portions of the parenting research is a daunting and risky one, liable to errors of omission and misinterpretation. The thousands of completed research projects span not only generations of researchers but substantial shifts in thinking about what are important influences on child development (Clarke-Stewart, 1998).

Different types of research projects make unique contributions to understanding the effects of parenting practices, and each approach has distinct benefits and limitations.

Interviews and Surveys

These play a critical role in gauging parent practices in large and representative segments of the population. When parents are questioned about parenting practices they currently use or their children's current behavior, the data are more reliable than when they are asked to remember events earlier in their child's development. Inevitably, concerns arise about parents' tendencies to report themselves and their children in socially desirable ways, as well as the probable underreporting of socially disapproved and illegal behaviors, such as abusive discipline.

Observations

Unstructured observations of parenting practices provide direct information on how parents and children behave and can be undertaken in familiar, everyday settings to enhance the applicability of the findings. Structured observations, often conducted in laboratories, might focus on parent–infant interaction during standardized separation and reunion episodes to provide information on the strength of the parent–child emotional bond. Or a parenting task—for instance, getting a child to pick up toys—can address fundamental questions concerning how parent behaviors affect children's compliance and how their compliance or noncompliance affects subsequent parent behavior. The implicit assumptions of observational research are that closely observed processes are very similar to nonobserved ones and that behaviors and interaction patterns observed in the short-term have long-term effects, though the latter assertion is rarely tested. Concerns about observational research include potential bias on the part of observers and alterations in behavior due to the observer's presence.

Correlational Studies

Because many naturally occurring variations in parenting practices (e.g., use of other-than-parent care) are of intense interest but not feasible (or ethically defensible) to impose as experimental procedures, there is an important role for correlational studies. Many of them consist of simple tests of associations between parenting practices and children's behavior, with measurements taken at the same time, making it impossible to establish causal relationships. More recently, regression analyses and sophisticated modeling techniques (LISREL, AMOS, EQS) have made it possible to estimate the role that parenting practices play in children's outcomes later in time, with statistical correction for the children's (and sometimes parents') initial behavior (Duncan, Duncan, Strycker, Li, & Alpert, 1999). Often multiple ratings or standardized assessments serve as measures of parenting concepts or children's behavior, for example, punitive parenting and child aggression.

Experiments

Always the easiest way to establish cause-and-effect relationships, true experiments are relatively uncommon in parenting research. This is in part because researchers cannot ethically impose random assignment to test key questions (e.g., the effects of corporal punishment) and in part because there would be serious questions about the generalizability of the findings obtained to typical family situations. In selected areas, such as the effects of television on children, experiments make substantial contributions to the body of evidence. Recently, a new generation of prevention experiments incorporating random assignment has provided important information on improving postdivorce family adjustment (Forgatch & DeGarmo, 1999) and preventing adolescent substance abuse (Dishion, Kavanagh, Schneiger, Nelson, & Kaufman, 2002), and there has been a call for more experimental research on parenting (Patterson & Fisher, 2002).

Research Reviews

Both qualitative and quantitative summaries of empirical research studies provide accumulated evidence relevant to parenting issues, and each has benefits and limitations (Light and Pillemer, 1984; Lytton, 1994). Qualitative summaries, or narrative reviews, provide a useful service in aggregating data, but the process of selecting studies for inclusion is necessarily subjective, as is resolving conflicts between studies. Quantitative summaries or meta-analyses synthesize the weighted results of individual research projects and are an effective and increasingly frequent method of drawing conclusions on well-researched topics in parenting. They permit calculations of effect size, the estimated strength of a relationship between two variables, say the hours of television watched per week and school grades. Because of their emphasis on yielding summary conclusions, research reviews often fail to yield the kinds of results that parents can work with. The answer to the question "How large an effect size does this type of parenting behavior generate?" may be important, but parents may really want the answer to the question "Will this work with my child?"

Issues in Interpreting Research

A basic difficulty in synthesizing child development research is bridging the gap between short-term and long-term empirical studies. Short-term studies yield critical information about interactions between parents and children and immediate causal relationships, and they provide representations of what might happen in the longer term with daily repetition of parenting behavior patterns. But if the ultimate test of effective parenting is how children turn out, then the answers to many important parenting questions lie in the findings of prospective, long-term studies of parenting. The problem is that because such studies of necessity take a long time, sometimes decades, and cost a great deal of money, they are few in number. On topics for which they are available, particular attention will be paid to them. Prospective long-term studies that begin with a group of families selected for their representativeness, rather than for the presence of child or parent problems, contribute importantly to the understanding of differences in family functioning that precede the onset of problem behavior in some families. Utilizing several research methods (direct observations combined with teacher and parent ratings and standardized assessment instruments) avoids the problem inherent in any one. Multiple sources of information—for example, having a parent, a teacher, and the target child rate aggression—provide for more reliable measures of concepts. Finally, measuring multiple concepts helps place behaviors in their larger context; for example, a child who scores higher than average on social actions may also score high on antisocial actions because of an overall high activity level. Unfortunately, relatively few empirical studies on parenting incorporate these more recently developed advances in research methods, but the number of such studies is increasing.

Inevitable disparities occur when multiple investigators with their particular orientations and methods are pursuing the same topics. Teams of researchers measure different behaviors, or sometimes even when measuring the same behaviors, researchers obtain results at odds with each other. Further, distortions routinely occur in the research summarization process. One is the well-documented bias toward reporting differences (Rosenthal, 1978), in this context parenting practices that are associated with better or worse outcomes. Studies with indeterminate findings or no differences wind up in the researcher's "file drawer." If researchers study some aspect of behavior that turns out not to have any effect on outcomes, most will not attempt to publish their results, and if they do, it is unlikely that they will be selected for publication in professional journals (Greenwald, 1975). For example, Roggman, Langlois, Hubbs-Tait, and Rieser-Danner (1994) demonstrated that studies that found no differences between children cared for at home by a parent and those attending day care were less likely to be published than those that did, leading to systematic exaggeration of the effects of day care.

Because of their extensive technical descriptions of procedures and the complexity of their statistical analyses, research reports do not lend themselves to distribution and easy digestion by parents, few of whom have either the time or the training to read them. And as Holden (1997) acknowledged, "no single parenting practice results in a universal child outcome; if that were the case, the effects of child rearing would be much better understood by now" (p. 110). The answer to the "Will it work with my child?" question that parents are interested in is obtained not by examining statistical averages across children, as empirical researchers typically do, but by examining the variable effects of parenting practices on widely varying kinds of children in a variety of situations. Thus, the parenting experts can play a valuable intermediary role in synthesizing and interpreting relevant research to the parenting public, to the extent they choose to do so.

WHICH MESSAGES GET THROUGH?

Of course, parents are not uniformly receptive to information regarding parenting (Goodnow, 1995). Nor is information related to parenting always attended to intensely; some is processed without scrutiny; some completely escapes attention. Parents seek information to meet their current needs (Deutsch, Ruble, Fleming, Brooks-Gunn, & Stangor, 1988). For example, information on toilet training is unlikely to attract more than a passing glance from the parents of adolescents. Parents' search for information is often motivated by pressing concerns (Showers & Cantor, 1985), as when a child is clearly not doing well or the family is in upheaval.

Fatigue, emotional arousal, and distraction by other tasks have all been demonstrated to affect parenting (Dix, 1991; Holden, 1983; Holden, Coleman, & Schmidt, 1995), and they likely affect the search for parenting information as well. Inevitably, parents who can calmly sift through alternatives and make rational decisions at 10 o'clock in the morning find themselves tired, exasperated, and sometimes literally at wits' end in dealing with their child at 8 PM or 3 AM. For the burgeoning number of families in which there are two working parents, parenting problems are likely to occur well after the office hours of pediatricians, counselors, or educators. The book on the shelf, the Web site, or the TV or radio show, may determine what parents do to deal with a 5-year-old who is toilet trained but wakes up with a wet bed.

CULTURAL AND SUBCULTURAL DIFFERENCES IN PARENTING

Any general book, TV show, parenting Web site, or media expert runs the risk of assuming that one approach to parenting invariably produces the best outcomes across all racial and cultural groups. It should be acknowledged that parenting experts write for those who they or their publishers think are likely to buy the books they write and the magazines in which they appear. They write little on dealing with racial discrimination against your child, obtaining reduced-price school meals, or coping with neighborhood gangs, and much on how to manage Little League-type sports, music lessons, and other enthusiasms of the middle class. Their audience is implicitly, though not explicitly, European American (or British in the case of Leach), and middle-class.

As Holden (1997) noted, the quality of parenting must be evaluated in relation to the culture, social class, and family environment in which the child is raised. Like the experts, those who have done empirical research on parenting in this country have largely focused on European American middle-class samples, with notable exceptions (e.g., Brody, Stoneman, & Flor, 1996; Chao, 1994; McLoyd, 1990). Yet cultural differences are pervasive—for example, the differences between Japanese and American parents in cosleeping arrangements or between Swedish and Canadian disciplinary practices. At the subcultural level, social class differences evident in this country have been associated with differences in disciplinary practices (Erlanger, 1974; Gecas & Nye, 1974). Even different neighborhoods elicit different parenting practices (Furstenberg, Eccles, Elder, Cook, & Sameroff, 1997). So is it simply a matter of different strokes for different folks, which would preclude any general prescriptions for parenting? Are parenting experts doing a disservice unless they carefully parenthesize their writings with qualifications concerning race and class differences? Steinberg (1996) has argued that there are some broad principles of effective parenting that transcend ethnic and racial differences, reporting that in his large research project, authoritative parenting is associated with greater school success within each of four ethnic groups (African American, Asian American, European American, and Latino American). Other large studies have produced findings of greater similarities than differences across racial groups in the relationships between parenting practices and child and adolescent outcomes (Amato & Fowler, 2002; Rowe, Vazsonyi, & Flannery, 1994). But not all researchers show similar patterns across groups, and group differences inevitably qualify parenting experts' advice.

HOW MUCH DIFFERENCE CAN PARENTS MAKE?

One of the implications of research on genetic influences on behavior is that even the most effective parents do not—indeed they cannot—totally control their children's behavior. The effects of parenting practices typically found in empirical research studies are surprisingly weak (Maccoby & Martin, 1983), usually weaker than genetic effects, typically in the range of 20%–40% in child outcomes. This flies in the face of the widespread belief on the part of parents, children, and those who study them that what parents do matters a great deal. A typical finding is that of Rothbaum and Weisz (1994), whose meta-analysis of 47 studies found parental behavior had only a small effect ($r = .24$; medium and large effect sizes would be $r = .30$ and $r = .50$, respectively; J. Cohen, 1988) on the differences in child aggression, hostility, and noncompliance. And there is accumulating data, particularly from comparing the similarities between identical twins and same-sex fraternal twins, that genetic factors account for substantial proportions of the individual differences among children in personality (Loehlin, 1992; Rowe, 1994) and intelligence (Fulker, De Fries, & Plomin, 1988). In the latter study, the identifiable contribution of genetic influences on IQ actually increased from infancy to childhood. Studies designed to assess genetic influences and those of the shared family environment typically yield evidence of both genetic effects and effects of shared family environment, with smaller shared family environment contributions to children's and adolescents' behavior than to the behavior of their parents (Deater-Deckard, Fulker, & Plomin, 1999; Ge et al., 1996; O'Connor, Hetherington, Reiss, Hetherington, & Plomin, 1995).

One possibility is that effects of parenting practices obtained from individual observations or assessments underrepresent their actual contributions, which are cumulative (Abelson, 1985). Or parenting may be most prominent at critical moments in parent–child interaction that are poorly captured by researchers (Maccoby, 2000). Different effects of the same parenting intervention on children who differ in age, sex, and temperament may be lost when data are aggregated (W. A. Collins et al., 2000; Maccoby, 2000). Maccoby (2000) rejects the assumption that when genetic effects are large, the effects of environmental factors such as parenting must be correspondingly small because genes and environment are inevitably interwoven in development. The effects of relatively short-term parenting interventions on children's behavior (e. g., Cowan & Cowan, 2002; Forgatch & DeGarmo, 1999) demonstrate that it would be a mistake to believe that parenting practices are trivial or inconsequential in affecting children's development.

There is an additional complication in understanding parents' interactions with their children. Despite the frequent assumption that parents are the instigators and children the targets of parenting practices, there is clear and convincing evidence that children's behavior affects the parenting they receive, for better or worse (Bell, 1968). Frequent findings that harsh, punitive parents have children who are difficult to control may reflect the fact that problematic child behaviors elicit harsh, punitive parenting (Lee & Bates, 1985; Patterson, 1986).

Scarr and McCartney (1983) described how children's physical and mental attributes and personalities can elicit behaviors from those around them. Thus, children with more active, less irritable temperaments tend to receive better parenting and mentoring than those not so favored (Werner & Smith, 1992). And when there is differential treatment of siblings, parents tend to favor the same child (McHale, Crouter, McGuire, & Updegraff, 1995), implying that attributes of individual children elicit similar behaviors from parents who differ in sex, in gender-shaped parenting roles, and many other attributes. Children establish their own developmental niches, which serve to further shape their abilities and personalities (Holden, 1997).

Compelling evidence of children's ability to elicit their mother's behavior comes from a study of parent–child interaction in which mothers of normal and conduct-disordered sons interacted in a laboratory playroom with their own sons, another boy of the same classification, whether conduct-disordered or normal, and a boy from the other classification. All mothers responded more negatively to the conduct-disordered boys. But the different types of mothers did not produce different behaviors in the boys, suggesting that the boys' behavior had more effect on the mothers' than vice versa. There was also evidence of past experience influencing the behavior of mothers of conduct-disordered boys: They were more negative with their own sons than with the other conduct-disordered boy (K. E. Anderson, Lytton, & Romney, 1986).

One thing is clear: When parenting behaviors and children's behaviors are studied, the wide variety in outcomes for children and adolescents cannot simply be attributed solely to parenting practices or genetically influenced temperamental qualities. An emerging consensus is that interactive effects are the rule, in that expression of heritable traits depends, often heavily, on parenting practices, as well as subcultural and cultural factors (W. A. Collins et al., 2000). For example, for infants and toddlers assessed as more temperamentally unmanageable, mothers' highly controlling parenting practices have been linked to lower levels of aggressive behavior during middle childhood (Bates, Pettit, Dodge, & Ridge, 1998). Children at risk because of perinatal difficulties and family problems improved in functioning when they had warm, responsive interactions with at least one parent figure (Werner & Smith, 1992). Interactive influences are inevitably more difficult to translate into simple recommendations for parental behavior, but oversimplification that emphasizes only effects of parenting practices or only genetic influences inevitably misrepresents the manner in which each contributes to children's outcomes (W. A. Collins et al., 2000).

It remains a cultural expectation, however, that parents shape their children's behavior and development. Parents themselves often subscribe to the belief that if they were parenting "correctly" their children would not have problems, and they are aware that family members, teachers, neighbors, and adults in the wider community are likely to believe so, too. Thus, parents are in a situation in which they are not always sure what to do and may in fact not be able to change their children's behavior very much, and yet their performance as parents is under public scrutiny. When people feel responsible for—and care deeply about—good outcomes amidst conditions of uncertainty, they are driven to seek both information and assurance. No wonder there is such enormous demand for books, newspaper and magazine articles, TV and radio programs, and videotapes on parenting.

OVERVIEW OF THE CHAPTERS

The book is topically organized, focusing on those issues about which parents frequently seek information and professional assistance. Parents report a greater information gap between the knowledge they have and what they need on parenting than on physical care (American Academy of Pediatrics, 2003; Young, Davis, Schoen, & Parker, 1998). This first chapter will conclude by briefly previewing the major topics that follow. The next chapter is focused on infancy, describing the substantial differences in coverage of the five experts and focusing on two key issues: persistent crying and toilet training. Infant crying contributes to parents' feelings of exasperation, depression, and helplessness and is a significant source of stress for new parents (Wilkie & Ames, 1986). In two nationally representative samples, 23% of parents of infants and young children wanted more information on crying (Schuster, Duan, Regalado, & Klein, 2000; Young et al., 1998). Research findings on the causes of crying, the interpretation of crying, and soothing techniques are compared with the experts' advice. Similarly, toilet training has been repeatedly identified as a topic on which many parents would like more guidance than that provided by their pediatrician (Bethell, Peck, & Schor, 2001; Schuster et al., 2000; Young et al., 1998). After a review of empirical research and best practice standards for toilet training and brief descriptions of the experts' advice, a public controversy between the experts that played out in the *New York Times* and other media is analyzed.

The third chapter considers day care, particularly for infants. Negative effects of early substitute child care are reported as a frequent or occasional worry by 50% of parents surveyed in their pediatricians' offices (Stickler, Salter, Broughton, & Alario, 1991). Although a topic for national discussion, only recently has large-scale data collection documented the effects of the early day care that is actually available in this country. These findings provide the centerpiece of the discussion of day-care effects on parent–infant relationships and the development of social and cognitive skills of infants and preschoolers. Professional standards for day-care quality will be described. The experts' advice on appropriate age of entry to day care, their description of what to look for in child care, and their assessments of day-care effects will be reviewed. In this area as in others, their advice is at odds with each other, and in two cases, with their own previously published stands, and the forces shaping their disagreements and position changes will be outlined.

Discipline is addressed in the fourth chapter, which covers research on effects of parental strictness, love and responsiveness in discipline, and discipline practices, with a section devoted to physical punishment. One of the largest gaps between the information that parents say they need and what they get from their pediatricians occurs for discipline (Bethell et al., 2001; Young et al., 1998). Seventy-three percent of parents report that they worry occasionally or frequently about their ability to provide appropriate discipline (Stickler et al., 1991). The review of the experts' advice on discipline provides a particularly striking depiction of their overall philosophy of parenting and the larger concerns that shape it.

The fifth chapter briefly reviews media effects on children's aggression, creativity, academic skills, and sexual behavior. The authors' universal concerns with public media and their strategies for dealing with it will be described, as will research on parents' TV management. Television worries are mentioned by 50% of parents (Stickler et al., 1991). Next, the sixth chapter, which focuses on adolescence, will be devoted to two key topics: teens' sexuality and substance misuse, both of which are highly ranked among parental concerns (Hughes & Durio, 1983). Empirical research on preventive effects of family cohesion, parental monitoring, and specific parent communications about sex and drugs will be compared with the authors' advice, and the controversy surrounding sexuality education in the schools will be briefly reviewed.

The last chapter sets out criteria for assessment, provides a review of each author's contributions, and identifies the persuasive appeals and ideologies that shape their advice. Finally, an argument is made for more broadly constructed and better publicized best practice standards on major parenting issues that would address the gap between the knowledge that professionals have and what parents need to know.

This not a book that needs to be read from beginning to end. The topical organization is designed to permit use when confronted with a specific problem, and particularly when having to sort out conflicting advice regarding that issue. The five public figures featured in this book do not have all the answers, but then neither do academic researchers or family counseling professionals or anybody else. It is only by synthesizing—and comparing and criticizing—the knowledge, prescriptions, and beliefs of experts, clinicians, and researchers that a base of information can be established to help parents make good decisions about their children. And even then, there will always be a gap between parents' knowledge of what is best for their children and what they actually put into practice.

There is no last word on parenting, no one expert, no sure system for sorting out all the advice. The focus ultimately has to be on what produces good outcomes for the individual children and their families. For every parent and any professional to have the best grasp on all they might face, everyone must become more willing to discuss, compare, and choose among different views. Like children, we all have a lot to learn.

CHAPTER 2
INFANTS AND TODDLERS

As PARENTS LOOK DOWN at their newborn, their feelings of joy and relief at having the delivery over are rapidly replaced by an awareness of just how much moment-to-moment care an infant requires. Their baby must be kept warm; it must begin to nurse; it needs to be changed, cleaned, soothed, and protected from harm. There has not been an infant born that is capable of meeting its basic needs or even of telling parents exactly what they are, so mothers and fathers are immediately faced not only with rounds of feeding, burping, and changing, but also with trying to figure out why their baby is crying and what he or she might need.

Meeting a baby's needs is especially difficult because parents initially know very little about their child. Over time they will learn his or her daily rhythms and preferences, what works in soothing, what is unsettling, and so forth. They will form ideas about their child's temperament that will subsequently shape their thoughts and actions. But right after birth parents know none of this, and they are likely to need information about normal variations in infant behavior and when to seek treatment for problems.

Just as this is the time when parents are likely to be most reliant on advice, it is also the time when the accuracy of that advice is particularly critical. Child care mistakes with infants are likely to lead to more serious and long-term consequences than mistakes with older children. Sending a child to school without warm enough clothing can result in referral to social service agencies; by contrast, failing to keep a newborn warm enough can result in depressed respiration and death. In addition, infancy is often characterized as a time of laying down developmental foundations, of sensitive periods in which fundamentals must be established for the child's subsequent success. Studies of infants in understaffed orphanages who are adequately nourished and clothed but denied emotional and social stimulation provide galling evidence of the retardation and mortality caused by inadequate attention to the very young (Dennis, 1973; Spitz, 1946). So those who would advise parents of infants certainly must instruct them about those parenting behaviors that maintain life, contribute to well-being, and prevent damage. Equally important, they must counsel parents in ways to promote growth and development.

Because infants are so vulnerable and their capabilities so drastically different from older children and adults, parents have a particular need for thorough descriptions of normal infant development. And much of what the experts communicate about infant care necessarily concerns mechanics: bathing, comforting, and maintaining physical safety. But even in their advice to parents on the rudiments of care, the experts show strongly contrasting approaches. Some emphasize parents' nurturing, shaping actions in socializing infants into appropriately subordinate social roles. Others emphasize the need for parental responsiveness to facilitate infant development toward positive outcomes. Even a question as simple as "Can you spoil a baby?" can reveal an expert's construction of infancy, which in turn reveals their assumptions about the social order both in the family and in the larger society.

THE BABY MANUALS

Three of the media experts, Spock, Brazelton, and Leach, provide "owner's manuals" for parents of infants, with thorough coverage of the physical care and nurturing of infants and discussion of parents' problems, including postpartum depression. Each acknowledges normal infant variations, including prematurity, as well as temperamental differences in infancy. Each volume is well organized and well indexed, so parents can find what they need in a hurry, and each provides specific helpful tips and general reassurance and support for parents. All endorse breast-feeding, with Spock and Leach providing extensive information on establishing breast- and bottle-feeding, and Brazelton recommending another book specifically devoted to the topic. With the assistance that a good hospital pediatric staff provides in getting feeding established, each would be adequate to support parents who need a first parenting manual.

Yet they are distinctly different in their advice. Brazelton's (1992) is the more developmental approach, the most explicitly research grounded, and the most geared toward helping parents anticipate their child's upcoming development. He writes in the role of the teaching pediatrician, getting parents to appreciate their infant's abilities. He acknowledges demands that compete with parents' care for infants, including work responsibilities and care for older children, and he emphasizes fathers' active role in care of infants. Substantial coverage of temperamental differences is provided, and Brazelton provides insightful advice on how to deal with babies who are extremely sensitive and difficult to soothe. His nutritional guidance and recommendation to put babies on their backs for sleeping are consistent with the advice of the American Academy of Pediatrics. Despite the lack of content on breast-feeding, *Touchpoints* provides a great deal of accurate, useful information on parenting infants.

Leach (1998) writes more as a naturalist documenting infancy and provides rich, complete descriptions and pictures of common newborn peculiarities in skin, head shape, and eyes. There also are excellent sections on everyday care, including carrying, feeding, dressing, and keeping babies clean, which are supported by step-by-step pictures. She is especially thorough in her explanation of getting breast- or bottle-feeding started. Advocacy for responsive care for infants is prominent in her coverage. She gives state-of-the-art advice on infant nutrition but has a particular concern about pesticide residues on foods for older babies and toddlers that may be unfamiliar and seem alarmist to American readers. Leach does not cover parental preparations and emotions during pregnancy, though both Spock and Brazelton deal with these topics. And even in the recently revised (1998) edition of *Your Baby and Child*, Leach writes little about fathers' contributions to the development of infants and young children. Given the intensity of care that infants require and the evidence that fathers and mothers interact with babies in distinctly different ways (Cowan, Cowan, & Kerig, 1993), the omission is puzzling. There are many pictures of fathers caring for infants in this richly illustrated book, and they are written about as labor coaches and advocates during delivery and as providers of bottle feedings, but when Leach writes to "you" the parent, there is little doubt that she is addressing mothers.

Spock's seventh edition (Spock & Parker, 1998) provides a thorough treatment of both parents' perception during pregnancy and an overview of equipment needed to care for an infant. He describes how newborns appear and how to care for them and does it in a friendly and reassuring manner. He urges fathers to participate in baby care and household tasks and writes extensively about fathers' responsibilities, their children's identification with them, and their role in discipline. He recommends demand rather than scheduled feedings and urges parents not to force babies to take more milk or formula than they want. He warns of the risks of cosleeping with infants in the same bed once they get past the age of 6 months, all positions that are fairly well-established.

In this edition, Spock takes conventional stands against low-fat diets for infants (consistent with the recommendations of the American Academy of Pediatrics [AAP] Committee on Nutrition, 1998) and against sugary foods, artificial flavors and colors, caffeine, corn syrup, and honey in children's diets. But he goes further, perhaps inspired by his perceptions of improvements in his own health with dietary changes. He argues against animal protein sources, including dairy foods, meats, and eggs for young children's diets. Instead he favors plant-based foods for older babies and children, including soy milk starting when babies switch from breast milk and formula at age 1 (Spock & Parker, 1998). These recommendations were controversial (J. Brody, 1998) and inconsistent with AAP guidelines (AAP Committee on Nutrition, 1998), which call for supplemental feeding with meat, as well as fruits and vegetables. In fact, the AAP's *Pediatric Nutrition Handbook* describes a vegetarian diet without adequate dairy products as putting children at nutritional risk (AAP Committee on Nutrition, 1998).

In summary, though all the infant manuals have much to recommend them, they have distinct differences in tone and coverage and particular shortcomings: Leach neglects pregnancy, Brazelton writes little about breast-feeding, and Spock includes his dietary enthusiasms, deemed by other pediatricians to be nutritionally risky. None can be considered the absolute standard on infant care, though they are arguably the best available.

In contrast with Leach, Brazelton, and Spock, Dobson provides incidental coverage of infant topics in responding to parents' questions, as will be described in the next two sections. In his first book, Rosemond (1990) covers important infant topics in a chapter, among them postpartum blues, breast- versus bottle-feeding, feeding schedules, introducing solid foods, getting babies to sleep, pacifiers, and day care for infants, but his coverage is issue-oriented rather than comprehensive.

Two problems in infancy reveal most completely the comparative accuracy and reliability of the experts' advice. As noted in the introductory chapter, persistent crying and toilet training are topics for which parents frequently seek advice. They have been identified as the two parenting situations that most frequently precipitate fatal child abuse (Krugman, 1983–1985). These two topics, which would seem very far removed indeed from the public arena, also reveal how the authors' advice may reflect their political beliefs. To assess empirical support for the experts' advice on these two topics, relevant empirical research will be reviewed.

PERSISTENT CRYING

Developmental Course of Crying

Crying actually increases in the first few weeks of life, peaks around 6 weeks of age in American babies, and decreases to a more stable level by the end of the 3rd month (Barr, 2000; Hunziker & Barr, 1986; Papousek & Papousek, 1996; St. James-Roberts, 2001a), which is a period of major neural and behavioral transformations (Papousek & von Hofacker, 1998). During the first 3 months, infant crying occurs most frequently during the evening, accounting for 40% of the daily crying total (Barr, 1990; St. James-Roberts & Halil, 1991). This evening peak consists predominantly of fussing rather than intense crying, but comes at a time of day when parents are likely to be tired and short on coping skills, even without the presence of crying.

At the 6-week peak, babies cry and fuss on average 2 hours a day (Alvarez, 2004; Brazelton, 1962; Hunziker & Barr, 1986; St. James-Roberts & Halil, 1991), but by the beginning of the 4th month, crying averages about half that amount (St. James-Roberts, 1993b). Good news for parents whose babies cry prodigiously in the early weeks is that their average levels of cortisol are not higher than average, which would indicate stress (White, Gunnar, Larson, Donzella, & Barr, 2000), and in most cases there is no significant relationship between the amount of crying in the early weeks and that occurring at 9–12 months (Hubbard & van IJzendoorn, 1991; Isabella, Ward, & Belsky, 1985). Irritability, however, is more stable across time (Fox & Polak, 2001; St. James-Roberts, 1993b).

Barr (1998) suggests that the early peak in crying may be "a behavioral universal of human infancy" (p. 426) characteristic of all cultures but not all infants within each culture. Even among !Kung San babies in the Kalahari desert who are held 80% of the day and breast-fed on demand, the amount of crying peaks and then subsides within the first 3 months of age (Barr, Konner, Bateman, & Adamson, 1991).

Variability in Crying

Colic is increased crying limited to the first 4 months of life, usually including unexpected, prolonged bouts of unsoothable crying (Barr, 1998).

The most commonly applied criterion for colic is crying and fussing more than 3 hours a day, for more than 3 days a week and for more than 3 consecutive weeks (Wessel, Cobb, Jackson, Harris, & Detwiler, 1954). Estimates of the number of babies engaging in colicky persistent crying range from 8% to 40% (Barr, 1998), depending on whether the "rule of threes" given above or a looser criterion is used. Crying increases parents' concerns about their infants, as indicated by the relatively high percentage of mothers (21% in one British study and 15% in another) seeking referral for problem crying (St. James-Roberts & Halil, 1991).

Impact of Crying on Mothers and Infants

A. R. Miller, Barr, and Eaton (1993) measured emotional distress in women in their third trimester of pregnancy and again after their baby's birth. There was no difference in the women's moods before birth, but those mothers whose babies met the clinical criteria for colic (more than 3 hours a day for 3 or more days) at age 6 weeks reported more distress than they had in pregnancy; mothers whose babies did not have colic actually reported less distress, and the two groups were now significantly different. So colicky persistent crying has measurable negative effects on the mother. Another sign of the difficulties created by problem crying is that parents' stress levels drop significantly in response to reductions in crying (Murray & Cooper, 2001).

Can Adults Tell Different Types of Cries Apart?

Adults can clearly differentiate the sounds associated with pain and hunger cries whether or not they have had experience with babies (Gustafson & Harris, 1990; Zeskind, Sale, Maio, Huntington, & Weiseman, 1985). But women in a caregiving simulation study (Gustafson & Harris, 1990) who heard cries of hungry babies and of babies in pain had difficulty responding appropriately in circumstances where there were no additional clues for distinguishing them (e.g., how long since the last feeding). They did not feed a baby following a hunger cry sooner or spend more time comforting a baby following a pain cry, indicating that they used a general repertoire of soothing behaviors, even if they could discriminate the two sounds. This suggests that parents in actual caregiving situations will be similarly unlikely to take effective caregiving steps, at least in the early weeks of their baby's life.

Causes of Crying

DIGESTIVE PAIN. Despite the widespread belief that early crying problems are due to digestive upsets, intestinal problems cause the pain responsible for colic in only a small proportion of cases (St. James-Roberts, 1993a). One estimate based on research is that less than 5% of early excessive crying cases can be accounted for in this way (Barr, 1996, 1998). Others are slightly higher (5%–10%, Gormally, 2001; 10%–15%, Wolke, 1993).

DEVELOPMENTAL FACTORS. The function of crying changes as infants develop in the months beyond birth: The initially reflexive, unlearned sign of discomfort and distress becomes a more differentiated behavior reflecting the development of emotional abilities (St. James-Roberts, 1993a). Persistent crying in early infancy apparently reflects a general but transient dysfunction in infants' regulation of their behavioral–emotional states (Papousek & von Hofacker, 1998). Around 3 months of age, reflexes evident at birth diminish, and cortical regulatory control over behavior becomes more pronounced (Lester, 1985; Prechtl, 1984). About this time, changes occur in brain organization so infants can inhibit crying more readily (Fisichelli, Karelitz, Fisichelli, & Cooper, 1974), but some babies make this transition easily and some do not (St. James-Roberts, 1993a). It has recently been suggested that persistent crying in the early weeks of life may be due to transient delays or disruptions in coordinating day–night rhythms in different body systems (Barr, 2000; White et al., 2000). The 6-week peak in persistent crying comes at a time when infants are developing daily sleep–wake cycles more like those of adults, and fatigue during longer waking periods also may contribute to the occurrence of late afternoon and evening crying (Parmelee, Wenner, & Schulz, 1964). In brief, recent discussions have emphasized central nervous system organization rather than the digestive problems in early differences among infants in crying (Barr, 2001; St. James-Roberts, 2001b).

TEMPERAMENT. Early research in temperament provided no direct evidence that difficult temperament underlies persistent crying (Thomas, Chess, & Birch, 1968). St. James-Roberts (1993b) notes that temperament alone cannot account for two of the main features of early persistent infant crying: evening crying and a decline in crying around 3 months of age. It seems more likely that temperament amplifies or modulates infants' responses to other stresses, so that they respond more strongly to late-day fatigue or have a relatively intense reaction to stressful stimuli (St. James-Roberts, 1993a).

Barr (2000) differentiates two types within the minority of babies with persistent crying. One is an "early excessive crying" type with increased crying that resolves by the 4th month of life. This includes the great majority of babies who show problem crying. Babies who cry persistently beyond 3 months are the second type and may have difficult temperaments, difficulties regulating their arousal levels, or, in some cases, organic risk factors, problems in feeding or sleeping, and evidence of mild developmental delay (Barr, 2000; Papousek & von Hofacker, 1998).

In a 3-year follow-up of a community sample of persistently crying infants identified at age 3 months, well after the normal developmental peak, there was an increased rate of sleep disorders, temper tantrums, interactional problems, and negative long-term effects on family functioning (Rautava, Lehtonen, Helenius, & Sillanpaa, 1995), suggesting that temperamental factors are involved in crying past the 6-week peak in early infancy. Babies with "persistent distress syndrome" show generalized irritability, persistent crying past the developmental peak, and feeding and sleeping problems, again potentially implicating temperamental factors. But their mothers reported higher levels of prenatal stress and anxiety and more conflicts with their marital partners during the pregnancy, suggesting that temperament may not be the only influence on their babies' crying (Papousek & von Hofacker, 1998).

PARENTING FACTORS. Prospective studies using infants drawn from the community (rather than clinically referred) have failed to find significant differences in early crying as a function of maternal age, personality, ethnicity, and social class (St. James-Roberts, Conroy, & Wilsher, 1995; Stifter & Braungart, 1992). However, particularly for babies who cry persistently past the waning of the 6-week developmental peak, parent attributes seem to affect how long babies cry. Mothers' anxiety (Carey, 1968) and misinterpretation of infant signals (Taubman, 1988) have been linked to persistent crying. A mother's prenatal reactivity (indexed by acceleration in heart rate) predicts her postnatal rating of her baby's difficultness and fussing and crying (Pederson, Huffman, del Carmen, & Bryan, 1996).

In summary, the pattern of findings suggests that persistent crying in the early weeks is not uncommon and reflects an underlying neuromaturational shift, whereas persistent crying past 3 months of age involves fewer babies, and temperamental and family factors are more likely to be involved.

Techniques for Reducing Crying

CHANGING DIET AND STIMULATION. If a baby does not tolerate cow's milk protein well when repeatedly tested, changing to alternative formula may be beneficial according to a quantitative review of controlled clinical trials (Lucassen et al., 1998). In one well-designed recent study, one quarter of colicky babies showed a substantial reduction in crying time when given lactase to aid in breaking down the lactose present in milk, suggesting that there is a subset of infants whose distress is due to transient lactose intolerance (Kanabar, Randhawa, & Clayton, 2001). Thus, if intestinal pain is a possibility, parents should consult their pediatrician. However, elimination of cow's milk protein or lactose should not be the first intervention attempted because the change makes no difference in the majority of cases (Wolke, 1993). Any rocking technique soothes infants more rapidly than either just holding the infant upright on the shoulder (thereby giving them body contact and warmth) or leaving them to self-soothe. Continuous horizontal rocking led to infant drowsiness in one study (Byrne & Horowitz, 1981); in two others, vertical rocking was used to quiet crying (Ambrose, 1969; Keefe, 2001). One study showed that carrying infants reduced their crying (Hunziker & Barr, 1986), but two studies, one with a community sample (St. James-Roberts, Hurry, Bowyer, & Barr, 1995), and one with problem-crying babies (Barr, McMullen, et al., 1991), did not.

Campos (1989) studied crying in 2-week-old infants and 2-month-old infants after needle pricks during medical procedures and found that using a pacifier was more successful than swaddling in terminating crying. Pacifiers were also more successful than rocking (Campos, 1994). Although any continuous, rhythmic noise seems effective in soothing newborns, white noise has been evaluated most thoroughly and probably works because it masks other external stimuli (Spencer, Moran, Lee, & Talbert, 1990). Tapes of uterine noises and other strategies to simulate the uterine environment seem effective but have not been well evaluated, according to leading researchers (Blakeslee, 2005; Wolke, 1993).

In some cases, irritable crying may be exacerbated by parents' attempts to soothe the baby, trying first one strategy and then another. When mothers of infants with "troublesome" crying were given instructions to cut down on stimulation, their babies cried less than those randomly assigned to a wait-list control condition (McKenzie, 1991). However, because mothers' ratings were used to assess crying rather than more objective measures, these findings should be interpreted conservatively (Wolke, 1993).

CHANGING PARENT–INFANT INTERACTION. Evidence demonstrating the importance of parental responsiveness comes from a longitudinal study on newborns who showed high levels or low levels of crying and fussing in response to a painful stimulus or when their sucking was interrupted (Fish,

Stifter, & Belsky, 1991). Their crying later in infancy was dependent in part on their mother's attitudes. Fussy newborns whose mothers were more positive in attributional style (crediting themselves for good events, not thinking bad events would recur) were more likely to show reduced crying by age 5 months. In the same research, lowest levels of newborn fussiness in response to negative events were found in babies whose mothers showed the most sensitive, responsive interactions with their babies (Fish et al., 1991).

Intervention studies provide the most compelling evidence that when parents increase their responsiveness to babies' crying, babies cry less. Wolke, Gray, and Meyer (1994) conducted a multifaceted intervention in which they provided parents of 2- to 6-month-old babies with information about normal crying patterns, recommended establishing a daily routine and pattern of activities for sleeping and feeding, reduced overstimulation when necessary, and provided a repertoire of soothing techniques. Depending on the intensity and suspected reason for the crying, they also counseled parents to wait 1 or 2 minutes after crying had begun before intervening to encourage self-soothing. Crying diminished significantly more in this multiple treatment condition than in a control condition administered by the same individuals who provided only empathy, and mothers reported greater problem reduction and improved relationships with their babies in the treatment condition.

Ian St. James-Roberts, a leading researcher in this area, suggests that the optimal strategy for dealing with crying changes with age. Early reflexive crying, which peaks at 6 weeks of age, should be responded to immediately. "As learning and social communicative abilities develop, however, a strategy of uncritical response will prevent the infant from learning differentiated social communicative skills and autonomous self-control, both of which are desirable in the longer term" (1993a, p. 37). So parents should try to determine the likely reason for crying and avoid rewarding irritable fussiness with attention. Hubbard and van IJzendoorn (1991) argue that an immediate response to intense, pain-type crying and a slower wait-and-see strategy to fretful, fussy behavior allow the child to learn self-soothing and other coping strategies. They point out that being responsive to other behaviors, such as exploratory play behaviors, might diminish irritable crying (Hubbard & van IJzendoorn, 1991). However, in a longitudinal study of 50 mother–infant pairs, mothers' delay in responding to crying in early infancy was not associated with frequency of crying later in the first year when the amount of earlier crying was appropriately controlled for (Hubbard & van IJzendoorn, 1991), so there is no indication that early delays in responding lead to less crying later.

To summarize briefly, research on persistent crying shows that parental strategies for coping with crying need to change over time, from that of always responding to crying in young infants that is largely reflexive, to more selective responding to crying in older infants that may be motivated by a wish for attention. Therefore, the parenting authors' advice can be both consequential and, if unvarying, potentially harmful.

THE EXPERTS' DISCUSSION OF PERSISTENT CRYING IN INFANTS

When helping parents deal with persistent crying, it is crucial that experts let parents know what they can expect concerning the amount and developmental course of crying, and help them accept individual differences in crying. Because babies cry the most in early infancy, when parents have the least experience, parents need some understanding of the challenge they face and reassurance to help them cope. Parents can benefit from information that will help them discriminate causes of crying, including those signaling the need for medical intervention, and they need effective techniques for soothing infants. They need guidance on when to attend to crying and when to let the baby cry it out. The sections on crying in Spock's, Brazelton's, and Leach's books are accessible and well organized so that parents can find them easily at 8:00 PM when their baby has been crying for 2 hours straight. The three also differ substantially from one another in dealing with infant crying.

Spock

The seventh edition of *Dr. Spock's Baby and Child Care* (Spock & Parker, 1998) treats infant crying as a separate topic. Parents are given accurate information about the waning of crying at 3 months and told that babies cry most in the afternoon and evening—the type of basic information parents need to recognize normality and variability. Spock notes that some babies (10% is the figure used) cry more frequently and inconsolably than do others and provides parents accurate and reassuring information that such babies usually are healthy and show normal growth patterns (Spock & Parker, 1998). According to Spock, crying does not always mean pain or sadness, and he enjoins parents to listen to the quality of the cry, describing hunger cries as insistent, loud, and high-pitched, and discontented cries as "softer, lower-pitched, and more melodic" (Spock & Parker, 1998, p.209), to determine which crying needs an immediate response. He writes that the environment does not cause persistent crying and briefly notes the immaturity of the baby's nervous and digestive systems to account for why crying waxes and wanes during the first 3 months (Spock & Parker, 1998). Fatigue, dirty diapers, digestive problems, and incipient illness are mentioned as causes of crying, and Spock provides an extended discussion of how to rule out hunger and digestion problems. "Hypertonic" irritable temperament is discussed, and reduction of stimulation to reduce crying is recommended. Several soothing techniques are described—more frequent feeding, rocking, using pacifiers, swaddling, carrying, massaging, playing music, reducing stimulation, and providing herbal tea for irritable babies (Spock & Parker, 1998)—but no information is provided about their likely effectiveness.

What should parents do when they have ruled out hunger, pain, and discomfort as causes of crying and used all their soothing techniques without apparent effect? Spock asserts that you cannot spoil babies during the first 6 months, perhaps the first 9 months of life, so that should not be a concern for the parents of young infants. "Whiny" babies should be left alone for 10 to 15 minutes to see if they can calm themselves before intervening with another round of soothing techniques (Spock & Parker, 1998). He recommends against picking up older babies whenever they fuss. Spock realistically describes parents' feelings of anger and helplessness in response to inconsolable crying and supports their need to occasionally escape from it. He repeatedly advises parents to avoid becoming overly focused on the baby and to attend to their own needs, by having friends in or making care arrangements so one or both parents can go out.

Spock's approach to infant crying is that of an active problem solver. He is accurate in describing the daily fluctuations and developmental course of crying. He is thorough in his treatment of the topic, reassuring, and genuinely helpful to parents trying to ascertain what might be the cause of crying and in giving specific techniques to deal with it. Spock tells parents that persistent crying comes from within, and he notes that early crying is a normal developmental phenomenon, assertions supported by research. His instructions on how to tell when a baby is hungry are particularly useful, since feeding is one of the first soothing strategies used even when adults hear a pain cry (Gustafson & Harris, 1990). He devotes much attention to infant intestinal discomfort when it is not a very frequent cause for persistent crying, though it is certainly a cause that parents should attend to. His advice to parents to occasionally seek a reprieve from crying helps safeguard against frustration escalating into abuse. His counsel that parents cannot spoil a young baby, but should avoid rewarding fussiness in older babies by not responding immediately, is supported by research (e.g., St. James-Roberts, 1993a).

Brazelton

Brazelton gives a clear, accurate description of the daily fluctuations and developmental course of crying, informed by his own research (Brazelton, 1962b; Brazelton, 1990) that is also consistent with data gathered by others (Hunziker & Barr, 1986; St. James-Roberts & Halil, 1991). He recognizes temperamental "hypersensitivity" as a contributing factor in crying (Brazelton, 1983; Brazelton, 1992). In *Touchpoints*, Brazelton identifies six different cries and writes that parents learn to tell them apart by finding out what makes them stop. He provides additional help as well; for example, the unique sound of the pain cry is described as a sharp scream, followed by a brief period of no breathing, then repeated cries that do not stop when the baby is picked up (Brazelton, 1992). Brazelton also provides an explanation for the evening crying in early infancy: "An immature nervous system can take in and utilize stimuli through the day, but there is always a little bit of overload. As the day proceeds, the increasingly overloaded nervous system begins to cycle in shorter and shorter sleep and feeding periods. Finally, it blows off steam in the form of an active, fussy period" (Brazelton, 1992, p. 63). This is complemented with information reassuring to parents who are trying to cope: in his research on early crying, the onset was largely inevitable in 85% of the babies (Brazelton, 1992).

His list of soothing techniques is similar to Spock's: Parents should feed a baby first, change him, give warm water to get a burp, and pick him up and carry him. He cautions parents against using too many soothing techniques and thereby incidentally increasing the baby's arousal rather than reducing it. For a baby who is hypersensitive, he recommends reducing stimulation, even to the point of feeding her in a darkened room (Brazelton, 1984). Babies who cry for longer periods and more intensely over time despite soothing efforts should be taken to the pediatrician, who can search for an allergy or other potential contributors. Much of his focus is on teaching parents how to assist their babies in self-comforting: "The parents' task is to determine how much each of these different cries demands attention from them, and how the infant can 'learn' to comfort himself" (Brazelton, 1992, p. 236). Parents can teach their babies to suck on a thumb or pacifier as a self-soothing technique. He writes, "I don't believe spoiling is possible in the first year" (Brazelton, 1992, p. 73) but cautions parents against responding in the 2nd year, or even in the first year, to crying that has no obvious cause except to demand their attention. Hovering, overly intrusive parents, he writes, slow down their toddler's development of a sense of his or her own competence (Brazelton, 1992).

Brazelton's treatment is more descriptive than Spock's, focusing on helping parents to cope and on how they can teach their baby to cope. It draws on his own research, with attention to infant temperament as a source of crying variations. He effectively places crying in the context of the baby's overall development, and information about the largely inevitable duration of infant crying in the early months is likely to be reassuring to parents. Much of his focus is on getting the baby to learn the skill of self-soothing as part of the development of emotional self-regulation. In this process, parents' role is necessarily secondary, and he enjoins them against hovering overprotectiveness. His advice that parents should respond selectively to older babies' crying is supported by research (Hubbard & IJzendoorn, 1991; St. James-Roberts 1993a). In his main parenting manual, Brazelton provides fewer specifics than Spock that would enable parents to diagnose the cause of crying and try different soothing techniques, perhaps because of his focus on infant skill development. In a recently published specialty book (Brazelton & Sparrow, 2003a), he provides more specific and helpful strategies. Like Spock, he gives parents permission to leave a crying baby alone for a short while to settle themselves, which gives them at least a brief respite.

Leach

Leach provides a full treatment of infant crying in three major sections of *Your Baby and Child*, and she describes an increase in crying and fussing in normal babies and a developmental peak at 2 to 3 hours a day at 6 weeks of life. Only when she describes colic does she identify evenings as a peak time of crying, and she acknowledges that some researchers do not consider colic anything more than the extreme end of a normal crying pattern. She identifies colic with intense crying during the evening, soothable by a variety of techniques that are only momentarily effective. As she describes colic, it is "not an illness; only a very distressing pattern of newborn behavior with no accepted cause, no generally agreed-on treatment and absolutely no ill-effects except on parents' nerves" (Leach, 1998, p. 120). But she warns parents against concluding their baby has colic when he or she cries in the evening, when there may be another, easily treatable source of discomfort. Parents of colicky babies should avoid repeated changes in their infant care routines in a search for the cause of crying, because they will likely be unsuccessful (p. 120).

In Leach's (1998) treatment of causes of crying, she writes that "Babies never cry for nothing. . . . But while crying always means that your baby is as least somewhat uncomfortable or unhappy, crying in these first weeks doesn't always mean that something is wrong. Recent research suggests that a lot of newborn crying is 'developmental' " (p. 113). She also describes parents' feelings of ineffectiveness and even of anger in response to crying they cannot soothe. On the basis of Wolff's (1969) observational study of 14 babies, Leach identifies causes of crying: hunger (which she identifies as the most frequent cause), pain, overstimulation, shock, fear, mistiming (e.g., bathing the baby when she is hungry), exposure to cold, reflexive jerking and twitching, or wanting to be picked up and held, and boredom and loneliness in older babies. She mentions discussing persistent colicky crying with a pediatrician, who might suggest a change in formula or the mother's diet if she is breast-feeding. She briefly notes temperamental qualities that might increase crying and discusses "babies who never seem happy" and their whimpering and fretfulness in a separate section on temperament. Leach gives descriptions of several techniques for reducing crying: feeding, carrying, swaddling, rocking, pacifiers, thumb sucking, rocking, sounds, and extra warmth. If a baby is hungry, she points out, only feeding will make the crying stop. About the baby who cries when she is put down, Leach writes: "The baby is not making unreasonable demands; if anyone is, you are. She is not crying to make you pick her up but because you put her down in the first place and deprived her of contact comfort. . . . Picking the baby up and cuddling her will almost always stop the crying" (1998, p. 116). Because a baby cannot be carried for hours on end, she recommends wrapping them tightly to provide the warmth and contact comfort of blankets.

As do Spock and Brazelton, Leach argues that babies cannot be spoiled, because they do not have the cognitive capacity to manipulate parents. She does not believe in letting babies "cry it out," warning parents that babies whose needs are not met or met after considerable delay will lose their confidence that they will be met and may become quicker to cry and slower to accept comfort (Leach, 1998, p. 220). For crying during the night, parents should feed the baby as soon as crying begins (Leach, 1989a, pp. 85, 187), both to soothe the baby and to get back to sleep as quickly as possible. To parents of babies with colic, she writes: "Sometimes nothing you do makes more than a minimal practical difference, but even then, if you listen to the note of sheer despair that develops if you put him down, it seems likely that your baby is aware when someone is (or isn't) there for him and trying to help" (Leach, 1998, p. 123). She does not give parents permission to leave in his or her crib a baby whose crying has no obvious cause and seems intractable and inconsolable, recommending that they take turns or ask for help from friends. Older crawling babies can be allowed to cry if prevented from activities that are unsafe or destructive, but even in this instance she recommends taking steps to head off their frustration.

Leach's coverage of infant crying is extensive, specific, well organized, and easy to access. Her tables, graphics, and illustrated instructions are extremely helpful in understanding infant behavior and are not available in any of the other authors' books. She gives accurate information on the developmental course and the amount of crying, but identifies daily fluctuations in crying only when she describes colic, as if only colicky babies show them. She provides clues on how to recognize different types of crying and correctly acknowledges that adults sometimes cannot discern a pain cry from other cries. Of the five experts, she is also the most demanding on parents. They should attend to and respond to their babies' crying no matter how ineffectual their soothing efforts are. If a baby wants to be carried, it is because the parents are depriving her of contact comfort when they put her down—this despite the fact that two of the three research studies on carrying found it did not reduce crying (Barr, McMullen, et al., 1991; St. James-Roberts, Hurry, et al., 1995). Research on persistent crying past the 6-week peak (Rautava et al., 1995) indicates that temperamental factors clearly contribute to crying in some infants, but Leach's (1998) discussion of babies who never seem happy is located in a separate section on temperament that parents may not find when their baby is crying at full volume.

Leach's advice discourages withdrawal from a baby whose crying cannot be soothed despite parents' thorough search for causes of discomfort or incipient illness. If followed, it increases pressure on parents, though she does discuss their need to take brief respites for their own well-being. This advice may help strengthen the infant–parent relationship, but it gives infants little opportunity to learn how to soothe themselves.

Dobson

Dobson has not attempted a comprehensive account of infant development and behavior. His coverage of infancy appears in a chapter entitled

"The Discipline of Infants and Toddlers" (Dobson, 1982) and is limited to responses to questions he selected for inclusion. In his answers, Dobson does not address the peak in evening crying in early infancy that most babies show. His discussion of infant temperament is restricted to one dimension—"strength of the will." Some children are "born with an easy-going, compliant attitude toward external authority" (Dobson, 1982, p. 93), while others "expect meals to be served the instant they are ordered, and they demand every moment of mother's time" (Dobson, 1982, p. 94). He acknowledges that "the expression of the will, whether compliant or defiant, is only one of an infinite number of ways children differ at birth" (Dobson, 1982, p. 94), but it is the only aspect of infant temperament that he discusses. Dobson does not address the causes of infant distress, including ones that might signal a need for medical attention, nor give parents techniques to deal with it. He advocates nurturant care in a general sense: The infant "needs to be held, loved, and most important, to hear a soothing human voice. He should be fed when hungry and kept clean and dry and warm" and provided with "security, affection, and warmth" (Dobson, 1982, p. 95). But Dobson gives parents few specifics about the care activities that will help provide these feelings. For example, he writes that an infant's cries are an important form of communication, telling of hunger, fatigue, pain, or the need to be changed, and he enjoins parents to "listen to the tone of her voice for the difference between random discontent and genuine distress" (Dobson, 1982, p. 95).

Dobson's responses to selected questions show his concern about providing warm, loving care for infants, but do not provide parents guidance about what actions to take. Nor does he advise parents to read other sources on the topic. Aside from his brief injunction to provide nurturant care, his primary concern about infant crying is making sure that parents are in control of a demanding child, even during the infant months. Possible medical causes for crying are not considered. He advises parents to discriminate between discontented crying and genuine distress, but does not tell them how to do so using either tonal or contextual cues, and there is research evidence that even experienced parents cannot necessarily do this (Gustafson & Harris, 1990).

The bulk of his coverage of infant crying concerns manipulative crying. Parents run the risk of creating a "fussy, demanding" baby by picking him up every time he cries: "If an infant is immediately picked up or rocked each time he cries, he may quickly observe the relationship between tears and adults' attention. How well I remember standing at the doorway of my infant daughter's nursery for several minutes, awaiting a momentary lull in the crying before going to her crib. By doing so, I reinforced the pauses rather than the howls" (Dobson, 1992, p. 115). In responding to a question from the mother of a fussy 8-month-old baby who cries when she is put down, he advises, "Don't be afraid to let her cry a reasonable period of time," noting that "it is important to strike a balance between giving your baby the attention she needs and establishing her as a tiny dictator" (Dobson, 1982, p. 95). He uses the idea of balance in several contexts to convey the idea of avoiding extremes, but here giving adequate attention is one pole, and "establishing her as a tiny dictator," the other. He does not consider the logical polar opposite, that in order to avoid spoiling, parents might not respond adequately to their baby's needs. Dobson clearly endorses nurturant care and attention for infants, so it is unclear how "giving your baby the attention she needs" can be considered extreme.

Older babies will cry long and hard when separated from their caregivers, but Dobson does not consider that this might be due to bonds of attachment. Instead, when advising the father of a 10-month-old who cried for hours when his mother left the house or when left in a nursery during church services, he writes that the infant "fits the pattern of an extremely strong-willed baby who has already learned how to manipulate his parents to achieve his purposes" (Dobson, 1982, p. 97). Because the only aspect of infant temperament that Dobson emphasizes is the strength of the will, parents who read him may be led to conclude that they must, as early as age 8 months, restrain their nurturant responses to avoid turning their child into "a tiny dictator." Dobson's lack of information about other factors, including attachment, that influence crying may lead parents to soothe less and babies to cry more than may the more responsive strategies of other experts. Ironically, when early crying subsides, parents may erroneously conclude that Dobson's advice helped them win an initial "contest of wills." Even if that is not a correct understanding of the baby's behavior, Dobson's interpretation may appear to be valid and become a framework for the parent–child relationship.

Rosemond

Rosemond devotes relatively few of his newspaper columns to infant care topics. In *New Parent Power!* he identifies the developmental course of crying in early infancy, although he states that it wanes by the fifth or sixth month, rather than by the third. He notes correctly that crying tends to increase in the evening (Rosemond, 2001b), and he acknowledges temperamental differences among infants, including the amount they cry. He does not give any advice pertaining to the persistently crying young infant (Rosemond, 2001b). By 3 months, he writes, most mothers can distinguish hunger cries from those due to boredom, but he gives no clues to parents to help make the discrimination. He briefly describes causes of crying: "Sometimes fussiness is caused by a readily identifiable source of discomfort. . . . Other crying is unrelated to physical discomfort and seems to be an attempt at self-stimulation—a way of asking for attention. Some crying can't be explained in terms of discomfort or deficiency. Sometimes babies cry for the sake of crying. Perhaps this is their way of announcing their existence—talking to themselves, so to speak" (Rosemond, 2001b, p. 234). Echoing Brazelton, he writes: "most babies cry some at bedtime. This is not necessarily an indication of discomfort, but may be a natural way of discharging tension and thus making the transition between waking and sleeping" (Rosemond, 1990, p. 60). His suggestions for soothing a crying baby are similarly brief: holding and gently rocking the baby, playing music or singing to the baby (which he says enhances language development), wrapping the baby snugly in a blanket, giving the baby a pacifier, and burping (Rosemond, 2001b).

Like Dobson, Rosemond devotes much attention to the question of when to attend to babies and when to let them cry it out: "If the cry is an attempt at communication, don't leave an infant to 'cry it out.' Make every reasonable effort to provide comfort. This responsiveness helps your baby develop a trusting attitude toward the world in general and toward you in particular" (Rosemond, 2001b, p. 241). He cites research to support his position: "Studies have shown that babies whose parents respond quickly to their cries for attention feel more secure and, consequently, cry less and less with the passage of time" (Rosemond, 2001b, p. 241). He agrees with Spock, Brazelton, and Leach on the low risk of spoiling an infant: " 'You can't spoil an infant,' which, while essentially true, doesn't mean parents should pick up a baby every time he or she cries. That's not only impractical, especially with a chronically fussy baby, but also unnecessary" (Rosemond, 1989, p. 37). If parents need to do something that they cannot do while holding a baby, there is no harm in putting the baby down for a few minutes (Rosemond, 1989). He notes that "there are definitely times when baby will cry, not because of discomfort or lack of attention, but simply for the sake of crying. When this seems to be the case, it is perfectly all right to let the baby fuss for a while" (Rosemond, 2001b, p. 241).

Rosemond offers a topically organized treatment of the period from birth to 8 months in a single chapter (Rosemond, 2001b). His information on daily fluctuations in crying is accurate, and he provides a list of soothing techniques, but he writes nothing on how to judge the cause of crying or on how to deal with babies who cry persistently. Nor does he mention going to a physician if the crying intensifies. Rosemond's general advice that you cannot spoil the younger baby, but to avoid slavish attending to older babies' and toddlers' fussing, is in accordance with advice given by researchers on crying (Hubbard & IJzendoorn, 1991; St. James-Roberts, 1993a) and consistent with the reflexive nature of early crying and the partly learned and partly temperamental nature of some of the crying and fussing in later infancy.

Rosemond notes research (Bell & Ainsworth, 1972) that babies responded to more rapidly by their mothers early in the first year cry less later in the 1st year. This study has been widely cited in research, practice, and educational articles and books. However, a larger, more appropriately analyzed study using the same procedures (Hubbard & von IJzendoorn, 1991) yielded results that indicate no connection between mothers' responding to infant crying early in the 1st year and later crying.

TOILET TRAINING

Few parents can muster enthusiasm for changing diapers. Fewer still are comfortable when their child stains the carpet or wets or soils their clothes in a supermarket or shopping mall. Managing the bodily functions of infants, toddlers, and older children adds "potty" words to parents' conversations and mopping-up skills to their repertoire of behaviors. It may also add to their anxieties: Ever since Sigmund Freud's identification of toilet training practices as a source of children's later psychopathology, parents have wanted to do toilet training right. But toilet training requires cooperation from the child, and parents may not know how to elicit it. And they may be hesitant about demanding proper toileting behavior before their child is physically mature enough. These considerations make toilet training a source of concern for parents. It is also a parenting topic on which there is a substantial information gap between parents' current knowledge and what they think they need (Bethell et al., 2001; Schuster et al., 2000; Young et al., 1998).

Furthermore, it is problematic that parents routinely expect that children will be toilet trained before they actually are (Stehbens & Silber, 1971). This raises the possibility of parent–child conflict and the potential for abuse, and in fact, toilet training conflicts are most frequently named as a precipitant for fatal abuse of children over age 1 (Krugman, 1983–1985). Yet community surveys suggest that parents who have recently toilet trained their youngsters did not find the process all that difficult. Seim (1989) found that 52% of his sample of 266 parents reported that toilet training was less difficult than they had expected, and only 13% reported that it was more difficult than expected.

Infants are typically unaware of passing urine and stools, and even when toddlers become aware of elimination functions, they may not be able to anticipate them in time to reach the toilet (MacKeith, Meadow, & Turner, 1975). Thus, maturational processes necessarily affect when toilet training can be started, though toilet training is typically completed before the bladder is fully mature (Berk & Friman, 1990). Peers can be influential in toilet training, particularly in day care settings in which children can observe successful toileting in older or same age children (Brazelton et al., 1999). Marked race, class, and cultural differences in the age at which toilet training is begun and completed provide further evidence for social influence (Oppel, Harper, & Rider, 1968; Robson & Leung, 1991; Schum et al., 2001). Thus, toilet training, the most mundane of parenting topics, provides an excellent opportunity to compare the experts' advice concerning a process in which both maturational forces and social expectations play important roles.

Evaluations informed by research findings and best practice standards are based on the assumption that those being evaluated did not themselves conduct the research or write the standards. On the topic of toilet training, however, that assumption does not hold. Brazelton (1962a) conducted one of the best known studies of toilet training and developed the training strategy most widely used in this country. He also contributed to the writing of the best practice standards published by the American Academy of Pediatrics (Stadtler, Gorski, & Brazelton, 1999), so on this topic the checks afforded by comparing the experts' positions with independently conducted research and professional standards are compromised. However, it is possible to test the accuracy of each expert's advice, including Brazelton's, because a number of independent researchers have conducted studies on toilet training topics, gathering data from a large number of children, including data from outside the United States, and collected prior to the publication of Brazelton's widely adopted toilet training practices. Some of the other experts recommend practices distinctly different from Brazelton's, and the comparisons are revealing and potentially helpful to parents.

What should be the criteria for successful toilet training and for judging expert advice on this topic? In some cultures, toilet training must be accomplished as soon as possible because the child is carried by the mother and diapers are not used. When parents are equipped with automatic washers and washable or disposable diapers, quickness of training should not be the only factor influencing the advice given to parents. Certainly, the minimization of children's medical complications from toilet training should be a first goal. Perhaps reducing parent–child toilet training conflicts and hassle is an additional appropriate standard for diaper- and washing-machine-equipped societies. Given that parents in the United States typically believe that children will be trained before they actually are, it is critical that media parenting experts give accurate advice on when most children are trained, how long training normally takes, and how to deal appropriately with toileting accidents. Media experts' advice must take into account children's different rates of physical maturation and how the overall parent–child relationship is likely to affect toilet training. Parental exasperation and child resistance need to be minimized to reduce the potential occasions for child abuse. And it is important that the experts' advice not unnecessarily delay the process nor increase the chances of toilet accidents or other toileting problems.

Typical Age and Length of Toilet Training

In their chapter reviewing research on bowel and bladder control, Mac-Keith et al. (1975) described this time line: 15-month-olds become aware of their accidents and demand to be changed; 18- to 24-month-olds call their parents' attention to soiled diapers and begin to use different words for urine and feces. At age 2, children also can announce their need to urinate, though often not in sufficient time to make it to the toilet and avoid an accident. At age 2½ to 3 years, children can feel urinary urgency and request assistance in time to use the toilet. By age 4, children use the bathroom appropriately, including closing the door and cleaning up afterward.

Baseline data on when children are actually toilet trained are important to evaluate the experts' advice on when to initiate training. Studies conducted in Europe (Klackenberg, 1971; Largo & Stutzle, 1977) suggest that by age 2 only 20%–25% of children are "practically always dry" or "completely dry," using the criteria of the two studies. Higher completion figures were obtained by Oppel et al. (1968) in a prospective interview study conducted with parents of 859 African American and European American children: 51% were dry in the daytime by age 2, 78% by age 3. Other studies with smaller samples (Stenhouse, 1988; Stephens & Silber, 1974) have obtained intermediate ages for bladder control, with 30% and 39% of children successfully trained by age 2, respectively. By comparison, in a recent study, only 1 child out of 496 was "completely trained" on bladder and bowel functioning by age 2, and a little less than 50% were completely trained by age 3 (Schum et al., 2001). African American parents began toilet training earlier than did other racial groups, at a median age of 21 months, and they reported that their children were completely trained at an earlier age, though there was little difference among races in duration of training. This earlier success may be due to earlier development of motor skills in African American children, or it may be due to attitude differences among parents: 50% of African American parents compared with 4% of European American parents agreed that it was important for a child to be toilet trained by the age of 2 (Schum et al., 2001).

In fact, in a study by Seim (1989), the child's evidence of readiness to toilet train was the reason given by 74.3% of parents for starting to train. In this study, parents reported that 24% of the children (68 cases) actually initiated toilet training themselves. Typically, toilet training is not a 1-day or 1-week process. It takes about 9 months to complete toilet training (Schum et al., 2001), and girls tend to complete the process sooner than boys (Largo & Stutzle, 1977; Martin, King, Maccoby, & Jacklin, 1984; Schum et al., 2001; Taubman, 1997). Nighttime dryness is achieved later than daytime dryness, and more accidents occur at night (Oppel et al., 1968).

When Seim (1989) interviewed parents about the toilet training methods they found to be successful, frequent prompting of the child was the most frequently named strategy (by 31% of the sample), and more parents of girls reported this to be successful than did parents of boys. Largo and Stutzle (1977) found that parents' prompting of their children to use the potty resulted in a higher percentage of completely bowel-trained children.

When parents of first children who have completed toilet training their children recently are asked what advice they would give to others, the most frequent response (by 38% of the parents) was to relax and be patient about it. The second most frequent response (35% of the parents) was to wait until the child was ready (Seim, 1989). So veteran parents favor a low-pressure approach, responsive to the child's developing abilities.

Does Starting Earlier Lead to Earlier Completion?

Largo and Stutzle (1977) provided compelling evidence that early training in healthy children does not lead to early completion. They found that 80% of their longitudinal sample of 413 Swiss children had been put on the potty by their mothers by age 9 months, but only 17% of boys and 22% of girls were completely dry during the day by age 2, and it was not until age 4 that 89% of the children were completely dry during the day (there were no measurements at ages 2½ or 3½ years). Klackenberg (1971) also found that early initiation of toilet training was not associated with early completion. In their review, Robson and Leung (1991) concluded that "no matter what age toilet training begins, most studies show that the majority of children will not develop control until after the age of two years" (p. 1264). In a recent study that was separated into age groups, there was a correlation between starting date and completion date only for children older than 27 months, suggesting that beginning training early provides no benefit (Blum, Taubman, & Nemeth, 2003). Taubman (1997) found that one of the predictive factors for his pediatric patients who were trained later was a later start date for training. However, the later start dates may have been attributable to his advice to parents in the study not to begin before age 2 and to delay onset of toilet training if the child showed resistance, so the later starting group consisted of resisting children. Thus, there are no apparent gains for early initiation, nor apparent risks for late initiation. There is also no indication that if parents wait long enough, most children will train themselves by an age that parents find acceptable.

Maturational differences may play a role in the shorter length of training and earlier successful completion for girls. When mothers of girls started earlier (and roughly half began before 18 months), the girls completed training earlier (Martin et al., 1984). But for boys, completion of toilet training was predicted by the maturity of their sleep patterns, rather than when they had begun training. Maturation of sleep cycle, the child's ability to wake up in time to void, may occur later in boys and may account for why they are more frequent bed-wetters (Martin et al., 1984).

Brazelton's (1962a) influential article in *Pediatrics* outlined a gradual approach to toilet training, dependent on the child's demonstrated readiness and understanding of the toileting process. The best publicized alternative procedure was developed by Azrin and Foxx (1974) and published in a book entitled *Toilet Training in Less Than a Day*. Azrin and Foxx's procedures have been criticized as unsuitable for unsupervised parents and caretakers, particularly with very young children, or where there is a likelihood of physical abuse (Howe & Walker, 1992; Matson & Ollendick, 1977). Surprisingly, there appears to be no published research that systematically compares Brazelton's and Azrin and Foxx's methods regarding the time it takes to train children, the number of toilet accidents they have, or the problems encountered with constipation (Christophersen, 2003).

Toilet Training Problems

Clinicians who write about the time to start toilet training focus on the risks of too early initiation: "For a parent to begin toilet training before a child has matured sufficiently is inviting failure and disappointment" (Christophersen & Rapoff, 1992, p. 409). Children whose mothers began toilet training after 20 months were less likely to be emotionally upset than those who started at 15–19 months, and training was completed more quickly (Sears, Maccoby, & Levin, 1957). Robson and Leung (1991) note that "sometimes children who resist toilet training are involved in a power struggle with their parents" (p. 1266) and warn parents against making toilet training a focus of an ongoing battle of wills.

Children's resistance to using the toilet is a source of frustration for parents, but it can also lead to serious medical complications. Stool toileting refusal (refusing for at least 1 month to use the toilet for stools) occurred in 22% of the children in a recent study (Taubman, 1997). Stool refusal is associated with later completion of toilet training, which means more hassles for parents. It is usually the result of constipation (Blum, Taubman, & Nemeth, 2004), and more problematically, it has been linked to stool withholding, which can worsen constipation and lead to chronic soiling (Taubman, 1997), a condition occurring in approximately 3% of the general pediatric population (Levine, 1975).

Several factors have been identified that lead young children to delay using the toilet for stools. Those who have a younger sibling or whose parents reported that they did not feel in control of the child's behavior in other situations (e.g., during meal times, getting them to sleep) were more frequent stool refusers (Taubman, 1997). Toilet training for these children was begun at a somewhat later age ($M = 26.2$ months) than for matched control children ($M = 23.0$ months), though both groups' training onset dates were close to the average for Taubman's (1997) larger study group. However, these 27 children did not show more behavior problems than did a matched group of 27 completely toilet trained children during a room clean-up task in the laboratory, a semistructured interview, or on temperament scales or the Child Behavior Checklist (Blum, Taubman, & Osborne, 1997). Putting the child back in diapers after having worn underpants was successful in 27 of 28 cases of stool toileting refusal (Taubman, 1997).

Toilet Training and Child Care

Most American children under age 6 are enrolled in nonparental care (U.S. Census Bureau, 1998). Child care providers and parents function most effectively in toilet training if they are consistent about timing and policies. Taubman (1997) found no association between a child's enrollment in substitute child care and the age at which they became toilet trained, but because of sanitation concerns for children in group settings, timely completion of toilet training is critical and some training strategies—for example, leaving the lower body naked—may be impractical. There is also evidence that children in day care can learn appropriate toileting behavior by watching older children: "In the most common scenario, children who are in 2-year-old groups have an ideal opportunity to observe peers who are nearly 3 and therefore are likely to imitate and master many toileting skills" (Brazelton et al., 1999).

THE AUTHORS' POSITIONS

Spock

Along with his position on many other topics, Spock's position on toilet training evolved with the times and with the accumulation of research on toilet training. In the first edition of his book (Spock, 1946), he recommended placing a child on the potty once she could sit well, around 7 to 9 months. The seventh edition uses Brazelton's method and credits Brazelton: "He has advised this method for thousands of children in his practice, and 80 percent of them achieved success at bowel and bladder training—abruptly and simultaneously—at an average age of twenty-eight months. They gained night control at an average age of three years. These are excellent results by any standards" (Spock & Parker, 1998, p. 511).

As Spock and Parker summarize it, "Dr. Brazelton's basic principle is that children should become trained of their own free will—without force, coercion, or criticism" (p. 511). "But remember, this does not imply an absence of expectations on the parents' part" (p. 512). Spock recommends use of a potty chair rather than the adult toilet, so that children do not feel precarious. He endorses modeling of appropriate behavior by an older brother or sister. Parents are to toilet train without urging or reproaching, and Spock recommends not flushing lest the child become fearful when the stools disappear. He advises parents to prompt the child to use the toilet by themselves when their readiness shows that they are ready to go without diapers, and to the praise child for success. "But don't overdo it. At this age a child doesn't like to be too compliant" (p. 511).

Spock's recent position on toilet training is explicitly derived from and closely aligned with Brazelton's. It is simple to implement and appears to be well supported by the limited research on this topic. For example, Spock recommends prompting children to use the toilet when they are first out of diapers (p. 514), which is a successful technique according to parents' reports (Seim, 1989).

Brazelton

Brazelton's approach is gentle, gradual, and child centered. He provides five readiness cues involving motor skills, ability to follow instructions, orderliness, and imitative abilities (Brazelton, 1992). Unless the signs of toilet readiness are evident, he recommends that parents not initiate toilet training before age 2. In *Touchpoints*, he gives an elaborate week-by-week sequence of successive approximations to the act of actually depositing the urine or bowel movement in the toilet. He also discusses the dangers of constipation and resultant anal fissures and gives preventive recommendations to keep stools soft. If constipation develops, he recommends putting the child back in diapers and getting a stool softener from the pediatrician. Brazelton stresses parents' responsibility to help children understand about toileting accidents and recommends using diapers as a way of relieving children of the fear of making a mistake. He cautions against putting children in pants until they have control. To avoid putting too much pressure on the child, Brazelton recommends avoiding power struggles when toilet training. His concern about oppositional behavior complicating toilet training is shared by other writers on the subject (Luxem & Christophersen, 1994). He cautions against pressure for nighttime dryness, but tells parents to take supportive steps when the child is committed to staying dry. He rejects the notion of a fixed time when every child should be dry at night (Brazelton, 1992).

Brazelton is the single most influential person in determining how American children are toilet trained. His emphasis on readiness and his information on timing of toilet training (about 24 months) and duration of training is well supported by many independently conducted research studies with children and their parents, including studies done outside this country. As noted earlier, the child's evidence of readiness to toilet train was the reason given by nearly three quarters of parents for starting to train (Seim, 1989), which is evidence that Brazelton's approach has had an impact.

Not surprisingly in light of the fact that Brazelton is one of the authors, the American Academy of Pediatrics' advice to practitioners on toilet training (Stadtler et al., 1999) is overwhelmingly consistent with the Brazelton approach. Child signals of readiness for training are emphasized, and parents are cautioned to avoid early training and to let their child's motivation and interest drive the process. Parents are instructed to give encouragement and praise and avoid pressure and punishment; they are told that toileting accidents should be accepted as a normal part of the process. If parent–child relationships are difficult, a 3-month pause in training is suggested as a possibility (Stadtler et al., 1999). The selection of Brazelton and colleagues to write the American Academy of Pediatrics best practice standards is a clear sign of the support for his approach among pediatricians.

Leach

As on other topics, Leach's advice about toilet training focuses on assisting the child to recognize and achieve mature behavior: "The process is not really a matter of training—of making the child do something for you, or to obey you—but a matter of helping her do something for herself. The end result is that she will take autonomous charge of her own toileting, recognizing her own full bladder or bowel and doing something socially acceptable about it" (Leach, 1998, p. 350). Like the latter-day Spock and other contemporary experts, she recommends against putting infants on potties early: "If you try to insist that she sit on that potty, you run a real risk of starting a battle that will actually *delay* your child's readiness to manage her own needs when she is physically able to do so" (Leach, 1998, p. 349). She writes that urination and defecation are automatic before 15 months and that children are ready to move toward toilet training at 24 months. "However early you start, your child is unlikely to be entirely reliable, even in the daytime, before the third year" (Leach, 1998, p. 350).

Leach describes one readiness signal: A child becomes aware when she is about to produce urine or a bowel movement, rather than being aware only after wetting or soiling her diapers. For the child to be successful in bladder training, he or she must be able to recognize the need to urinate while there is still time to get there. Her toilet training steps are similar to Brazelton's. Show the child the potty and when she is ready to sit on it "don't insist on taking her diapers off" (Leach, 1998, p. 351). Leach advises parents that bowel training is far easier for a child than bladder training because there is a longer delay between first urge and the bowel movement. She recommends that parents show low-key reactions to their child's success and failure and avoid expressing disgust about feces or using laxatives to speed up the process.

Leach characterizes bladder training as a long, slow process, accomplished by using procedures similar to those employed for bowel training. She recommends against disposable training pants: "Some of these absorb urine so efficiently, and keep the toddler feeling so dry while they do so, that instead of helping 'training,' they set it aside" (Leach, 1998, p. 354).

After a few days with occasional successes in using the potty to urinate, Leach recommends taking the child out of diapers when he is at home and awake. If a child uses the toilet and wants to flush it, that is good: "the more she feels that the whole business is up to her, the better" (Leach, 1998, p. 352). She cautions against nagging: "A lot of reminders don't help anyway. You are trying to help her recognize her own need to go and do something about it for herself. If you keep reminding her, you are doing her thinking for her. You may actually delay the moment when she is fully and independently reliable" (Leach, 1998, p. 355). For a child with toileting refusal and chronic soiling, she recommends seeing a doctor for stool-softening medications.

Leach's approach is similar to Brazelton's, with less focus on readiness. Her description of toilet training as an area in which to assist the child in acquiring self-mastery is consistent with her approach to other parenting issues. When she deviates from Brazelton's general gradual approach, her advice is unsupported by research or contradicted by parent report. For instance, Leach states that parents should refrain from reminding their children, but Seim (1989) found that parents of 3- to 5-year-olds named this most often as contributing to their child's toilet training success. Leach argues that leaving children in disposable training pants slows down toilet training, but there is no systematic evidence that this is the case. Taubman's (1997) intervention of putting stool-refusing children back in diapers suggests that it is a very effective intervention with them, but Leach does not mention this in her response to parents with a boy who has refused to use the toilet.

Dobson

Dobson has very little to say about toilet training in his books, a significant omission given parents' frequent concerns about it. His approach to the subject is captured in his response to a question about a 24-month-old boy: "Should we spank him for using his pants instead of the potty?" Dobson writes:

> It is entirely possible that your child *can't* control himself at this age. The last thing you want to do is spank a two-year old for an offense which he can't comprehend. If I had to err on this matter, it would be in the direction being too late with my demands, rather than too early. Furthermore, the best approach to potty training is with rewards rather than with punishment. Give him a sucker (or sugarless candy) for performing properly. When you've proved that he can comply, then you can hold him responsible in the future. (Dobson, 1982, p. 100)

Dobson has an awareness of developmental stages, and he clearly values the use of rewards. His answer allows parents leeway about when to start training, and presumably it would not be too difficult to fade out the sweet treats once toilet training is established. It is not clear, however, what the phrase "hold him responsible" means. Should parents punish children for accidents? If so, what punishment is appropriate? This is a potentially risky gray area. Dobson's emphasis on behavior modification and concern about holding the child responsible is characteristic of his advice, but he does not provide enough description for parents to apply those principles in toilet training.

Rosemond

Rosemond's hundreds of newspaper columns in the early and mid-1990s made little mention of toilet training, other than a discussion of how to deal with children who are partly trained and have accidents. In these columns, parents are advised to be calm, matter-of-fact, and insist that their children clean up after themselves. A 4-year-old who has once-a-week bowel accidents and no physiological complications should clean up after himself and should be confined to his room for the rest of the day and go to bed 1 hour early (Rosemond, 1994c). In Rosemond's first book (1990; originally published in 1981) his advice is consistent with the Brazelton approach: "There is no 'normal' age for toilet training, and there can be no prescriptions for when this learning must take place or how long the process should take. The important variable is not age. It is the child and the signals she will send to let you know when she is ready to give potty sitting a try" (p. 203). In a book focused on 2-year-olds (Rosemond, 1993b), his advice again emphasizes waiting until the child is ready, with instructions on how to recognize when that is. The child's readiness "defines the most opportune time for learning toilet independence. This critical period usually emerges between twenty-four and thirty months. It varies approximately six months in either direction, and lasts from eight to twelve weeks, typically. During this phase, the child is 'primed' for learning toilet skills and needs only support and encouragement from parents to do so" (Rosemond, 1993b, p. 117). According to Rosemond, this is the critical window of opportunity and misreading readiness in either direction is likely to cause problems. But other than that, children train themselves: "Learning to use the toilet is an exercise in 'I can do it myself.' For this exercise to work well for all concerned, the child must be given almost total control over it. Parents need do little more than arrange things so the child can use the toilet easily and be there to help when help is requested" (Rosemond, 1993b, pp. 115–116).

For children who are not training themselves, Rosemond recommends regular voiding prompted by a timer and use of an outside authority figure—the doctor—as source of the expectations that it is time to be toilet trained. When a 2½-year-old refused to use the toilet for bowel movements and asked for a diaper, Rosemond (1990) advocated a "cold turkey" approach: "Under no circumstances would he ever again be allowed to wear a diaper. When he demanded to know why, they said 'Because we won't let you.' Period. End quote. As in 'We are in charge here, and we know what's best for you.' Trust us" (p. 212). In this case, when the child had a bowel movement in his pants, he had to bathe, hand wash any soiled clothing, put on his pajamas, and go to his room for the rest of the day. For children who are not keeping the bed dry at night a year after they are day trained, he recommends putting them to bed without diapers. "This will increase the likelihood that she will be sensitive to the pressure of a full bladder while she's sleeping and 'hold' until she wakes up" (Rosemond, 1993b, p. 122).

In 1997, Rosemond reaffirmed 24–30 months as the appropriate time for training (Rosemond, 1997b) and offered two signs for parents to use to assess their child's readiness (Rosemond, 1997a). Then, suddenly, he reversed his position. In a series of newspaper columns beginning in the fall of 1998, Rosemond argued that "only a child knows when he's ready to walk, but the only people qualified to determine when a child is ready for toilet training are parents" (Rosemond, 1998e, p. 3E). "When you sense that your child is ready (in most cases, sometime between 20 and 30 months), buy a child's potty and tell him he's no longer going to wear diapers during the day" (Rosemond, 1998d, p. 3E). However, in this series he gave no clues to parents on how to sense the child's readiness. In a later column he wrote, "As for the matter of 'readiness signs,' I am now convinced this is so much psychobabble" (Rosemond, 2000, p. E03).

In Rosemond's "Naked and $75" method of toilet training, the child is allowed to run around the house with his or her lower body uncovered (Rosemond, 1998d). According to Rosemond, urine and feces running down children's legs are so unpleasant to them that they will train themselves. "During the week or so that this method typically takes, keep your distance. Nothing is more counterproductive to successful training than a hovering, anxious parent" (Rosemond, 1998d, p. 3E). He reported that "typical of their peers, my children, Eric (29) and Amy (26), were fully trained at 28 and 24 months, respectively. . . . Some 25 years later, it's not at all unusual for a 3-year-old to still be wearing diapers during the day" (Rosemond, 1998e, p. 3E). But he did not mention that it took 4 months to train Eric and that he had written about it previously (Rosemond, 1993b) in these terms: "When Eric, our first, turned two, my wife and I decided, quite arbitrarily, it was time for him to use the toilet. . . . The more we pushed, the less he cooperated, and the more we pushed. . . . I cringe to think of the havoc we created in the process" (p. 116). He reported that Amy was trained in less than a week (Rosemond, 1998e) but did not mention that she was trained by attending to the very "child-centered" readiness cues that he formerly endorsed and now argues against. In this column, he claimed that there has been a significant increase in toilet problems since "child-directed" training became popular. He argued that "the contention that 'early training'—between 22 and 30 months of age—is potentially harmful is myth" (Rosemond, 1998e, p. 3E).

Quick results are promised by using his method: Working parents, with sufficient attention, can achieve results in a weekend, or might have to take a day or 2 off work. He offers no advice on how to cope with a child who is not trained by the time that the parent has to go back to work (Rosemond, 1998d). The claim is also made that diapers slow down training. In one column, Rosemond quoted from a letter from a mother who toilet trained her child starting at 7 months and reported that he was urine trained at 18 months, without commenting on the fact that it apparently took 11 months (Rosemond, 1998c, p. 3E).

In a subsequent column, Rosemond attacked Brazelton as the purveyor of "child-centered parenting" for disseminating a gradual, child-oriented approach to toilet training. In a *New York Times* article, he chided Brazelton for serving as a consultant to Procter and Gamble and appearing in commercials for their Pampers diapers—"I think it's a fairly blatant conflict of interest" (Goode, 1999)—despite the fact that Brazelton's first article recommending a child-oriented readiness approach (Brazelton, 1962) appeared long before his connection with Procter and Gamble.

Rosemond reports that he and Brazelton are in agreement that toilet training problems have increased markedly in the last decade. "He says it's because people like me advocate putting premature pressure on kids to use the toilet" (Rosemond, 1998a, p. 2E). In fact, Brazelton argued that many toileting problems arise because day care centers require a child to be toilet trained before enrollment, leading parents to pressure children not to wet or soil their clothes. Brazelton told a *New York Times* reporter, "Parents are feeling very guilty, and people like Rosemond are making them feel more guilty, not less" (Goode, 1999). Rosemond's insistence on age rather than readiness became more firm as he contested Brazelton's position. "It's a slap to the intelligence of a human being that one would allow him to continue soiling and wetting himself past age 2. There is simply no excuse or justification for this" (Rosemond, 1998a, p. 2E). But in his column a few months earlier (Rosemond, 1998e) and in his earlier book (Rosemond, 1993b), he asserted that children might not be ready to start toilet training until 30 months, that this constituted early training and did not cause problems. And in a subsequent column, Rosemond mentioned that his own grandson was being trained at 30 months (Rosemond, 1999a, p. 6E), 6 months past his 24-month deadline.

As part of his attack, he systematically misrepresented Brazelton's position: One contention "at the heart of the Brazelton's/Pampers' position [is that] . . . the typical child is not ready, either physically or psychologically, to be toilet trained between 24 and 30 months" (Rosemond, 1999b, p. 3E). "Someone recently told me she'd followed Brazelton's plan with her 3-year-old and the child was trained in two weeks. That misses the point, which is not whether his plan works, but that waiting until age 3 insults the child's intelligence, delays mastery in other areas (i.e., toilet training is prerequisite to acquiring, among other things, certain social skills), and prolongs the child's dependency upon his parents" (Rosemond, 1998a, p. 2E). But Brazelton's position has never been to wait until age 3; he initially recommended (Brazelton, 1962a) not beginning toilet training before 18 months and subsequently (Brazelton, 1992) not beginning before milestones typically achieved by 24 months, in the range (20–30 months) that Rosemond himself suggested (in his revised advice). Nor does Rosemond describe which social skills are delayed or provide research or clinical evidence to back up his claims about social skills and dependency.

In a later column, he claimed, "In 1955, more than 90 percent of children were toilet trained by 24 months. There is no evidence, anecdotal or otherwise, to suggest this was stressful, much less harmful" (Rosemond, 1999a, p. 3E). In fact, data from the 1950s suggest that Rosemond is incorrect. Oppel et al. (1968), in a 12-year prospective study of 859 children born in 1952, found that only 55% of children were bladder trained by age 2 and only 84% were by age 3. In an earlier study, only 60% of 705 2½-year-olds (born 1944–1946) were bladder trained, and only 88% of children were bowel trained (Roberts & Schoellkopf, 1951). Rosemond also asserts that "research has demonstrated that when parents fail to properly train by 30 months, children are more likely to resist learning to use the toilet" (Rosemond, 1999b, p. 3E). Of the researchers in this area, only Taubman has stated publicly that he has a hunch, though without data to support it, that if parents wait too long to toilet train (past 30 months) it may take longer (Goode, 1999). Alternatively, parents may wait later to train children who have problems with compliance and then find that they are not compliant with bladder or bowel training either.

By drawing Brazelton into a dialogue, Rosemond obtained front-page exposure in the *New York Times*, and pointed out that Brazelton created at least the appearance of a conflict of interest. He also may have caused a wider audience of parents to be more confused than before on this topic.

Rosemond's recent pronouncement that 24 months is the right time to toilet train is aligned with the average age at which contemporary American parents start training in research studies, but the average time to achieve training is more than 6 months. There is no research evidence that toilet training can be achieved in 1 week at 20 or 24 months of age by using Rosemond's procedures, and setting up such an expectation is likely to increase parents' feelings of frustration and children's feelings of failure when bladder and bowel training are not achieved so quickly. The best empirical evidence available from the 1940s and 1950s (before disposable diapers allowed more flexibility) indicates that children were not toilet trained at the early age that Rosemond describes. He argues that leaving children in diapers will delay toilet training, a position for which there is no systematic evidence. Nor is there evidence that "delayed" toilet training retards social skill development and impedes the acquisition of discipline. Rosemond does not address the problem of children in day care, for whom the "naked and $75" procedure is not feasible because of concerns about sanitation.

There is no change in research findings nor a general societal trend that can account for Rosemond's sudden shift from a "readiness" child-initiated approach, similar to but less structured than Brazelton's, to a draconian parent-oriented "quick fix" for toilet training. Rosemond's sudden change in his advice on toilet training, offered without rationale or supporting research, may be attractive to parents who (figuratively and perhaps literally) want to wash their hands of the process, though they will probably wind up washing the floor instead. But the difficulties encountered by parents with other "quickie" toilet training methods (cf. Azrin & Foxx, 1974) suggest that Rosemond's approach is unlikely to be successful in most cases, and the expectations of quick success are likely to produce disappointment in parents and feelings of failure in children.

ASSESSMENT: FINDING A CONSENSUS ON INFANT AND TODDLER CARE

Among Spock, Brazelton, and Leach, there is a remarkable but perhaps not surprising correspondence between their current advice and the findings of toilet training research. Their recommendations on the time to start training are consistent with the results of large research studies that demonstrate that most children are not trained by 2 years of age, but that the proportion trained accelerates rapidly between 2 and 3. Brazelton's plan is the most elaborate, but given the apparent ease with which most parents report that their children are trained (Seim, 1989), the many steps he suggests may not be necessary. Dobson says little on this topic, but he does not push early training and relies more on rewards than do any of the other writers.

Of the five authors, only Rosemond offers the hope of quick toilet training but with little evidence that his procedures actually produce the results that he promises. Spock's, Brazelton's, and Leach's descriptions of gradual training, acquired in stages, fit with the research descriptions of the typical course of toilet training in American and European children. All five experts recommend praise or rewards for successful performance. Only Rosemond's "naked and $75" procedure is parent centered, with its insistence on a fixed timetable and parent-determined readiness without regard for individual differences between children. He increases stress on parents and children to tell a story of parental permissiveness and child irresponsibility in contemporary society, but that story is not supported by research on toilet training.

Thus, when the experts converge in their advice, it agrees closely with what has been established in the research on this topic. When they venture advice that differentiates their positions from the others, they are more likely to be contradicted or at least not supported by research findings.

Spock, Brazelton, and Leach teach parents how to effectively manage infant crying. In their approach, parents should learn to discern infant capabilities and limitations, to time interventions appropriately, and to structure interactions that assist the infant in acquiring mastery of basic tasks. They clearly have strong beliefs about what infants and children are being socialized for, but their advice focuses on infant attributes that parents must deal with, rather than projecting infants into future family and social roles. Of the experts discussed here, they are the ones who have written baby manuals. Parents are arguably most in need of expertise in dealing with infants, whose needs can be difficult to discern and who are more vulnerable than older children to errors in caregiving.

Rosemond's and Dobson's lack of attention to infant crying may simply be due to the fact that they never dealt with babies professionally, either as clinicians or as researchers. It is surprising, though, in light of how problematic it is for parents (Lucassen et al., 1998). But more likely they pay little attention to unique attributes of infancy because their focus is not on babies themselves but on preparing them for adult roles in family and society. Dobson's advice on crying defines the parent–infant relationship as a power struggle that parents need to win. Parents' exercise of leadership in their early relationships with their infants is emphasized, as is babies' early development of respect for their parents' leadership. Whatever their baby's temperamental attributes, parents bear the final responsibility for making sure they are appropriately socialized, and that is where Dobson focuses his attention.

Research has provided many helpful insights into normal infant behavior—for instance, that adults must learn to discriminate hunger and pain cries (Gustafson & Harris, 1990). Research has established that early crying reflects individual differences in neurological maturation and self-soothing (Barr, 2001) and that later crying is more volitional (St. James-Roberts & Halil, 1991) but can be predictably elicited by separation from a caregiver. Babies are not normally trained by age 2 (Oppel et al., 1968), and there are proven techniques than parents can use to coax them to use the toilet (Brazelton, 1962). But this information is buried in journals and books not generally accessible to parents, and that is when the experts make their great contribution. The authors of the three baby manuals—Spock, Brazelton, and Leach—provide parents of infants with a solid foundation concerning what they need to know.

CHAPTER 3
EARLY CHILD CARE

IT MAY CREEP INTO parents' consciousness during the months after a baby's birth, that nagging awareness that bank accounts are dwindling and the mother's income will be needed to pay the bills. Or it may come up when parents realize that the money simply is not there to buy a home for the family of three that has replaced the married couple ensconced in their apartment. It may arise when a former coworker drops by and lets slip news of a job opening that would be "right up your alley" or "a good step up." The months of caregiving certainly make parents aware of the demands that a baby makes on their time, and the most substantial competing demand is parents' need to earn a living. One of the great ironies of domestic life is that parents typically make the most money when their responsibilities for moment-to-moment parenting are long past, and earn so little when their children need so much care.

THE EASY DECISION AND THE USUAL CASE

Under some circumstances, the child care decision is clear. If family income is adequate to buy the child and her parents a safe home and neighborhood, with money set aside for rainy days and long-term eventualities, those factors may tilt the balance toward one parent staying at home with the child during the preschool years. If a parent works in a field where movement in and out of the work force is easily negotiated and work opportunities are abundant, the costs of stepping out for the early childhood years may be minimal, far outweighed by the opportunity to directly nurture and enjoy his or her own children. If a parent is a sensitive, devoted caregiver, the child can clearly benefit. It makes the decision easier if a parent is not heavily invested in work or so heavily invested in the role of parent that he or she cannot function effectively if the child is in substitute care. Of course, if a parent is a sensitive, devoted caregiver but currently has little earning power, there is not much to be gained financially by placing the child in nonparental care. If child care is simply not available, as is the case in many rural areas and small towns, no decision is needed. In addition, for parents of children with congenital problems severe enough that substitute care cannot accommodate their needs or would be risky for them (Booth & Kelly, 1998), the decision is clear. But these circumstances, ones that would make it easy to decide against the use of nonparental care in infancy and early childhood, are relatively rare. Usually parents have to make a choice, and it is not an easy one. For those parents and professionals who work with them, it is critical to consider what is currently known about nonparental child care.

There remains a substantial gap between the experts' advice on child care choices and the complexity of parents' situations. Whereas the experts focus on the child's immediate needs, many factors necessarily influence parents' decisions: long-term needs such as educational costs, as well as parents' work schedules and commutes, the schools their other children attend, the quality of care that is actually available within driving distance, and so forth. Contemporary popular wisdom often traps parents in an apparent either/or dilemma: one parent stays at home during a child's infancy and preschool years, which is deemed best for the child, or the child is placed in substitute care, which is believed to be best for the parents. But in reality the choices are more complicated. Higher family income when both parents work enables the purchase of housing in safer neighborhoods with better schools. Thus, one parent staying home may simply be trading off the child's long-term interests in favor of short-term ones. Forty percent of births in this country are unplanned (Forrest & Singh, 1990), and parents often wind up raising children when they thought they would be completing school or working. Many parents may not be able to take extended leaves from businesses or professional practices without losing not only their jobs but their careers as well. Some parents, because of their difficult personalities, mental disturbances, or abusive tendencies, provide care that is decidedly worse than that in most child care settings. In the lives of most families, deciding whether children's interests are best served by being at home with a parent or in substitute care proves to be more complicated than it seems to outsiders.

On no topic is there a greater need for expert advice, and on no topic is there more disparity among the experts or, for that matter, greater change in individual experts' positions across time. This topic also is one that provides perhaps the best opportunity to empirically evaluate the accuracy and utility of the experts' advice, because recent large-scale research studies on early child care have provided extensive information about the type and quality of care that parents are able to obtain and their effects on parent–child relationships and children's social and cognitive development. As will be seen, research findings provide evidence of child care effects that match neither the dire foreboding of some experts nor the naive optimism of others.

The demographics of parental employment shifted so radically in the 1980s that the need for large-scale research on its effects on children became unmistakably evident to foundations and federal agencies that fund research. This gave rise to a new generation of larger, long-term investigations that documented not just the "showcase" early childhood programs that most parents can only dream of, but also the child care that large numbers of parents are actually able to obtain. Taken together, the earlier, smaller research projects and the later, larger ones report findings that can be used to guide decision making for the great majority of parents whose circumstances render one-parent-stay-at-home care difficult or impossible.

A WORD ABOUT CHILD CARE RESEARCH

Separating the effects of child care from the competing influences of interwoven family variables is a daunting task. There are ethnic and family income differences in the type of care used (U.S. Bureau of the Census, 1998), and parenting practices are related to the selection of different forms of child care (Fuller, Holloway, & Liang, 1996). Parents whose relationship with their infant is more difficult before the baby is placed in substitute care tend to place him or her in care that, on the average, is poorer in quality, raising the question of whether subsequent differences are effects of nonparental care or the original infant–parent relationship (Howes, 1990). Some maternal personality variables (extroversion, agreeableness) also predict earlier enrollment in child care (NICHD Early Child Care Research Network [ECCRN], 1997c). After enrollment, child care quality can also influence the quality of parenting because young children in better quality care may develop enhanced cognitive and social skills that then elicit more sensitive parenting. Or parents may learn better caregiving practices from child caregivers. If child care quality affects parenting, as well as vice versa, then controlling for parenting variables might result in underestimates of the relationship between child care quality and children's outcomes because of the overlap between the two (Burchinal & Nelson, 2000).

Adding to the complexity is the sheer variety of child care arrangements, from a grandmother's care of her grandchildren but no other children, to center-based care with trained caregivers whose activities may be directed toward enhancing preacademic skills. In addition, the paths that infants and toddlers actually take through child care arrangements vary widely and nonsystematically, altered by the birth of siblings, the availability of care, and parents' circumstances as their jobs and residences change. In the largest study of child care to date, families used center-based care, child-care homes, relative care, and maternal care, singly and in combination. For children in substitute care arrangements, there was movement toward center-based care when children were between 2 and 4 (NICHD ECCRN, 2004b), but there were actually 260 different paths through these types of care (NICHD ECCRN, 2001d). Moreover, child care research suffers from the same limitation that frequently besets other early childhood research: emphasis on mother–child interaction, with relatively little attention to fathers' roles. For example, comparative assessments of emotional ties are almost always conducted with mothers and alternate caregivers.

Given the range of child attributes and variability of child care arrangements, is there one effect of child care? Almost certainly not (Lamb, 1998). Can effects of nonparental care be estimated in ways that will be helpful to parents? Almost certainly, given modern statistical tools and willingness to acknowledge that individual effects will vary.

RECENT LARGE RESEARCH PROJECTS

Of the hundreds of research studies that crowd the research literature on child care, recently published large-scale studies are disproportionately significant. Unlike many of the smaller research projects, they investigate care in a variety of regions and attempt to control for many family factors that correlate with child care (e.g., parental education, race, family income, marital status of parents, and maternal depression). They are more likely to be reported on national media because of the legitimation conferred by their sponsoring agencies. They are probably also more likely to have their findings selectively reported and oversimplified. Considering their procedures and their strengths and limitations is essential to understanding what is known about child care effects and what is not.

The National Institute of Child Health and Human Development Early Child Care Research Network Study (NICHD ECCRN)

Participants were recruited from 31 hospitals located near 10 research sites scattered throughout the eastern, midwestern, and coastal western United States. Hospital visits were made to all mothers who had given birth within selected 24-hour sampling periods, but some families were excluded from the study: if the mother was under 18 years of age or did not speak English or if the family lived in a neighborhood deemed unsafe for researchers to visit. In addition, the family was excluded if the mother had a multiple birth or if the infant had obvious disabilities or remained in the hospital for more than 7 days after birth. Single mothers, minority mothers, and those who had less than a high school education were oversampled to avoid the distortions that can result from small sample sizes. Of the 5,416 mothers who met the eligibility criteria for the study, 1,364 mothers were sampled to ensure that the recruited families matched the demographic diversity (economic, educational, and ethnic) of the area surrounding each study site (NICHD ECCRN, 1996; NICHD ECCRN, 1997a).

Families in the study were visited in their homes at 6, 15, 24, 36, and 54 months. The quality of mother–child interaction and the home environment were assessed, mothers were interviewed, and they completed questionnaires about their beliefs and attitudes, their emotional well-being, their children's development, and family demographic characteristics. At 6, 15, 24, 36, and 54 months, children who were in child care for 10 or more hours a week were observed in one or two visits to their care setting, during which the quality and quantity of their interactions with caregivers were recorded during 44-minute observations. Children were later observed in their first grade classrooms (NICHD ECCRN, 2003c). Caregivers were also interviewed and completed questionnaires concerning their education, child care training and experience, and their "modern" versus "traditional" child-rearing beliefs (NICHD ECCRN, 1996). They also described the child who was the focus of study and the care setting. Children were observed in laboratory playrooms at 15, 24, and 36 months in structured situations to assess their attachment, compliance, and willingness to delay gratification. Every 3 or 4 months during the first 4½ years, mothers were interviewed by telephone to check on their current child care arrangements, their employment, and family circumstances. Yet despite the massive resources devoted to this research, it has some limitations: The sample is not truly nationally representative and excludes the most potentially vulnerable infants because they are physiologically compromised at birth. As is the case with any correlational study, there could be unmeasured factors that would account for the observed relationships between child care variables and children's behavior. And, of course, the child care arrangements are specific to the United States, which provides relatively little government funding for early child care for families above the poverty line. Different effects of child care have been found in other countries (Love et al., 2003).

Cost, Quality, and Child Outcomes Study

Rather than recruiting and studying individual children beginning at birth, the Cost, Quality, and Child Outcomes (CQO) Study focused on children in 401 child care centers (Helburn et al., 1995). The economics of the child care industry was a major focus of this research, but child care quality and children's social and mental skills were extensively assessed. Centers from four different regions (the Los Angeles area; the Hartford, Connecticut, area; the Front Range of Colorado; and the Piedmont region of North Carolina) were selected because they operate in widely varying economic and regulatory climates. For example, when the study began, mandated staff:child ratios for 4-year-olds varied from 1:10 in Connecticut to 1:20 in North Carolina (Peisner-Feinberg, Huffman, del Carmen, & Bryan, 2001). Approximately 50 for-profit and 50 nonprofit child centers were randomly selected from state licensing lists of the four states. Process quality was observed in 228 infant/toddler classrooms (those with children less than 2½ years) and 521 preschool classrooms, randomly chosen from those serving those ages at each center (Helburn et al., 1995). Participating children have been followed through the end of second grade. The major limitation of this study is its focus on center-based care when so many other care arrangements are used, particularly for infants. Nor were the children assessed before they entered care, making it difficult to separate effects of care from family differences that might have existed beforehand.

In brief, the NICHD and the CQO studies have followed children over time, and both of these large studies have focused on the child care that parents actually purchase, rather than model programs available to only a few parents. Therefore these studies, combined with many smaller research projects addressing specific child care topics, provide answers to critical questions: Should infants and toddlers be placed in nonparental care? What is the best age for entering care? What are key aspects of child care quality? What is the best type of care? These questions are addressed in the following sections.

SHOULD INFANTS AND TODDLERS BE IN NONPARENTAL CARE 30 HOURS OR MORE A WEEK?

The sharpest controversy in child care has swirled around the topic of substitute care for the very youngest children, whose vulnerability is greater than at any subsequent point in their lives. For many families, the decision of whether to put infants in substitute care occurs very early (NICHD ECCRN, 1997a). Research on the effects of substitute child care for infants falls into three major categories: research on attachment, cognitive and language development, and social behavior.

IS THE PARENT–INFANT BOND WEAKENED BY SUBSTITUTE CARE?

Many parents fear that if they put their infant or toddler into child care, the child's emotional connection with them will be weakened and the child will grow to love their substitute caregiver as much or more than the parent. Jealousy of the child care provider is not an unknown emotion. Moreover, if parents have left their older baby or toddler with a babysitter for an evening out, they have probably witnessed their children's distress and know that they will resist being separated. The protest crying that many babies and toddlers show when parents place them in child care tears at the heart strings of even those parents who are most committed to working. Ironically, after adjustment to child care, parents can encounter painful episodes at the other end of the day when the child with whom they have come to be joyfully reunited throws a tantrum and does not want to come home with them, at least not just yet. But infants and toddlers adapt, their distress is reduced over time, and after-work reunions become less and less often ambivalent ones (Vandell, Dadisman, & Gallagher, 2000).

Attachment theory and research (Ainsworth, Blehar, Waters, & Wall, 1978; Bowlby, 1969) has provided the conceptual and methodological framework for assessing the emotional connection between infant and toddlers and their parents. Attachment is an infant's enduring relationship to specific people characterized by seeking closeness, especially when afraid or stressed, and becoming distressed when separated from them. According to the theory, attachment fosters compliance with parents, and failures in attachment commonly result in more disobedient and problem behavior (Ainsworth et al., 1978; Arend, Gove, & Sroufe, 1979; Londerville & Main, 1981). The dominant procedure used to test the quality of attachment is the Strange Situation (Ainsworth et al., 1978), involving seven 3-minute episodes in which infants are tested for their reactions to separation from their parent (almost always their mother) and their reaction to the presence of a stranger. Strange Situation testing is typically done when children are from 12 to 18 months of age, though adapted versions have been used with preschoolers. It is controversial as a measure of attachment for children in substitute care (Clarke-Stewart, 1989) because one criterion for secure attachment is distress when separated from a parent, and separation is an everyday occurrence for children in substitute care.

Is there empirical evidence that emotional connections between infants and their parents are compromised by placement in nonparental care? The NICHD study provides the best evidence on effects of child care on attachment because of its large size, nationally distributed sample, recruitment of participants at birth, and frequency of measurements. To quote from the research reporting attachment assessments when infants were 15 months old: "There were no significant differences in attachment security related to child-care participation. Even in extensive, early, unstable, or poor-quality care, the likelihood of infants' insecure attachment to mother did not increase, nor did stable or high-quality care increase the likelihood of developing a secure attachment to mother" (NICHD ECCRN, 1997a, p. 875). This failure to find an overall effect of substitute child care is critical because the sample size is large enough that even subtle differences should be detectable, certainly by 15 months, an optimal time to assess infant attachment. Child care status had no overall effect on attachment, but children of mothers who were lower in psychological adjustment and lower in sensitivity–responsiveness were less likely to have children who were securely attached, a finding consistent with previous attachment research (Belsky, Rosenberger, & Crnic, 1995; Clarke-Stewart, 1988).

Child care status did have small but statistically reliable effects that emerged in combination with other variables: Children were less likely to be securely attached when mothers were low in sensitivity–responsiveness and they were in poor-quality, less stable, and more extensive child care. There was also evidence that very good quality child care made secure attachment more likely for children whose mothers were lower in sensitivity and responsiveness (NICHD ECCRN, 1997a, 1997b). Thus, the NICHD research puts effects of child care in the context of other factors affecting children's attachment to their mother. The general pattern of findings was replicated in a smaller Canadian sample of infants (McKim, Cramer, Stuart, & O'Connor, 1999): There were no overall effects of child care, but there were negative effects of nonparental care on attachment for those infants who received the least sensitive mothering prior to entering such care.

One potential reason why the NICHD research did not reveal greater disparities in attachment between children who were experiencing extensive substitute care and those who were not is that differences in direct mother–infant interaction time were much smaller. Mothers in the at-home group spent an estimated 7.51 more hours per week with their infants in instrumental care, including discipline and supervision, than did mothers whose infants were in substitute care at least 30 hours a week, and the at-home mothers spent 4.75 more hours in social interaction, according to time-use interviews with 326 mothers when their infants were 7 months old. A comparison of weekday and weekend data showed that mothers whose infants were in substitute care during the week spent 22% more time with their infants in social interaction on weekend days (2.67 vs. 2.18 hours), in an apparent effort to compensate for time missed during the week. So actual hours spent interacting were much less discrepant than possible hours because mothers of infants at home did not spend most of the "extra" time interacting with them (Booth, Clarke-Stewart, Vandell, McCartney, & Owen, 2002).

By age 3, differences emerged in mothers' and children's behaviors in semistructured observations. During the observed interactions, mothers whose children had experienced more nonparental care were lower on sensitivity, a composite measure of responsiveness, positive regard, and nonintrusiveness (NICHD ECCRN, 1999), and the more hours their child spent in substitute care, the less likely their child was to be positively engaged with them during an observational session. The negative effects of more hours in child care accounted for a much smaller percentage of the variability in maternal sensitivity (2%) than the positive effects of maternal education (12%) (NICHD ECCRN, 1999).

Moreover, the probability that a child's attachment would be classified as ambivalent was increased slightly if they were in more hours of care *and* their mother was less sensitive, a pattern similar to that found at 15 months (NICHD ECCRN, 2001b). In past attachment research, mothers who were moody, unpredictable, and therefore less consistently available were more likely to have infants who showed ambivalent attachment (Cassidy &

Berlin, 1994), but the NICHD research team noted that more extensive use of child care did not in itself lead to higher rates of ambivalent attachment. Rather, they concluded that more hours in child care were an additional risk factor for children whose mothers were already less sensitive and responsive (NICHD ECCRN, 2001b). The stability of attachment classification from 15 to 35 months was, to use the authors' word, "modest" (p. 858), but the small group of children whose attachment classification changed from secure to insecure during that interval were more likely to have entered into 10 or more hours per week of child care, though the effect was not strong (NICHD ECCRN, 2001b).

To briefly summarize, infants, even those in extensive care at early ages, do show strong attachments to their mothers and prefer their mothers to substitute caregivers. In general, placing an infant or toddler in child care does not seem to impede the formation of attachment, but those mothers who are having difficulty connecting with their babies may put their relationship at additional risk by placing their child into 30 or more hours of care per week. By age 3, there is evidence that the mother–child interaction has been negatively affected to a modest but detectable degree by more hours spent in substitute care, though such negative effects are small compared with those of family factors such as maternal education.

SOCIAL COMPETENCE, COMPLIANCE/CONFLICT, AND BEHAVIOR PROBLEMS

April 19, 2001, was a day full of child care headlines and features on *Good Morning America*, in the *New York Times*, and in hundreds of other media outlets. The big news was the release of findings by the NICHD Early Child Care Research Network. There was good news and bad news, but the story that captured national attention and resonated in public commentary was the bad news: Children with a history of 30 or more hours in child care per week during their first 4 years showed less social competence, more conflict in relationships with adult caregivers and teachers, and more problem behaviors than did children who averaged less than 10 hours per week, even after controlling for family factors that might provide an alternative account for such problems. Were the negative findings unexpected? Some associations between more hours in care and caregivers' ratings of more behavior problems had emerged at age 2, though they were not evident at age 3 (NICHD ECCRN, 1998a). But these findings at age 4½ and during kindergarten were reported differently and treated more seriously, perhaps because they might reflect cumulative effects of substitute care and because caregivers *and* now kindergarten teachers detected more problems among children who had been in more hours of care, suggesting poorer adjustment across settings and effects that might be long lasting. And what was the good news? As will be described subsequently, better quality child care and center-based care were associated with positive effects on cognitive and language development (NICHD ECCRN, 2002b), but this went virtually unnoticed.

Social Skills

In the NICHD research project, children's social skills were determined by rating their cooperation, assertion, responsibility, and self-control, including interactions both with children and with adults (NICHD ECCRN, 2003b). When social skills were assessed at age 2, there were no effects of hours in substitute care after controlling for family, child, and selection factors. When children in the study were age 4½, even after controlling for child and family attributes, including the quality of parenting, there was a small negative relationship between hours spent in substitute care and social skills, as rated by both mothers and caregivers. This relationship was not attributable to differences in the quality of care, proportion of time spent in care with peers, or more frequent changes in care (NICHD ECCRN, 2003b). When the children were assessed in the first grade, small negative effects of more hours in substitute care were still apparent in teachers' ratings of social skills (though this time not in mothers'). Furthermore, more hours in nonmaternal care before school entry predicted decreases in teachers' ratings of social skills, even when current after-school care was controlled (NICHD ECCRN, 2003c).

The CQO Study provided evidence of the connectedness of social competence with peers and with adults. Children who had good relationships with their care providers also tended to have good relationships with their peers (Howes, Phillips, & Whitebook, 1992). Greater teacher–child closeness in child care classrooms was related to later sociability in kindergarten, though differences washed out by the second grade (Peisner-Feinberg et al., 2001). Furthermore, children who were enrolled in better quality child care classrooms were more sociable (extroverted) over a 5-year period, even after adjusting for child and family characteristics, though effects were modest by the second grade (Peisner-Feinberg et al., 2001). Because children in this research were recruited through their child care centers, comparisons were not possible with other types of care or differing amounts of substitute care. Findings from this research were consistent with Lamb's (1998) earlier review of shorter term studies: Enrollment in high quality care was associated with better relationship skills in children.

Compliance/Closeness/Conflict With Adults

Several studies (see Lamb, 1998) have measured compliance with mothers' requests during home and laboratory observations, with child care teachers, and with unfamiliar researchers. Frequent research findings of instability in compliance across relationships suggest that it is not a trait of the child but is highly related to the degree of adult–child harmony (Lamb, 1998). In the NICHD study, neither of two structured observation measures of compliance showed apparent effects of child care at 36 months, after controlling for factors related to selection (income:needs ratio, parents' psychological adjustment), child (gender, temperament), and family (attachment, sensitive parenting) (NICHD ECCRN, 1998a). The NICHD researchers necessarily change measures to ensure that they are age appropriate, and by first grade, compliance was replaced by closeness (the degree of warmth, positive feelings, and open communication between child and teacher). There was no relationship between earlier child care hours and closeness to the teacher (NICHD ECCRN, 2003c). The other side of compliance and closeness is adult–child conflict. The number of child care hours that 4½-year-olds had experienced was more predictive of conflict with caregivers than the most potent parenting factor (maternal sensitivity), but by kindergarten, the effect of number of hours was smaller, though still significant (NICHD ECCRN, 2003b). When data from the first 2 years of school were analyzed, controlling for children's social functioning at age 4½, the amount of child care they had experienced was related to modest but significant increases in conflict from kindergarten to first grade (NICHD ECCRN, 2003c).

Behavior Problems

Of all the findings that attracted media attention, the link between hours in early child care and increases in behavior problems at age 4½ years and in kindergarten probably caused the most immediate concern. Initial reports described the negative effects of increasing hours in substitute care on externalizing (aggressive, destructive, and oppositional) behaviors as larger than the effects of a composite measure of positive parenting (NICHD ECCRN, 2001d; NICHD ECCRN, 2002b). Given the widespread use of early child care, this finding raised the specter of a generation of mean kids growing into mean adults wreaking havoc on their families and communities. The NICHD researchers used the Child Behavior Checklist (Achenbach, 1991), a widely adopted measure of behavior problems with versions for mothers and teachers. An exploration of the relationship between child care hours and behavior problems revealed that it was not due to unstable child care arrangements, nor to the amount of time spent in care with at least two other children. Externalizing behaviors were generally more affected by substitute care than internalizing behaviors, such as anxiety and depression (NICHD ECCRN, 2003c). Child care hours were related to behavior problems in a straightforward, linear manner, with no discernible minimum number of hours below which the relationship was not evident. Children who had more hours in child care were more likely to score above the "risk" cutoff score for externalizing problems (one standard deviation above the mean). Specifically, kindergarten teachers rated 15% of children who had been in substitute care 30–45 hours a week over the risk cutoff compared to 9% children in substitute care 0–9 hours a week (NICHD ECCRN, 2003b). But the overwhelming majority of children, even those in early and extensive hours of care, did not score in the at-risk range (NICHD ECCRN, 2003b; NICHD ECCRN, 2004b). Better quality care was also associated with fewer teacher reports of problems and less conflict (NICHD ECCRN, 2003b).

Effects of quantity of care on externalizing problems were more likely to be detected by teachers than mothers (NICHD ECCRN, 2003b). One interpretation of this discrepancy was that some children who spend a lot of time with other small children develop a repertoire of negative, contentious peer interaction behaviors that are specific to peer group settings and that their mothers are less likely to be aware of (NICHD ECCRN, 2004b).

Recently published findings on trajectories of aggression from 24 months to third grade (NICHD ECCRN, 2004b) provide evidence that in the overwhelming majority of children, nearly 90%, aggressive trajectories are established early, and that high aggression trajectories are statistically linked to family risk factors that are detectable at age 24 months, such as lower income and less maternal education (Arsenio, 2004). Child care quantity or quality had no systematic effects on children's aggression trajectories. Children in the highest aggression trajectory group did not experience more hours of child care, and changes in aggression were not associated with changes in child care hours. When aggression levels at age 9 were examined, the amount of substitute care children had experienced was not a significant predictor (NICHD ECCRN, 2004b).

There are at least two reasons for the discrepant findings of this latest report and earlier reports (NICHD ECCRN, 2002b, 2003b). Aggression ratings in the latest study were obtained from mothers only; the ratings from caregivers and teachers had provided the greatest evidence of child care effects in earlier research. But mothers' ratings of children's physical aggression turned out to be good predictors of several social and cognitive outcomes in the third grade, so it is not that mothers are poor at rating their own children (Arsenio, 2004). As mentioned earlier, it is possible that behavior problems among kindergarten and first graders are specific to group settings that mothers are less likely to observe, and they are similarly likely to be ignorant about group behavior when their children are 9-year-olds. But a more likely account for the reduction over time in the differences between children with extensive substitute care and those without it is that the kindergarten and first grade findings reflect a transient adjustment bump in the transition to elementary school that is more marked for children with earlier child care experience (Arsenio, 2004). They may have acquired negative interaction skills in group settings that are resocialized during the first three years of elementary school.

There had been earlier studies linking more hours in substitute care to behavior problems, though none were as large and comprehensive, with so many design and statistical controls in place. An earlier study found that more hours in care, as reported by mothers just before kindergarten, were associated with higher rates of aggression even after controlling for family stress, socioeconomic status, and child gender, though this study did not control for the quality of care, nor was the relationship consistently obtained (Bates et al., 1994). Vandell and Corasaniti (1990a) found that third graders who had been in more extensive early child care received poorer conduct grades and more negative sociometric nominations, but the quality of care could not be assessed and child care standards were relatively lax in Texas when the study was conducted, as they have been in many other states (Vandell & Corasaniti, 1990b).

Lamb (1998) argued that associations between child care in infancy and toddlerhood and later problem behavior may be affected by the poor relationships with child care providers and not reflect effects of separation from the mother. As he notes, "Because nonparental care experiences are not reliably associated with insecure infant–mother attachment, the speculation that nonparental care fosters insecure attachment that in turn fosters subsequent misbehavior is not supported" (Lamb, 1998, p. 115).

Findings of the CQO Study lend support to Lamb's (1998) interpretation. Those children who had closer relationships to their child care teachers showed fewer problem behaviors through the second grade (Peisner-Feinberg et al., 2001). Though the overall effect of quality child care classrooms was not significant, there was a statistical interaction, with better early child care environments associated with fewer problem behaviors in kindergarten, though the effect declined in subsequent years (Peisner-Feinberg et al., 2001). For this sample of children, Howes (2000) reported similar relationships between teacher–child interaction at age 4 and social competence in the second grade, but also found weaker, though significant, effects of socio-emotional climate in the preschool classroom, suggesting that quality of care makes an independent contribution.

Recent reports from child care researchers have emphasized children's early development within a broad framework of child, family, child care, and school factors as shaping subsequent social behavior. Child, family, and parenting qualities are emphasized as more important than child care experience. For instance, maternal sensitivity measured from 3 to 54 months has been proven to be the strongest and most consistent buffer against externalizing problems and the strongest associate of social skills during the early school years (NICHD ECCRN, 2003b, 2003c) and plays "a fundamental role . . . in shaping social and self-regulatory skills in early childhood" (NICHD ECCRN, 2003c, pp. 1654–1655). Maternal education and family income:needs ratio predict children's outcomes as strongly as any child care factor (NICHD ECCRN, 2003b). Behavior problems are also more common when mothers report more depression symptoms (NICHD ECCRN, 2003b, 2003c).

So where do these findings lead? Effects of hours spent in substitute care on social functioning are small but often negative. They persist through kindergarten and first grade years, but there is evidence that negative effects of early child care on aggression fade away by the third grade year.

COGNITIVE AND LANGUAGE DEVELOPMENT

It has been demonstrated repeatedly over the past 30 years that high-quality, educationally oriented early child care programs have positive effects on cognitive skills, particularly for children from disadvantaged backgrounds (Clarke-Stewart & Allhusen, 2002; Lamb, 1998). Lost among the headlines about problem behaviors is the fact that better quality care has been associated in a number of studies with better cognitive and language skills, not just for disadvantaged children but for children across the range of family income and child ability levels. Again, the most compelling findings come from the NICHD study, which assessed both the quantity and quality of care for children who were recruited at birth.

The NICHD study demonstrated that better linguistic, cognitive, and preacademic functioning was predicted by higher quality care. Children in higher quality care had better preacademic skills $(d = 0.24)$ and language $(d = 0.15)$ than did children who received low-quality care. Not surprisingly, both receptive and expressive language were also associated with more stimulating home environments as early as age 3 (NICHD ECCRN, 2000b).

By age 4½, positive effects of child care quality were observed on children's language skills in structural equation models, but parenting quality showed effects that were nearly five times greater (NICHD ECCRN, 2004a). Maternal caregiving (a composite measure of maternal sensitivity, overall level of stimulation and responsiveness, and nonauthoritarian child-rearing beliefs) was a strong predictor in models of cognitive competence at this age (NICHD ECCRN, 2002a). In the NICHD study, the effect size for substitute caregiving was only about 22% of the maternal caregiving effect for preacademic skills, memory, and language. These findings suggest that whatever positive effects early child care is having, family factors are far more important in determining children's cognitive skills.

The CQO Study revealed similar effects of quality of care on receptive language ability, math ability, and cognitive and attention skills, with children who attended better quality child care classrooms being more advanced in math skills in second grade, though effects of quality of care were modest and diminished over time (Peisner-Feinberg et al., 2001).

SUMMARY OF RESEARCH ON CHILD CARE EFFECTS

In his extensive review of research on child care, Lamb (1998) argued, "The diversity of family circumstances, the disparate array of nonparental care arrangements that exist, and the complex effects of endogenous differences among children all ensure that day care per se is unlikely to have clear, unambiguous, and universal effects, either positive or negative, when other important factors are taken into account" (p. 74). Research published since that time has validated that statement. Effects are varied and inevitably qualified by family and child factors (Clarke-Stewart & Allhusen, 2002; Vandell et al., 2000, pp. 98, 117). By the late preschool years, small negative effects can be observed in mother–child interactions and larger ones in children's peer and adult interactions. At the same time, there are small positive effects of better quality early child care on language and cognition. Even if the negative effects could be reduced or eliminated and positive effects enhanced in excellent quality child care settings, the fact remains that the quality of care that families are actually able to obtain produces both negative and positive effects, at least in the short term. The long-term effects, if any, remain unknown.

At the end of his review, Lamb (1998) noted that the quality of care and interaction that children receive at home continues to be the most important nurturing influence on the development of young children, even for children who receive extensive nonparental care. Subsequent research has confirmed this empirically with structural equation models: Family factors were as influential for children in 30 or more hours of care as they were for children in 10 hours of care or less (NICHD ECCRN, 1998b). So it is not the case that extensive time spent with substitute caregivers reduces the importance of parenting practices and other family attributes in influencing children's cognitive and social behaviors. The recently published kindergarten and first grade findings confirmed the strongest, most consistent effects for maternal sensitivity in children's outcomes, effects that were stronger than those of quantity and quality of substitute child care (NICHD ECCRN, 2003b, 2004a). The preeminence of family variables was also established in the most recent findings from the CQO Study (Burchinal, Peisner-Feinberg, Pianta, & Howes, 2002). No matter how much or how little children are in substitute care, parents' contributions are the ones that matter most.

THE AUTHORS' ADVICE

The first key question that the experts address is whether infants and toddlers should be placed in full-time child care (30 hours a week or more).

Spock

In the various editions of his books spanning more than 50 years, Benjamin Spock was shaped by his times, even as he came to shape them in his role as a political activist. The early editions of his book (Spock, 1946) provide reassuring words to mothers caring for their infants and children at home. By the seventh edition, entire sections are devoted to discussions of substitute care. Spock recognizes the competing attractions of work life: "Parents who know that they need a career or a certain kind of work for fulfillment should not simply give it up for the sake of their children. Their children would not benefit from such a sacrifice" (Spock & Parker, 1998, p. 603).

Spock acknowledges both sides of the early child care controversy and then presents a qualified defense of child care for infants: "Where I stand . . . I believe that infants are resilient creatures, up to a certain point, and that there is no reason why high-quality day care should harm their development. Children need adults who are devoted to them most of all, whether it's a single parent or a group of day-care teachers" (Spock & Parker, 1998, p. 606). One issue not addressed by this statement is whether infants are capable of becoming attached to a group of day care teachers. He also argues that some children could be differentially benefited by child care: "Group care is particularly valuable for the only child, for the child without much chance to play with others, for the child who lives in a small apartment, and for the child whose parents find her difficult to manage" (Spock & Parker, 1998, p. 604). On the decision to place an infant in child care, Spock leaves the ultimate decision to families: "Should you send your child to day care? I think this is a very personal decision that must be based on your family's needs. If you want to send your infant to a day care, I wouldn't feel at all guilty about it. He'll do just fine, so long as the quality of the care is high" (Spock & Parker, 1998, p. 607).

Brazelton

Brazelton was the first of the experts to respond to the rising numbers of mothers entering the workforce when their children were very small. He was the first of the experts to devote a book to the topic, *Working and Caring* (1985), and was an early and frequent advocate for improvements in both the quality of care and humane parental leave policies, including the Family Leave Act. In his 1992 parenting manual, *Touchpoints*, Brazelton's attitude toward substitute care is reassuring: "Parents who must return to work often have deep fears that their babies might be damaged. I can say with conviction that, as long as they find a really nurturing, caring person for him, the baby can adjust without permanent trauma. It will not be the same as having one parent all day, but that can be pretty conflicted for the baby and parent, too" (Brazelton, 1992, pp. 103–104).

In a 1998 interview, Brazelton seemed to be wavering on the issue of early child care, arguing essentially for compensatory parenting time for infants in nonparental care. When asked by the interviewer whether "child care is the best thing for kids," he answered:

> I think we aren't in a position to answer that yet. What we are in a position to ask is: What kind of back-up for families can we give them that will make it work?... Three months is just a start for being home with a new baby. But even if you're there for three months, and you know that child and know that that child knows you, then you can back up your relationship every day when you come home, every weekend, and you can do things to make up that time missed. (Healy, 1998)

In his recent advocacy book (Brazelton & Greenspan, 2000) addressing early childhood issues, Brazelton is still giving parents options on substitute child care: "Again, I think it needs to be a case-by-case decision, weighing this or that, rather than simply telling people what to do. Some parents are better parents if there is an outlet for them. But we do need to provide the children with an optimal secondary caregiver" (Brazelton & Greenspan, 2000, p. 25). But he and Greenspan are firmer in their recommendations for a parent to stay at home with infants: "We recommend a leave of most of the first year of life for one parent. . . . We do not recommend full-time day care, 30 or more hours of care by nonparents, for infants and toddlers *if* the parents are able to provide high-quality care themselves and *if* the parents have reasonable options" (Brazelton & Greenspan, 2000, p. 48).

The authors never clarify what they consider "reasonable options," though in a recent newspaper column, Brazelton acknowledges the bind that many young families are in: "In far too many families, there is no choice. Both parents must work just to pay the bills, to stay off welfare or to cover their benefits. These families are not working for luxuries. No family today can dare to be without health insurance and other 'benefits' of the work force" (Brazelton, 2001). Brazelton and Greenspan's (2000) rationale for their recommendation that infants should stay home cites the quality of early child care currently available: "More important than mere numbers are reports regarding the quality of this care. These are not encouraging. The most comprehensive study of the quality of day care [citing the CQO Study] reported that the vast majority of center-based care was not of high quality (over 85 percent was not of high quality for preschool children and over 90 percent was not of high quality for infants and toddlers)" (Brazelton and Greenspan, 2000, pp. xii–xiii). Brazelton's most recent parenting manual, *Touchpoints Three to Six* (Brazelton & Sparrow, 2001), reports statistics on the scarcity of high quality care, but also recognizes that more than half of preschool age children are in substitute care, and provides extensive tips for parents to find better quality care.

Dobson

In his books on discipline and parenting, Dobson apparently never directly addresses the topic of early child care, other than to point out the importance of full-time motherhood and domestic roles for women:

> I know some families which just can't seem to pay their bills without a supplement to the father's paycheck, but children need their mother more than they do a newer car or larger house. . . . What activity could be more important than shaping human lives during their impressionable and plastic years? I'm afraid I have little patience with the view that domestic responsibilities are not worthy of a woman's time. The hand that rocks the cradle rules the world, yet mom is now told that she should chase around after some additional source of fulfillment. . . . The traditional concept of motherhood, *full-time* motherhood, still sounds like a pretty good idea to me. (Dobson, 1970, p. 54)

As did the other experts, Dobson changed with the times: In the 1992 version of this book, these remarks were edited out.

Dobson clearly remains concerned about mothers taking jobs outside the home that might interfere with the domestic responsibilities that he assigns primarily to them: "The great movement of women into the labor force has left millions of mothers on the brink of nervous collapse as they attempt to combine full-time employment with full-time responsibilities at home. . . . When the demand for energy exceeds the supply, for whatever reason, burnout is inevitable. And children are almost always the losers in the competition" (Dobson, 1987, p. 132). This message has been repeated more recently in newspaper columns (e.g., Dobson, 1997) describing the demanding double load of full-time employment and a second shift of family work for mothers. Could fathers' family work reduce the load? "Well, he may be working a fifteen-hour day at his own job. Getting started in a business or a profession often demands that kind of commitment. Or he may simply not choose to help his wife. That is a common complaint among working mothers. 'Not fair' you say. I agree, but that's the way the system often works" (Dobson, 1997, p. D3).

So rather than advising fathers to work more reasonable hours and do their fair share at home, Dobson shrugs his shoulders while leaving mothers with full responsibility for parenting and housework: "The issue, then, is not whether a woman should choose a career and be a mother, too. Of course she has that right, and it is nobody's business but hers and her husband's. I would simply plead that you not allow your family to get sucked into that black hole of exhaustion" (Dobson, 1997, p. D3). Apparently because Dobson believes that women's parenting and domestic roles are so much more demanding than men's, he never considers the question of whether a man can choose a career and be a father without getting "sucked into the black hole of exhaustion." Not surprisingly, Dobson's writings are silent on the issue of timing of child care entry, the relative advantages of types of care, and how to assess quality.

Leach

Leach is unique among the experts for having stayed home with her children for at least part of their early years. In her parenting manual, she emphasizes both the importance of the initial primary attachment to the caregiving parent and the additional benefits of child care: "Every baby needs at least one special person to attach himself to—and more are better. . . . As long as your baby does have at least one special person, he can make other people special too. His capacity for love is not rationed any more than yours is. The reverse is true. Love creates love" (Leach, 1998, p. 144). Child care expands the infant's emotional horizons:

> Sharing your time between the baby and paid outside work will not threaten it or the baby's well-being provided that he continues to be—and to feel that he is—your primary concern, and that the care that fills in for yours is enthusiastic and genuinely loving. Sharing your baby's care with your partner, with other relatives and/or with a caregiver whom you pay to act like family is a modern version of the way babies used to be cared for in extended families. (Leach, 1998, p. 145)

Nor should parents be concerned about losing their children's affection when they place their infant in child care: "They are indeed your children and spending the working days without you will not change their awareness of that or their feelings about you. Children's love for adults is not rationed or channeled. It cannot be used up or diverted. Indeed, the more people children have to love and feel loved by, the more lovable and loving they are likely to be" (Leach, 1998, p. 316). But she also acknowledges the important role that substitute caregivers play in caring for a child: "His self-esteem, discipline and learning will be influenced almost (though not quite) as much by her as by you. You need to choose accordingly" (Leach, 1998, p. 318).

Thus, Leach's position on substitute child care in her parenting manual is temperate and reassuring about the use of substitute care. The strongly negative tone of her advocacy writing, however, stands in marked contrast to the manual:

> The spiraling strands of development that transform helpless newborns into sociable and socialized small people are plaited into their relationships with known, loved and loving adults. Those adults do not have to be parents or relations but, unfashionable and unpalatable though the fact may be, it is much easier if they are. . . . That does not make every natural mother or father a "good parent" nor handicap every infant raised otherwise, but it does stack the odds and should inform the debate. Whoever it is who cares for infants, they need to have permanence, continuity, passion and a parentlike commitment that is difficult to find or meet outside the vested interests and social expectations of family roles and cannot be adequately replaced by professionalism. (Leach, 1994, p. 83)

The impact of child care transitions for infants is compared to bereavement:

> The grieving of a baby who loses her one and only special person—her lone mother who dies, for example, or the lifelong foster mother from who she is removed—is agonizing to see because we know we are looking at genuine tragedy. But the pain of the separations we arrange and connive at every time we change caregivers or leave a baby in the daycare center that has new staff—again—or with an agency baby-sitter she has never seen, may not be as different as we assume. (Leach, 1994, pp. 87–88)

Leach, as the title of *Children First* implies, puts infants' interests ahead of those of their mothers and writes with humor about how her public statements against nonmaternal care for infants led her to be regarded:

> In public, for example (though rarely by individual women in private), it is generally assumed that women's rights take precedence over infant needs: not just that they *should,* but that they self-evidently *do.* To suggest that a baby may temporarily have a greater right to his mother's time than she has to her own, places the speaker with the "family values" lobby of the extreme Right unless it is coupled with a proposal of financial support for mothers at home, in which case the speaker is briskly moved to the extreme Left. . . . There are plenty of individuals, including many within the women's movement, who speak out for mothers' right to *choose* to stay with their babies but few who suggest that that decision might be of value to the *baby* or that, if it was, that could be sufficient reason to make it. (Leach, 1997, p. 15)

Leach's rejection of care for infants by anyone other than their mothers is grounded in her belief in the preeminent importance of the mother–child relationship for young infants:

> Most daycare advocates gloss over babies' need to be breast-fed and to establish the primary attachments on which later development depends. . . . The baby will be fine if he has a single, continuously available, long-term alternative person to attach himself to (his father, perhaps, or the rare kind of in-home caregiver who really is psychologically part of his family). The mother will be fine if she feels no sense of long-term loss. But those are large ifs. (Leach, 1994, pp. 96–97)

But her position also reflects her view of the quality of care currently available for infants and its frequent failure to provide dependable alternative adults for an infant to become attached to: "That vital continuous one-to-one attention can rarely be achieved in group care, however excellent the facility may be. . . . In most countries, the majority of daycare centers for infants are not excellent . . . there is such constant staff movement that babies are likely to be handled by several different people each day and are unlikely to be handled by those same people all week" (Leach, 1994, pp. 88–89). In summary, her objections to child care for infants focus on the failure of most child care arrangements to provide sensitive caregivers for infants to become attached to over the long term. Such attachments, she argues, are the foundation for optimal development.

Rosemond

Prior to late 1992, Rosemond's position on early child care was consistent with his theme that children do not need close attention from parents as much as parents think that they do. During the late 1980s and early 1990s, he contrasted his position with the more conservative one of another parenting book author: "Developmental psychologists agree there is no truly adequate parent substitute during the first few months of life, but don't feel there's any real danger to leaving older babies and toddlers with competent, attentive secondary care-givers, such as in-home sites and trained day-care staff" (Rosemond, 1989, p. 26). In support of his position, he notes that "most research indicates problems can be minimized, if not eliminated, if the day care responds to the infant's needs" (Rosemond, 1990, p. 62). Further, early child care could have positive effects on the early mother–child relationship: "In fact, day care can help the mother–child relationship by giving a mother a chance to feel adequate outside the home. The self-fulfillment a mother such as you derives from a satisfying career will, in all likelihood, have a positive effect on her baby" (Rosemond, 1990, p. 63). Parents were enjoined to seek the best quality child care available for their children (Rosemond, 1990, p. 63). In response to a reader's question concerning whether young children needed an at-home mom, Rosemond wrote in his newspaper column:

> I think children need mothers who are a model of self-fulfillment. In that context, whether a mother is at home during the day or at a job is largely irrelevant. The ideal of a previous generation's at-home mom is a fantasy. Whereas most of these women were not employed outside the home, they were not doting on their children during the day. . . . They did not feel obliged to pay constant attention to their children. . . . Quite the contrary, they expected their children to occupy their own time and solve their own problems with playmates. (Rosemond, 1992a, p. 2)

But then came his sudden and dramatic shift of position: "For reasons having to do with research I did during the writing of this chapter, I am now convinced that parent-care during the first three years of life is clearly in the best interest of a child" (Rosemond, 1993b, p. 161). One justification for this shift was nostalgia for the family of former days, presented as an

undeniable truth: The American family worked better when there was a parent in the home during the day. In past generations, the parent was almost always female, but gender is irrelevant to the purpose of our discussion. That all-but-constant adult presence provided for greater family stability, smoother internal transitions, more effective overall time management, better supervision and care of children, and more efficient delegation of responsibilities, not to mention a lower level of stress. (Rosemond, 1993b, pp. 162–163)

Rosemond frequently evokes nostalgic themes in his writing, but these contradictory passages make it clear that parents of the past were *always* better, whether they provided closer supervision and care *or* avoided doting and left children to occupy their own time.

After the switch, he expresses a new appreciation for the special connection between parents and children: "I would argue that in all but the most extreme cases there is no one more in tune with the child, and therefore more capable of properly responding to this process [of development] than the child's parents. The good intentions of the most well-trained day-care workers simply do not compare" (Rosemond, 1993b, p. 164). He also now warns about the potential of early child care for producing serious problems in children, from depression to attention-deficit/hyperactivity disorder (ADHD):

What, therefore, are the *possible* consequences of placing an infant or toddler in day care? First, lacking in care-givers who are adequately tuned to the child, the child may not develop a sufficient sense of trust. The environment, therefore, appears threatening, rather than nurturing and inviting. Insecurity prevents the child from moving creatively out into the world. Either the child withdraws, becoming depressed and clinging, or his explorations appear driven and chaotic, rather than creative and purposeful. In this regard, it is interesting to note that as the number of infants and toddlers in day care has increased, so has the incidence of childhood depression and behavioral disorders, including attention-deficit hyperactivity disorder (ADHD) which is characterized by a preponderance of driven, chaotic activity. (Rosemond, 1993b, p. 165)

Nor are the children the only ones at risk. Suddenly, the beneficial effects of early child care are negative for mothers as well as for their children: "Twenty years of family counseling tells me that a mother is far more likely to be guilt-ridden when she works outside the home during her child's early years than when she does not. The working mother often overcompensates by paying excessive attention to, and doing too much for, her child when she is at home. It is not the mother's presence, but these anxious over-compensations that set the stage for co-dependency" (Rosemond, 1992b, p. 2E). Thus, use of substitute care sets the stage for mutual dependency, which is described in the clinical language of addiction.

One fascinating aspect of his shift on the child care issue is that it came at a time when there was little new evidence on the overall quality of substitute care or negative effects of early child care. As part of his position change, Rosemond claims that the parenting public had long been the victim of deception:

> For the last twenty years or more, the professional community has been engaged in a cover-up concerning these issues. Not wishing to offend anyone, much less appear out of step with the time, developmental psychologists, early-childhood educators, and the like have acted as if home care and day care workers were fundamentally equivalent. The impression created has been that if parents know what to look for in a day-care center, a young child will be as well off in the care of strangers for forty-plus hours a week, fifty weeks a year, as in the care of a parent. That's a myth. It's myth that serves the needs of day-care providers, employers, and to some extent, women, but it's a myth, nonetheless. (Rosemond, 1993b, p. 164)

Rosemond embraced his alternative stand without a hint of irony about his own role as a member of the professional community who published and spoke widely as a parenting expert. If there was a cover-up as he alleges, he was either hoodwinked by his fellow professionals, unusual for an expert to admit, or he participated in it. Nor does he seem troubled by his new identification of his own former, oft-repeated position as being based on "myth."

Later in the 1990s, when larger, better controlled research on child care documented concerns about the quality of care in child care centers and some negative effects of early child care, Rosemond used the findings to bolster his position. He noted evidence, apparently from the CQO Study

(Helburn et al., 1995), that the quality of care available for infants and toddlers is not good: "Only 8 percent of centers serving children under age 3 provide care of high quality, where emotional nurturing is concerned" (Rosemond, 1998b, p. C3). The widely reported NICHD finding (NICHD ECCRN, 2001c) that children in more hours of substitute care scored higher on externalizing was summarized thus: "children who spend lots of time in day care during their preschool years are three times as likely to be aggressive as children whose moms care for them at home" (Rosemond, 2001c, p. E10).

Summary of the Experts' Positions on Placing Infants in Substitute Care

The findings of recent research, particularly the massive NICHD-sponsored study, suggest mixed effects of child care that match none of the experts' recent positions. Spock is the most optimistic about high-quality substitute care for infants. The recent advocacy writings of Brazelton (in collaboration with Greenspan), Leach, and Rosemond are alarmist concerning child care for infants, but research findings do not support their positions, though research clearly shows the risks of poor quality care and negative effects of extensive child care on social adjustment during the early school years that fade over time. Their expressed concerns about extensive hours of child care ignore the much smaller difference in time spent in instrumental and social care between mothers at home with their children and those in the workforce 30 or more hours a week (Booth et al., 2002).

Leach's description of child care placement and re-placement as being equivalent in the infant's mind to the death of the parent or caregiver makes her point dramatically but does not correspond with the accommodations that infants themselves make to child care. They increase their sleeping time while in care and save their social awake time for their parents (Brazelton, 1992, p. 104), who in turn compensate by spending more social time with their children when they are at home than parents at home full time do (Ahnert, Rickert, & Lamb, 2000; Booth et al., 2002). Leach warns about child care's threat to attachment security, and there is modest evidence of less secure attachment by age 3 if children are in full-time care, but only if their mothers are low in sensitivity (NICHD ECCRN, 2001b). The failure to find an overall negative effect of substitute child care on attachment provides little evidence of the risks that Leach warns about. Considering her advocacy writings on the critical importance of the parent–infant connection, her parenting manual is surprisingly accepting of substitute care, and to the extent that child care research can test her ideas, there is better support for the moderate position on early substitute child care taken in the parenting manual.

Dobson's failure to acknowledge the reality of substitute child care during the years from birth to age 6 is unrealistic in light of families' current high usage rates, and it is a disservice to those parents who value his advice. Rosemond's radical about-face on child care preceded the mixed-to-negative research findings of the late 1990s on hours in substitute care and may reflect his increasing identification with and appeal to one particular segment of the parenting public: social and religious conservatives. He exaggerates the negative effects of more hours of day care on externalizing behavior. Rosemond's suggestion that increased use of child care has led to a higher incidence of depression and ADHD can be taken only at face value since he provides no evidence of a causal connection. Could substitute child care cause ADHD? In light of the consensus that there are important genetically influenced neurological influences on ADHD development (Barkley et al., 2002), child care seems an unlikely sole cause for the disorder. Elsewhere in his writing (see chapter 5), Rosemond blames ADHD on too much TV viewing by young children.

WHAT IS THE BEST AGE FOR INFANTS OR CHILDREN TO ENTER CHILD CARE?

Research on Age of Entry

Data on when children are actually placed in child care show that it happens early: During the first year of life, 58% of infants in the NICHD study were in child care at least 30 hours per week, full-time or close to it, and they entered substitute care early, at an average age of less than 4 months (NICHD ECCRN, 1997a). But does early entry pose special risks? Put another way, is there an age beyond which any potential risks associated with substitute care are minimized?

One risk to be considered is early illness. Children who are in substitute care during the first 2 years of life experience more colds, ear infections, and gastrointestinal flu than those in parent care, though differences are reduced by the 3rd year (NICHD ECCRN, 2001a). Children between ages 3 and 4½ with more child care experience show lower rates of illness than do those newly enrolled, but even at this older age, care in larger groups is associated with increased rates of colds, ear infections, and gastrointestinal flu. The key factor seems to be simply the amount of exposure to illness-causing pathogens (NICHD ECCRN, 2003a).

Direct evidence of behavioral effects is limited and must be extracted from the research on the effect of cumulative amount of hours in care. When the two can be separated, as in the NICHD research, the effects of age of entry on attachment at age 15 months are small or nonexistent (NICHD ECCRN, 1997b, 1998a). In a review of research on early child care, Belsky (2001) concluded that age of entry into care was less predictive of behavior than number of hours of care per week, or the cumulative amount of child care received. Findings of the NICHD study when the children were age 4½ suggest that the cumulative quantity of substitute care is more predictive of socio-emotional adjustment rather than the amount of time spent in care during any particular time period (NICHD ECCRN, 2003b).

One study of mothers whose babies had entered child care early revealed that very early entry (earlier than 6 weeks) may be a risk factor for some babies—and their mothers. A group of 198 mothers who had returned to work by 4 months after their child's birth were videotaped as they fed their infants, and their sensitivity and positive affect were rated. How long they had taken off work by itself did not predict their sensitivity with their infants, but mothers who had shorter leaves (less than 6 weeks) and who had a difficult infant or elevated depressive symptoms were less sensitive and positive in their interactions with their babies (Clark, Hyde, Essex, & Klein, 1997).

In his review of child care research, Lamb (1998) concluded that the earlier nonparental care is initiated, the greater the likelihood of noncompliant behavior, particularly for infants in poorer quality care. But as noted earlier, compliance rates change across situations, and Lamb noted several findings that contradicted the general pattern. A case in point would be the NICHD study, in which children who entered child care later had *more* behavior problems as rated by caregivers at age 2, but age of entry did not significantly predict behavior problems at age 3, after controlling for family income, maternal personality and depression scores, and child gender and difficult temperament (NICHD ECCRN, 1998a).

It has recently become possible to obtain direct measures of young children's stress in child care by measuring salivary cortisol, a major hormone associated with stress. It is clear that entry into child care is stressful for toddlers as shown by cortisol increases as well as by increases in fussing and crying. Even when mothers were present as children were being adapted to child care, a recent study found that cortisol levels were elevated in group care settings, and even 5 months after enrollment they were still higher than the earlier established home level of cortisol (Ahnert, Gunnar, Lamb, & Barthel, 2004). Findings suggest that long days in child care may produce elevations in cortisol and that the toddler age group is most at risk. From midmorning to midafternoon, children below age 4 did not show predictable changes in salivary cortisol levels, and children age 4 or older showed predictable small decreases (Gunnar & Donzella, 2002). But cortisol levels increased markedly from midmorning to midafternoon for 71% of toddlers enrolled in child care centers full-time, though when in parental care at home on weekends these children did not show similar increases (Watamura, Donzella, Alwin, & Gunnar, 2003). Infants enrolled in substitute child care did not show this increase in cortisol, older preschoolers (beyond 36 months) showed less of an increase, and early elementary school children showed decreasing cortisol levels from midmorning to midafternoon (Gunnar & Donzella, 2002; Watamura, Sebanc, & Gunnar, 2002).

The researchers note that peer interactions intensify during this age period and believe the increase in cortisol for toddlers in child care centers may reflect their difficulties in managing interactions with other children who are also socially incompetent. In support of this point, they found that the largest increases in cortisol over the day occured in those children whom teachers, parents, and observers found to be less socially competent and less capable of regulating negative emotions, such as anger, and who showed more aggressive behavior (Dettling, Gunnar, & Donzella, 1999). Children with greater cortisol increases played less often with other children, and controlling for age, these children were rated higher by their teachers in social fearfulness (Watamura et al., 2003), though as the authors report, previous research has not invariably found a link between fearfulness and cortisol. The authors note that cortisol increases do not occur in all children, and the pattern suggests that children grow out of them.

These preliminary findings might argue that entry into child care centers should be delayed past the toddler years, especially for those children who have difficulty with peer social interactions. But it may be difficult for parents to know before child care entry whether their children will have problems with peers. These findings are based on comparisons of children at different age levels and deserve further investigation with a larger group of children followed longitudinally.

What the Experts Say about Timing

Spock argues for delaying reentry to the work force, but for a surprisingly short time:

> Though parents can return to outside jobs at any stage after the baby's birth, a good rule is the later the better. Taking three to six months off is great if you can manage it. This gives the baby time to settle in to pretty regular feeding and sleeping routines and to get used to the rhythm of her family. It also gives the mother time to adjust to her own physiological and psychological changes and to establish nursing or switch from breast to bottle, if she wants to before returning to work. (Spock & Parker, 1998, p. 603)

For older preschool-age children, Spock is equally firm about the advantages of group care:

> By the age of three, every child needs other children of the same age, not just to have fun with but also to learn how to get along with. This is the most important job in a child's life. . . . Few children nowadays enjoy all these advantages at home. Good group care is crucial to the parents as well as to the child in the growing number of families in which both parents work outside the home. (Spock & Parker, 1998, p. 604)

Brazelton's position has changed over the years: In *Working and Caring* (1985), he wrote: "If there can be a choice, I suggest a mother choose a time when her baby is not learning a new, demanding task. . . . For instance, good times for change might be (1) at nine to ten months, after stranger anxiety and after self-feeding, sitting and crawling are achieved; or (2) eighteen months to two years, after walking, negativism and the heightened fear of separation of the twelve-to-sixteen month period" (p. 61). But his recent advocacy book coauthored with Stanley Greenspan recommends later entry:

> We believe that in the first two years of life full-time day care is a difficult context in which to provide the ongoing, nurturing care by one or a few caregivers that the child requires. Part-time day care, on the other hand, may be quite helpful. . . . But the 35-plus hours a week

for infants and toddlers makes it very difficult to have the consistency of caregiver and the depth of nurturance required, or the amount of facilitative interaction with the environment or direct interaction that we believe is healthy for infants and toddlers. (Brazelton & Greenspan, 2000, p. 46)

In her advocacy writings, Leach argues strongly for delaying full-time child care entry: "It is clearly and certainly best for babies to have something close to full-time mother care for six months at least—conveniently linked with breast-feeding—and family care for a further year and better two" (Leach, 1994, pp. 78–79). She warns of the dangers of too-early placement in too-long hours of care: "Three hours a day in an understaffed nursery where he is special to nobody is far from ideal for a newborn, but nine hours a day is far more likely to damage his development" (Leach, 1994, p. 85). Group care is problematic even for older infants: "Everyone who lives or works with toddlers knows that they are not well adapted to group life" (Leach, 1994, p. 92). She argues that "the appropriate use of professionally staffed daycare centers is for children who are well into their third year or more" (Leach, 1994, p. 92).

But note the marked contrast with her parenting manual, which never directly addresses the question of whether early child care entry is risky for infants and toddlers: "You can be quite sure that even the most clingy one-year-old will eventually take sympathetic day care in his stride if you can give him enough time to adapt" (Leach, 1998, p. 318).

Rosemond's ideas about timing of entry correspond with his ideas about the advisability of early care. Before his change of position in late 1992, his ideas were flexible: "Ideally, parents should take primary care of their children for as least the first year of their children's lives. Realistically, however, if that's not possible because of economic pressures, or you truly feel your own mental health is at stake, stay home for at least six weeks and then go back to work" (Rosemond, 1989, p. 26). His shift in position reflected not a rejection of all other-than-parent care for young children, but really a change in timing: "Parent-care during the first three years of life is clearly in the best interest of a child" (Rosemond, 1993b, p. 161). His arguments for parent care in the first 3 years of life focus on it as a developmentally sensitive period: "Parents are throwing the dice whenever they entrust the day care of an infant or toddlers to someone other than themselves. The first three years of life constitute the single most critical, precedent-setting of all developmental periods. Of utmost importance to the child's developmental integrity are parents who are first, available, and second, properly responsive to the child's needs during this time" (Rosemond, 1993b, p. 165).

In summary, regardless of the experts' position changes over time, there is not strong research evidence identifying a particular age as better or worse for child care entry, nor is there definitive evidence that later entry leads to better outcomes. Other child care variables (hours per week and quality of care) seem to be more crucial. Published research reports do not provide evidence that delaying entry until 36 months provides beneficial effects. On the other hand, if the higher cortisol levels reported by Gunnar and coauthors (Gunnar & Donzella, 2002; Watamura et al., 2002, 2003) are supported in future research, parents should avoid placing 2-year-olds, especially less socially competent 2-year-olds, in group care.

QUALITY AND TYPE OF CARE

What Are the Effects of Quality of Care on Children's Cognitive and Social Skills?

In child care centers that offer good quality care, children are more likely to be emotionally attached to their caregivers and to be socially competent with peers (Howes et al., 1992), though it is possible that these stronger connections are attributable to the fact that better parents choose better quality centers for their children (Howes, 1990). Even after controlling for social class and other aspects of the family background, children in higher quality, as opposed to poorer quality, child care center classrooms in the CQO study showed better receptive language and social skills (Helburn et al., 1995, p. 33), and as noted earlier in the section on cognitive and language development, this study showed better math ability and cognitive and attention skills. However, effects of quality of care were modest and diminished over time (Peisner-Feinberg et al., 2001). But these studies are concerned solely with center-based care.

In the NICHD study of children followed from birth whose parents selected different types of child care, those children who had attended higher quality child care scored higher on social competence and showed fewer externalizing problems and less conflict with adult caregivers and kindergarten teachers (NICHD ECCRN, 2003b). They also scored higher on tests of preacademic skills and language at age 2, 3 (NICHD, 2000b), and 4½ (NICHD ECCRN, 2002b). Changes in care quality were linked to changes in children's early cognitive performance: "Children whose child care increased in quality over time had better pre-academic skills, whereas pre-academic skills were lower for children whose child care decreased in quality over time" (NICHD ECCRN, 2002b, p. 151).

What Is the Quality of the Care That Parents Are Able to Obtain?

Because it was done in four states with varying regulatory climates, the CQO Study (Helburn et al., 1995) provided some of the earliest data that could be extrapolated to the broader population of children in the United States. It presented a grim picture of the quality of care in child care centers, particularly in infant and toddler classrooms, with only 8% of the classrooms providing care that was excellent or even good. However, only a small fraction of infants in substitute care are cared for in centers: The National Household Education Survey found that 7% of infants under a year of age are in child care centers, with higher numbers for 1-year-olds (11%) and 2-year-olds (19%) (National Center for Education Statistics, 1996). For children in child care homes, the rates of children receiving care deemed inadequate was 35% in one national study devoted just to this type of care (Kontos, Howes, Shim, & Galinsky, 1995) and 41% in the NICHD sample. When data were pooled for all the children in the NICHD study, whose parents chose a variety of child care arrangements, the results were not much better. Positive substitute caregiving was deemed highly characteristic for only 12% of the sample and somewhat characteristic for an additional 32% of the sample. For over half the sample (51%), positive caregiving was "somewhat uncharacteristic" (NICHD ECCRN, 2000a). There is widespread concern among child development professionals about the quality of care. One recent estimate is that as few as one third to one fifth of the programs studied in research used developmentally appropriate practices identified by the National Association for the Education of Young Children (Dunn & Kontos, 1997).

Toddlers become attached to and prefer stable caregivers over nonstable caregivers, as evidenced by both behaviors in distress situations and more social initiatives in nondistressed play situations (Barnas & Cummings, 1994; Raikes, 1993). Howes and Hamilton (1993) found that preschoolers were more likely to be socially withdrawn or aggressive with peers if they had experienced more caregiver changes over a 3-year period (the average number of changes was 2.4). A survey of a nationally representative sample of child care centers, though, revealed that in 61% of the centers, none of the infants stayed with the same teacher when they moved up to the toddler classroom. And 70% of the centers indicated that none of the toddlers stayed with the same teacher when they were advanced to the next class (Cryer, Hurwitz, & Wolery, 2000).

What Are the Important Dimensions of Quality?

In the summary of their findings on child care quality, members of the NICHD research network concluded that, "Positive caregiving was more likely when child-adult ratios and group sizes were smaller, caregivers were more educated, held more child-centered beliefs about childrearing, and had more experience in child care, and environments were safer and more stimulating" (NICHD ECCRN, 2000a, p. 116).

The strongest and most consistent predictor of positive caregiving was the child–adult ratio (NICHD ECCRN, 2000a). When there were fewer children for each adult, the nature of child–caregiver interaction changed qualitatively: Caregivers were more likely to be sensitive and warm in their interactions with children (Howes, 1997; NICHD ECCRN, 1996). In the NICHD study (1996), when the ratio of caregivers to infants was 1:2, only 17% of the caregivers were rated as highly sensitive; when the ratio was 1:4, only 8% were. Caregivers with more education and more child-centered beliefs about childrearing provided more positive caregiving, though the relationship was less strong and consistent than child:adult ratio (NICHD ECCRN, 2000a). Children in child care homes with better educated and trained providers scored better on tests of cognitive and language development (Clarke-Stewart, Vandell, Burchinal, O'Brien, & McCartney, 2002). The importance of caregiver attributes increased as the children got older: At ages 6, 15, and 24 months the child:staff ratio was most important in determining the quality of care, but by 36 months the association with the number of children and positive caregiving became significantly weaker, and caregivers' education, experience, and beliefs became relatively more important (NICHD ECCRN, 2000a).

In one of the few instances in which child care researchers directly addressed the implications of their findings for what is arguably their most important audience, the members of the NICHD network recommended that "parents would be well advised to select care arrangements that are characterized by a low child-adult ratio, a clean and orderly physical environment, a variety of toys and learning materials, and a caregiver with a college education" (NICHD ECCRN, 2000a, p. 134).

Type of Care and Pattern of Usage

Whatever appreciation there is for children's care by their mothers in their own homes during the infant and preschool years, only 8% of the children in the NICHD study were exclusively in their mother's care for the period between birth and age 4½ (NICHD ECCRN, 2004c). Only about one quarter of the families were able to rely primarily on coparental care to meet child care needs when their toddlers were 15 months of age, and these tended to be families in which the mothers were less well educated (NICHD ECCRN, 1997c). For those families who used nonparental care, there was abundant evidence that child care arrangements were affected by many factors aside from the child's welfare. Relatively few of the families followed a pattern of care of one type in the infant or toddler years with a switch to center care at the preschool age level. Only 4% of the children moved from a child care home to a child care center, which is the pattern recommended by some of the experts (NICHD ECCRN, 2004c).

Does One Type of Child Care Provide a Higher Quality of Care Than Another?

At 15 and 24 months, the highest level of positive caregiving was provided by in-home caregivers, including fathers and grandparents, if they cared for only one child, closely followed by family child care homes with relatively few children per adult. The least positive caregiving was found in center-based care for which there were typically higher ratios of children to adults. "By 36 months of age the significance of child–adult ratio decreased, and in-home arrangements became less positive" (NICHD ECCRN, 2000a, p. 116).

Those child care centers with the smallest child:adult ratios (fewer than three children per adult) were not significantly different from home-based care in the rating and frequency of positive caregiving (NICHD ECCRN, 2000a). Positive caregiving ratings for child care center caregivers improved from 15 to 36 months, whereas ratings of home-based caregivers decreased, so that by age 3 there were no significant differences (NICHD ECCRN, 2000a). In a large study of child care homes, when care provided by relatives was compared with that provided in child care homes, relative care-givers were lower in sensitivity and responsive involvement with their charges and higher on restrictiveness (Kontos et al., 1995).

What Are the Effects of Different Types of Care on Child Cognitive and Social Skills?

In the NICHD study, relative care did not appear to be either benefi-cial or detrimental to children's early cognitive, language, and social de-velopment. For family child care homes, there was a negative relationship between number of hours in care and Woodcock–Johnson Word Identifi-cation at 36–54 months; scores on the Preschool Language Scale were also negative for 36–54-month-old children, suggesting that continued time in home-based care that is frequently less structured and lacks preacademic activities may be a factor in the lower scores for preschoolers (NICHD ECCRN, 2001d).

Positive effects of child care on cognitive and language development were associated with more time in child care centers, not merely any substitute care (NICHD ECCRN, 2002b). Children who had more experience in child care centers showed better receptive and expressive language skills and better short-term memory for sentences. The positive effects of child care center experience on language ($d = 0.29$) and memory ($d = 0.34$) were small but positive (NICHD ECCRN, 2002b). A reanalysis of these data (NICHD ECCRN, 2004c) that controlled for different parenting variables (adding mothers' endorsement of "traditional" beliefs on child obedience and parental authority, maternal reports of harsh control, and deleting ma-ternal sensitivity) showed only two positive associations with outcomes at age 4½. More hours in center care in infancy (1–17 months) were associ-ated with lower preacademic skills, and more hours in center care during the early child years (between 18 and 35 months) were associated with bet-ter language skills. This illustrates the dependence of apparent effects of substitute care on which parenting processes are statistically controlled for, a significant methodological issue when the two are invariably correlated. Controlling for variability associated with maternal authoritarian beliefs markedly reduced the small positive association between hours in center care and better cognitive and language development. Given that child care providers with authoritarian beliefs provide poorer quality care (NICHD ECCRN, 1996), if parents with authoritarian beliefs pick child care providers with beliefs similar to their own, then statistically removing variability due to parental authoritarianism may also reduce variability due to caregiver authoritarianism and lead to underestimates of child care effects. The small effects found in the NICHD research stood in contrast to Clarke-Stewart, Gruber, and Fitzgerald's (1994) finding that children in child care centers were 6 to 9 months more advanced on measures of intellectual competence than children cared for in child care homes or even those cared for by their own mothers.

Though generally the most potent child care variable predicting social functioning is simply number of hours in substitute care, the proportion of time that children spent in child care centers independently predicted first grade teachers' reports of more externalizing behavior (NICHD ECCRN, 2003b; NICHD ECCRN, 2003c), though it had no systematic effect on aggression trajectories through Grade 3 (NICHD ECCRN, 2004b).

THE AUTHORS ON TYPE AND QUALITY OF CARE

Spock

Spock writes with conviction about the importance of quality of care and what is necessary to maintain it: "The quality of day care is critical for children's well being. . . . Responsive, nurturing, stimulating, consistent care is vital and can be provided only by a stable, well-trained staff in a well-funded day-care setting" (Spock & Parker, 1998, p. 606). But then he acknowledges how little good quality child care is available: "Unfortunately there are nowhere near enough day-care centers with such high standards. And what few there are are too expensive for the average family. The only solution is unending political pressure for local and federal substitutes" (Spock & Parker, 1998, pp. 606–607). Spock was a veteran of activist campaigns and was undoubtedly aware how slowly such massive changes would occur, but this answer may not help families who are faced with difficult and pressing child care choices. He also expresses the need for continuity of care for infants and toddlers: "They need consistency in their relationships, but this can be provided at home and in many day-care centers" (Spock & Parker, 1998, p. 606).

When he gives parents criteria for selecting child care, he recommends considering whether or not the caregivers use physical punishment and whether there are

> warm, nurturing interactions between the caregivers and children, appropriate supervision and safety measures, and whether activities are

appropriate to the children's developmental levels. Are the children relaxed? Do they trust the teachers and turn to them for help? Do they cooperate with other children and get involved in few fights? A friendly relationship between teachers and children will show in the relationships among the children. (Spock & Parker, 1998, p. 608)

Spock recommends a ratio for children to staff that is tougher than most current state standards: "under the age of two is 3:1; 25 to 30 months, 4:1; 31 to 35 months, 5 to 1; three-year-olds, 7:1; four- and five-year-olds, 8:1; six- to eight-year-olds, 10:1" (Spock & Parker, 1998, pp. 608–609). His idea of the optimal pattern of substitute care also may be difficult for many parents to achieve:

My own preference for care of children under the age of two or three is for family care. Ideally, the child's own mother and father between them would care for the children as least half of their waking hours by means of adjustments of the parents' work schedules. The rest of the day, whether this means two hours or eight hours, the child could be cared for by a live-in or live-out caregiver or in family day care with another family. (Spock & Parker, 1998, p. 608)

Brazelton

In his parenting manual, Brazelton recommends at-home child care during the first year if the parents can afford it and ratios of three to four babies or fewer for each adult caregiver in a child care home or center. More than four toddlers per adult is "hopelessly chaotic" (Brazelton, 1992, p. 447). He gives pointers on picking out better child care arrangements: "Home day care is entirely dependent on the quality of the caregiver and her ability to relate to each child. . . . Teachers at day-care centers should be trained, supervised, caring, and well paid" (Brazelton, 1992, p. 447). His parenting manuals provide chapters that include extensive tips on evaluating caregivers and a checklist for parents to use in choosing a child care center or child care home (Brazelton, 1992, pp. 449–450; Brazelton & Sparrow, 2001, pp. 333–338), and he devotes a chapter in another of his books (Brazelton, 1985) to evaluating child care. In their recent advocacy book, Brazelton and Greenspan identify critical aspects of quality in child care that need to be improved: "lower child/caregiver ratios, better training and salaries, and maintaining the same caregiver from birth to roughly age 3" (Brazelton & Greenspan, 2000, p. 46).

Leach

Leach emphasizes the intimacy and consistency of a "key worker" who provides the primary care for each infant, with everything possible done to provide training to caregivers and minimize their turnover: "Changing caregivers does not just mean going through the getting-to-know-her process all over again; it also means losing somebody who has become important. Of course, you cannot leave your baby with someone unsuitable, but do choose as carefully as you possibly can in the first place" (Leach, 1998, p. 318). Care arrangements should allow for individual differences in diet and napping patterns (Leach, 1998, p. 218), and Leach provides a list of things to look for in a child care center (Leach, 1998, pp. 543–545). Her recommendations for child:staff ratios are also tougher than many state standards in the United States: "Babies should be in rooms containing groups of no more than six children (and two adults). Young toddlers may be in groups of nine children (still with three adults). From around 18–36 months the usual recommendation is an adult: child ratio of 1:4 and group size of up to 12 children (and three adults)" (Leach, 1998, p. 218).

Rosemond

Before his conversion on the child care issue, Rosemond recommended that parents attend to the child:staff ratio, caregivers' training and certification, whether there are enough varied play materials, and caregivers' discipline policies (Rosemond, 1989, pp. 26–27). He also mentioned the importance of staff responsiveness, rotation, and turnover: "Consistency of care allows the infant to form a secure attachment to the caregiver" (Rosemond, 1990, p. 64). His recommendations for child:staff ratios were the highest of any of the experts: "For infants in child care centers, the ratio should be no greater than five-to-one" (Rosemond, 1989, p. 26).

Rosemond also had firm recommendations for child care of the youngest children: "For infants, I recommend a family home in which the caregiver is looking after no more than two or three children. A small-scale home setting all but guarantees that each child will receive enough individual attention. . . . Because there is no staff rotation or turnover in a home setting, an infant can form a more secure attachment to the caregiver. Few children also means the caregiver can accommodate varied sleep, feeding, and activity schedules" (Rosemond, 1990, p. 62).

Summary of Quality and Type Concerns

Quality of care clearly makes a difference, and the experts are relatively close to each other in identifying critical dimensions of quality: child:staff ratio and caregiver education. Each expert who addresses child care (Spock, Brazelton, Leach, and Rosemond) provides helpful tips on how to select quality care. These tips, in fact, turn out to be related to the overall quality of care and predictive of children's outcomes. They all emphasize the importance of caregiver continuity, though there are few findings documenting its importance. But their recommendations are very difficult for parents to follow: There is little excellent quality care available, and continuity of care for infants and toddlers is rare among the 331 child care centers responding to a recent survey (Cryer, Hurwitz, & Wolery, 2000). Rosemond's recommended ratios for care providers would be considered lenient by most professionals in the field, though they were more strict than minimal 6:1 standards for infant care in his home state of North Carolina at that time (Helburn et al., 1995). Spock recommends a pattern of shared parental care, which very few families are able to accomplish. He also recommends a sequence of care arrangement in which children are moved from a child care home to a child care center as they become older preschoolers. Reports on the quality of care offered in the two settings suggest this would be beneficial, but only 4% of the NICHD families used that pattern of care (NICHD ECCRN, 2001d).

Spock insists on high quality care yet admits that such care is hard to find. He emphasizes continuity and stability in care, without addressing the fact that it is rarely available. His writing is unrealistically optimistic in light of the limited amount of good quality care available, a problem that he acknowledges in passing. As it turns out, he is wrong in one particular: Difficult-to-manage children are also likely to have problems in group settings and may find them more stressful than other children do (Gunnar & Donzella, 2002). Spock (and, in earlier days, Rosemond) recommends early care in family child care homes, and there is some evidence that the child:

adult ratios and quality of care in child care homes are better at earlier age levels (NICHD ECCRN, 2000a) than what is provided in most centers. But by age 3, child care centers are providing better quality care than child care homes, though few parents apparently choose to follow this sequence of care arrangements (NICHD ECCRN, 2004c).

The American Public Health Association (APHA) and the American Academy of Pediatrics (AAP) collaboratively produced standards for practices and settings in child care (APHA & AAP, 1992). Their standards recommend that, unless there are extraordinary circumstances, children not be placed in out-of-home care before 6 weeks of age (APHA & AAP, 1992). Their standards emphasize the importance of small groups of children, with sufficient staff to offer warm, responsive care. In the case of family child care homes with one care provider, this means not more than six children (including the provider's own children), with no more than two children under age 2 (APHA & AAP, 1992). The National Association for the Education of Young Children (NAEYC), the National Association of Family Child Care (Burchinal, Howes, & Kontos, 2002) and the Zero to Three Project (Lally et al., 2003) offer nearly identical recommendations for child:staff ratios. They recommend a ratio of 3:1 for children from birth to age 2 (4:1 is allowable in the NAEYC guidelines), 4:1 and 5:1 ratios for the first and second half of the third year, a 7:1 ratio for 3-year-olds, and an 8:1 ratio for 4- and 5-year-olds (APHA & AAP, 1992). Recommended group sizes call for a maximum of two staff per group; for example, the maximum infant–toddler group size would be six children and two adults.

AAP and APHA standards recommend staff with college educations in fields related to early childhood education, or a combination of supervised experience working in the field supplemented by college coursework. Assistant teachers, who count in the ratio requirements above, merely need to be 18 years old, have a high school degree, and to participate in ongoing training (APHA & AAP, 1992). Facilities should provide space, materials, and equipment to support active learning and becoming well-adjusted psychologically. Safe, adaptable, and age-appropriate play equipment that can support motor development and creative expression are emphasized (APHA & AAP, 1992).

Continuity of care that gives children the chance to develop long-term, trusting relationships with care providers is acknowledged as important in both the APHA–AAP standards (1992) and the accreditation standards of the NAEYC (1991).

CONCLUSION

Most parents face difficult choices regarding the substitute care of their infants and young children. Research does not support the extreme statements about negative effects of substitute care made by some of the experts who write on this topic. It does not impair the formation of attachment bonds in infants, nor does it lead to attention deficit disorder. Family factors contribute far more to children's outcomes than child care factors do. But there is cause for parents to be concerned. There is increasing evidence that early childhood is a critically important period of development, and large national studies converge on the conclusion that the quality of substitute child care often is not good, especially for infants and toddlers. In light of these findings, families should weigh the option of having a parent stay home during their children's infant and toddler years, but they also have to consider the long-term consequences for their children of lost income and benefits. Children need the guarantee of good health care, safe neighborhoods, good schools, and opportunities for higher education. Almost inevitably, these are easier for parents to provide with the income provided by two salaries. Perhaps it is most important that parents insure adequate levels of safety, health care (including insurance), and education. If they can manage these while having a devoted, caring, and competent parent at home with the children during their infant and toddler years, they can avoid the risk of some behavior problems. As an alternative, they can educate themselves and choose selectively from among the relatively scarce child care settings with good child:staff ratios that offer superior opportunities for social as well as cognitive development.

The four parenting authors who write about substitute care provide accurate advice on the aspects of child care that make a difference in children's outcomes. The experts, researchers, and best practice standards converge on what parents who use substitute care should look for in selecting care: lower ratios of children to caregivers; caregivers who are better educated, especially in early child development; and caregivers who provide warm and responsive care. The NICHD findings offer evidence that encouraging appropriate social development is every bit as important as supporting cognitive development, which is the current emphasis of many early childhood programs in this country (Maccoby & Lewis, 2003). There is also convergence on the importance of a safe setting with developmentally appropriate play materials. These are the things on which parents should not compromise. Parents may well have to compromise on factors that they actually name as most important in their selection of substitute care: low cost and convenience (Gable & Cole, 2000; Leslie, Ettenson, & Cumsille, 2000). Here their children's needs should come first. Good quality care is worth paying for and worth driving farther for.

The best research studies suggest that good quality care is relatively rare and that the overall quality of care is wildly discrepant from the worst settings to the best ones. So the choices parents make for early substitute care may be critically important, especially in light of the vulnerability of infants and young children, who cannot tell parents when things are going badly. Continuity of care for infants and toddlers, which most of the experts advocate, is at this point more than most parents can hope for if they choose center-based care. The NICHD data and two of the experts suggest moving children from family child care homes early on to child care centers, and that pattern of enrollment may be beneficial for cognitive and language development. It may also avoid the stress that some 2-year-olds experience in group settings as the day wears on. When possible, parents should adjust their schedules to shorten time in day care. Because current low wages in child care lead to high turnover, they need to frequently monitor the quality of care that their child is receiving.

The bottom line from experts and researchers who favor substitute child care, or at least recognize that parents are using it, is that there needs to be increased support for better quality child care. Our national ambivalence about substitute care for infants and young children, despite its wide use, makes it less likely that substantial improvements in future child care will occur. Just as working parents of young children are often short on money, they have even less time. They are usually far too busy raising their own families to be advocates for children in general. Better parent education in the future might lead to better child care choices, but if improvements are left to the efforts of parents alone, they will be a long time coming. This is a situation where concerned professionals and an enlightened public can make a difference.

CHAPTER 4
DISCIPLINE

EVERY PARENT HAS HAD some of those moments, and some parents have hours of them. Their child breaks a rule: You do not take things from the baby, you do not tease the dog, you do not draw on the wallpaper, you do not run out in the street. It often seems as if those moments come at the end of the day, when dinner is being cooked, or when parents are otherwise distracted. Parents simultaneously deal with their flash of anger, especially if there have been several such moments that day, and try to figure out what to do. A clear explanation of why, exactly, that was a bad thing to do ("It hurts the dog when you pull his tail")? Yes, but that explanation has been given at least five times. Time-out? But that did not seem to work yesterday. No more crayons until a year from next Sunday? But maybe the child did not really understand what crayons do to living room wallpaper. Time for a spanking? But does that teach her that hitting is okay? After all, I do not want her hitting the baby. Parents decide on some course of action, but there is often the mental dialogue afterward: Was that the right way to handle the problem?

Advice to parents on how to discipline their children goes back at least to biblical times and has echoed through public writings on the family ever since. Contemporary print, television, and electronic media have become a marketplace for the burgeoning number of new discipline programs that promise ease of application, parent control, and a minimum of tears and upsets. Each is invariably illustrated with two or three "makeover" stories of tantrum-throwing terrors transformed into polite, manageable children. Life-changing outcomes are reported from programs of every stripe, whether they recommend firm control in a home-as-boot-camp atmosphere or advocate discarding even milder forms of discipline, such as time-out. Public concern and media discussion of parenting practice reaches a fever pitch after episodes of child and youth violence, as when two Columbine High School students murdered 12 of their classmates and a teacher. Postevent analyses probe for character flaws, mental illness, and, inevitably, parent oversight and discipline.

Public media offer an abundance of warnings to parents about what can go wrong with children, from statistical evidence of illicit drug use in middle adolescence to cautionary tales of slavish conformity to peer group norms leading to juvenile crime. Reports of increasing discipline problems in the schools and the dosing of behavior problems with Ritalin and similar medications at ever-earlier ages (Goode, 2000) also fuel concerns about the lack of parent-supplied discipline. Parents are offered the prospect of their children growing up to join a future generation of deadbeats whose undisciplined behavior causes social chaos. For those who argue that the family is the fundamental unit of society, these apparent signs of lack of parental authority are ominous precursors of the decline of Western civilization and a signal of the need for parental action.

Public discussions of parental discipline have been dramatically altered by social recognition of child abuse. Since it has become illegal to physically punish children beyond societally determined limits, discussions of the harmful effects of subabusive punishment have become more prevalent in public media, and advocacy for making all corporal punishment of children by parents illegal has increased (Straus, 1994). Movement toward such legislation has not been swift, nor is it likely to be, in light of the fact that 90% of parents in the United States still use corporal punishment (Straus, 1994). Corporal punishment has been as much a concern for those who emphasize preventing harm to children as lack of parental discipline has been for those concerned with preserving families, schools, and religious organizations as fundamental social institutions.

Because discipline inevitably involves situations in which parents' and children's wishes are at odds, it defines how conflicts are managed in the family and helps set the emotional tone of family life. All five parenting authors distinguish between discipline and punishment. Discipline involves guiding a child toward better behavior, internalization of adult standards, and self-regulation; punishment is the administration of unpleasant consequences following a child's action. Discipline is a central concern for all of them and, for two of them, the reason they became publicly prominent as parenting experts. Discipline policies also reveal the authors' basic approaches to all parenting concerns, approaches that differ markedly from one another and from the parenting research.

CRITERIA FOR EFFECTIVE DISCIPLINE

There is ample evidence that disciplinary practices differ along a number of social and demographic factors: Corporal punishment is used more often with boys, by younger parents, in the South, and among religious conservatives (Ellison, Bartkowski, & Segal, 1996; Giles-Sims, Straus, & Sugarman, 1995). Yet many parents firmly reject the discipline practices that their parents used or those prescribed by their ethnic or class socialization, but are unable to intuit acceptable substitutes.

In contrast to actual discipline practices, it is important to address the question of what is the best discipline policy. Ideally, discipline policy should be simple, clear, and easy to apply, because of the lack of interpersonal skill and the cognitive and language limitations of some parents. It should provide general boundaries for child behavior, telling parents when to draw the line, when they should discipline and when they should leave well enough alone. Parents need specifics on effective disciplinary methods that can both produce immediate compliance and the internalization of adult standards of behavior, and give children a sense of the underlying moral principles that govern right behavior in relation to other people and the larger society.

In light of the risk of abuse, one of the fundamental injunctions of advice on discipline, echoing the Hippocratic oath taken by physicians, must be "First, do no harm." Most episodes of physical child abuse begin as corporal punishment episodes (Kadushin & Martin, 1981; Straus, 1994). Recommendations for discipline that include corporal punishment or that lead to intensified anger during punishment episodes can potentially facilitate child abuse. All the experts in this volume have made strong statements in public and in print against parental violence and abuse, but a key question to be addressed is whether their disciplinary methods actually reduce its likelihood. Given that parenting experts are remote from the domestic scenes of parent–child conflict, it is critical that their advice not be perceived as justifying abusive punishment.

Expert advice needs to be responsive to the type and the seriousness of child misdeeds and flexible enough to deal with children who vary widely in activity level and impulse control and therefore in manageability. Effective discipline should be linked to the current developmental level of the child and take into account the child's construction of the situation, even if it is incorrect from the parent's perspective. Effective discipline should have positive outcomes in both the short-term and long-term for the child, for the parents, and for the family system. Guilt, depression, or residual anger on the part of the child or the parent should be minimized.

This chapter is divided into four issues in discipline: strictness or laxness, the role of parental warmth and responsiveness, effective disciplinary policies (further split with subheadings), and corporal punishment. For each issue, findings of empirical research and review articles will be summarized; then media parenting experts' advice will be reviewed as a prelude to a description of areas of agreement or, more often, areas of disagreement among the experts, and in some cases between experts and empirical research findings. The chapter summary addresses the experts' widely varying constructions of discipline, the relationship between their advice and research on children's compliance and internalization of parental standards, and the likely effects of applying the experts' discipline advice.

IS STRICTNESS OR LAXNESS IN DISCIPLINE BETTER FOR CHILDREN?

When parenting experts are reduced to a one-dimensional evaluation, the focus is often on their supposed strictness or laxness, and parents who pick one expert to rely on undoubtedly seek a person who matches their conceptions of how strict they should be. Norman Vincent Peale's characterization of Spock's parenting recommendations as permissive followed Spock the rest of his life (Spock & Morgan, 1989), though Spock frequently restated in public and in print that he was not permissive either as a parent or in his recommendations for discipline. All the authors address the question of parental strictness, and comparison of their positions reveals their fundamentally different constructions of the parent–child relationship.

Research on Strictness

To evaluate the effects of strictness, it is important to distinguish *strictness* from *restrictiveness*. Strictness refers to "consistent control, reasonable restrictions with clearly defined limits, combined with latitude for individual action" (Grusec & Lytton, 1988, p. 173). Restrictiveness involves directiveness, critical interference, and demands for orderliness (Grusec & Lytton, 1988) and overall constraints on the child's behavior (Rothbaum & Weisz,

1994). Consider strictness as establishing high expectations for behavior and setting consistent limits, and restrictiveness as the number of prohibitions a child must abide by and the degree of intrusive direct supervision the parent provides. Strictness might involve consistently enforcing the policy that older children must complete their homework before they can play, whereas restrictiveness might involve the parent requiring that the homework be done under their supervision, that it be done to their standards, and then refusing to let a child play if he or she fails to do so. This discussion focuses on parental strictness and its demonstrable relationships with children's behavior.

Public discussion has historically favored strictness; laxness has been associated with antisocial and irresponsible behavior. In her research on preschool children with effective behavior, Diana Baumrind (1971) worked backward to identify the parenting practices that contributed to desirable outcomes. Parents fell into one of three types: authoritative parents, who were both demanding and responsive; authoritarian parents, who also demanded much of their children but were less responsive; and permissive parents, who were responsive to their children but made few demands on them. Maccoby and Martin (1983) further divided the permissive parents into types: those who were warm and indulgent, like the permissive parents in Baumrind's research, and those who made few demands on their children because they were cold and indifferent. The latter group, they argued, constituted a distinct fourth type of parents: the uninvolved, who were not very responsive to their children but also made few demands on them. Both authoritarian and authoritative parents demand and expect much from their children, leading them to be characterized as more strict than permissive and uninvolved parents. These four classifications of parenting and the predictions that follow from them describe the European American parents that Baumrind originally studied. Not surprisingly Asian American parents (Chao, 1994) and African American parents (G. H. Brody et al., 1996) show distinct patterns of parenting, and different relationships emerge for children's behavior, in particular the finding that high levels of both warmth and control promote better outcomes.

When parents and children have been directly observed, laxness, characterized by use of bargaining and lack of rule enforcement, has been associated with noncompliance displayed by 18- to 30-month-old children (e.g., Kuczynski, Kochanska, Radke-Yarrow, & Girnius-Brown, 1987; Lytton, 1977). More generally, the permissive style of parenting has been linked to poor short-term outcomes: higher levels of impulsiveness and aggression, as well as less self-reliance. Uninvolved parenting has been associated with lower self-esteem, external locus of control, and uncontrolled behavior (Maccoby & Martin, 1983). Lax parenting has been correlated with intermittent punitiveness (Smith & O'Leary [1995] found a correlation of .45) and with heightened aggression in children (R. R. Sears et al., 1957). Harsh punishment has also been associated with negative outcomes (Amato & Fowler, 2002; Schneider, Cavell, & Hughes, 2003). In sum, a long line of empirical research suggests that either punitively strict or consistently lax parenting, or the two in combination, are associated with bad outcomes for children (e.g., Baumrind, 1971; Baumrind & Black, 1967; Kuczynski et al., 1987; Lytton, 1977).

Thus, child behavior is best when parents avoid the extremes of punitive, severe strictness but exercise firm and consistent control. Laxness indicative of disengagement and consequent poor supervision has been linked repeatedly to poorer outcomes in children.

The Experts' Positions on Strictness

As in the research studies, the experts' writings on strictness focus on firm control in discipline, rather than parental directiveness, interference, and constraints on the child's behavior. Of the experts, Spock has written the most about strictness, perhaps because he thought that his advice had been mischaracterized in public media: "I don't believe that strictness or casualness is the real issue. Good-hearted parents who aren't afraid to be firm when it is necessary can get good results with either moderate strictness or moderate casualness. On the other hand, a strictness that comes from harsh feelings or an excessive permissiveness that is timid or vacillating can lead to poor results" (Spock & Parker, 1998, p. 429).

Brazelton emphasizes the importance of limits that provide firm guidelines about acceptable behaviors, particularly during the toddler and preschool years. In discussing a child who has thrown a temper tantrum, he writes: "Children sense that they need discipline and will go to great lengths to compel their parents to set limits" (Brazelton, 1992, p. 253). In a passage devoted to how to parent an "active" baby, Brazelton (1983) writes: "There is no time when he needs firmness in boundaries as much as he does in this negative period [of testing]. These will help him find his own limits and decisiveness eventually cuts down on the very indecision that throws him into these tumultuous situations" (pp. 278–279).

Dobson (1992) is at pains to reject extreme punitiveness: "Let me say again with the strongest emphasis that aggressive, hard-nosed, "Mommie Dearest" kinds of discipline are destructive to kids and must not be tolerated. Parents who are cold and stern with their sons and daughters often leave them damaged for life. . . . May all doubts be dispelled. *I don't believe in parental harshness.* Period!" (p. 12). But he is very clear about the type of child behavior that must be responded to immediately and definitively: "when he openly defies his parents' spoken commands! If he runs the other way when called, purposely slams his milk glass on the floor, dashes in the street when being told to stop" (Dobson, 1992, p. 66). Whatever else may be put up with, child behaviors that signal apparent defiance are ones that Dobson feels must not be tolerated in order for parents to establish firm, consistent control early in the parent–child relationship.

All the experts mention the importance of rules or limits established well in advance. Leach writes:

> But making sure that limits limit is a prime adult responsibility and reneging on them with bribes and punishments is a betrayal. Nothing young children can do can actually force parents into acting against their own convictions if those convictions are strong enough, but are they? Parents often maintain that they "cannot stop" crawling babies playing with the TV, but how many turn up at the hospital because they failed to prevent them playing with the space heater? (1994, pp. 124–125)

But as to day-to-day rules: "Be consistent in your principles but don't worry about the details. As long as you know the kinds of behavior you think desirable and are consistent about those, it does not matter if daily life finds you allowing an activity one day and forbidding it the next. . . . The principle is that certain activities are only allowed sometimes" (Leach, 1989b, p. 212).

For Rosemond, strictness means "defining rules clearly and enforcing obedience to them" (1990, p. 11) and sets the stage for a respectful relationship between parents and children, but the terms of respect are quite different for the two generations: "Children respect their parents by obeying them. Parents, on the other hand, respect their kids by insisting they obey" (Rosemond, 2001b, p. 47). He believes that "truly strict parents do their children great service," though he notes that "strict parents must be disciplined themselves, practicing no less than they preach" (Rosemond, 1990, p. 11).

Aside from taking pains to identify their positions as moderate, when the experts write about strictness, they focus on setting rules or limits. Dobson has a particular concern with child defiance, which sets him apart from the others. Brazelton and Leach focus on limit setting as a major parent responsibility, but the particular limits set are typically left up to parents, within the bounds of safe behavior.

Moderate strictness seems to be associated with the best outcomes, and though the experts differ in degree, they avoid the extremes of harshness or laxness. The question remains of what other dimensions of discipline help to insure short- and long-term compliance and internalization of parental values and whether they are captured in parenting experts' advice.

WARMTH, RESPONSIVENESS, AND CHILDREN'S BEHAVIOR

Research on Conscience Development and Shaping Good Behavior

Parents' love for their children has been widely celebrated for its qualities of devotion and self-sacrifice, but it has not always been viewed by parenting experts as being good for children (Hulbert, 2003). Parenting advice in the early 20th century focused on the risks of spoiling children (Watson, 1928) and recommended care regimes that would be rejected today as overly harsh—for example, rigid 4-hour feeding schedules for infants (L. Holt, 1914). By contrast, numerous studies have implicated parental affection or warmth in preventing misbehavior and enhancing compliance (as reviewed by Grusec & Lytton, 1988; Maccoby & Martin, 1983).

The term *warmth* captures parents' affectionate feelings for their children, whereas *responsiveness* describes how parents interact with their children, the mutual shaping of behavior initially to maintain proximity and subsequently to promote communication (Bowlby, 1969). Extensive research examining individual differences among mothers (and sometimes fathers) in parent–infant interaction patterns provides evidence that parental responsiveness is key in promoting close relationships between infants and their parents (Ainsworth & Bell, 1969; Isabella, 1993; van IJzendoorn, Goldberg, Kroonenberg, & Frenkel, 1992).

Kochanska has done a systematic longitudinal program of research on the contributions of attachment and responsive parenting to the development of conscience in infancy and the early childhood years. In one study, mothers' reciprocity with their young children was observed when the children were 32 months and 46 months old. Mothers who were high on reciprocity during both observations less frequently used power assertion as a control tactic. Their children also showed more internalization of moral rules, as demonstrated by resisting tempting toys that they had been prohibited from playing with and cooperating with their mother's request to clean up toys (Kochanska, 1997). Kochanska (1995) found an overall positive relationship between both attachment and use of gentle discipline (reasoning, requests, distractions, and incentives) and measures of the internalization of moral standards. However, temperament played a role as well: Gentle discipline was a better predictor of internalization for more fearful children, and security of attachment was a better predictor for more fearless children.

Recently, Kochanska and colleagues have demonstrated that the initial relationship between infants and their parents influences the impact of parenting practices. When children are securely attached to their mothers at age 14 months, there is a strong positive relationship between their mothers' responsiveness and avoidance of power assertion during four observations in their 2nd and 3rd years and a composite measure of children's moral reasoning and moral behavior at age 4½. No such relationship is obtained, however, in insecurely attached children (Kochanska, Aksan, Knaak, & Rhines, 2004). Kochanska et al. (2004) argue that two processes are critical in the emergence of morality: The first is the formation of a trusting secure relationship with the caregiver that makes the child receptive to the parent's socialization attempts; the second is an adaptive parenting style incorporating warmth, responsiveness, and avoidance of power assertion to promote the internalization of moral standards.

Evidence for the latter connection also emerges in other observations of interactions between mothers and their young children in laboratory settings. When mothers asked their children if they needed help, attempted to persuade them, or explained the task to them, they were more successful in obtaining their child's compliance in completing tasks (Crockenberg & Litman, 1990). Maccoby and Martin (1983) summarized evidence suggesting that children are more likely to comply if they perceive that they are participating in a reciprocal relationship in which the parent complies with their requests. In a related experiment, half the mothers were trained in play behaviors. They decreased the number of commands they issued and increased their responsiveness and compliance to their children, and they were subsequently more successful in obtaining compliance than mothers not so trained (Parpal & Maccoby, 1985).

Compelling evidence for the importance of responsive parenting with children comes from a short-term longitudinal study by Pettit, Bates, and Dodge (1993). Their research team observed parents and children prior to kindergarten entry and found that family interaction patterns characterized by coercive and intrusive behavior by parents, particularly the mother, most strongly predicted later aggressive, destructive, defiant, and overactive behaviors as rated by kindergarten and first grade teachers, whereas positive parenting patterns (e.g., teaching, social conversation, responsiveness) predicted lower levels of such behaviors. Even after statistically controlling for the child's initial levels of aggression, hostility, and noncompliance, those children who had experienced the most negative and coercive parenting showed the greatest increase in these behaviors from kindergarten to first grade.

Rothbaum and Weisz's (1994) meta-analysis found several caregiving behaviors, including approval, guidance, use of motivational strategies, synchrony, affection, and lack of coercive control, clustered together as a factor they labeled acceptance–responsiveness. Not surprisingly, higher parental acceptance–responsiveness was associated with less aggression, hostility, and noncompliance in children, but it was also significant that this factor accounted for the largest portion of the individual differences in aggression and related behaviors. These authors excluded studies of clinic-recruited children from their meta-analysis, so the findings cannot be attributed to extreme behaviors that led to referrals for these children and their parents. Rothbaum and Weisz (1994) also found that experimental studies showed stronger relationships between parental responsiveness and child compliance than did correlational research. They argued that stronger effects occurred in experiments because multiple aspects of responsiveness were manipulated and because parents are more likely to be vigilant and distraction-free in short-term situations than they are on a daily basis (Rothbaum & Weisz, 1994). Of the experiments, however, the only one that directly examined a disciplinary situation (Pfiffner & O'Leary, 1989) found weaker connections. Based on their meta-analysis, Rothbaum and Weisz (1994) concluded that "parents who are rejecting and unresponsive increase their children's learning of and motivation to use socially unacceptable behaviors" (p. 66), but they also acknowledged that children's aggressiveness and noncompliance may reduce parental acceptance and responsiveness.

Similarly, in their review of the role of attachment in the development of disruptive behavior, M. T. Greenberg, Speltz, and DeKlyen (1993) note that "there appears to be a growing recognition that the absence of positive parenting behaviors may be as important as the presence of coercive cycles in the etiology of disruptive behavior" (p. 196). Thus, parental warmth and responsiveness play a critical role in the effectiveness of discipline.

Responsiveness in parenting has been studied much less frequently than warmth, especially after the preschool years. In their review of discipline in parenting, Chamberlain and Patterson (1995) contrasted warmth with contingency, the correlation of parent reactions to what their children are doing, and argued that in a contest between the two in the shaping of children's behavior, contingency, essentially responsive parenting to maintain good behavior, is ultimately more important. Lytton (1980) found that parent responsiveness to a child's needs predicted compliance but that warmth did not. In extensive studies of conduct disordered children (e.g., Patterson, 1982), lack of contingency (responsiveness) was more directly implicated in conduct problems than lack of warmth. Consistent with the behavioral orientation of this research group, contingency incorporates shaping behavior with reinforcement. "Based on three decades of intervention with aggressive children, we are convinced that the only reliable method of changing antisocial behavior is to change the relative rates of reinforcement for that behavior" (Stoolmiller, Patterson, & Snyder, 1997, p. 224).

Thus, for most children, affection for parents is established first and motivates compliance to avoid parental displeasure, but particularly for children with a history of difficult behaviors, parental warmth may be less important than responsiveness and appropriate contingencies in managing their behavior. Both individual studies and reviews, done with normal and clinic-referred children, offer consistent evidence that responsive parental behavior is essential and that warm affect is important in obtaining compliance and minimizing negative behaviors.

Experts' Positions on Warmth and Responsiveness in Discipline

Do the experts' writings acknowledge the importance of the affectionate, responsive relationship between parents and their children in promoting compliance? Despite substantial differences in their philosophies, most of the experts cluster together on this issue. Spock gives a central role to nurturance in discipline: "Children need the love of parents more than anything else" (Spock & Parker, 1998, p. 431). He writes that "punishment is never the main element in discipline. . . . The main source of good discipline is growing up in a loving family—being loved and learning to love in return" (Spock & Parker, 1998, p. 435). Brazelton's position is similar: "Next to love, a sense of discipline is a parent's second most important gift to a child" (Brazelton, 1992, p. 252).

Dobson (1992) writes more specifically about activities that help prevent punitive interactions:

> The *best* way to get children to do what you want is to spend time with them before disciplinary problems occur—having fun together and enjoying mutual laughter and joy. When those moments of love and closeness happen, kids are not as tempted to challenge and test the limits. Many confrontations can be avoided by building friendships with kids and thereby making them *want* to cooperate at home. (P. 75)

Leach writes similarly: "The best possible foundation for later discipline is early love, love which is as mutual, as secure, as predictable and as enjoyable (for all concerned) as you can possibly make it" (1989b, p. 209). She emphasizes the primacy of the parent–child relationship: "Learning how to behave—and to be more comfortable behaving that way—depends on parental influence rather than power, on the warmth of the relationship adults offer rather than the clarity of the order they impose" (1994, p. 117). Clearly rules are secondary in this construction of discipline.

Rosemond writes little about parents' love for their children, and his description suggests more disengagement than engagement: "To properly love a child is to act in the child's best interest. Two of a child's foremost interests are, first, that his parents take excellent care of themselves—and if there are two parents in the home, their marriage. Second, that he learn to stand on his own two feet" (Rosemond, 1991). In Rosemond's construction, "parental authority must be clearly established before the full potential for affection with the parent–child relationship can be released. Unresolved disciplinary issues force a child to constantly test his parents' authority. . . . Resolve the discipline problems, therefore, and affection will follow. So if you want your children to know you love them, discipline them well" (Rosemond, 1991). In this passage, discipline makes a child lovable, rather than love for a child leading the parent to want to make the child behave. Rosemond mentions that "love gives a child reason to strive. Authority provides direction to the child's strivings" (Rosemond, 1989, p. 49). He emphasizes a balance of love and discipline, but in his advocacy for a "benevolent dictatorship" form of parenting, benevolence—that is, warmth and nurturance—is a way to make the household dictatorship work.

So consensus on the importance of warmth as a foundation for discipline is not complete, with Rosemond arguing that discipline enables the full development of an affectionate relationship. The authors focus on parental warmth when they write about discipline in their advice books and do not separate out the effects of responsiveness per se in establishing discipline. But many researchers do not do so either, on the grounds that they are closely linked empirically (e.g., Grusec & Lytton, 1988; Rothbaum & Weisz, 1994). The preeminent effectiveness of responsiveness over warmth may emerge most strongly in preventing negative behaviors in at-risk and clinical samples (Patterson, 1982), but the importance of responsiveness in establishing discipline deserves more attention from those who would advise parents.

WHAT WORKS IN GAINING COMPLIANCE AND INTERNALIZATION OF VALUES?

Research on Disciplinary Practices

For years, researchers have been observing parents interacting with their children in discipline encounters in laboratory settings, in their homes, and in community settings. Parents use bribes, they spank, they reward good behavior, and they try to head off misbehavior or ignore it when it happens. In short, they use a wide variety of disciplinary strategies, and not always effectively.

DETERMINANTS OF DISCIPLINE. Parents who are observed interacting with their children provide ample evidence of inefficient and sometimes counterproductive discipline techniques, especially among high risk families. For example, Lytton (1980) found that young children's compliance and non-compliance was followed most often by no response by parents within the following 20 seconds. Snyder and Patterson (1995) found that mothers of aggressive boys were more likely than other mothers to withdraw when their sons acted aversively toward them. When they did so, their sons' aggressive behavior increased. By withdrawing, the mothers did not only not *punish* their sons' bad behavior; they actually *rewarded* it by ceasing to interfere, and not surprisingly for those familiar with learning theory, the rewarded behavior increased. So available evidence from families of normal and clinically referred children suggests that parents do not always use effective discipline strategies available to them. Research on families drawn from neighborhoods with relatively high juvenile arrest rates also demonstrates the importance of the child's contribution to the disciplinary interaction (Vuchinich, Bank, & Patterson, 1992). In this study, preadolescents' antisocial behavior had a substantial negative impact on parent discipline. Though the size of the effect was smaller, there was evidence that parents' ineffective discipline practices influenced child antisocial behavior, suggesting that the two maintain each other.

Parents' punishment choices are systematically affected by their appraisals of their children, appraisals that are in turn shaped by broader attitudes. For example, Dix, Ruble, and Zambarano (1989) asked mothers to respond to vignettes about negative behaviors that might be performed by their own or other children. Those who had higher expectations of their children and inferred higher levels of child knowledge, capacity, and responsibility reported that they would be more upset with the child, would respond with greater sternness, would give longer time-outs, and thought that punishment was more desirable. In other words, mothers who inferred that the child understood the rule that he or she was violating showed less enthusiasm for reasoning with the child or explaining the bad behavior and more frequently recommended use of power-assertive punishments. These mothers also scored high on a self-report measure of authoritarian parenting, so variations in discipline reflect underlying parental belief systems.

The picture that emerges from empirical research studies is of parents who clearly have ideas about how they should be disciplining, which they can report on attitude surveys (Holden et al., 1995; Holden & Edwards, 1989), but who vary in their use of effective techniques to shape behavior consistently and effectively, even when they know their behavior is being observed and recorded. Some of the difference between research evidence and parent practice is clearly due to parents' underlying beliefs about their children and the nature of the parent–child relationship, so parenting experts in their public information roles can potentially play an important role. Research on discipline has provided a clear idea of what the content of their message should be by identifying the most effective discipline practices.

PREVENTIVE MEASURES. One effective strategy that parents can use to head off disciplinary encounters is to think ahead and either structure situations to minimize conflict or avoid altogether situations that are likely to elicit misbehavior. Research on what mothers actually do in natural circumstances provides evidence that some mothers are very effective at proactive discipline strategies. Holden (1983) observed 24 mothers and their 2½-year-old children in trips to the supermarket. Children of mothers who most frequently used proactive control techniques, such as talking to the child or providing them with food or an object to hold, made fewer requests and exhibited fewer undesirable behaviors. Techniques less frequently used by mothers included steering down the center of the aisles so the child could not reach items on the shelves, avoiding aisles that contained particularly tempting food items, and spending as little time at the supermarket as possible. Eighty percent of the mothers took their children shopping in the morning because they thought they would behave better then. Fewer disciplinary encounters should be necessary when parents use proactive preventive discipline strategies, but Holden (1983) suggests that there is a hidden benefit as well: "Mothers who exhibit a high rate of proactive controls may be socializing their children into concordant relationships" (p. 239).

THE ROLE OF REASONING. Despite parents' best efforts to plan ahead, inevitably there are situations when children and parents will disagree about what the child wants to do or has done and parents exert their control. How do parents most appropriately respond? In his review of research on discipline, Holden (1997) concluded that "at a global level, there is widespread agreement that the central attribute of effective discipline is a reliance on reasoning" (p. 122). Reasoning may include descriptions of the negative effects of the child's behavior on others or for the child him- or herself, explanations for why it is important for a child to do or not do some behavior, an account of what would constitute better behavior and why, and rationales for the parent's intervention. As a proactive discipline strategy, when reasoning is added to instructions to children, it enhances effectiveness. One example of this comes from an experiment on resistance to temptation (playing with attractive toys) in which the provision of reasons not to play with the toys resulted in less toy play than the absence of reasons (Parke, 1969).

Grusec and Lytton's (1988) review found that moral rules were more likely to be internalized when punishment is accompanied by explanations or rationales for the rule that was broken or when the punishment is tied to the logic of the situation (Lytton, 1997). Reasoning works better if it takes into account the child's point of view: "Strategies that combine a clear statement of what the parent wants with an acknowledgment of the child's perspective (even implicitly) are quite effective in both effecting compliance and avoiding defiance" (Crockenberg & Litman, 1990, pp. 970–971). There is also evidence of the consequences of failing to combine reasoning and control. Parents of toddlers in families subsequently classified as troubled were least likely to use simple commands with reasons for them (e.g., sit down before you fall and hurt yourself) and had children who were more disobedient and escalated their responses to parental control tactics (Belsky, Woodworth, and Crnic, 1996).

Quickly and effectively gaining compliance is a pressing concern for parents, but potentially more important is the question of the long-term self-regulation and internalization of adult values. Here, telling effects of not giving reasons to the child emerge. Kochanska, Padavich, and Koenig (1996) studied children's development of conscience during two time periods (26–41 months and 43–56 months) by using children's responses to moral dilemmas, observed moral conduct, and maternal reports drawn from a community sample of mothers and young children. They found that children who had been observed receiving relatively direct and forceful maternal discipline (verbal commands and physical restraints) as toddlers produced fewer themes of commitment to rules and standards of conduct and concern about good behavior in their narratives, both in contemporaneous measurements and when subsequently assessed at preschool age. In observations, they showed less evidence of internal moral standards and were rated by their mothers as having a less developed conscience (Kochanska et al., 1996). This difference emerged despite the fact that the authors controlled statistically for children's initial levels of defiance.

Having a parent focus on the child's internalization of controls has itself been demonstrated to succeed in enhancing compliance. Kuczynski (1984) observed 64 mothers and their 4-year-old children's performance on a laboratory task under two conditions: one in which the mother was told that her child's cooperation and distractibility would be observed both in her presence and later in her absence, and one in which the mother was told only that the child's behavior would be observed in her presence. When mothers thought their child's task performance would be observed in their absence, they acted more nurturantly prior to the task and more frequently used reasoning in their interactions with the child. Characteristics of the child also made a difference in the tactics mothers used. Boys more frequently received power assertions: direct commands, use of force or threats, maternal behaviors designed to direct attention to the task, or bribes. Children whose mothers worked for compliance while they were absent actually showed more compliant and fewer negative behaviors during *both* the mother-present and mother-absent sessions. This suggests that parents who work toward self-regulation in their children are likely to enjoy both immediate and longer term benefits.

DEALING WITH NONCOMPLIANCE. Observations of disciplinary sequences provide valuable information on how parents interpret child misbehavior and how they respond to it to avoid further escalating the conflict. In research on the interactions between 95 mothers and their 2-year-old children in laboratory and home observations, Crockenberg and Litman (1990) focused on self-assertion, in which the child indicated her or his unwillingness to do what the parent wanted—in other words, the child said "no" to a parental request. When relationships among the children's behaviors were analyzed, self-assertion was positively related to constructive behaviors—for example, asking for help or information and positive communication—suggesting that the child's decision to say no is actually a positive development. The authors distinguished self-assertion from child defiance, which they described as "any response to the mother's control attempt that intensifies the original behavior, or that is directly opposite to what the mother wants" (p. 964), including expression of anger and aggression toward the mother. Their analyses of behavior sequences revealed that when children showed self-assertion and mothers responded with negative control (that was intrusive or conveyed anger or annoyance toward the child, including threats and corporal punishment), child defiance was the most common response among children. Thus, child defiance may sometimes be a response to parental negativity and forceful control, rather than an attempt by the child to test limits and elicit a parental response.

This does not imply that parents have to tolerate frequent naysaying by children as a healthy development. Kucynski et al. (1987) found that children's noncompliance decreased with age from 14 to 44 months of age. When they observed mother–child interactions, mothers' direct commands were associated with higher rates of direct defiance ($r = .29$) than were other control strategies, such as providing explanations ($r = .01$), offering alternatives ($r = .07$), and bargaining ($r = -.03$), none of which showed a significant association. Lytton and Zwirner (1975) found that mothers' physical restriction or control and critical remarks were particularly likely to lead to noncompliance. Similarly, Lytton (1980) found that when mothers added negative control to suggestions or commands, they became less effective in controlling children's behavior. When mothers accompanied their commands with smiles or praise, their children were more compliant.

But advice to parents must acknowledge that children differ greatly in their defiant tendencies. Lee and Bates (1985) provide the strongest evidence of the impact of child temperament on parental disciplinary practice. Temperament assessments were made by mothers at 6, 13, and 24 months. Toddlers who were rated by their mothers as difficult at these three assessment points were found during in-home observations at 24 months to more frequently approach breaking household rules or cause mild damage to persons or property. And the more difficult that toddlers were perceived to be by their mothers, the more likely they were to resist their mothers' control attempts. So mothers' descriptions of their children as difficult reflect not merely the mothers' own perceptions but have a basis in the child's behavior, including the child's resistance to disciplinary control. Attributes of individual children clearly cannot be disregarded in considering disciplinary practice.

CAN DISCIPLINE BE EFFECTIVE WITHOUT PUNISHMENT? Most authorities acknowledge at least in passing that parents dislike having to punish their children. But can parents achieve compliance and internalization without using some form of punishment, some consequence for undesirable behaviors that makes them less likely to recur? In her review of discipline strategies, Baumrind (1996) argues that "because children's wishes often conflict with those of their caregivers, the notion that children can or should be raised without using aversive discipline is utopian" (p. 409). She argues that the exercise of control accompanied by reasons leads to the acquisition of parental values more effectively than reasons alone do.

Many parenting researchers would agree that reasoning is a necessary but not sufficient component of discipline. Empirical support for Baumrind's argument comes from an observational study by Crockenberg and Litman (1990). When children refused to comply in a laboratory task (picking up toys) or an in-home observation, mothers who followed up children's refusals solely with requests and reasons were not as effective in gaining compliance. The authors' interpretation was that a request ("Could you put the toys in the box?") appears to offer the child a choice, rather than serving as a clear expression of the parent's wishes (Crockenberg & Litman, 1990). Kuczynski et al. (1987) similarly reported that suggestions, requests, and polite commands, which they labeled as indirect commands, were more strongly correlated with simply saying no (nonangry refusals) by children than direct commands, suggesting that young children do think that their compliance is optional. In a structured diary study of 2- to 3-year-olds' misbehaviors and their mother's responses, the longest interval between recurrences occurred when mothers responded to misbehaviors with a combination of reasoning and punishment, rather than using either punishment or reasoning alone (Larzelere, Schneider, Larson, & Pike, 1996). In a 20-month longitudinal follow-up controlled for children's initial levels of oppositional and physical aggression, mothers' earlier use of explanations and descriptions of consequences without use of punishment was positively associated with children's oppositional and aggression scores (Larzelere, Sather, Schneider, Larson, & Pike, 1998).

Clinical studies also provide evidence on the effects of rewards and punishments. In a parent-training program for mothers of clinic-referred preschool children, adding time-out to a program of contingent attention was associated with a tripling in children's compliance rate, from 25.5% to 81.6% (Roberts, Hatzenbuehler, & Bean, 1981). On the basis of research with at-risk and clinic-recruited children and youth, Stoolmiller et al. (1997) argue that parents should consistently use punishments that work, such as time-out, point loss, or natural consequence.

For punishment to be maximally effective, it is important for parents to reward alternative behaviors that are acceptable to them before they introduce any punishments deemed necessary and children must be capable of discriminating appropriate and inappropriate behavior (G. Martin & Pear, 1999). Introducing intense punishment after the first transgression or using sharp increases in punishment intensity (Azrin & Holz, 1966) suppresses undesirable behavior most rapidly. Punishment is most effective when delivered immediately and following every incident of undesirable behavior, requiring considerable attention and consistency on the part of parents. Punishment does not establish new desirable behaviors; it only suppresses old misbehaviors and tends to have negative side effects: higher levels of aggressive behavior (Berkowitz, 1988) and avoidance of the person using punishment. In clinical and institutional settings, punishment is used as a last resort to suppress self-damaging behaviors that must be eliminated quickly (Martin & Pear, 1999).

In summary, there is solid research evidence on the effectiveness of disciplinary practices against which the experts' advice can be compared. First, parents should use proactive prevention strategies to minimize disciplinary encounters and positive attention to shape behaviors. Second, when a young child says "no," it is a positive form of self-assertion that can be distinguished from defiance, and defiance itself is often elicited by parental negative and forceful control. Third, children differ markedly in their resistance to control and receptiveness to discipline. Fourth, discipline that includes reasons and some incorporation of the child's perspective leads to better immediate and long-term outcomes. Finally, punishment should be used if necessary, it is best administered immediately, and it has potential negative side effects.

The American Academy of Pediatics (AAP) considers discipline important enough that its Committee on Psychosocial Aspects of Child and Family Health published discipline strategies for pediatricians to give to parents. Committee members are typically practitioners interacting directly with parents, and they review relevant research in formulating policy statements, which include a set of AAP-recommended best practices against which the experts' advice can be compared. The Committee's (1998) report identifies three elements of discipline: (a) positive, supportive parent–child relationships, (b) teaching and strengthening of desired behaviors, (c) decreasing undesired or ineffective behaviors. Daily routines of activities and interaction are emphasized as a way to reduce resistance. Parent strategies to help children learn positive behaviors are recommended, such as giving positive attention; careful listening; reinforcing desirable behavior; modeling orderly, appropriate behavior; and providing choices to children when they exist. Time-out and removal of privileges are identified as disciplinary procedures effective in reducing undesirable behavior. Strategies to reduce undesirable behaviors are similarly named: clarity about the problem behavior and the consequences for it, following through with consequences immediately and consistently, and providing a reason for a consequence for a specific behavior to children beyond toddler age (AAP Committee on Psychosocial Aspects of Child and Family Health, 1998).

The Authors' Positions on Disciplinary Practices and Punishment

SPOCK. As Spock describes it, "The everyday job of the parent is to keep the child on the right track by means of firmness and consistency" (Spock & Parker, 1998, p. 435). He is clear about what he believes to be the source of discipline:

I urge parents to count on mutual love and reasoning as the best ways to motivate a child to behave. These will, in the long run, preserve and enhance the child's spirituality, make him or her the kind of adult who will deal with his or her family, co-workers and others in a friendly, cooperative, honorable way. This, in turn, will bring out the best in other people. I say this not because of a theory, but because I've known dozens of children who were never punished or humiliated and they turned out to be as cooperative and considerate as you could wish. (Spock, 1994, p. 161)

Spock advocates both proactive controls and reasoning: "When your child is young, rely most heavily on physically removing her from dangerous or forbidden situations by distracting her to something interesting but harmless. . . . As she grows a little older . . . if she wants an explanation or a reason, give it to her in simple terms. But don't assume that she wants an explanation for every direction you give" (Spock & Parker, 1998, p. 442). He suggests that parents not use requests when commands are called for because if the child refuses, the parents will have "to persuade the child to give in to something that was necessary anyway" (Spock & Parker, 1998, p. 440). He asserts that "shaming, humiliating and shouting angrily at children erodes their self-esteem and is permanently harmful" (Spock, 1994, p. 161).

On the issue of disciplining without punishment, Spock suggests that parents' own experiences growing up, rather than specific discipline strategies, can lead them to be successful in avoiding punishment: "A lot depends on how the parents were brought up. If they were punished occasionally for good cause, they naturally expect to have to punish in similar situations. And if they were kept in line by positive guidance alone, they are apt to find that they can do the same with their children" (Spock & Parker, 1998, p. 435). Spock acknowledges individual differences between children that affect the likelihood that parents will need to use punishment: "In automobile terms, the child supplies the power but the parents have to do the steering. Some children are more challenging than others—they may be more active, impulsive, and stubborn than most—and it takes more energy to keep them on the right track" (Spock & Parker, 1998, p. 436). He also suggests an acid test for the effectiveness of punishment: "The best test of a punishment is whether it accomplishes what you are after, without having other serious effects. If it makes a child furious, defiant, or worse behaved than before, then it certainly isn't working. If it seems to break the child's heart, then it's probably too strong for him" (Spock & Parker, 1998, p. 436).

Spock's advice on discipline calls for parents to provide reasons when children want them, and, in fact, research demonstrates that this leads to better immediate compliance and greater internalization of parental values by children. His writing emphasizes proactive control to head off problems, a technique supported by research on mothers' management of children in supermarkets (Holden, 1983). Spock minimizes the role of punishment but acknowledges that it may be necessary, and there is evidence that in some situations, using punishment as a backup for explanations and description of consequences may be associated with less need for punishment later (Larzelere et al., 1998). His injunction to parents to evaluate how a particular punishment is working with their child helps ensure that parenting is responsive rather than formulaic. In short, his advice is well supported by research studies, including those that contributed to the AAP guidelines on effective discipline.

BRAZELTON. Brazelton emphasizes what children learn through discipline, but he includes the possibility of punishment in program of discipline. "*Discipline* means 'teaching,' not punishment. What you do about any single incident is not as important as what you teach on *each* occasion. Punishment may need to be part of discipline on certain occasions, but it should follow promptly on the misbehavior, be short, and respect the feelings of the child" (Brazelton, 1992, p. 253).

The goal for Brazelton is the child's acquisition of self-discipline, which is accompanied by testing: "Small children search for limits on their behavior. . . . When they begin to sense that they are getting out of control, or when they do not know how to stop themselves, they begin to tease or provoke the adults around them" (Brazelton, 1984, p. 82). Brazelton argues that parents should understand their child's actions in terms of the child's stage of development and fit the discipline to that stage. A child over 2 needs an explanation: "Try to figure what triggered the child's aggressive behavior, and give her a chance to understand it herself" (Brazelton, 1992, p. 259). Consistent with his recognition of children's individual differences, he advises that the punishment must suit the child: "Make use of what you know about your child's temperament and sensitivities. A sensitive child will be devastated by punishment that is geared to a more active, wound-up child" (Brazelton, 1992, p. 259). He recommends use of time-out: "Putting him in his room 'to cool off' gives you both a chance to collect yourselves" (Brazelton, 1984, p. 89).

Brazelton focuses on the teaching possibilities of discipline, with insight as the immediate objective for both parent and child and long-term self-regulation as the goal for the child. There is extensive research evidence that teaching and explanation is beneficial in producing short-term compliance (Grusec & Lytton, 1998; Kuczynski, 1984) and internalization of moral standards consistent with self-regulation over a 1- to 2-year period (Kochanska et al., 1996). His advice that punishments for young children, if they are necessary, should be prompt and brief is well supported by clinical research (Martin & Pear, 1999). He recommends time-outs, which do allow anger to subside and may help prevent abuse that can follow when young children resist parents' control.

DOBSON. Dobson's emphasis in discipline is less on the acquisition of self-control as a personal attribute and more on the child's acquisition of respect for authority. The early interaction between children and their parents takes on special significance as a template for later hierarchical relationships: "*Developing respect for parents is the critical factor in child management*. It is imperative that a child learns to respect his parents—not to satisfy their egos, but because his relationship with them provides the basis for his later attitude toward all other people. His early view of parental authority becomes the cornerstone of his future outlook on school authority, law enforcement officers, employers" (Dobson, 1992, p. 18). Dobson favors the establishment of rules well in advance, ones that children clearly understand, and mentions the use of proactive controls: "It seems foolish to leave an expensive trinket where it will tempt him, and then scold him for taking the bait. . . . It is much wiser to distract him with something else than to discipline him for his persistence" (Dobson, 1992, p. 66). He also mentions the wisdom of understanding the child's point of view: "The primary parental task is to get behind the eyes of the child, thereby tailoring the discipline to his unique perception" (Dobson, 1992, p. 71).

The essential structure of his disciplinary practice comes from applied behavior analysis, which deemphasizes the child's perspective in discipline exchanges and focuses on observed compliance. Children's good behaviors are strengthened through rewards, which should be granted quickly: "Many adults are reluctant to utilize rewards because they view them as a source of bribery. . . . Rewards make responsible effort worthwhile. That's the way the adult world works" (Dobson, 1992, p. 87). Children are given stickers or pennies for chores completed, required to give a portion of any money received to charity or their church, and required to save a portion. Required household tasks and rewards change as the child matures. He believes that children should be given age-appropriate responsibilities, and those who show irresponsible behavior should suffer the consequences of their acts: "When Barbara misses the school bus through her own dawdling, let her walk a mile or two and enter school in midmorning (unless safety factors prevent this). If Janie carelessly loses her lunch money, let her skip a meal" (Dobson, 1992, p. 117).

Dobson describes A. Thomas et al.'s (1968) three temperament types (easy, difficult, and slow-to-warm-up) and writes that "they confirm my own observations" (Dobson, 1987, p. 28), but consideration of the slow-to-warm-up child is shunted aside as he focuses on the contrast in temperament between compliant and "strong-willed" children. The focus is not on regularity in biological functions or responses to new stimuli as in Thomas et al.'s classification of easy and difficult children, but on how manageable the child is. Strong-willed children are those that resist their parents' attempts at control: "A child's resistant behavior always contains a message to his parents, which they must decode before responding. The message is often phrased in the form of a question: 'Are you in charge or am I?' A distinct reply is appropriate to discourage future attempts to overthrow constituted government in the home" (Dobson, 1992, p. 29).

Dobson recommends use of proactive controls, which can help head off many problems (Holden, 1983). When Dobson insists that children respect parental authority and advises parents to deal forcefully with noncompliance, he makes young children's developmentally appropriate self-assertion into a threat to the integrity of the parenting role and, inevitably, into a contest of wills. This increases the likelihood of highly charged emotional interchanges that may escalate to abuse. In fact, research demonstrates that firm parental control is the likely *cause* of defiance, and a parental harsh response only escalates conflict (Crockenberg & Litman, 1990). Defiance fades over the years of early childhood in normal children, and negotiation rather than firm control seems most helpful in reducing its frequency. Dobson claims that strong parental response to defiance leads to its suppression, but research findings (e.g., Kucynski et al., 1987) suggest that it diminishes with age without intervention.

Dobson's equation of child resistance to parents with adult rebellion against constituted government reveals his tendency to frame family issues in terms of the larger social order and to treat family socialization as a means to instill in children an appreciation for societal hierarchies. His focus on gaining the child's respect as a disciplinary objective focuses on what parents should gain from discipline and treats compliance and internalization of values as by-products of child's respect. Even basic temperamental differences among children are recast solely in terms of children's controllability. Despite Dobson's instruction to get behind the eyes of the child, his discipline strategies take little account of the child's perception. Dobson's disciplinary advice carries some real risks. Because of his focus on respect for adults and stamping out resistance to parental authority, a child's self-assertion, which actually clusters with positive behavior (Crockenberg & Litman, 1990), is likely to be misinterpreted as defiance. As is clear in the next section, Dobson has a ready method for dealing with a child's defiance but fails to consider what parents might have done to provoke it, whereas systematic observation reveals that parent threats, criticism, physical intervention, and anger are the most common precipitants (Crockenberg & Litman, 1990).

LEACH. Leach's goals for discipline present a striking contrast to Dobson's: "Worthwhile discipline has to be self-discipline because the kind that keeps him safe and good when you are standing over him will not help when he is on his own. As he gets older, then, it is important not to be too hooked on obedience as a prime childish virtue" (1989b, p. 208). Her focus on self-regulation leads her to attempt to reframe discipline: "If for example, you stop calling it 'discipline,' but call it 'learning how to behave,' the whole business stops being something which is imposed on children and becomes something which, with our help, they do for themselves" (Leach, 1989b, pp. 205–206). In this context, the parent becomes facilitator of the child's acquisition of a broader set of standards for behavior, standards of self-control and right behavior to which the parent must also adhere. Disciplinary encounters become opportunities for the child to learn to cooperate with the parent instead of necessary clashes between parent and child whose successful resolution is indicated by the parent's will persevering and the child complying.

Leach pays close attention to the child's interpretation of the situation when misbehavior occurs, offering five possible reasons why children might misbehave that reflect their own cognitive limitations and conflicts of interest rather than disobedience. Consistent with her focus on the child's conscience development, she emphasizes providing reasons when disciplinary actions are taken:

Whenever there is time, tell him your reasons. Apart from emergencies you insult your child's intelligence if you ask for unthinking obedience and you also make it impossible for him to begin to fathom those vital basic principles of behavior. . . . If you tell him why, he can add this snippet of behavior into his knowledge of how to behave. If you just say "because I say so" he learns nothing except that adults are incomprehensible. (Leach, 1989b, p. 212)

In the same vein, she opposes trying to make children feel ashamed of their behavior because it makes them feel incapable of the more mature behavior that discipline is supposed to encourage (Leach, 1989b).

Leach also draws on learning theory fundamentals: "Make sure that behaving well is nicer for him than behaving badly" (1989b, p. 211), and she describes giving prizes to small children for getting through difficult situations, such as having a tooth out or getting stitches. "It is not the *object* that matters, it is having something nice dangling just the other side of the nasty few minutes" (Leach, 1989b, p. 223).

She clearly describes a lower age limit for discipline. Concerning toddlers, she writes: "No conventional kind of 'discipline' actually *works* with this age group though. You need patience, humor and parent-upmanship to survive unscathed but, if you can muster them, your child will emerge, at two-and-a-half or three perhaps, *ready, willing and able to learn how* to behave" (Leach, 1989b, p. 209).

Leach mentions consequences for bad behavior: Toys played with too roughly get broken; a toddler who bites others in the sandbox is removed to the swing; a temper tantrum in the line to get ice cream means no ice cream. However, she takes a strong stand against punishment: "Should there be any punishments, then? No, not if 'punishment' is seen as the deliberate infliction of pain, physical or mental. There are many kinds of action parents can take in the interests of children's safety, social acceptability and eventual social learning. Many of these are punishments in the true, psychological sense of reducing the likelihood of the child offending again, but they do not have to be perceived as punitive to be effective" (Leach, 1994, p. 129). Furthermore, she writes that if parent and child are in a cooperative relationship in learning how to behave, "you [the parent] will seldom need to think up a deliberate punishment because he will be working for your approval and your disapproval will make it clear to him when he has gone wrong" (Leach, 1989b, p. 224).

Leach also argues against punishment on the ground that it is ineffective: "In fact punishment is a very inefficient way to bringing about lasting change in peoples' behavior and, as those behaviorist psychologists soon found with their maze-running rats, vastly inferior to rewards. . . . Punishments do not inspire remorse or motivate effort; they seldom reform people—criminals, citizens or children; indeed they often backfire and make people angry and obstinate instead" (Leach, 1994, p. 119). Leach rejects time-outs, widely recommended in behaviorally based discipline programs, as difficult to implement. She recommends disengaging from a child who is misbehaving or suggesting to the child that he or she disengage, for instance by running around the yard, but Leach argues that use of heavy adult control is inappropriate if the purpose is the child's acquisition of self-control. Effective parents, then, should work to maximize their children's understanding of correct behavior and to understand occasional misbehaviors, and if they are successful, they should be able to minimize punitive consequences for their child.

Leach's statement that toddlers cannot be effectively disciplined before age 2½ or 3 is contradicted by research showing that parents do, in fact, effectively discipline their toddlers by using reasons to support their statements and that children thus disciplined have better outcomes (Belsky et al., 1996). She argues against the necessity of punishment, but research demonstrates that for many children, compliance is more likely to occur when aversive consequences are a part of the disciplinary mix (Larzelere et al., 1996). Punishments have side effects, and those that are arbitrary or unaccompanied by an explanation do not promote self-regulation, her goal for parenting. However, there is evidence for most children that punishments accompanied by a rationale do help shape their behavior. Leach rejects time-out for its heavy reliance on adult control. In fact, giving chronically noncompliant young children more control—for instance, by allowing them to decide how long to stay in time-out—leads to more subsequent misbehavior (and timeouts) than if the duration is fixed by adults (M. W. Roberts & Powers, 1990). She is correct that time-outs may be difficult to administer when the child resists going to time-out or comes out early, but confinement serves as an effective backup technique for children who refuse to stay in time-out (Roberts & Powers, 1990). Time-outs may constitute a "least-worst" punishment procedure that gives both child and parent necessary time to cool off.

ROSEMOND. Rosemond's disciplinary practice emphasizes rules and involves parents staking out a clear position of authority relative to their children: "Parents need to consistently demonstrate their power to their children, because children feel more secure with parents who are clear on where they stand and where they want their children to stand. . . . The moment a parent steps into a power struggle with a child, the parent loses all power. The child wins, because he has pulled you [the parent] down to his level" (Rosemond, 1993f, p. 3E). "Parental authority consists of nothing more than establishing and enforcing rules, routines, and responsibilities. . . . These three are the essence of discipline" (Rosemond, 1990, p. 19).

Without these three things, a child cannot become fully secure and cannot develop "complete self-esteem." What Rosemond calls "the three *R*s" "give the child a sense of direction and purpose, and they are the framework in which his life takes form and substance" (Rosemond, 1990, p. 20).

As a consequence of children's cognitive immaturity, rules, responsibilities, and routines must be justified by parental authority, not the force of reason: "Until a child is mature enough to understand a certain explanation, no amount of words will successfully convey that understanding. In that case, it is in the child's best interest for the parent to say 'Because I said so' or words to that same effect. . . . When a child is old enough to understand the explanation, he's also old enough to figure it out on his own" (Rosemond, 1989, pp. 45–46). According to this argument, then, parents *never* need give an explanation because of their children's immaturity or because the children will eventually be able to (somehow) correctly discern their parents' reasons and motivations. The possibility that children might misinterpret parental disciplinary actions is not considered. He acknowledges that "Some people don't like the idea of saying 'Because I said so' to a child. They argue that it isn't a reason. I disagree. Not only is it a reason, it's often the only reason. Let's face it, most of the decisions parents make are arbitrary" (Rosemond, 1989, p. 46).

In a later book, Rosemond argues that acceptance of parents' decisions without explanation is adaptive for children: "The primary function of being a parent is that of acquainting children with reality. Part of that reality is that, even in a democratic society, authority figures—teachers, lawmakers, employers—frequently impose arbitrary decisions" (Rosemond, 1993b, p. 94). Thus, from Rosemond's perspective, the well-socialized child (and, by extension, adult) is one who accepts his or her position in a social hierarchy in which others hold higher positions, and who does not challenge authority, however willful and unreasoned it may appear.

In elaborating his position, Rosemond also changes it: "Now hear me clearly: *I'm not saying that parents should never give reasons to children.* I'm saying parents should make no attempt to *reason with* children. . . . No amount of words will instill an appreciation for an adult point of view into the mind of a child" (Rosemond, 1993b, p. 95). In this more recent statement, Rosemond at least tolerates the provision of explanations by the parent but rejects parent–child disciplinary encounters in which the parent attempts to persuade the child, who is treated as a status equal. But this is different from his earlier and oft-repeated reliance on "because I said so" as a basic parenting strategy. Nonetheless, in Rosemond's description of the household with well-disciplined children, the flow of information is largely one way: "Children should be seen (allowed to listen to most adult conversation) but not heard (not allowed to interrupt). Understanding that when all is said and done, they will obey not because of bribe, brutality or successful explanation, but because their parents 'say so'" (Rosemond, 1993c, p. 3E).

Rosemond recommends using time-out to punish children. A list of misbehaviors for which the child is to be sent to time-out should be posted "on the refrigerator door or some other easily visible place (it is irrelevant whether the child can read)" (Rosemond, 1990, p. 37). How the list can be effective if children cannot read it is not explicated. He is unusual in his advice relying on the use of punishments rather than rewards to shape children's behavior. He maintains that rewards work for only a short time with misbehaving children and that "research has failed to verify the efficacy of reward-based discipline" (2001a, p. E10). Punishments are arranged in an escalating "three strikes" procedure in which children are allowed one misbehavior, then given time-out or loss of privileges, until the third strike, which results in restricting the child to his or her room for the rest of the week, except for meals and educational activities (Rosemond, 1996).

Rosemond emphasizes parent power and rules as the effective framework for discipline—not, as noted earlier, the warm responsive relationship that motivates rule adherence (Holden, 1983). Household life for those who follow his advice is more likely to be arranged around rules: restating them, administering them, dealing with transgressions, and revising them as the child's abilities develop. Rosemond is unique for his reliance on "because I said so" (Rosemond, 1989, p. 46) as a reason for rules. Like Dobson, he focuses on establishing parental authority as a step in preparing children for their eventual rungs in the social hierarchy. His nonsensical statement that children should be sent to time-out for violating posted rules, even if they are too young to read them, is incompatible with an understanding of discipline as involving teaching. Rosemond ignores the negative side effects of punishment (Martin & Pear, 1999), and his reliance on it does not support the development of positive alternative behaviors in children. As a result, parents are likely to need to punish more, rather than less, and their discipline is likely to be perceived by their children (and others) as heavy-handed.

Implications of the Experts' Advice on Disciplinary Practices

The five authors differ markedly from one another in their constructions of disciplinary interactions and their strategies for dealing with disciplinary confrontations with children. Spock, Brazelton, and Leach recognize that parents' disciplinary controls should be accompanied by reasons, which, in fact, lead to greater internalization of parental values by children. Leach's arguments against punishment fly in the face of evidence that it may be necessary for some young children on some occasions and that it may play a role preventing subsequent misbehavior. Dobson's strict behavioral approach to discipline emphasizes consequences for children and neglects the role that parental explanations might contribute to children's understanding and acquisition of self-discipline. There is substantial research evidence that applying Rosemond's command-reliant discipline and advice against parental explanations would lead to delayed development of conscience and more transgressions when adults are absent (Kochanska, Padavich, & Koenig, 1996; Kuczynski, 1984). This is an instance in which the same parenting strategy—that is, using "because I said so" as a reason—is strongly endorsed by one author (Rosemond) and explicitly rejected by another (Leach), demonstrating the wide divergence among the experts on key disciplinary strategies.

TO SPANK OR NOT TO SPANK? WHAT ARE THE KNOWN HARMS AND BENEFITS?

Research on Harsh and Mild Physical Punishment

Research on punishment provides evidence that aversive consequences are occasionally necessary, but the question of what type of punishment is most effective is still to be addressed. Tremendous controversy has raged among parents, child welfare advocates, and legislators concerning the use and abuse of spanking and other forms of corporal punishment. However, in survey studies, the overwhelming majority of parents (more than 90%) have used spanking and believe it to be effective (Graziano, Hamblen, & Plante, 1996; Straus & Stewart, 1999). Even those parenting experts who eschew punishment generally, in favor of discipline as teaching, have published comments on the use of corporal punishment.

PREDICTORS OF SPANKING. The research literature on spanking does not provide information on when spanking constitutes good discipline, but it does reveal who spanks when and for what reasons, when its effect is minimized and maximized, and how it compares with other forms of punishment.

Spanking, as actually administered by parents, is influenced by attributes unrelated to the child's behavior. The prevalence of spanking is higher for children brought up in southern states in the United States than for children brought up in the northeast, north central, or western states (Giles-Sims et al., 1995), and spanking frequency varies inversely with family income (Gunnoe & Mariner, 1997). A greater percentage of African American mothers spank their children than do mothers from other ethnic groups (Giles-Sims et al., 1995). Parents who believe that the Bible is the inerrant word of God and that it provides answers to all human problems spank more than parents with less literal religious beliefs (Ellison et al., 1996).

Spankings are twice as likely to occur at night, when family members' fatigue levels are higher, than in the morning or afternoon (Holden et al., 1995). Holden and Miller (1997) identified two predisposing reasons for spanking—instrumental (because parents believe that it controls behavior) and emotional (because parents get angry)—and found that instrumental spankers spank 55% more often than do emotional spankers. In one questionnaire study of predominately white, middle-class parents and their children, 85% of the parents reported feeling moderate to high anger, remorse, and agitation while physically punishing their child. And even in this presumably lower risk sample, 5% of parents admitted raising welts and bruises during their most severe punishment (Graziano et al., 1996).

Child attributes clearly make a difference in how much spanking occurs: Boys are spanked more than girls, and younger children are spanked more than older children (Day, Peterson, & McCracken, 1998). What children do clearly contributes: Behaviors that are deemed out of control, disobedient, or disrespectful of adults (Graziano et al., 1996) and child aggression and rights' violations (e.g., taking away another child's toy, refusing to take turns or share) are those most likely to elicit a spanking (Holden et al., 1995).

HARSH PUNISHMENT EFFECTS. A recent review argues that few differences in children's behavior occur when parents do not use corporal punishment or use it sparingly, but parents' frequent use of corporal punishment is associated with, and to some degree responsible for, negative child behaviors, particularly aggression (Deater-Deckard & Dodge, 1997). For example, toddlers whose mothers relied primarily on corporal punishment scored lower both on impulse control and on the Bayley Scales of Infant Development (Bayley, 1969) administered 7 months later, but there were no differences between toddlers whose mothers used corporal punishment occasionally and those who never used it (Power & Chapieski, 1986). Deater-Deckard and Dodge (1997) noted the lower correlations between corporal punishment and aggressive behavior obtained in children drawn from the general population (Rothbaum & Weisz, 1994) and the higher correlations between frequent high-intensity corporal punishment and child aggression in clinic-referred children (Loeber & Stouthamer-Loeber, 1986).

In fact, one of the clearest connections in punishment research is between parents' use of overly harsh punishment and child aggression. For example, B. Weiss, Dodge, Bates, and Pettit (1992) had home interviewers rate the punishment the child received, on a scale from *nonrestrictive* to *severe, strict, often physical* punishment. They found that children who had been harshly punished as assessed at a home visit before kindergarten were more likely to be rated as aggressive by their teachers 6 months later, even when child temperament and socioeconomic status were statistically controlled for. Along with socioeconomic status, parents' use of severe punishment was predictive of peer rejection in kindergarten, but when children's aggression and academic and social skills were entered into the analysis as a block, the effect of parent punishment disappeared (Pettit, Clawson, Dodge, & Bates, 1996). And parent punishment practices played less of a role in social status when these children were first graders (Pettit et al., 1996), suggesting that effects of parents' behaviors may diminish in significance as experience with peers increases. High scores on persistent temperament, defined as resistance to intrusion and persistence in pursuing forbidden activities, interact with mothers' harsh discipline to predict child aggression, hostility, and noncompliance in the first 6 years of school (Deater-Deckard & Dodge, 1997). Thus, parents' punishment practices may exacerbate the behavior of children with difficult temperaments.

Similar evidence of the importance of child attributes comes from long-term studies that confirm a relationship between early harsh punishment and adult violence and criminality (Eron, Huesmann, & Zelli, 1991; Farrington, 1995). When the child's own aggressive or antisocial behavior is statistically controlled for, however, parent punishment practices no longer predict outcomes. The pattern of findings, then, indicates that difficult children may influence the harsh parental punishment they receive in an increasingly coercive cycle (Patterson, 1982).

There is also the possibility that other psychological variables could account for the apparent connection between use of harsh corporal punishment and bad outcomes for children. Parental warmth has been implicated as a potential hidden variable. Deater-Deckard and Dodge (1997) argue that the effect of corporal punishment in the context of a nurturing relationship is likely to be negligible, whereas in the context of a cold, unresponsive parental relationship, its effect will be magnified, and there has been support for this from longitudinal research (McLoyd & Smith, 2002). Pettit et al. (1993) measured warmth with positive verbal statements, positive emotions when speaking about the child, positive physical contact with the child, and positive acceptance of the child's physical approaches. This type of warmth was negatively related to measures of later child aggressive behavior, even when disciplinary practices were controlled for.

In a sample of boys in an impoverished urban environment, who were first studied when they were 10½ years old, warmth was indexed by whether the "parent interacted frequently with the child, without being generally critical" (McCord, 1997, p. 215). Not surprisingly, there was a negative relationship between parental warmth and punitiveness for both parents: 35% of 108 punitive mothers were warm, whereas 60% of 116 nonpunitive mothers were warm (McCord, 1997). Later rates of criminal behavior were lower if the mother was warm; similar results were obtained for fathers. However, the use of corporal punishment by parents was associated with higher rates of later criminal acts, even when the parents were warm (McCord, 1997). It is not clear whether the boys' initial misbehavior levels were controlled for in these analyses, so the possibility that more difficult boys elicited more punishment cannot be ruled out. Similarly, Lytton (1997) argues that frequent punishment is related to parental rejection and that rejection is ultimately responsible for the negative effects of punishment.

Evidence to support Lytton's point emerged from data collected from a sample of 281 working-class, Southern children in grades 3–12, 54% of whom were African American (Rohner, Bourque, & Elordi, 1996). In these older children, when they viewed parental punishment as a form of rejection, corporal punishment was associated with measures of poor psychological adjustment, but neither the frequency nor the severity of corporal punishment was directly linked to adjustment.

Despite the seeming strength and consistency of the relationship between harsh corporal punishment by parents and aggression and antisocial behavior in children and youth, corporal punishment per se may not be the causal factor in subsequent outcomes. In three clinical or at-risk samples, Stoolmiller et al. (1997) found that inept (noncontingent) discipline had stronger relationships to teachers' and mothers' ratings of a child's antisocial behavior and observed child aversive behaviors in the home than did the mother's abusive discipline (humiliation and corporal punishment). Their results showed that "harsh abusive discipline, by itself, plays no causal role except perhaps in families characterized by out-of-control children and unskilled parents. Even here the effect is small relative to the effect of inept discipline" (Stoolmiller et al., 1997, p. 228). Parental use of harsh punishment, then, is part of a larger pattern of inept parenting in which parents do not control their children effectively because their discipline attempts do not respond appropriately to the child's bad behavior (Stoolmiller et al., 1997).

MILD OR MODERATE PUNISHMENT EFFECTS. Most parents, especially those who care enough to read parenting manuals or parenting columns in their newspaper, do not endorse the use of harsh corporal punishment. The operative question then becomes whether mild punishment, such as spanking, has effects that are discernible from no spanking at all.

In an important study of spanking (separated from other forms of corporal punishment) in a predominately European American (81%) and African American (17%) sample of 273 children and their mothers (and fathers, if present), Strassberg, Dodge, Pettit, and Bates (1994) found that parents who reported during a prekindergarten interview that they used spanking had children who showed more reactive and bullying aggression in kindergarten than did children of parents who did not use spanking, though aggression scores were unrelated to the frequency of spanking. This relationship was obtained even when socioeconomic status was statistically controlled for. Again, it is possible that more difficult children elicit corporal punishment.

On this topic it is inappropriate to generalize from European Americans to other ethnic groups. Day et al. (1998) found that African American mothers (but not fathers) reported using corporal punishment more than did European American mothers and fathers. But among African American parents, use of corporal punishment has been viewed as acceptable and nonabusive; perhaps because of these factors, the correlation between parental corporal punishment and child aggression, hostility, and noncompliance emerges only in those African American families demonstrating a relatively cold parent–child relationship (Deater-Deckard & Dodge, 1997). In a large national survey research study, the association between parental spanking and number of fights children got into was statistically significant only for older (age 8–11) European American boys in single-mother families. No significant relationship between spanking and fights emerged for African American children (Gunnoe & Mariner, 1997). Longitudinal research revealed an association between use of physical punishment before age 6 and higher subsequent levels of problem behavior, including aggression and trouble with school authorities and police. But this relationship was obtained only for European American youth and not for African American youth (Lansford, Deater-Deckard, Dodge, Bates, & Pettit, 2004). These studies taken together suggest that the effects of corporal punishment are not universal and absolute, but must be considered in the context of the broader parent–child relationship and subcultural norms for parents' behavior.

What about media advice concerning spanking? Is there enough evidence on the negative effects of spanking to warrant instructions not to spank? In his review of corporal punishment research, Larzelere (1996) concludes that "there are not enough quality studies that document detrimental outcomes of nonabusive physical punishment to support advice or policies against this age-old parental practice" (p. 827). Other researchers impose a stricter criterion for acceptance of spanking as a parenting practice. Lytton (1997) writes: "In truth, there is very little evidence for any harmful effects—either immediate or in the long term—arising from minor use of physical punishment, such as parents might inflict in passing, apart from the adverse effects of power assertion in general. . . . On the other hand there is no evidence for its usefulness" (p. 212). Huesmann (1997) agrees: "The real issue must be whether punishment accomplishes anything positive or not" (p. 203). Importantly, in one research study comparing types of punishment, the combination of reasoning and noncorporal punishment worked as well as reasoning and corporal punishment in preventing recurrences of fighting and disobedience among toddlers, suggesting that the punishment need not be corporal to be effective (Larzelere et al., 1996).

Gershoff's (2002) widely reported meta-analysis on 88 studies of the short- and long-term effects of parental corporal punishment found associations between its use and children's aggressive, antisocial, and delinquent behavior, as well as negative associations between corporal punishment and moral internalization and mental health. One of the largest composite effect sizes ($d = 0.69$) occurred for the association between parental use of corporal punishment and physical abuse of the same child. However, there was a strong positive association between physical punishment and the immediate cessation of misbehavior ($d = 1.13$), which demonstrates why parents may get "hooked" on its use to quell disobedience. Nor did all the associations fade away over time: Corporal punishment during childhood was positively associated with aggression ($d = 0.57$) and criminal and antisocial behavior in adulthood ($d = 0.42$), effect sizes similar in magnitude to those observed in children. Gershoff's critics (e.g., Baumrind, Larzelere, & Cowan, 2002; Larzelere, Kuhn, & Johnson, 2004) argue that the undesirable associations could be due to untested or inadequately controlled variables, including those discussed elsewhere in this chapter (parental warmth, child temperament) and note that Gershoff's analysis does not distinguish between severe and mild corporal punishment (open-handed spanking). Even the critics' reanalysis of the association between nonsevere punishment and child aggression, though, shows a small association between the two, with an effect size of $d = .30$ (Baumrind et al., 2002).

PUNISHMENT OR INEPT DISCIPLINE EFFECTS? As noted earlier, parents' ineptness in discipline may be to blame in children's outcomes rather than whether corporal punishment is used. In a sample of 206 families with sons at risk for abuse, parent aggression toward sons (as rated by in-home observers) and parent-reported punitive parenting was significantly related to parents' reports of ineffective discipline, but not to such potentially complicating factors as parental irritability or the stress that parents were under (Greenwald, Bank, Reid, & Knutson, 1997). The sons' coercive behavior did not contribute directly to excessively punitive parenting, but ineffective discipline did, and there was evidence of bidirectional effects between children's coerciveness and ineffective discipline. In short, whatever roles child attributes or family contexts play, ineffective discipline may be a key factor contributing to punitive parenting.

The linkage of parent's use of corporal punishment to their ineffectiveness as disciplinarians has implications for interventions as well. Legal or social prohibitions on mild corporal punishment would be unlikely to lead to better outcomes in children, because they would not be addressing the effective cause of children's misbehavior. Even Straus (1994), arguably the best-known opponent of corporal punishment by parents, acknowledges that nonspanking parents are more engaged with their children, use reasoning more, and act in ways that promote positive parent–child relationships. So the practice of spanking in itself is far from the only cause for spanked children's seemingly poorer outcomes. Promoting positive parent disciplinary behaviors (use of reasons and positive contingencies) may be more effective and certainly less controversial than prohibiting mild, subabusive corporal punishment. And some discipline researchers would argue that existing research does not warrant a blanket prohibition on spanking (Baumrind et al., 2002; Larzelere, 2003).

The AAP Committee on Psychosocial Aspects of Child and Family Health (1998) acknowledges that spanking is prevalent and controversial and argues that it is ineffective and associated with bad adult outcomes, such as spousal abuse and substance abuse. Its harshest words, though, are reserved for other forms of physical punishment, such as jerking a child's arm, striking a child with an object, or striking a child someplace other than on the buttocks, which it views as unacceptable and dangerous to children's health (p. 726). Two parenting books written by committees of AAP members contain identical statements that the AAP is strongly opposed to parents striking a child and recommend that if parents spank in the heat of the moment, they should later explain why they did it and how angry they were. They suggest that parents apologize for their loss of control because it can help the child understand the spanking (Schor, 1999; Shelov, 1998). The book in this series focusing on parenting adolescents (Greydanus, 2003) mentions the AAP's opposition to corporal punishment and goes so far as to suggest that "parents who become physically aggressive with a teenager should seek the help of a mental-health specialist" (p. 22).

In brief, spanking is widely used and is more likely to be elicited by children whom parents regard as more challenging. Spanking has to be interpreted in ethnic and family contexts; it seems to have its worst effects when there is widespread disapproval of spanking in the family's ethnic group and when the child interprets corporal punishment as parental rejection. On the other hand, any good effects of spanking seem to be limited to immediate compliance, and there is little evidence that spanking accomplishes disciplinary goals that could not be achieved by using other techniques. Parents' use of harsh corporal punishment may be a signal of erratic, ineffective parenting, and the American Academy of Pediatrics advises against its use.

The Authors' Positions on Corporal Punishment

The parenting experts split on the topic of corporal punishment in ways that make it clear that considerations other than research findings and clinical practice are influencing their positions.

SPOCK. In recent editions of *Baby and Child Care,* Spock takes a strong position against corporal punishment: "It teaches children that the larger, stronger person has the power to get his way, whether or not he is in the right. Some spanked children then feel quite justified in beating up on smaller ones" (Spock & Parker, 1998, pp. 437–438). He emphasizes its negative effects on the overall parent–child relationship: "Physical punishment means hurting children to try to make them behave when other forms of management have failed. It relies ultimately on the parent's superior size and strength. So it teaches that might makes right and that it is acceptable to inflict pain to get one's way. This tends to destroy love and spirituality" (Spock, 1994, pp. 161–162). Spock also mentions that reliance on spanking as a discipline technique "may be one reason that there is much more violence in our country than in any other comparable nation" (Spock & Parker, 1998, p. 438) but does not present evidence to support this statement.

Spock's stand against corporal punishment is stronger than research findings support, but it is reasonable in light of the fact that spanking has few demonstrated benefits that cannot be achieved by using other techniques. Moreover, spanking would be strongly inconsistent with his overarching goal of a cooperative relationship between child and parent that leads to ethical and prosocial behavior in children. His antispanking stand also minimizes chances for abuse, which often occurs when punishment episodes go awry.

BRAZELTON. Brazelton takes a strong stand against corporal punishment: "Remember what it means to a child to see you lose control and act physically aggressive. It means you believe in power and physical aggression" (Brazelton, 1992, p. 260). "Spanking is no good, as we've said before. It says you believe in settling things by force—and I don't believe in that" (Brazelton, 1992, p. 170). He urges parents to defuse situations in which they might be tempted to corporally punish by interrupting ongoing activity before the situation reaches a crisis and sitting down for a quiet minute with the child or putting him or her in their room to cool off (Brazelton, 1984).

Brazelton's emphasis on defusing situations that might lead to spanking is good policy, again because it reduces the chances for abuse. Like Spock, he insists on alternatives to brute assertion of physical power by parents, as inevitably occurs when children are spanked, and lays the groundwork for more cooperative parent–child relationships.

DOBSON. Perhaps the most distinctive aspect of Dobson's parenting advice is his reliance on corporal punishment as a fundamental child control strategy. His stand on corporal punishment is well developed in *Dare to Discipline*, the book that launched his public career, and it is reaffirmed in the 1992 revision and in subsequent books, tapes, and videos.

Dobson describes the use of mild corporal punishment with young children in sufficient detail so that parents can easily apply his advice:

When a parent's calm request for obedience is ignored by a child, Mom or Dad should have some means of making their youngster *want* to cooperate. For those who can think of no such device, I will suggest one: it is muscle lying snugly against the base of the neck. Anatomy books list it as the trapezius muscle, and when firmly squeezed, it sends little messengers to the brain saying, 'this hurts: avoid recurrence at all costs.' The pain is only temporary; it can cause no damage. But it is an amazingly effective and practical recourse for parents when their youngster ignores a direct command to move. (Dobson, 1992, p. 38)

His writings are full of other examples of the application of physical pain to keep children safe and command their attention. Suppose, writes Dobson, that they are reaching toward an electric socket and ignore a shouted "No!": "You can see the smile of challenge on his face as he thinks 'I'm going to do it anyway!' I'd encourage you to thump his fingers just enough to sting. A small amount of pain goes a long way at that age and begins to introduce children to realities of the world and the importance of listening to what you say" (Dobson, 1992, p. 65). Dobson reports that his 15-month-old daughter three times disobeyed his wife's command to stand in an open doorway rather than come outside in the rain where his wife was fetching wood. The punishment: "Shirley stung Danae's little legs a few times with a switch" (Dobson, 1992, p. 36). She then held the toddler and rocked her for 15 minutes and during that time talked about the importance of obedience (Dobson, 1992). Dobson's typical examples of spankable offenses involve physical safety issues or failing to obey adult authority but do not consider the child's perspective, in this case bonds of attachment that would make a child of this age resist separation from their parent.

However, he writes that "spankings should be reserved for a child's moments of greatest antagonism, usually occurring after the third birthday" (Dobson, 1992, p. 66). He sets a lower age limit for corporal punishment: "There is no excuse for spanking babies or children younger than fifteen to eighteen months of age. Even shaking an infant can cause brain damage and death" (Dobson, 1992, p. 65). Children over the age of 6 should be spanked rarely, teenagers should never be spanked, and spanking is to be done on the buttocks only. Spanking is to be done with a switch or a paddle because "the hand should be seen as an object of love—to hold, hug, pat, and caress" (Dobson, 1992, p. 64). He is also clear that a spanking should cause pain: "If it doesn't hurt it isn't worth avoiding next time. . . . While being careful not to go too far, you should ensure he feels the message" (Dobson, 1992, p. 72).

Spanking is also an option to deal with a child's protest at being punished. In response to a question concerning how long should a child be allowed to cry after being disciplined or spanked, Dobson (1992) writes that "crying can quickly change from inner sobbing to an expression of protest aimed at punishing the enemy. Real crying usually lasts two minutes or less, but may continue for five. After that point, the child is merely complaining, and the change can be recognized in the tone and intensity of his voice. I would require him to stop the protest crying, usually by offering him a little more of whatever caused the original tears" (p. 70).

Dobson apparently recognizes the potential for abuse in endorsing even limited use of physical punishment: "Corporal punishment that is not administered according to very carefully thought-out guidelines is a dangerous thing. Being a parent carries *no* right to slap and intimidate a child because you had a bad day or are in a lousy mood" (1992, p. 60). He decides that "just because a technique is used wrongly, however, is no reason to reject it altogether. . . . In those situations when the child fully understands what he is being asked to do or not to do but refuses to yield to adult leadership, an appropriate spanking is the shortest and most effective route to an attitude adjustment" (Dobson, 1992, pp. 60–61). Dobson argues that corporal punishment is not harmful and in fact helps promote obedience to authority as an adult: "Not only does this response not create aggression in a boy or girl, it helps them control their impulses and live in harmony with various forms of benevolent authority throughout life" (Dobson, 1992, pp. 60–61).

Dobson's focus on challenges to parental authority and his one-dimensional characterization of children for disciplinary purposes as strong-willed or compliant is likely to lead to more, not fewer, control encounters with young children. His descriptions of using corporal punishment for ignoring parental commands and for children's unsafe actions signifies that corporal punishment will be used frequently with young children, despite his injunctions to the contrary. He fails to consider the child's understanding of a situation (not wanting to be separated from a parent) or to offer nonviolent alternatives, such as saying "No!" loudly and removing a child from the proximity of the electric outlet.

Dobson's belief that corporal punishment should reflect thought-through guidelines does not reflect the reality of spankings, which occur when parents and children are fatigued and therefore more prone to anger and less capable of considering alternate ways to resolve conflict (Holden et al., 1995). His advice to spank with an object, a procedure that the AAP Committee report on discipline (1998) labels unacceptable, means that parents do not have direct feedback on how hard they are spanking, making bruises and lacerations more likely. His instruction to quiet crying after spanking by threatening more spanking does not consider the child's real anger and the risk of suppressing it by force. Though there is research evidence that corporal punishment in the context of the warm parent–child relationship that Dobson espouses is not as damaging as that which occurs in the context of parental rejection and disengagement (Deater-Deckard & Dodge, 1997), there is little evidence that corporal punishment is more effective than noncorporal punishment or the only way to achieve compliance.

Dobson argues that corporal punishment helps children live in harmony with authority. By this logic, the children and youth who have received the most corporal punishment should show lower levels of aggression and be highly compliant children and law-abiding adults. But even in research that controls for child or family attributes that might lead to more spanking, no such relationship is obtained (Eron et al., 1991; Farrington, 1995; Strassberg et al., 1994). In fact, the empirical data argue just the opposite: Longitudinal studies clearly show that high levels of parental corporal punishment are associated with later higher levels of aggression and delinquent acts (Eron et al., 1991; Farrington, 1995).

LEACH. Leach opposes corporal punishment of children, using language that suggests that they are social, if not developmental, equals of parents: "Would you swat your spouse or a co-worker? Why should we treat our children with less consideration?" (Kennedy, 1997, p. 84). In her advocacy book, *Children First*, she writes: "If the whole concept of punishment is foreign to the self-discipline parents want children to acquire, then physical punishment cuts at its very foundations, highlighting people's reluctance to regard children as fully human—as people just like themselves except for youth and inexperience—and their ultimate readiness to abandon cooperation for the naked assertion of painful power" (Leach, 1994, p. 126).

Her overall position is that discipline is most importantly an educational process, and she rejects the idea that punishment itself promotes learning because children do not remember what they were spanked for and the pain and the indignity cause them to be angry: "Smacking, therefore, cuts right across any attempt at cooperation and certainly across anything you are trying to teach about using strength gently or relying on words rather than blows" (Leach, 1989b, p. 224). She specifically rejects the idea that corporal punishment should be used to help children understand dangers to their physical safety: "Many parents regard the assertion of that painful power as a necessary part of keeping small children safe, rather on a par with stair gates or car seats.... Stair gates and car seats prevent injury; they do not punish children for risking it.... This kind of punishment is not education for children but post-traumatic stress relief for parents" (Leach, 1994, p. 126).

Leach condemns corporal punishment—"smacking"—because it so upsets children that it prevents the use of discipline to teach children about co-operation and self-regulation. Her position against corporal punishment is the only one that makes sense in the context of her larger stand against punishment.

ROSEMOND. Rosemond's position on corporal punishment includes statements about his own parenting practices, his advice on how to physically punish children, and his pronouncements on how and when parents should use corporal punishment. On his own use of spanking he is straightforward: "As the occasion warranted, I spanked my children. I did so not because I had given it a lot of thought or believed that children needed to be spanked or reached the end of my rope, but simply because I *felt* like it. I have learned, during twenty-two years of raising my own children, to trust my feelings" (Rosemond, 1990, p. 12). Rosemond's (1994e) book on spanking identifies the type of behaviors that warrant spanking:

> One cannot afford patience when it comes to disrespect, defiance, tantrums, and anti-social behavior. These must be dealt with swiftly and, more often than not, dramatically. The child must know that these behaviors will not, under any circumstances, be tolerated, not because they are threatening to the parent, but because they threaten the child's ultimate ability to succeed.... True success comes to those who respect authority as well as their fellow man, know when and how to obey as well as when and how to lead, and are in control of themselves. (p. 48)

He also rejects the idea that spankings can produce antisocial behavior: "The social, economic, political, and psychological factors that combine to produce criminals, child abusers, bullies, and emotional cripples are far too complex.... To suggest that spankings play a major role in shaping that kind of social behavior is ludicrous" (Rosemond, 1990, pp. 12–13).

According to Rosemond, the main problem is that parents do not spank correctly: "It is possible to spank a child *well*, to do it *right*, and to make it *work*.... The problem with spanking is that most parents make a sorry mess out of it" (Rosemond, 1990, p. 13). In a newspaper column, he elaborates: "I believe in spanking as a first resort, spanking in anger, of spanking only with one's hand, of spanking only the child's rear end; of administering no more than two spanks at a time" (Rosemond, 1992c, p. 2E). He argues that spanking preemptively as soon as the child commits an act of defiance—for example, spitting on an adult—helps reduce the chance that the spanking will become abusive (Rosemond, 1992c). According to Rosemond, "The idea is *not* to cause the child pain, but to (1) quickly terminate undesirable behavior, (2) remind the child of your authority, (3) express, in a relatively low-key way, your anger, and (4) grab the child's attention for a moment of plain talk" (1990, p. 14). Rosemond recommends spanking only occasionally, on the buttocks, and pairing spanking with other punishment (Rosemond, 2001b, p. 82). Children should be spanked in private rather than in public, not before age 18 months and not after age 9 or 10 (Rosemond, 1994e).

Despite his assertion that it is possible to make spankings "work," Rosemond writes that "spankings are a lousy form of discipline. In fact, they do not warrant being classed as discipline at all. At best, a spanking is nothing more, nothing less, than a dramatic form of nonverbal communication" (Rosemond, 1992d, p. 2E). Most of his short book on spanking concerns the public controversy surrounding it, Rosemond's opposition to antispanking legislation, and stories of his successful use of spanking with his own two children (Rosemond, 1994e).

Rosemond's contradictory advice (i.e., spanking is lousy discipline, but I spanked when I felt like it and it worked for me, and if you are going to do it, here is how) includes some very risky elements: spanking preemptively, which is likely to escalate child noncompliance, and spanking in anger, when emotional overreaction, intensified by the physical actions of spanking and the child's reaction, are frequent precipitants of abuse. Rosemond pays little attention to establishing a warm, loving relationship with children, treating it as only an offshoot of good discipline. In light of the repeated demonstrations that effects of corporal punishment are particularly likely to occur and particularly likely to be damaging in the context of a detached or hostile parent–child relationship (Deater-Deckard & Dodge, 1997; Rohner et al., 1996), this is a serious oversight. Like Dobson, Rosemond recommends spanking when children show a lack of respect for adult authority, yet there is little evidence that the assertion of superior physical power by parents leads to better internalization of moral standards, and plenty of evidence that older children who have a history of corporal punishment are actually more likely to engage in antisocial and delinquent acts.

The Experts and Physical Punishment Research: A Summary

All five authors take a stand against frequent, harsh corporal punishment. Spock's, Brazelton's, and Leach's stands against any corporal punishment do not have strong support from research on child outcomes, in that there seem to be few differences between those children spanked only occasionally and those not spanked. The best research evidence against mild corporal punishment is that children who are spanked (but are not otherwise physically punished) are more aggressive in kindergarten (Strassberg et al., 1994), even after socioeconomic status was controlled for. This finding was not related to the frequency of spanking, and the possibility exists that more aggressive children elicited more spanking.

Given the relative dearth of research evidence on negative child outcomes for mild corporal punishment, is there sufficient reason to accept these three experts' stands against it? Huesmann (1997) and Lytton (1997) raise the issue of using corporal punishment in the absence of research demonstrations of its positive benefits. The AAP Committee on Psychosocial Aspects of Child and Family Health (1998) argues that spanking is ineffective. Larzelere et al. (1996) found that noncorporal punishments were as effective in preventing recurrences of misbehavior as corporal ones, and there is little or no research demonstrating that corporal punishment works better than time-out or removal of privileges. Religious beliefs, family income, ethnicity, parents' aggressiveness, and even the time of day influence spanking practices, suggesting that factors other than the child's undesirable behavior and spanking's effectiveness in eliminating it are important in its actual occurrences, when effectiveness should be the most important criterion if the child's well-being is paramount. Particularly in light of the number of instances in which corporal punishment incidents turn abusive (Gershoff, 2002; Graziano et al., 1996; Kadushin & Martin, 1981), a stand against the use of corporal punishment is prudent for media parenting experts. If parents do use occasional mild corporal punishment, Spock, Brazelton, Leach (and Dobson, as discussed below) all emphasize the importance of warm interactions with the child as a foundation for discipline, which research suggests attenuates negative effects of mild (or even harsh) corporal punishment.

THE EXPERTS' ADVICE AND THE RESEARCH ON DISCIPLINE: COMPARISON AND CONCLUSIONS

For the experts' discipline policies to be maximally effective, they need to offer strategies for parents that are most likely to lead to desirable outcomes for children and parents, providing positive guidance. They should recognize the circumstances under which parents actually use discipline and consider the ways in which their advice is likely to be used in order to prevent possible negative effects.

The media experts' advice on discipline reveals major differences in their conceptualizations of parent–child relationships. Spock, Brazelton, and Leach focus on self-regulation with the long-term goal of internalization of parental values. To motivate that internalization, they count on the child's love for the parent and the parents' realization that they can strengthen the affectionate bond and accomplish their long-term goals more effectively by influencing their children than by asserting their power as adults. They advocate giving reasons for parents' disciplinary actions and recommend not using corporal punishment, which has no evident advantages and increases parental guilt. Their policies are associated with a lower risk of abuse and greater degree of internalization of moral standards, but they may be challenging to implement with children who have poor impulse control.

For Dobson and Rosemond, the immediate goal of discipline is developing respect for the parents with the long-term goal of being able to function effectively in a hierarchically organized society. For Dobson, subordination of the child to the parent is preparation for the grown child's subordination to authority figures and ultimately to God, envisioned as the final lawmaker and rule giver. His advice can be implemented by parents who do not have sufficient forethought to prevent conflicts or the language skills to explain why an act is wrong. The practices he recommends rarely consider the child's perspective, and his relatively quick escalation to corporal punishment preempts the search for other discipline strategies. Negative effects of corporal punishment can be attenuated by parental warmth, which Dobson endorses, but there is no research demonstrating that corporal punishment is the only effective method for attaining compliance and much research suggesting that it carries its own risks. For Rosemond, the parent's establishment of a powerful position early provides the foundation for subsequent obedience and makes children lovable, but his neglect of positive discipline strategies in favor of punishments is likely to lead to more of the latter. His reliance on commands and reluctance to give reasons to children concerning rules and misdeeds is a significant deviation from optimal disciplinary practice. The American Academy of Pediatrics standards (1998), derived from research findings and a conference consensus, recommend giving children reasons for discipline to children over toddler age. Research studies have repeatedly linked command-reliant discipline without explanations to delays in children's internalization of adult standards, an important goal of discipline (e.g., Kochanska et al., 1996; Kucynski, 1984).

Thus, the two experts who built their reputations on their discipline advice are the two whose discipline recommendations diverge substantially from available research findings and from best practice standards. But obviously many parents are attracted to their punishment practices, perhaps because they are closer to the practices those parents actually use and want to see validated. It is a measure of the lack of influence of both child advocacy groups (most of which oppose spanking) and academic researchers that media experts' positions that are so widely divergent are viewed as not only legitimate, but authoritative.

CHAPTER 5
ELECTRONIC MEDIA

PARENTS WHO ARE CONCERNED about the effect of television and other media on their children have their work cut out for them. There are televisions in 98% of American households (Nielsen Media Research, 1998). A typical American child age 8–18 spends more than 6 hours a day engaged in media use, and about two thirds have television sets in their bedrooms (Rideout, Roberts, & Foehr, 2005). Even the youngest children live in media-rich environments. Two thirds of children under the age of 6 live in homes where the TV is on half the time or more, and nearly half (48%) of the children in this age group have used a computer (Rideout, Vandewater, & Wartella, 2003). Recent TV content analyses provide evidence that the electronic media offer child and adolescent consumers a menu generously sprinkled with sexual content (Kaiser Family Foundation, 2002) and spiked with large helpings of violence (Kunkel et al., 1999; National Television Violence Study, 1996, 1997, 1998). Television provides most children with their first glimpse of their society, and that view includes images that most parents believe children should not be exposed to.

The explosion of media in the last 20 years—the VCR tapes, the Nintendos, Super Nintendos, Segas, Play Stations 1 and 2, X-Boxes, computer games, the new cable channels—ensures that today's parents face choices about their children's entertainment that their own parents never had to consider. The push-button access of most media, the presence of children of different ages in most families, and children's access to media in other children's homes can frustrate parents' intentions to control exposure. Such policies have to be instituted early: 3-year-olds who cannot reliably tie their shoes can easily operate TV remote controls and video cassette recorders. Thus, parenting experts have a potentially important role to play, if parents are disposed to follow their advice. Since the experts discussed here are at least a generation older than the parents they counsel, their media advice is one indication of whether they are current on the issues that affect children and their parents in these media-pervasive times. This chapter will review the research on several of these issues to see what the experts cover well and what they miss.

This chapter, like the others, is one of contrasts. The starkest contrasts are not among the experts, though differences are certainly evident on individual issues. Concerning electronic media, both the experts and media researchers are a long way apart from most parents who, despite their ambivalence about the appropriateness of TV content, typically control very little of their children's media exposure. If parents were reading for themselves the massive amounts of research data on negative effects of media, they might play closer attention to what their children are watching, but maybe not. One of the best known phenomena in media research is the "third person effect," the belief that mass media affects other people more than it affects the self (Davison, 1983). Perhaps most parents believe that electronic media do not really affect their children. Or it may be that media are so pervasive that they do not want their children to be sheltered from the "real" world, which they believe, rightly or not, is reflected in the small world of television or computer screens (Farkas, Johnson, & Duffett, 2002).

DOES MEDIA VIOLENCE CAUSE CHILDREN TO BECOME MORE AGGRESSIVE?

Television

Concerns about media violence go back all the way to the early years of television. The first report to the Surgeon General about television violence was made in 1958, and nearly half a century later the controversy still simmers. Meanwhile, global news coverage of war and terrorism becomes more immediate and more graphic, and entertainment violence is enhanced with special effects that do not just pierce bodies with bullets, but shatter them. The National Television Violence Study found that about 60% of cable and broadcast TV programming in the United States contained violence (National Television Violence study, 1996, 1997, 1998; Wilson et al., 2002), with an average of 6.8 violent incidents per hour. Lower rates of violence might be expected in programs directed at children, but they actually registered the highest rates of violent incidents, especially in cartoons, which were more likely to show unrealistically low levels of harm to the victim. Children's programs also contained a higher proportion of scenes in which violent acts were immediately rewarded (Wilson et al., 2002). These findings are based on a content analysis of over 8,000 hours of programming, so the more children watch television, the greater the likelihood that they will view violence, unless parents take active steps to prevent it (C. A. Anderson & Bushman, 2002; National Television Violence Study, 1998).

Forty years of research, involving over a thousand studies on TV violence, should enable solid conclusions, and in fact, summary findings are remarkably consistent. Five meta-analyses combining data from hundreds of TV studies and reducing them into effect size measures (Andison, 1977; Hearold, 1986; Hogben, 1998; Paik & Comstock, 1994; Wood, Wong, & Chachere, 1991) all concluded that viewing violence is related to increases in aggressive emotions, attitudes, and behaviors. The effects are larger for experimental studies, and because participants are randomly assigned to media exposure and comparison conditions, experiments also have the advantage of demonstrating precisely under what conditions media exposure can cause aggression. In a meta-analysis including only those experiments in which the outcome measure was aggression against another person who was physically present, the overall effect sizes were small to medium: $d = 0.27$ (weighted for sample size) and $d = 0.40$ (unweighted) for 12 studies for which effect sizes could be calculated (Wood et al., 1991). In a restricted meta-analysis of studies published since 1980, Hogben (1998) tested the hypothesis that effect sizes would be larger for children than for adults. He found that children showed a larger, near-medium effect size ($d = 0.44$; based on 10 studies with 16 effect sizes) than the small effect found for adults ($d = 0.12$; based on 8 studies with 12 effect sizes).

On the basis of these and many other studies, there is a general consensus among both quantitative and qualitative reviewers (e.g., C. A. Anderson et al., 2003) that the effect of media violence on children's and adults' aggression is certainly positive and small to medium, depending on aggressive behavior that is measured. The effects are evident both in cross-sectional studies of immediate effects and in longitudinal research on longer term effects. Bushman, C. A. Anderson, and coauthors (C. A. Anderson et al., 2003; Bushman & Anderson, 2001; Bushman & Huesmann, 2001) have pointed out that media violence effects are similar in size to those of cigarette smoking on lung cancer, and larger than the effects of calcium intake on bone mass or of lead exposure on IQ in children.

One concern is that early experiences of any kind, but especially those experiences that are emotionally intense as media are for young children, will have especially lasting, potentially "hard-wiring" effects on behavior. The best data to support or refute such concerns comes from studies that follow children from the media exposure that they get in early childhood to adulthood, when aggression is most fully expressed. The first of the longitudinal studies investigating media effects, begun in Hudson, New York, in 1960, is one of the few studies capable of providing evidence, and it shows the importance of early viewing. Children's preference for viewing violent shows at age 8 proved to be a better predictor of aggressive behavior at age 18, and even 30, than adult viewing of TV violence, making the case for the disproportionate contribution of early violent TV exposure to later aggression (Huesmann & Miller, 1994).

This best-known longitudinal study on early aggression measured TV viewing preferences and aggression at age 8 and found that for boys, early preferences for violent television predicted aggression 10 years later, but early aggression did not predict later preference for violent television (Eron, Lefkowitz, Huesmann, & Walder, 1972). Their subsequent longitudinal research with a different sample of American children provided early evidence of bidirectional effects, largely for boys, in that measures of aggression also predicted later viewing of violence (Huesmann & Eron, 1986a). Data collected from this second sample 15 years later when they were between 20 and 25 years of age demonstrated that early viewing of violent television (measured between ages 6 and 9) predicted scores on a composite measure of adult aggression (including both physical and verbal aggression) for both men and women, even when childhood aggression was statistically controlled for. Relations were strongest for those adults who viewed the most violent television as children. The relationship between early viewing and later aggression could not be accounted for by such potential confounding factors as parental aggression, parental rejection, or parental TV-violence viewing (Huesmann, Moise-Titus, Podolski, & Eron, 2003).

Adolescent viewing is apparently not innocuous either. In a longitudinal study including measures of aggressive behavior and hours spent watching television, time spent viewing at age 14 was a significant predictor of boys' acts of violence against other people at age 16 or 22, even after controlling for earlier TV viewing hours, childhood neglect, low family income, low parental education, neighborhood violence, and psychiatric disorders. This was not an experiment, so other contributors cannot be ruled out, and in fact there was evidence of interactive effects. Prevalence of subsequent aggressive acts was greatest among those boys who were heavy TV viewers *and* who had a history of prior aggression, suggesting that they may be most susceptible to violent TV effects (Johnson, Cohen, Smailes, Kasen, & Brook, 2002).

Media researchers agree that children's aggressive acts are the product of multiple influences: biological predispositions, peer and family interactions, and trigger points in the immediate situation, such as frustrations, misunderstandings, insults, or the availability of weapons (e.g., C. A. Anderson et al., 2003; Bushman & Huesmann, 2001; Huesmann et al., 2003; Slater, 2003). Media are only one of the contributing forces to violence, and it is also clear that many children and teens are attracted to violent shows. The observed association between violent television and aggression is undoubtedly due not only to the effects of viewing on attitudes and behavior, but also to the preference for violent viewing by aggressive individuals (Huesmann & Eron, 1986b; Huston & Wright, 1998; Slater, 2003).

But even if parents cannot eliminate their children's aggressive tendencies, modifying their TV viewing is one way in which parents can attempt to reduce them. Two school-based intervention projects provide evidence of this. One simply promoted an initial 10-day media-free period, followed by a 7-hour per week limit on media usage. This simple restriction in media exposure reduced aggression among third and fourth graders, probably because contemporary media are sufficiently saturated with violence that more hours watching means more viewing of violence (Robinson, Wilde, Navracruz, Haydel, & Varady, 2001). A school-based series of guided discussions for third and fourth graders who were heavy viewers of violent television accomplished the same end of reducing their levels of aggression (Huesmann, Eron, Klein, Brice, & Fischer, 1983).

The risk that TV violence leads to imitative aggression is not the only concern. There is clear evidence that TV violence also desensitizes children to aggressive behavior, making behavior most adults find unacceptable somehow more expected and tolerable. Children who are frequent viewers show less physiological arousal in response to televised violence than do peers who are infrequent viewers (Cline, Croft, & Courrier, 1973). But four experiments by Drabman and Thomas in the 1970s (Drabman & Thomas, 1974a, 1974b, 1976; M. H. Thomas & Drabman, 1975) are most compelling because they studied children's tolerance for violent acts committed by other children. In these experiments, third- through fifth-grade children were brought to a laboratory and led to believe that they were responsible for monitoring the behavior of two younger children whom they could see on a TV monitor. The younger children seen on the monitor (child actors in a taped portrayal) played quietly for a while, then engaged in a series of escalating interactions that became increasingly hostile and destructive. Children who saw a violent 8-minute segment from a TV Western featuring gun battles, shootings, and fist fights delayed significantly longer in reporting the younger children's behavior to an adult than children who had not seen the TV show segment beforehand.

A recent replication obtained the same findings with updated materials, comparing the effect of a truncated version of the movie *Karate Kid* or active but nonviolent scenes from the summer Olympics (Molitor & Hirsh, 1994). The desensitization research gets much less attention than that on imitative violence, but its implications are equally disquieting: Children who have watched a lot of TV violence may enable peers' aggressive acts by simply failing to stop them.

Electronic Games

Electronic games have become pervasive in households with children much more recently than television, and only in the last several years have there been enough research studies to draw conclusions about the effects of video games. Video games clearly merit parenting experts' attention: More than two thirds of American children ages 2–18 live in homes that have them (Woodard & Gridina, 2000; Kaiser Family Foundation, 1999). Use is especially frequent among older boys at more than 7.5 hours per week (Rideout, Foehr, Roberts, & Brodie, 1999), and almost half of boys (49%) name a favorite game that is violent, versus 20% of girls (Gentile, Lynch, Linder, & Walsh, 2004). Teens who score higher on trait hostility play more violent video games and report getting into more physical fights and more arguments with their teachers, so unless they are controlled, dispositional factors may contribute to apparent video game effects (Gentile et al., 2004). C. A. Anderson and Bushman's (2001) meta-analysis addressed the effects of violent video games on aggression, drawing on 35 research reports that included 54 independent samples of participants. About half the research participants were over 18 years of age, but age of the participant made no difference in the magnitude of the observed effect. For 21 experimental studies, the average effect size, calculated as a pooled correlation, was $r = .19$, indicating that violent video games caused at least a small to medium increase in aggression. The pooled correlation for the effect was substantially larger ($r = .41$) if the target was an inanimate object than if it was a person ($r = .14$). In a separate meta-analysis of 25 studies, Sherry (2001) reported similar effects of violent video games with a nearly identical estimate of the effect ($r = .15$) for violent video games with human antagonists. In this analysis, more recent studies yielded larger effect sizes. Sherry found a positive correlation between participant age and effect size for studies whose participants ranged from age 4 to adulthood. In an up-dated meta-analysis, Anderson (2004) found that better designed video game research studies actually yielded a larger average effect size ($d = 0.26$) than did weaker studies ($d = 0.20$).

Three research projects might serve as illustrations of the design and out-comes of video game research with children. In a small study of 28 4- to 6-year-olds, Silvern and Williamson (1987) found that playing an aggres-sive video game (Space Invaders) increased children's aggression compa-rably to watching a violent TV cartoon (from the Road Runner series). Physical, verbal, and object aggression in a free-play situation nearly doubled immediately after exposure as compared with baseline levels.

Irwin and Gross (1995) split 60 second graders into two groups that played either a martial arts or a motorcycle racing game. Children who played the violent game (Double Dragon) showed more violent play with toys after exposure and more often showed verbal aggression toward a con-federate in free play. When provoked in a frustrating competitive situation, they also showed more physical aggression toward a confederate. Using a sample of 52 third and fourth graders, Kirsch (1998) found that after play-ing a violent electronic game (Mortal Kombat, toned down to prevent blood spurting after injuries and mutilation moves) children were more likely to attribute negative intent to the ambiguous actions of others (e.g., a child hit in the back with a ball), but on some measures (e.g., amount of pun-ishment recommended) there were no apparent effects. Thus, most exper-imental studies and most but not all measures showed that children immediately increased the aggression after playing violent video games (Funk, Buchman, Jenks, & Bechtoldt, 2003).

Organized Medicine Speaks Up

Providers of children's physical and mental health services have recently voiced their concerns about media violence. Six major professional soci-eties—the American Academy of Pediatrics, the American Academy of Child and Adolescent Psychiatry, the American Academy of Family Physicians, the American Medical Association, the American Psychiatric Association, and the American Psychological Association—issued a joint statement:

> At this time, well over 1,000 studies . . . point overwhelmingly to a causal connection between media violence and aggressive behavior in some children. The conclusion of the public health community, based on over 30 years of research, is that viewing entertainment violence can lead to increases in aggressive attitudes, values, and behavior, particularly in children. Its effects are measurable and long-lasting. Moreover, prolonged viewing of media violence can lead to emotional desensitization toward violence in real life. (Joint Statement, 2000, p. 1)

The American Medical Association had earlier published *A Physician's Guide to Media Violence* (Walsh, Goldman, & Brown, 1996), making essentially the same arguments and urging physicians and parents to educate children about media violence, so the organized medical community has taken a strong stand on this issue.

THE EXPERTS' POSITIONS ON MEDIA VIOLENCE

Of the experts, Spock takes the most emphatic stand against media violence, decrying parents' tendency to leave children in the care of "an electronic baby-sitter" that "tells our children that violence is an acceptable way to solve problems" (Spock & Parker, 1998, p. 647). He expresses concern about its effects on society: "For the wholesale violence that is becoming even greater, I blame television and movies first of all. We know for a fact that the average child has watched 8,000 depictions of murder before finishing elementary school. And each viewing makes the child more callous" (Spock, 1994, p. 81). He acknowledges the teaching value of some electronic media but complains that "many of today's electronic video games simply encourage a sense of perversity and brutality" (Spock, 1994, p. 75). The risk of children and teens playing such games, he notes, is "not that they will go out and commit the same kind of mayhem, but large doses of vicarious violence will condition them to some degree to accept real violence as one of the solutions to life's problems" (Spock, 1994, p. 76).

Brazelton expresses concern about media violence, noting the numerous research studies demonstrating a link: "Children today who watch television see so many shootings and murders they are likely to think of these as normal adult behavior. Study after study has shown that aggression and warlike behavior in young children is significantly more likely after a television show that portrays aggression or warfare. Limiting television is therefore important, although it will not stop aggressive behavior" (Brazelton & Sparrow, 2001, p. 452).

Dobson's primary concerns are about television as a force of moral decay. Like Spock, he cites research on children's exposure to TV violence: "According to Dr. Gerald Looney, University of Arizona, by the time the average preschool child reaches fourteen years of age, he will have witnessed 18,000 murders on TV, and countless hours of related violence" (Dobson, 1982, p. 243).

Leach, too, is concerned about media violence, suggesting that "the main classes of ill effect that researchers have identified—increased aggression, indifference toward real-life violence, fear of being a victim and a growing appetite for increasingly violent viewing—can be avoided by controlling what children watch" (Leach, 1998, p. 521). She also acknowledges that TV violence is not the sole cause of children's aggression: "The truth is probably that a violent *society* produces violent people *and* screens violent 'entertainment'" (Leach, 1989b, p. 677).

Describing the TV violence controversy, Rosemond writes that "the so-called smoking gun, the tie that could forever bind television violence to aggressive behavior in children has yet to be found" (Rosemond, 2001, p. 217). He suggests that "the relationship between television and aggressive behavior in children may have more to do with process than content, more to do with the watching than with what's being watched" (Rosemond, 2001, p. 217). Children who spend long hours per week sitting and staring at the television, he argues, have reduced opportunities for fantasy play. He mentions findings that children who engage in frequent fantasy play are less aggressive and argues that curtailed play opportunities may be responsible for the apparent effects of media: "It is distinctly and disturbingly possible that television can so isolate a child from the world (while seeming to bring the world closer) that rage or retreat are, ultimately, the child's only options" (Rosemond, 2001, p. 218).

Spock, Brazelton, Dobson, and Leach all write about the negative effects of media violence, and Spock and Leach show an awareness that media can condition children to accept violence without intervening to prevent it. Rosemond maintains that there is no strong connection between children's viewing of violent television and aggressive behaviors, although meta-analyses on experiments comparing the effects of violent and nonviolent television reveal small to medium effect sizes (Wood et al., 1991). More importantly, because experiments hold constant factors other than the amount of TV violence in the clips they show, it is possible to infer that the violence is what causes subsequent aggression. As the Joint Statement (2000) notes, the link between TV violence and aggression has been demonstrated in over 1,000 research studies, and meta-analyses have shown an unusual degree of consensus on the strength of the connection. But could there be a causal link between displacement of fantasy play by TV watching and increases in children's aggression, as Rosemond suggests? It is impossible to rule out this indirect connection on the basis of current data, but direct effects of violent television and video games are clearly evident, so content does makes a difference.

RESEARCH ON MEDIA EFFECTS ON CREATIVITY AND IMAGINATIVE PLAY

Television programs and video games are generally understood to be creative products, designed to draw children into story lines and hold their attention. But do they stifle or encourage creativity in the children who watch or play them? Six correlational studies have shown that TV viewing is negatively associated with creativity, but because such studies always carry the possibility of bidirectional and third-variable influences, they should not be considered definitive (Valkenberg, 2001). Most experiments have found that exposure to television produces less creative story completions than does radio or written text (Valkenberg, 2001), though not all experiments find a relationship (Runco & Pezdek, 1984). Television may lead to less creative completions of stories because of the greater concreteness and specificity of the visual images (Comstock & Scharrer, 1999). It is important to note that only one of the experimental studies completed to date has found that children produce *more* creative products after TV exposure and that was exposure to an educational TV program rather than general viewing.

Two major long-term studies of the link between TV viewing and creativity yield evidence that the relationship is dependent on what is measured and what children watch. When television was introduced in a town where previously there was none, there was a decrease over 2 years' time in verbal creativity (the ability to generate many alternatives) among children in grades four and seven at the start of the study (Harrison & Williams, 1986). These children had initially scored higher on verbal creativity than did children in towns that had television, but 2 years later their scores were reduced to levels similar to those children who had always had television access. However, a test of visual pattern fluency did not show a similar decline. Some analysts, however, note the lack of a correlation between viewing time and creativity for these children and suggest that any changes in creativity were likely to be transitory, the result of a "novelty bubble" that often occurs when television is introduced in a culture (Comstock & Scharrer, 1999).

One experiment (Tower, Singer, Singer, & Biggs, 1979) showed that *Mister Rogers' Neighborhood* led to immediate increases in imaginative play. In two large samples of children whose viewing preferences were assessed in early childhood and adolescence, preschool-age viewing of *Mister Rogers' Neighborhood*, a show that encourages pretending and imagination, was positively associated with creativity among adolescents ages 15–19 (C. A. Anderson et al., 2001). By contrast, viewing *Sesame Street*, with more rapid pacing and little emphasis on creativity, had no similar beneficial effect. Those preschool-age girls who were heavy viewers of general entertainment programs scored lower on creativity during adolescence. Of course, it is possible that more imaginative preschoolers would be drawn to the *Mister Rogers'* show, though these effects were obtained after controlling for parents' education, birth order, and, in some analyses, the child's Peabody Picture Vocabulary Test (C. A. Anderson et al., 2001). In brief, TV effects on creativity clearly depend on what is being watched.

Qualitative reviewers do not agree on the relationship between TV viewing and creativity. Valkenberg (2001) concluded that there was a negative link, but other reviewers have argued that there is no demonstrable relationship: "Television may offer more specific and concrete elements for use in story completions, but the medium appears to have little effect on children's ability to generate novel and original ideas" (Huston & Wright, 1998, p. 1009; see also Comstock & Scharrer, 1999).

THE EXPERTS ON MEDIA AND CREATIVITY AND IMAGINATIVE PLAY

Not all the experts address the effects of television on creativity. Spock, though, is emphatic: "Another subtle but worrisome effect TV has on its viewers is its tendency to promote passivity and a lack of creativity. . . . The viewer becomes a passive receptacle for whatever images the TV chooses to display. Watching TV is incompatible with creativity" (Spock & Parker, 1998, p. 649). Brazelton (1992) worries that too much television just does not leave enough time for creative activity: "It cuts down on the time a child might devote to exploring his own fantasies. . . . Television forces a child into a kind of overwhelmed passivity" (p. 325). He accuses television of "numbing the child's own imaginative adventures" (Brazelton, 1992, p. 325). Neither Dobson nor Leach address any effects of media on creativity in their books. Rosemond indicts television for a multitude of sins, reducing creativity among them: "Television-watching inhibits the development of initiative, curiosity, resourcefulness, creativity, motivation, imagination" (Rosemond, 2001b, p. 202). He concludes that "television-watching is a deprivational experience for young children. It deprives them of the opportunity to discover and take delight in developing their natural potential for giftedness. And the sad fact is, that once that 'window of opportunity' closes, it can never again be fully opened" (Rosemond, 2001b, p. 203).

This is one topic on which the experts who offer their advice render judgments that are stronger than research would support.

RESEARCH ON MEDIA USE AND ACADEMIC ACHIEVEMENT

General Television Viewing

The overarching generalization that emerges from research on television's apparent effects on academic achievement is that it depends on the content that is being watched (Huston & Wright, 1998). More entertainment TV viewing is related to less social interaction, less reading, and fewer educational activities, but no such relationship is obtained for educational TV viewing (Huston, Wright, Marquis, & Green, 1999). Those children who watch more educational television get higher school grades, place more value on achievement, and read more books (C. A. Anderson et al., 2001). At the same time, it is difficult to ignore the competing conclusion that children are selecting the type of shows that they watch largely because of their interests, and those children who like to watch educational programming and watch it frequently are likely to have a better aptitude for school-based learning experiences. And school curricula and educational media use undoubtedly reinforce each other, so that television provides opportunities for enhancement of school-based content, and school curricula, because they are more comprehensive than television, consolidate themes and examples provided by educational programming.

Clearly, time spent viewing is, in itself, insufficient to predict the effects of television on academic performance. Overall, the relationship between the time spent viewing television and school performance is surprisingly modest, a median correlation of $r = -.06$ (Williams, Haertel, Walberg, & Haertel, 1982). A negative association between hours spent watching and school achievement may occur, however, among those children who are heavier viewers. Comstock and Scharrer (1999) reported data from 281,907 California sixth graders on the relationship between television and reading achievement in middle and upper grades and found an overall negative relationship that was more marked when children were viewing 3–4 or more hours per day. What children watch may also be a factor: Heavy viewers report viewing more entertainment programs and light viewers report viewing more educational programming (Fetler, 1984).

When television is introduced into a culture, the "novelty bubble" may lead to negative effects on new readers, probably because they are so attracted to the new medium that reading time diminishes (Corteen & Williams, 1986; Hornik, 1978). In studies of societies where television is well entrenched as a medium, in which the researchers use appropriate controls for individual and family characteristics, there is little or no relation between TV viewing and reading or math achievement (C. A. Anderson et al., 2001). In a 3-year longitudinal study of three cohorts of elementary school children in grades 2, 3, and 6 at the start of the study, time spent viewing television did not predict reading ability or reading time (Ritchie, Price, & Roberts, 1987).

Any link between television and school performance is dependent on both what children watch and their gender. In a comprehensive longitudinal study of TV effects on academic performance (C. A. Anderson et al., 2001), there was a positive relationship between preschool viewing of educational television and adolescents' grades in English, science, and math in two large samples, one from the east coast and one from the midwest. On the other hand, there was a negative relationship between early entertainment viewing and grades on these subjects. These associations remained after taking into account family background, other categories of television that preschool-age children watched, and their current media use as adolescents (C. A. Anderson et al., 2001). The relationships were in the same directions for both genders, but the positive effects of educational television were much stronger for boys and the negative effects of entertainment television were much stronger for girls. The authors argue that effect size is maximized when the direction of early viewing runs counter to the typical developmental course, as it is when boys are heavy viewers of educational programming and girls are heavy viewers of entertainment programming. Interpreting these findings, Bickham, Wright, and Huston (2001) suggest that educational programs may provide boys entering school with much-needed self-control and desire to learn, whereas girls, who typically do better on self-control, inhibition of impulses, and following directions, do not get the same benefits. In their review of TV effects, Huston and Wright (1998) conclude that the empirical case for overall negative effects of television on school achievement is a weak one.

One final question is whether watching large amounts of television could cause learning disabilities or attention problems that could contribute to school achievement. One study that has been done on this question finds that children who are learning disabled have problems with television's time-leap mode of presentation that are not related to how much they watch, but that nonlearning-disabled children show better understanding the more they watch (Abelman, 1995). Recently, an analysis of longitudinal data demonstrated a connection between hours of television watched at ages 1 and 3 and parents' reports of higher levels of attention problems at age 7 (the odds ratio was 1.09 for the increased risk of attentional problems; Christakis, Zimmerman, DiGiuseppe, & McCarty, 2004), even after controlling for maternal depression, maternal education, cognitive stimulation in the home, parents' emotional support, and other child and family factors. The authors note that causal inferences cannot be drawn because it is a correlational study, and the research was controversial because of its criterion for attentional problems and other measurement issues (Bertholf & Goodison, 2004; Mehmet-Radji, 2004), so this connection deserves further study.

Sesame Street

Among the educational TV programs that might demonstrate beneficial effects of television, *Sesame Street* is arguably the most important. Among 2- to 4-year-olds sampled in the early 1990s, 80% of their educational TV exposure was to *Sesame Street* (Bickham et al., 2001). Just as it has been the most widely acclaimed and copied internationally, it has also attracted the most criticism, particularly for its rapidly paced magazine format.

Sesame Street was designed to provide children with skills relevant to early school success—notably, knowledge of the alphabet and numbers, sorting and classification skills, knowledge of relational terms, and form recognition—and extensive research demonstrates that it is successful. In an early experiment testing its effectiveness, an ethnically diverse sample of nearly 1,000 3- to 5-year-old children, largely from disadvantaged backgrounds, were randomly assigned to conditions in which they were either encouraged or not encouraged to watch *Sesame Street* during a 26-week period (Ball & Bogatz, 1970). Afterward, teachers rated their school preparedness (e.g., verbal readiness, quantitative readiness, attitudes toward school, relationships with peers), without knowing which children had been *Sesame Street* viewers. Frequent viewers were rated by their teachers as better prepared for school than were their non- or low-viewing peers (Ball & Bogatz, 1970). Before and after comparisons demonstrated that 3-year-olds gained the most, that those children who watched the most gained the most, and that the greatest gains occurred for letter recognition, the skill that *Sesame Street* had emphasized. Critics pointed out that much of the gain might be due to parental "encouragement" leading to more coviewing and discussion of content (Cook et al., 1975), but even in the critics' reanalysis controlling for other potential contributing factors, the academic enhancements that resulted from viewing *Sesame Street* remained significant (Fisch, Truglio, & Cole, 1999). Longitudinal research has demonstrated that *Sesame Street* has apparently beneficial effects on children's vocabulary growth, especially among 3- to 5-year-olds, even after controlling for parent education, older siblings, and parents' positive attitudes toward television (Rice, Huston, Truglio, & Wright, 1990).

Those first and second graders who watched *Sesame Street* as preschoolers "were more likely to be reading storybooks on their own and less likely to be receiving special help in school for reading problems" (Zill, 2001, p. 124). These data from the parents of about 10,000 children nationwide showed that preschool-age children who viewed *Sesame Street* were more likely to be able to count to 20 and recognize letters of the alphabet, even after the effects of other contributing factors (e.g., parental reading, family income, preschool attendance, parental education) were statistically controlled (Zill, 2001). The differences between viewers and nonviewers are not large (7%), however, and because this was a cross-sectional survey other factors cannot be ruled out.

Sesame Street has been controversial because of its rapid pacing. However, when fast- and slow-paced program segments were systematically compared, the pacing of segments was found to have no effects on perseverance, impulsivity, or sustained play afterward (D. R. Anderson, Levin, & Lorch, 1977).

THE EXPERTS' POSITIONS ON MEDIA AND ACADEMIC SKILLS

Despite his negative views on television, Spock acknowledges its educational potential: "There is no question that some programs, usually on the public broadcasting stations, provide wonderful learning experiences for children. . . . Unfortunately these shows are in the minority" (Spock & Parker, 1998, pp. 648–649). Dobson has written approvingly about particular shows, and Leach appreciates the learning potential of television in general: "The very qualities which make it seductive also make it a superb medium for education in its very widest sense" (Leach, 1998, pp. 520–521). Consistent with his focus on infancy and early childhood, Brazelton has written little in his advice manuals about the educational effects of television and other media.

Rosemond acknowledges a role for television in the education of older children: "Once literacy has been fairly well-established, I see no problem with letting a child watch programs which represent life in a realistic manner and which broaden the child's understanding of the world" (Rosemond, 2001b, p. 210). Concerning the general effects of television, though, he argues that it impairs children's learning and contributes to what he believes is a decline in the American educational system (Rosemond, 1993; Rosemond, 2001, p. 206). Parents are probably going to turn off shows with sexual or violent themes, he writes, but the problem is not with program content but with the process of watching television. Rosemond argues that television impairs sequential thinking

> because the action on a television set shifts constantly and capriciously backward, forward, and laterally in time (not to mention from subject matter to subject matter), television fails to promote logical, sequential thinking, which is essential to an understanding of cause-and-effect relationships. This causes difficulties in both following directions and anticipating consequences. Once again, these failings are the same regardless of whether the child is watching *Sesame Street*, an adult movie on late-night cable, or a video rental. (Rosemond, 2001, p. 203)

Because of the rapid scene shifts, "television-watching interferes significantly with the development of the attention span" (Rosemond, 2001b, p. 202).

Rosemond links the great increase in television viewing to national declines in literacy and achievement test scores and a "nearly epidemic" increase in learning disabilities over the last 45 years (Rosemond, 2001b, p. 204). He also ties the perceptual, social, and logical problems of learning disabled children to television viewing: "In short, an almost perfect parallel exists between the list of competency skills that television fails to exercise and the symptoms characteristic of a population of learning-disabled children" (Rosemond, 2001b, p. 205). He acknowledges that television is not the sole cause of this epidemic of ignorance and learning disabilities but nonetheless declares that "it would be naïve to ignore the obvious connection between the deficiencies inherent to the *process* of watching television and the deficiencies in competency skills that characterize not only the learning-disabled child, but seemingly this entire generation of television-overdosed children" (Rosemond, 2001b, p. 206). From his perspective, television clearly is damaging, whatever the content being shown. Even educational television is damaging, and Rosemond has particularly harsh words for what he believes are the pretensions of such programs as *Sesame Street*: "The notion that preschool children can learn the alphabet, numerals, and even a basic reading vocabulary from *Sesame Street* is nothing more than hype, brought to you by the same folks who tell us that a certain toothpaste will make us more appealing to persons of the opposite sex" (Rosemond, 2001b, p. 211).

COMPARING THE EXPERTS WITH RESEARCH ON TELEVISION AND ACADEMIC ACHIEVEMENT

There is evidence that time spent watching television is negatively related to academic achievement when children are watching a lot of television, more than 3–4 hours per day. Children who watch educational programming during the preschool years are likely to do better in school, but it is also likely to be the case that those children who choose to watch educational shows will have greater tolerance and perhaps greater aptitude for all sorts of educational experiences (C. A. Anderson et al., 2001) and come from more stimulating home environments (Huston et al., 1999). The largest longitudinal study that has examined the categories of programs that young children watch provides evidence that television as a medium is not the problem, and that its effects may be moderated by gender. Early viewing of educational television was linked to good school performance in adolescence, particularly for boys, whereas girls who were heavy viewers of violent television as preschoolers had lower grades in adolescence (C. A.

Anderson et al., 2001). In their discussions of TV effects, Spock, Leach, Dobson, and Rosemond rightly acknowledge the educational potential of television, which seems to have positive effects on children of both sexes.

Rosemond's strong statements on the negative effects of TV watching as a process, his argument that it may shorten attention span, and his implication that it produces learning disabilities among young viewers are not supported by a large number of research studies on these topics. For some assertions—for example, his indictment of *Sesame Street*—there is strong empirical evidence against his claims, both from field experiments and longitudinal studies of children's naturally occurring TV preferences. It is clear that children who watch *Sesame Street* do better academically. The research finding that children who watch 3–4 hours or more a day of television are lower in achievement provides limited support for his position that TV watching is likely to cause academic problems, and many American children do watch that much. It may well be that at high viewing levels, children watch so much television that there is little time for homework. And children who are heavy viewers watch relatively more entertainment television (Fetler, 1984), possibly because they are poorer readers. If the problem with television is in its attention-shortening process, as Rosemond asserts, there should be no relationship between what children watch and their academic outcomes, and there is substantial evidence that content does matter.

ELECTRONIC MEDIA AND PREMATURE SEXUAL ACTIVITY

Research on Media and Teen Promiscuity, Pregnancy, and Sexually Transmitted Diseases

Direct and indirect references to sexual acts have become more prevalent and explicit in broadcast television over the past 20-plus years (Farrar et al., 2003; Huston & Wright, 1998). In one of the most extensive research projects conducted to date of sexual content on television, an analysis of more than 1,100 shows (newscasts, sports, and children's shows were excluded), 64% of shows that were surveyed included sexual content. The percentage rose to 83% among the top 20 shows among teens. Most instances involved only talking about sex, but roughly one in three (32%) included sexual behaviors (Kaiser Family Foundation, 2002).

Only 9% of the reviewed shows included some sexual content involving teens, and 9% of all characters involved in sexual intercourse were teens, so there is far more talk about sex than there are depictions of sexual behavior among teens (Kaiser Family Foundation, 2001b). Talk is not innocent, however. Children who are interested in sexual topics will be old enough to draw inferences from scenes in which intercourse off-camera is strongly implied (Kunkel et al., 1999), an interpretation supported by focus group research with children as young as 8 (Kaiser Family Foundation, 1996). Nearly three quarters (72%) of a nationally representative survey sample of 505 teens reported that sexual behaviors on television influence the sexual behaviors of teens their age "somewhat" or "a lot," though less than one quarter thought it influenced their own sexual behavior (Kaiser Family Foundation, 2002). There is also far more discussion of sexual risks and responsibilities when teens are depicted talking about or engaging in sexual intercourse than is the case for adult characters. However, positive influences of these discussions, much like negative influences, have been difficult to demonstrate (Kaiser Family Foundation, 2001b).

There are apparently only a few published studies on the link between TV sexual content and sexual behavior in early and midadolescence, and most document a connection without clarifying the causal role of television. One three-wave longitudinal study of junior high students reported a positive correlation between the proportion of TV viewing with sexual content and teens' sexually permissive attitudes and reported intercourse, although total viewing time was not related to these outcomes (Brown & Newcomer, 1991). This relationship was still significant after researchers statistically controlled for past sexual experience not involving intercourse and for friends' perceived influence. A recent 1-year longitudinal study produced similar findings for sexual initiation (R. L. Collins et al., 2004). Because these studies are correlational, the possibility cannot be ruled out that teenagers who are already sexually interested are selecting TV programs with sexual content, although both studies attempted to control for self-selection. An additional possibility is that other unmeasured variables, such as social desirability in reporting, might be responsible for the associations (Malamuth & Impett, 2001).

Another longitudinal study, however, found no relation between viewing television in general or sexual content in particular and adolescents' initiation of sexual activity (J. L. Peterson, Moore, & Furstenberg, 1991). What influenced sexual initiation in this research was parents' discussion of TV content. They found that girls who less often discussed television with their parents had nearly twice the sexual experience rate of those who discussed it more often. Furthermore, girls who did not watch television with their parents were more than three times more likely to be sexually experienced (Peterson et al., 1991). For boys there was a strong positive correlation between viewing time and sexual experience but only among those who viewed television apart from their parents. But again these are associations, so reciprocal influences and unmeasured variables cannot be ruled out. The lack of coviewing may imply that parents are less engaged with their children and that engagement, family cohesiveness, and parental monitoring have protective effects for several adolescent risk behaviors (see chapter 6).

There is preliminary experimental evidence that sexual content strengthens permissive attitudes. Bryant and Rockwell (1994) randomly assigned 13- to 14-year-old boys and girls to conditions that viewed either 15 hours of TV programming depicting sexual relationships among unmarried partners, 15 hours depicting nonsexual relationships among adults, or a comparison condition in which participants read books or magazines. They were then asked to judge the morality of TV segments depicting mild to severe sexual violations (infidelity was a severe violation). Teen participants were asked how bad they judged the transgression to be. Those who had previously watched TV programs depicting sex between unmarried partners rated the sexual indiscretions or improprieties in the vignettes to be less severe transgressions than did participants who had watched nonsexual content or even depictions of married sex. But if the teen's family had an open communication style, the effects of exposure to sexual TV programming were reduced. Importantly, the researchers also included outcome measures assessing moral judgments of nonsexual, criminal, and antisocial behaviors, and the effects were found only for sexual acts. Since significance levels for their findings were not reported, however, it is unclear whether future research would produce the same results; a similar experiment found no effect of exposure to sexual scenes on teens' beliefs (B. S. Greenberg, Linsangan, & Soderman, 1993).

Experts' Positions on Sex in Television

Spock repeatedly voices concerns about the sexual content of media, warning parents that television tells children that "sex is especially exciting when it occurs without love and, besides, there are no real negative consequences anyway" (Spock & Parker, 1998, p. 647). His advocacy book goes even further: "Sexuality is being despiritualized, coarsened and brutalized. Teen promiscuity, teen pregnancy and venereal diseases are being fostered by television and movies because lawmakers are afraid of accusations of censorship" (Spock, 1994, p. 158).

Brazelton, whose books focus largely on parenting young children, mentions imitation as a problem: "If the program contains sexually explicit language, children will test it out afterward" (Brazelton, 1992, p. 411). Dobson's writing is concerned with social decay. He argues that television programming loaded with sexual content plays a role in the decline of the family and Christian morality: "Each program director is compelled to include all the avant-garde ideas—go a little farther—use a little more profanity—discuss the undiscussable—assault the public concept of good taste and decency. In so doing, they are hacking away at the foundations of the family and all that represents the Christian ethic" (Dobson, 1982, p. 243). He argues that it is impossible to shield teens from permissive attitudes: "The sexual urge is stronger during adolescence than in any other period of life. . . . Television brings every aspect of sexual gratification into the sanctuary of one's living room, and the details of immorality and perversion are readily available in the theater or from the neighborhood video store" (Dobson, 1992, p. 216). Dobson uses the easy availability of media sexual portrayals to make a case for parents providing sexuality education.

Leach does not address the negative effects of media sexuality in her parenting manual for older children. Rosemond's concern is that TV exposure will preempt the child's moral development: "By watching television, today's child is able to learn how to engage in sex prior to developing a value system that will properly govern sexual behavior" (Rosemond, 1994b, p. 3E).

Comparing the authors' positions with research findings is problematic. Spock provides the only testable assertions, that sexuality on television contributes to promiscuity, pregnancy, and sexually transmitted diseases. Unfortunately, because of the correlational nature of most of the research and the incomplete description and design problems of experiments on this topic, there are insufficient data to conclude whether Spock is correct. None of the research provides evidence that TV sexuality raises young people's moral standards. However, given the bias against the publication of null effects, there may be many studies investigating a possible link tucked in researchers' file drawers because no reliable connection could be demonstrated.

WHAT SHOULD PARENTS DO ABOUT CHILDREN'S MEDIA VIEWING?

Research on Parents' TV Management

Parents are actually present only 25% of the time when children are watching child audience programs (St. Peters, Fitch, Huston, Wright, & Eakins, 1991). When parents and children watch television together, they are more likely to watch adult programs than children's programs (St. Peters et al., 1991). Coviewing is actually more likely to happen with older children whose viewing preferences are more similar to those of adults (Dorr, Kovaric, & Doubleday, 1989). However, as Huston and Wright (1998) note, "There is little evidence that naturally occurring coviewing has strong beneficial effects" (p. 1041).

It is not that coviewing could not help, if it were done right. Adult interpretative comments improve comprehension of television's social content (W. A. Collins, Sobol, & Westby, 1981; Watkins, Calvert, Huston-Stein, & Wright, 1980). Children whose parents reported that they made negative comments about violent TV shows scored significantly lower on generalized aggression and marginally lower when they were tested for aggression after watching a cartoon with humorous violence (Nathanson, 1999). Why, then, does coviewing not lead to beneficial effects for children? Apparently because there is very little discussion of TV program content between parents and their children while they watch together (Mohr, 1979). Only rarely do parents explain content, discuss values, or interpret programs (Comstock, 1991; Desmond, Singer, & Singer, 1990; Messaris & Sarett, 1981).

In general, parents have few restrictive rules about television viewing (Dorr, Rabin, & Irlen, 2002). In a recent national survey of 8- to 18-year-olds, about half the respondents reported that their families have no rules about TV watching and only 20% reported that rules are enforced most of the time. The 20% of children in families with consistently enforced TV rules watched 2 hours less television per day than did other children (Rideout, Roberts, & Foehr, 2005). In a study of midwestern families with preschool-age children, if parents regulated television viewing, children watched less child entertainment programming, but not less child educational programming, and less television overall (St. Peters et al., 1991). All measures in this study were based on parents' reports, though viewing diaries were completed on occasions separate from questions about parents' TV practices. Not surprisingly, parents surveyed in pediatric clinics report higher frequencies of coviewing and more restriction of violent and sexual

TV content (Cheng et al., 2004). Nathanson (1999) found that children whose parents restricted viewing of violent television scored lower on measures of generalized and TV-induced aggression. However, viewing restrictions accounted for no more than 3% of the variability in aggression after controlling for the child's age, gender, violent TV viewing, and parental education.

More recently, after the advent of recent TV ratings and V-chips, about half (56%) of all parents reported that they had used the TV rating system to control the TV content that their children watched (Kaiser Family Foundation, 2001a). According to recent large phone surveys, few parents have actually used V-chip technology to reduce the amount of objectionable television their children watched: in the most recent research, only 15% of parents reported having done so (Rideout, 2004); in another study, 21% of parents reported using the V-chip (Woodard & Gridina, 2000).

In most studies, parents' TV restrictions have been associated with desired viewing choices: watching less TV overall, watching better programs, and active viewing selection (J.D. Brown, Childers, & Bauman, 1990; Desmond et al., 1990; St. Peters et al., 1991; Stranger, 1997). However, many children watch forbidden programs anyway, especially if they think that their parents are too controlling (Krcmar, 1996). A recent meta-analysis on the effects of ratings on children's and teen's attraction to media demonstrated that for children over age 8, especially boys, ratings signaling objectionable content may actually be somewhat of an enticement to watch the program (Bushman & Cantor, 2003).

Concerning the use of electronic media, the AAP recommends that its member pediatricians advise parents to view television selectively themselves and coview programs with their children, teaching them critical viewing skills while watching. The AAP also encourages parents to emphasize activities that can serve as alternatives to television. Parents are advised not to permit televisions in children's bedrooms and to discourage TV watching by children under the age of 2 (AAP Committee on Public Education, 2001). The AAP has also recommended several times in recent years that children's and adolescents' media time be limited to 1 to 2 hours of quality programming daily (Hogan, 2001).

Guidelines for parents published by television researchers are similar: (a) Parents should model the viewing behavior they hope to see in their children; (b) they should emphasize other activities; and (c) they should inculcate their own values, beliefs and attitudes in their children rather than let media socialize them by default (Dorr et al., 2002). Jordan (2004) recommends that parents maintain awareness of what and how much their children are watching and help them find educational programs. On the basis of their research on fear-inducing effects of media, Cantor and Mares (2001) recommend limited viewing and argue that parents should be especially concerned about viewing before bedtime. They further caution that parents should not allow children to have a television in their bedroom, and should use the V-chip that has been built into recent model televisions.

Experts' Positions on Managing Television and Other Media

Spock is one of three experts to recommend no television for young children, describing the prohibition as a "logical solution" for parents of young children, though he recognizes that "this solution is far too extreme for most of you" (Spock & Parker, 1998, p. 649). For parents who choose not to give up television, he advocates restricting viewing to shows and videos that parents approve. He recommends viewing with children to interpret media content. "The most important thing you can do as a parent is to help your children understand and make proper sense of what they see, read, and hear in the media" (Spock & Parker, 1998, p. 648). For shows with sexual content, parents should emphasize how easy sexuality is a distortion of what happens in real life. He also advocates prohibiting the viewing of violence: "Parents should flatly forbid their children to watch violent programs" (Spock & Parker, 1998, p. 650). Spock recommends that parents use the V-chip to limit access to violent shows. Total viewing time should be limited to 1 to 2 hours after the child's homework and chores are completed (Spock & Parker, 1998, p. 649). Spock advocates reading as a substitute activity that promotes imagination (Spock & Parker, 1998, pp. 466–467).

Brazelton's advice to parents on dealing with media focuses on its physiological and attentional demands and ability to induce emotional arousal, particularly fearfulness in young children. Toddlers should not watch for more than a 30-minute period (Brazelton, 1992, p. 198) and older children not more than 1 hour a day and not more than 2 hours on weekends. "Half of this viewing time should be 'family time' in which the adult members watch too. After it is over, there is an opportunity to exchange ideas and to discuss the issues" (Brazelton, 1992, pp. 412–413). Children can be allowed to help choose the program they will watch (Brazelton, 1992, pp. 412–413). And he reminds parents that children will imitate their viewing habits, so alternative family activities are called for: "In families where parents are enthusiastically involved with their children, in cooking, playing games, exploring the outdoors, or relaxing and chatting, the lure of the screen will be reduced" (Brazelton 1992, p. 413).

Dobson recommends monitoring the quality of the shows that children watch, restricting the quantity, and including the children in the decision making. On time restrictions, he draws from his own parenting days, and recounts that when they were in elementary school, his children could watch one half-hour on weekday afternoons and 1 hour Saturday mornings. In the same book, he suggests a more elaborate regulation system, which parallels his system for regulating chores and homework. Parents should sit down with children and select from a posted list of approved shows. Then TV programs are a currency to be controlled:

> Either buy or make a roll of tickets. Issue each child ten tickets per week, and let him use them to "buy" the privilege of watching the programs on the approved list. When his tickets are gone, then his television viewing is over for that week. This teaches them to choose carefully what he most wants to spend his time on. . . . This system can be modified to fit individual home situations or circumstances. . . . You might also give extra tickets as rewards for achievement or some other laudable behavior. (Dobson, 1982, p. 245)

Parents are urged to watch television with their children to help them understand what they are experiencing (Dobson, 1982, p. 244).

Leach remarks on the mismatch between fast-paced media presentations and the cognitive limitations of toddlers and very young children. Like Brazelton, Leach emphasizes a balance between media use and other activities, but she also asks "the usually unasked question. . . . What would your child be doing if she were not watching TV? If the honest answer is 'Squabbling with her sister,' or 'Moping around waiting for me to come home from work,' it's difficult to see how viewing is wasting her time, or to avoid seeing that it's saving your sanity" (Leach, 1998, p. 521). She recommends controlling what children watch and viewing television with children to help them recognize media stereotypes and discern which content is real and which is fictional (Leach, 1998, p. 521). She recognizes the demands of selective watching with adult coviewing: "If you know that highly selective and companionable television viewing is an ideal that's unachievable in your household, your child may be better off watching (and rewatching) carefully selected videos on her own than unselected TV programs" (Leach, 1998, p. 522). She recommends against rationing viewing time: "Rigid rationing of viewing-time . . . only increases the likelihood of children seeing television as a constant good of which they cannot get enough. Furthermore, a 'ration' contradicts the central idea of selective viewing: that the family watches television when, but only when, there is a program people genuinely want to see" (Leach, 1989b, pp. 677–678).

Rosemond suggests prohibiting television for young children and, unlike Spock, does not present a more moderate "fall-back" position in his parenting manuals: "First of all, I don't believe there's any justification for letting a preschool child watch any television at all. In fact, I think it makes sense to keep a child completely away from television until he or she has learned to read, reads fairly well, and enjoys reading. For most children, that point will be reached between third and fifth grades" (Rosemond, 2001b, p. 210). For children who can read well, time spent viewing should be limited to no more than 5 hours of television a week (Rosemond, 2001, p. 210). In response to a question about a child's problematic video game usage, Rosemond writes, "you can limit his game time to, for instance, thirty minutes a day on nonschool days only. Or better yet, you can tell him, 'We made a mistake,' and take it away completely. Perhaps he'd agree to let you sell it and replace it with something of equal dollar value" (Rosemond, 2001b, p. 223).

As for parents' viewing with their children and interpreting what is being watched, Rosemond is dismissive: "The terms *watch* and *together* are also incompatible. You don't watch television together. You watch alone. Regardless of how many people are in the same room watching the same television, each has retired into a solitary audiovisual tunnel" (Rosemond, 2001b, p. 208).

THE EXPERTS ON MEDIA: THE LIMITS OF ADVICE

All the authors are largely negative about television, regardless of their political ideology, and their attitudes are largely shared by American parents (Komaya & Bowyer, 2000). Yet they all recognize television's mesmerizing attractiveness for young children and understand the inevitability of parents coming to terms with their children's media use.

They all mention negative effects of media violence on children, and extensive research bears out its short-term and long-term effects on aggression. On creativity, the experts raise concerns that are only weakly supported by research: *What* children watch turns out to be more important than the fact *that* they watch. For example, watching *Mister Rogers' Neighborhood* was positively associated with both immediate and later creativity, but watching lots of general entertainment television was negatively associated with later creativity among girls. Many parents report concerns about television's negative effects on school achievement, but most of the experts correctly do not assert that there is a strong link between amount of television viewed and poor school performance. The evidence suggests, however, that parents whose children watch television more than 3 hours a day should be concerned about its effect on school performance. Rosemond's contention that the *process* (and not the content) of TV viewing is harmful for preliterate children is overwhelmed by research findings (e.g., C. A. Anderson et al., 2001) that viewing some types of television (i.e., that with educational content) is reliably associated with better educational outcomes. His statement that television impairs attention has received limited support in one recently published study, but his suggestion that television causes learning disabilities remains unsupported by data.

On one point, two authors contradict each other, with Dobson recommending a system in which TV allotment is limited with extra shows for good behavior, much as many parents limit candy or snacks with extras for holidays, whereas Leach argues that TV restrictions may actually increase children's attraction to the medium. In each case, the advice reflects other elements of the author's perspective. Dobson frequently relies on behavior modification with its emphasis on reinforcement for good behavior. Leach's advice fits easily with her emphasis on coviewing—where restriction would be social exclusion as well. And each has a point. Dobson's approach may work well with younger children, whose parents are less likely to watch shows with them, while restrictions may be difficult to enforce or produce a negative reaction from older children when parents are watching a show that their children want to watch as well.

There is at least one controversy about media that the authors have left largely unaddressed in their advice to parents. They are largely silent on the topic of gender stereotyping in media portrayals, which often exaggerate gender differences to the detriment of body images in both sexes (Hofschire & Greenberg, 2002; Polce-Lynch, Myers, Kliewer, & Kilmartin, 2001).

On media usage there is a greater gap than on other parenting topics, or perhaps one that is better documented, between what the authors recommend and what parents actually do. The experts suggest coviewing. It rarely happens for children's shows. The authors recommend mediation, and apparently that rarely happens either. The authors recommend no more than 1 or 2 hours of viewing per day, and average American children watch more than 3 (Nielsen Media Research, 1998; Rideout, Roberts, & Foehr, 2005), with additional time devoted to video and computer games. The authors recommend selective viewing, and just over half the parents report that they use the TV rating system to select what their children watch. Many parents may believe that children should make their own media choices. The substantial proportion of parents who own V-chips but do not use them may have these beliefs, or they may simply never have activated the V-chip because they do not realize their television has V-chip capability. There is preliminary evidence, though, that when parents do exert control by restricting viewing, the quantity of viewing goes down and the quality of viewing goes up.

Some of the gap between advice and parents' actual practice may be due to the genuine difficulty of sharing children's TV time and regulating it when parents are pulled in several different directions by competing responsibilities. In addition, about half of American children have televisions in their bedrooms (Rideout et al., 1999), so parents are often unaware of what children are watching on television or playing on their electronic game systems. It is not that parents cannot say no but that they often do not know what their children are watching because children's media access is so direct. Those who set rules have to say no very often because so much media content is not appropriate for children.

On this topic there is agreement among most of the authors and the researchers: Media violence has bad effects, educational television has good effects, and selective viewing of a limited number of shows is better for children. Despite this consensus, data from large national surveys make it clear that children's media choices are often underregulated by parents. The fact remains that neither the researchers' and clinicians' warnings nor the experts' advice has had discernible effects on parent practice. Having grown up by the glow of the television set themselves, contemporary parents may see little harm in their children's media immersion. On this topic though, what parents do does make a difference, and better media choices for their children can enrich the time spent watching and help promote a more active, engaged family life.

CHAPTER 6
ADOLESCENCE

ADVISING PARENTS OF TEENAGERS offers parenting experts a new set of challenges. If parents' interactions with children involve negotiating a shifting balance of controlling and letting go, by the time that sons and daughters are in their adolescent years, the balance has clearly shifted toward parents relinquishing some control. During the elementary school years, parents may be acquainted with their child's friends, but during adolescence, their children enter a wider social world, much of which may be unknown to parents. Teens enter increasingly larger middle and high school environments, pursue extracurricular activities away from school, and join the work world in entry-level jobs. Learning to drive allows easier contact with friends and romantic partners away from the supervision of parents. And increasingly their friends and partners are unknown or little known by their parents, and the peer cultures that develop often include norms about sexual behavior of which parents may or may not approve.

ADOLESCENT SEXUALITY

Among the issues of adolescence, the parenting experts write the most extensively about sexuality education. One reason may be that the parenting experts have built their professional careers and established their public personae as advocates for better family life. Sexually active teenagers run the risks of sexually transmitted diseases and pregnancies that end either in abortions or in premature parenthood. Such outcomes are a clear threat to the better family life that the experts are trying to bring about.

Research on Parenting and Adolescent Sexual Initiation, Contraceptive Behavior, and Pregnancy

Research on adolescents' developing sexuality differs markedly from research on less confidential topics and that conducted with young children. Outcome measures such as sexual intercourse and pregnancy obviously do not lend themselves to experimental procedures, so causal inferences are more difficult to establish. Information about adolescents' sexual feelings and sexual behaviors is much more likely to obtained by administering surveys to hundreds, sometimes thousands, of teens. Surveys are most frequently used because they are perceived to safeguard the confidentiality and therefore the honesty of the responses. The National Longitudinal Study of Adolescent Health (Add Health) study of 20,745 students in grades 7 through 12 is an outstanding recent example of research that provides a profile of teen attitudes, self-reported behaviors, and family relationships across years, while permitting statistical controls for numerous complicating variables (e.g., family income, parental education) that contribute to adolescents' sexual behaviors (cf. Davis & Friel, 2001). The Add Health project is one of the few longitudinal studies that provides data that can be used to tease apart causal relationships.

Much of the research on adolescent sexuality is relatively recent, and review articles summarizing parents' interactions or educational interventions with their teens on sexuality issues (e.g., Bennett & Assefi, 2005; Kirby, 2002; B. C. Miller, 2002; B. C. Miller, Benson, & Galbraith, 2001) are largely limited to tallies of studies showing positive effects, no effects, or, rarely, negative effects, because problems with incomplete reporting of data often preclude estimates of effect sizes. Some moderating variables, such as race and gender, have been identified in longitudinal research—for example, 40% of teen girls reported getting sexual information from a parent, whereas only 25% of teen boys did (Kaiser Family Foundation, 1998)—but explorations of potential mediators have begun only recently. Four aspects of relationships between parents and adolescents have been investigated as associates of sexual behavior in adolescence: support and cohesiveness, parental supervision and monitoring, the extent of communication on sexuality-related topics, and parents' values concerning adolescent sexual activity (B. C. Miller et al., 2001).

FAMILY SUPPORT AND COHESION. Parents' cohesive and supportive relationships with their teenage children have frequently been associated with longer delays in sexual initiation (Davis & Friel, 2001; B. C. Miller et. al.,

2001), though the relationship is frequently qualified by other factors. An initial report of 1-year longitudinal data from the Add Health study, drawn from a stratified random sample of 134 high schools and their feeder middle schools, found that mothers' satisfaction with the parent–teen relationship was an important factor in 14–15 year-old daughters' first reported sexual intercourse (reducing the odds ratio nearly in half to .56) but had no predictive power for sons (McNeely et al., 2002). The authors speculated that boys might be less influenced by maternal communications of values. They also described a residual form of the double standard in which mothers were equally opposed to their sons and daughters having sex, but were more likely to discuss sexual risks with their daughters and more likely to recommend specific methods of birth control to their sons.

Among teens who are sexually active, those who have closer relationships with their parents are more likely to use contraceptives consistently and have fewer sexual partners, which reduces the risk of sexually transmitted diseases (B. C. Miller, 2002; B. C. Miller et al., 2001). But it is also clear from the large Add Health study that adolescents' first occurrences of sexual intercourse predict changes in the adolescent–parent relationship, notably an increase in problem-focused interactions and a decline in the closeness of relationship with parents (Ream & Savin-Williams, 2005).

Several studies have found that when there is better parent–teen support and cohesiveness, teens have better impulse control, less positive attitudes toward having intercourse, and more involvement in academic and prosocial activities, all of which are associated with delayed sexual initiation among teens (B. C. Miller et al., 2001). When there is low parental support and cohesiveness, there is more substance use, especially for boys; more depression, especially among girls; and more association with sexually active peers, all of which are associated with teen sexual initiation and pregnancy (Whitbeck, Conger, & Kao, 1993). Several authors have argued that a lack of closeness in the parent–teen relationship increases the influence of peers on teens' sexual activity (Benda & DeBlasio, 1991; Feldman & Brown, 1993; Whitbeck et al., 1993; Whitbeck, Hoyt, Miller, & Kao, 1992).

PARENTAL MONITORING. The awareness of their teens' activities and companions, has been linked in several studies to later timing of first sexual intercourse (Hogan & Kitagawa, 1985; B. C. Miller et al., 2001). In a large majority of research studies, parental monitoring has been associated with reduced exposure to sexual risk (B. C. Miller et al., 2001) and among sexually active teens with having fewer partners and using contraception (Huebner & Howell, 2003; Luster & Small, 1994; Rodgers, 1999). Recently analyzed data from over 2,000 mother–teen pairs interviewed for the Add Health Study revealed that communication with the parents of a teen daughter's friends was associated with later sexual initiation, suggesting that parent social network plays a role, albeit an indirect one (McNeely et al., 2002). Other recent longitudinal studies suggest that monitoring during the preadolescent period may be most important (Longmore, Manning, & Giordano, 2001) but becomes less effective from 8th to 10th grade in delaying adolescent sexual activity (Whitbeck, Yoder, Hoyt, & Conger, 1999). Proactive parental awareness and monitoring may be more important than reactive attempts to control sexual activity among adolescents once they have started dating.

But as Stattin and Kerr (Kerr & Stattin, 2000; Stattin & Kerr, 2001) have pointed out, parental monitoring (often measured as parents' knowledge about daily activities of their adolescents) is strongly associated with adolescents' positive adjustment. Teens' spontaneous disclosure of information accounts for more of the association with teen adjustment than parents' surveillance. In short, monitoring may not have as much preventive effect as is frequently assumed by researchers, but rather teens' willingness to disclose their activities and whereabouts to parents indicates that they are less likely to engage in activities disapproved of by parents, including premature sexual activity (Laird, Pettit, Bates, & Dodge, 2003). There is recent evidence of both direct and indirect effects of parental monitoring on adolescent problem behavior (Fletcher, Steinberg, & Williams-Wheeler, 2004), so there is controversy over how much risk is reduced when parents monitor.

PARENTAL COMMUNICATION. The effects of parents' communication about sexuality with their adolescents have been mixed, with roughly equal numbers of studies finding positive effects of communication or no detectable effects and a few finding negative effects, perhaps because, similar to vigilance, communication happens proactively and reactively. Some parents become communicative only in response to a teen sexuality "crisis" when the adolescent may already be sexually active or on the brink (Kirby, 2002; B. C. Miller, 2002; B. C. Miller et al., 2001). Since few longitudinal studies have measured parent–teen communication about sexuality, it has been difficult to confirm or disconfirm this pattern of behavior.

It is clear from a small number of studies that when parent and teens communicate about sexuality, parents' and teens' values *do* make a difference in teens' sexual initiation (B. C. Miller et al., 2001). Several studies have documented an association between greater religiosity among teens and later and less risky sexual behavior (Lammers, Ireland, Resnick, &

Blum, 2000; Wills, Gibbons, Gerrard, Murry, & Brody, 2003). In a study of 625 teenage boys, ages 15–19, who were not yet sexually active, those not expecting to initiate intercourse in the next year most commonly gave as a reason the desire to wait until marriage (named by 32% of the "delayers"). These delayers were more likely to report attending church and having strict parents. This group of boys was less likely to actually initiate sexual activity in the next year, seemingly because of perceptions about the costs and benefits of sexual activity (Forste & Haas, 2002). Data from the Add Health study shows that parent values are also important: A mother's strong disapproval of her daughter having sex was associated with later sexual initiation, though no similar relationship was observed among sons (McNeely et al., 2002).

The Experts on Parents and Adolescent Sexuality

SPOCK. Some of Spock's first major writings on the topic appeared in his 1970 book, *A Teenager's Guide to Life and Love*, which he was recruited to write by his publishers (Spock & Morgan, 1989). It was his only book devoted solely to advising parents about adolescents and reflects remnants of traditional imbalances in sex roles and responsibilities, with cautionary instructions given most urgently to adolescent girls. Parents of girls are warned that "the strong instinct of boy or man is to keep progressing toward greater and greater physical intimacy, unless he is stopped decisively," and a girl "must remember that the male is designed to be intrusive and to have to prove his boldness up to the limit she sets" (Spock, 1970, pp. 35, 89). Spock's psychoanalytic training undoubtedly influenced his writings about the biological drives of adolescent sexuality. Use of "strong instinct" and the notion of "biological design" clearly condones boys' sexual assertiveness, even aggressiveness, and puts the onus of constraints and responsibility on adolescent girls, whose own sexual feelings are largely ignored. Boys' parents are given no similar admonitions to teach their sons to respect those limits, nor are they warned about the problems that might be caused by their sons' impetuous tendencies. If unplanned, unprotected sexual activity occurs repeatedly, however, both partners are condemned as immature; those with "a sense of responsibility manage to control their feelings" (Spock, 1970, p. 81).

But *Teenager's Guide* also expresses Spock's belief that there is a greater good to be taught teens than just sexual gratification. "I still think it's good for young people to hear about sex—not only the anatomical and physiological aspects, but the tender, spiritual and moral aspects" (Spock, 1970, p. 186). This theme was still a core message 24 years later in his advocacy book: "To point out that sex and marriage are as much spiritual as physical does not mean that the physical pleasure will be limited: it may in fact be enhanced. In cultures that postpone sexual intimacy until couples are committed to sharing their lives and aspirations, people may become passionate lovers for life" (Spock, 1994, p. 115). The language of the seventh edition of his parenting manual is similar, if a bit more restrained: "At the same time, parents can speak about their own ideals, explaining that sex is as much spiritual as physical, that they, as do many young people, think it is better for young people to wait until they are confident that their love is deep and long-lasting before having sexual relations" (Spock & Parker, 1998, p. 460). In his book for parents of adolescents, Spock emphasizes the parents' importance as role models regarding their children's sex education: "The most important part of sex education, in the broad and true sense, is the example the parents set for their children. I mean the respect and tenderness they show for each other (even though they may have quarrels), the selfless cooperation in the care of the family, the mutual loyalty. If children have this kind of image of married love before them, they are getting a good basic education" (Spock, 1970, p. 186).

At the same time that he promotes the spiritual side of sexuality, Spock's more recent writings are equitable for the two genders and acknowledge the intense sexual feelings of adolescence: "In adolescence the biological pressures compel children to be preoccupied with sexual and romantic interests again. . . . Before children have become secure about their sexuality and integrated it into their personality, it remains a rather awkward, compelling, separate instinct. They feel a nagging curiosity about sex and a compulsion to find out by experimentation. These feelings run counter, of course, to their idealistic emotions" (Spock & Parker, 1998, pp. 457–458). Nor does contemporary popular culture convey healthy messages: "Sexuality is widely trivialized, despiritualized and coarsened, particularly in the popular media" (Spock, 1994, pp. 114–115).

As part of their conversations with teens, parents should discuss the consequences of unplanned pregnancies for the teens themselves and for the babies that might be conceived (Spock, 1994, p. 112). Spock believes that sexual activity should embody idealistic principles and serve a higher purpose as the foundation for family life.

DOBSON. Dobson is extremely concerned about early sexual activity among teens in a culture that he believes to be saturated with depictions of easy sexuality without consequences: "Of all the dimensions wherein we have mishandled this younger generation, none is more disgraceful than the sexual immorality that has permeated the world in which they live. There is no more effective way to destroy the institution of the family than to undermine the sexual exclusivity on which it is based" (Dobson, 1992, p. 206).

As noted in chapter 5, Dobson blames public media, among other forces, for the sexualized context in which contemporary adolescents find themselves. He assigns parents the primary role in children's sexuality education and believes that it should begin early: "Particularly in the matter of sex education, the best approach is one that begins in early childhood and extends through the years, according to a policy of openness, frankness, and honesty. Only parents can provide this lifetime training" (Dobson, 1992, p. 217). He warns parents against giving too much education too early because it may lead to overstimulation: "Young people can be tantalized by what is taught about the exciting world of grown-up sexual experience" (Dobson, 1992, p. 223). Further, simply providing such information can lead to early, premarital sexual activity: "If eight-year-old children are given an advanced understanding of mature sexual behavior, it is less likely that they will wait ten or twelve years to apply this knowledge within the confines of marriage" (Dobson, 1992, p. 223). Instead, "it seems appropriate that the amount of information youngsters are given should coincide with their social and physical requirement for that awareness. The child's requests for information provide the best guide to readiness for sex education" (Dobson, 1992, p. 223). At the same time, parents whose children do not ask questions should instruct them in any case: "If a child is uninterested in or doesn't ask about sex, the parent is not relieved of responsibility" (Dobson, 1992, p. 224).

Furthermore, the process of sexuality education should be completed early: "Parents should plan to end their formal instructional program about the time their child enters puberty. . . . Adolescents usually resent adult intrusion during this time . . . *unless* they raise the topic themselves" (Dobson, 1992, p. 225). Thus, parents should educate their adolescent children on topics that might seem inappropriate for preadolescents, such as avoidance of sexually exploitative relationships, if their teens bring up the topic themselves. Or, parents can look for help from their churches, if the churches endorse premarital abstinence and marital fidelity. Church youth workers are recommended as people who might offer guidance to teenagers on sexuality issues.

Establishing a healthy parent–child relationship is a fundamental element in teaching morality, and adolescents should respect their parents enough to accept what they recommend, including their standards for premarital sexual behavior (Dobson, 1992, p. 228). But he also invokes "a God of justice. If we choose to defy His moral laws we will suffer certain consequences . . . for 'the wages of sin is death.' An adolescent who understands this truth is more likely to live a moral life in the midst of an immoral society" (Dobson, 1992, p. 228). When Dobson writes for teens themselves, his advice is straightforward and fortified by biblical quotations. After describing sex as "a wonderful, beautiful mechanism," he writes: "However, I must also tell you that God intends for us to control that desire for sexual intercourse. He has stated repeatedly in the Bible that we are to save our body for the person we will eventually marry, and that it is wrong to satisfy our appetite for sex with a boy or girl before we get married. There is just no other way to interpret the Biblical message" (Dobson, 1989, p. 80).

In marked contrast to Spock and Dobson are the writings of Leach and Rosemond. Their discussions of adolescent sexuality concern the practical values of maintaining credibility and a good relationship with the adolescent, smoothing relationships with parents of dates, and avoiding disasters (pregnancies).

LEACH. Although Leach takes a distinctly different approach to adolescent sexuality than Dobson, she, too, worries about educating children about sexuality too early, particularly concerning sexual risks: "But surely children should have time to come to terms with the concept of sexual activity as a life-enhancing, life-creating pleasure for the future, before they face it as a life-threatening danger? Should prepubertal children who are not yet comfortably familiar with the practical workings of any kind of sex nor yet at risk from it really be exhorted to 'safer sex,' complete with condoms?" (Leach, 1994, p. 153). Like Spock and Dobson, Leach advises parents to accept the powerful sexual feelings of adolescents: "The sheer strength of adolescent sexual feeling, for example, is something most adults choose to ignore. Good sex education may deal with 'love' as well as with 'the facts of life' but it seldom deals with lust; with the fact that the adolescent will *want* sex. You can accept the existence of a feeling without necessarily encouraging its expression and it is better if you do" (Leach, 1989b, p. 85).

Leach emphasizes the different timing of puberty for girls and boys: "The difference in the rates at which girls and boys mature means that girls are often looking for romantic/sexual contacts long before their male peers are ready for them" (Leach, 1989b, p. 86). This discrepancy means that

> young girls who go out with boys in their own age group are likely to have to "do the chasing," but will be doing so with boys who, because they are themselves still anxious about sexual activity, are unlikely to allow matters to go further than either of them truly wants. Eventually a boy will cease simply to be overwhelmingly interested in sex and his body's reactions to sexy sights and feelings; he will become interested in girls as people, and in one girl in particular. Then and only then will he be ready to share the kind of romantic closeness which his girl-peer has been dreaming of for so long. (Leach, 1989b, pp. 86–87)

Of the four experts who write about adolescent sexuality, it is Leach who considers peer norms for adolescent sexuality: "Whatever sexual behavior you think you are seeing in your adolescent and/or his or peer group, do remember that the group will itself have sexual customs and mores. If you can come to understand what these are, you may find them both comforting and surprising" (Leach, 1989b, pp. 85–86).

More than the other experts, Leach discusses negotiating the considerable issues involved in making sure that adolescent girls have contraceptive protection without making it seem that they should be sexually active. She also discusses the pros and cons of female versus male contraception. In summary, though Leach mentions romantic, loving relationships as the goal for teens, she devotes much attention to managing the practical side of adolescent sexuality.

ROSEMOND. Rosemond takes a pragmatic approach to dealing with adolescent sexuality, one that may have been influenced by Spock's writing, but which has elements that are consistent with his focus on the marital bond and a more hands-off approach to parenting in general. As Spock did in his adolescent book in 1970, Rosemond writes that sexuality education in the broadest sense should begin early and parents should model a healthy relationship:

Basically, we tried to get across to both of them that the secret to be a successful sexual relationship with someone has less to do with techniques and biology than with attitude and values—specifically, how well you respect yourself and how well you respect the other person. You can't package that attitude in one fact-filled conversation. It's something you model for them every day in what you say and what you do. In that sense, a child's sex education begins the day he or she is born. (Rosemond, 2001b, p. 404)

Rosemond does not leave it to modeling values, however. Parents also have some responsibility regarding the basics of sexuality. Rosemond describes how he taught his son: "All I want to say is that when you have questions or anything at all you want to discuss concerning women and men and sex, I'd like you to ask me. I'd rather you asked me instead of one of your friends, because their answers and opinions might not be correct. And remember: There's no such thing as a dumb question" (Rosemond, 2001b, pp. 403–404). He reports that his son did ask questions and that when answering, Rosemond took the opportunity to make additional points. Rosemond does not address the question of how to manage sexuality educa-tion for the child who is too intimidated to ask a question or seemingly uninterested until her or his first romantic relationship. He notes that "girls areconsiderably more vulnerable than boys when it comes to dating. Rules are definitely needed, but rules alone are likely to backfire. The most positive, productive, and preventive approach is one that educates the young girl on her responsibilities" (Rosemond, 2001d, p. 196). Later in the same section he describes his goals for the sexual education of his son: open communication on sexuality and relationships, a respectful attitude toward himself and toward the young women he dated, and an appreciation of the concerns of a teenage girls' parents (Rosemond, 2001d, p. 198). Nowhere in this recent book is there acknowledgment that a teenage boy's responsibilities might be commensurate with a teenage girl's.

Other than that, Rosemond recommends maintaining good relationships with both sons and daughters, noting that "a girl who feels approved of and respected by her father is not only less needy of approval from boys but also better able to 'just say no' and stick to her guns" (Rosemond, 2001d, p. 197). But he places more emphasis on parental structure than on parent–child communication. He supports his position by mentioning research that found that good discipline and supervision were more a deterrent to precocious sexual activity than good parent–child communication

(Rosemond, 2001d, p. 202). In general, Rosemond's advice on this topic is less demanding than that of the other experts because parents have to take few proactive steps to deal with their teens' sexuality. Parents should offer to answer questions, make their views clear, and make sure that their adolescents respect themselves, their dates, and their dates' parents.

Comparing the Authors and the Research on Parenting and Sexuality Education

Despite the limitations of current research surrounding parenting predictors or, more typically, parenting correlates of adolescent sexual initiation, it is clear that there are better and worse ways for parents to approach sexuality education. Spock's and Dobson's emphasis on communicating parents' values to adolescents is supported by several large research studies, which have consistently demonstrated that parents' values, and particularly their disapproval of early sexual initiation, are linked to later onset of sexual intercourse. Though Spock's and Dobson's discussions of adolescent sexuality do not mention the importance of family closeness and support, they write frequently about it elsewhere, notably in their discussions on discipline, and research findings have repeatedly demonstrated that cohesive relationships with parents are closely connected to better sexual outcomes for teens (later sexual initiation, fewer partners, fewer pregnancies).

Although Spock and Dobson's politics are worlds apart, they argue equally vigorously for postponing teens' sexual involvement until marriage. Their advice to parents who wish their teens to do so is on target, to the extent that current research can provide definitive support. Spock's 1970 book reflects the traditional double standard for sexuality, but his recent writings have clearly moved beyond it. By contrast, Rosemond's *Teen-proofing* (2001d) maintains it. Rosemond mentions that girls who are close to their fathers are more likely to "just say no," but most studies on this topic suggest that perceived support from both parents is important, and generally mothers' communications with adolescent girls concerning sexuality have a greater impact. Rosemond's advice to parents to let teens initiate the conversations about sexuality and relationships is risky if teens never bring up the topic. Some teens may not initiate such discussions until they are dating, perhaps on the brink of sexual involvement, when it is harder to remain abstinent, or, worst yet, in the midst of a pregnancy scare. These and other possible scenarios underscore the importance of Rosemond's emphasis on maintaining good relationships with both sons and daughters.

Leach's discussion of parents' role in sexuality education is even more reactive, focused on managing rather than preventing adolescent sexual activity. In the absence of the perfect contraceptive and considering the risks of sexually transmitted diseases, assuming that teens will have sex and attempting to manage it seems less desirable than persuading them to delay sexual initiation, and Leach's advice does not give parents the tools to do so. Leach wrote about adolescent sexuality in *Your Growing Child*, published in 1989, so it is unclear how her advice might differ today. Surprisingly, all four of the experts miss the importance of monitoring, that is, of simply keeping track of children's friends, activities, and whereabouts, in preventing sexual initiation, but in light of recent findings that parents' surveillance is dependent on teens' willingness to allow surveillance (Stattin & Kerr, 2001), perhaps the experts more appropriately focus on maintaining closeness in family relationships so that teens will report in.

MANAGERS AND MORALISTS

The four experts who write about adolescent sexuality could be classified in two camps, and not along the familiar liberal/conservative divide. Two of the experts are clearly *managers*. Managers' advice to parents is concerned with making adolescents aware of the social context of sexuality and their responsibility toward their partners. They devote attention to sexual mechanics: advocating for abstinence or advising how to cope with a sexually active adolescent's risk for contracting sexually transmitted diseases and becoming pregnant or causing a pregnancy. Their discourse is overwhelmingly concerned with practical matters. If parents follow their advice and teens do as their parents tell them (which certainly can never be guaranteed!), good outcomes should result: less problematic dating relationships, diminished likelihood of contracting sexually transmitted diseases, avoidance of being either a victim or a perpetrator of sexual exploitation, and fewer unwanted pregnancies.

By contrast, two of the experts are *moralists*. They invoke larger ethical and spiritual concerns in their discussions of adolescents' sexual activity, and their writing resonates with themes of sexuality in its support of marital and family life. The primary risk of sexuality in the media and premature sexual activity among teens is that the adolescent will embrace the coarsened and degraded sexuality of popular culture and thereby cheapen that which has great value: a long-term sexual relationship with a loving partner, one consecrated with matrimonial ties. These experts deal with the management aspects of adolescent sexuality, including the health risks of unprotected sexual activity, but their central message is clearly not that of effective coping to minimize problems, but rather of the incorporation of budding sexuality into a larger system of values that support marital fidelity and family stability.

The missing fifth expert is Brazelton, who has focused primarily on the years from birth to age 6 throughout his career. He has written occasionally on adolescent topics in a syndicated newspaper column but little that systematically addresses the adolescent topics addressed in this chapter.

Spock and Dobson emerge as the two moralists who emphasize the ethical and spiritual side of adolescent sexuality. Variously inspired by New England ethical progressivism in Spock's case and down-South biblical conservatism in Dobson's, they share a forthright belief in marriage as the context in which a loving sexuality should be expressed. Leach's attention to managing the practical aspects of sex differences and contraceptive use makes her more of a manager than either Spock, who is emphatic about the spiritual and ethical expression of sexuality, or Dobson, who counts on sexuality to cement marriages as part of God's larger plan for humanity. Similarly, Rosemond, who is concerned that teens not make sexual mistakes because of misinformation or because of lack of respect for themselves and that relationships among parents not be disrupted by teens' sexual misdeeds, comes across as more of a manager.

Teaching About Contraception and Outside-the-Family Sexuality Education

Spock, despite his advocacy for abstinence, writes with equal conviction about the need to teach adolescent sons and daughters about contraception: "I believe that the parents must take the initiative. They must not only instruct their children, or arrange for instruction, but also reemphasize from time to time, especially if they expect their teens to engage in sexual activity, that *people who have intercourse must take serious responsibility for birth control on every single occasion*" (Spock & Parker, 1998, p. 460). Dobson does not mention providing contraception information to teenagers in his advice to parents, probably for concerns similar to those outlined below that led him to reject sexuality education programs in the public schools. As explained in a *USA Today* ad placed by Focus on the Family and quoted approvingly in *The New Dare to Discipline*, Dobson's emphasis on abstinence is absolute: "There is only one way to protect ourselves from the deadly diseases that lie in wait. It is abstinence before marriage, then marriage and mutual fidelity for life to an uninfected partner" (Dobson, 1992, p. 211). The ad goes on to ask:

> But if you knew a teenager was going to have intercourse, wouldn't you teach him or her about proper condom usage?
> No, because that approach has an unintended consequence. The process of recommending condom usage to teenagers inevitably conveys five dangerous ideas: (1) that safe sex is achievable; (2) that everybody is doing it; (3) that responsible adults expect them to do it; (4) that it's a good thing; and (5) that their peers know they know these things, breeding promiscuity. These are very destructive messages to give our kids. (Dobson, 1992, p. 212)

Leach apparently has never written publicly about the desirability of abstinence for teenagers, though she mentions the special risks of early sexual initiation for young girls, notably on blind dates and mixed-sex trips when girls are not prepared with contraception (Leach, 1989b). In interpreting this apparently permissive attitude (how many adults would have sex on a blind date?), it should be noted that her most extensive advice to parents about adolescent sexuality was written in 1989 before the AIDS epidemic put sexually active teens at risk not just for other sexually transmitted diseases and unplanned pregnancy, but for lingering death as well. She warns against putting young girls on oral contraceptives as a routine preventive measure: "To suggest that a thirteen-year-old should 'go on the Pill' may be to suggest that you not only expect but even recommend sexual activity. She may be bitterly hurt by what strikes her as a lack of caring. She may be shattered at your lack of trust" (Leach, 1989b, p. 87).

Leach is emphatic that "both sexes should be taught that whatever the circumstances, *protection against pregnancy must be discussed in advance* of intercourse and that if neither partner has contraceptives available it cannot take place" (Leach, 1989b, p. 88). Warning that sexual intercourse sometimes takes place even though neither partner had fully intended it beforehand, she admonishes parents, "If you really want to ensure that your adolescent neither causes nor experiences an unwanted pregnancy, you will need to be extremely hard-headed in your thinking and frank in your advice" (Leach, 1989b, p. 87). She summarizes the arguments against putting young female adolescents on oral contraceptives and the difficulties of other types of reliable female contraception and concludes that "responsibility for avoiding very early pregnancies has to lie with boys, and therefore with their parents, even though the dread of pregnancy is so much more real to girls and their parents" (Leach, 1989b, p. 88). Parents of sexually active older girls should make it clear that they are not against using oral contraceptives, because girls who have to obtain them in secrecy are less likely to obtain and use contraception regularly (Leach, 1989b, p. 88). Again, Leach wrote these words before much of the publicity concerning negative effects of oral contraceptives.

The opinions of the three experts who write about sexuality education in schools differ markedly. Leach may not write about this issue because it is less controversial in the United Kingdom. But Spock, Dobson, and Rosemond all weigh in strongly on the topic. For Spock, the effects of sexuality education in schools have been positive but too limited: "Sex education has generally focused on the physiology of sex, birth control, disease prevention, and undoing the fear and guilt about normal sexual behavior. All of this has been of great value. However, . . . the vast, complex, rich field of spiritual aspects of sexuality have been left out, ignored. This is unfortunate" (Spock, 1994, p. 115).

By contrast, Dobson expresses deep concerns about sexuality education in the public schools, opposing programs that include anything besides abstinence promotion:

One of the problems with sex education as it is currently taught in public schools is that it breaks down the natural barriers between the sexes and makes familiarity and casual sexual experimentation much more likely to occur. It also strips kids—especially girls—of their modesty to have every detail of anatomy, physiology and condom usage made explicit in co-ed situations. Then, the following Friday night when the kids are on a date and attend a sexually explicit movie or watch a hot TV program showing teenagers in bed with one another, it is just a tiny step to intercourse. . . . In short, the way sex education is handled today is worse than no program at all. Look at what has happened to the incidence of teen pregnancy and abortion since it was instituted! (Dobson, 1992, p. 218)

In *Children at Risk* (1990), his advocacy book, Dobson argues that those who fail to promote abstinence as the only option are not doing so because they believe teens may become sexually active and want to minimize sexually transmitted diseases and unplanned pregnancies. They are not even given credit for being well intentioned but misguided. According to Dobson, their motives are more cynical:

> Why do bureaucrats, researchers, and Planned-Parenthood types fight so hard to preserve adolescent promiscuity? Why do they balk at the thought of intercourse occurring only in the context of marriage? Why have they completely *removed* the door marked "Premarital Sex" for a generation of vulnerable teenagers?
>
> Their motivation is not that difficult to understand. Multiplied million of dollars are generated each year in direct response to teenage sexual irresponsibility. Kids jumping into bed with each other are supporting entire industries of grateful adults. . . . At the top of the list of those who profit from adolescent irresponsibility, however, are those who are purportedly working to fight it! Planned Parenthood and similar organizations would simply fade away if they were ever fully successful in eliminating teen pregnancies. (Dobson & Bauer, 1990, p. 13)

Rosemond takes a similarly strong stand against anything besides abstinence promotion, attacking most public school programs that are comprehensive or "abstinence-plus," combining advocacy of abstinence with information about contraception: "There is no evidence that traditional sex-ed programs work, and a growing body of evidence that such programs may actually contribute to *increased* teenage sexual activity" (Rosemond, 2001d, p. 201). In support of this statement, he mentions "two federal studies" by Douglas Kirby "that have found comprehensive sex-education programs cannot claim to have accomplished anything" (Rosemond, 2001d, p. 202).

Research on Parents' Advice and the Efficacy of School-Based Education Programs Concerning Sexuality

Have existing sexuality education programs been effective? Douglas Kirby has written extensively about teen sexuality programs, as Rosemond notes. The findings of Kirby's most recent review (2002) are clearly mixed concerning the effectiveness of instructional comprehensive sexuality education. These are the most common type of programs, ones that do not involve individualized sessions in a clinic and therefore can reach far more teens. He evaluated comprehensive (abstinence plus contraceptive information) instructional programs for teens that included an appropriate control group and measured the program's impact on behavior, not just intentions for future sexual activity. Of 28 studies that met these and similar criteria for evaluation, 9 studies were tallied as having delayed sexual initiation, 18 found no significant impact, and 1 increased the rate of reported intercourse among sixth grade through 10th grade girls. The increase in intercourse occurred in a comprehensive health program for middle-school students that also addressed drug use and nutrition, and the authors speculated that the multiple health messages may have offset and diluted each other and contributed to oversaturation of the prevention message (Moberg & Piper, 1993).

Describing his findings, Kirby writes: "In sum, these data strongly indicate that sex and HIV education programs do not significantly increase any measure of sexual activity, as some people have feared, and that to the contrary, may delay or reduce sexual intercourse among teens" (Kirby, 2002). Since that review Kirby and coauthors have published findings of two large school-based comprehensive sexuality programs with control groups that followed teens over a 2- to 3-year period. One program delayed sexual initiation among boys but not girls (Coyle, Kirby, Marin, Gomez, & Gregorich, 2004), and the other found that HIV education also had a greater impact on boys' sexual behaviors than on girls' and greater effects on Hispanics than on other ethnic groups (Kirby et al., 2004).

Kirby (2002) also reviewed research evidence on abstinence-only sexuality programs, sticking with the same criteria used for comprehensive programs to allow for an accurate evaluation of outcomes. Only three programs met these criteria, and none of them found significant effects on behavior. Despite this apparent lack of success, Kirby cautions against making generalizations about abstinence-only programs, noting that they are extremely discrepant in their length, the intensity of their religious message, and their emphasis on just postponing sexual initiation or eliminating sexual intercourse outside of marriage. In another recent review (Bennett & Assefi, 2005), which was limited to 11 abstinence-plus (contraceptive information) and 3 abstinence-only pregnancy-prevention programs with randomized controlled trials, the authors concluded that delays in the onset of sexual activity were shown in only 2 abstinence-plus programs and 1 abstinence program. Again, only the comprehensive health program reported by Moberg and Piper (1993) lowered the age of sexual initiation (Bennett & Assefi, 2005).

One recent study has demonstrated that virginity pledges predicted later onset of sexual activity, but only if pledging was relatively non-normative, that is, if fewer than 30% of the students in the high school had pledged. The authors' interpretation of this finding was that pledges were more likely to be adhered to if they contributed to a sense of identity, which does not occur when a majority of teens pledge (Bearman & Bruckner, 2001).

In a 2001 policy statement, the AAP recounts the less-than-stellar statistics concerning sexual practices among American adolescents: high percentages of birth to unmarried girls, rates of sexually transmitted diseases that are among the highest in the industrialized world, and relatively low usage of barrier contraceptive methods that might prevent such diseases among sexually active teens. Low levels of parental supervision are identified among other factors leading to earlier sexual activity. Recommendations to pediatricians are to encourage parents to offer their children developmentally appropriate discussion of sexuality and sex-related issues. Parents are to be advised to initiate discussion about sexuality with children at relevant opportunities—for example, at the birth of a sibling—and children's questions should be answered fully and accurately (AAP, 2001b). As children get older, parents should discuss their expectations for their children's abstinence, delay of sexual initiation, and responsible sexual behavior (AAP, 2001b).

The AAP argues for the benefits of comprehensive sexuality education programs, stating that they delay the onset of sexual activity and increase use of birth control among sexually active teens (AAP, 2001b). Pediatricians are advised to encourage schools to provide "effective and balanced" sexuality education (p. 501). They are encouraged to consider presenting contraceptive information in schools because such information is not presented in one third of school districts. The AAP states further that abstinence-only programs have not been effective in delaying onset of sexual activity or preventing high-risk sexual behavior (AAP, 2001b). Thus, the AAP's policy statement is in accordance with the majority of published research in recommending age-appropriate and comprehensive sexuality education during adolescence.

The Experts' Advice and Research on School-Based Sexuality Education

Obviously if teens are abstinent, as Spock, Dobson, and Rosemond advocate, the threat of unplanned pregnancies and sexually transmitted diseases is eliminated. It is difficult to argue with Spock's and Leach's position that *if* teens are going to be sexually active, parents should instruct them to use contraception on each and every occasion. Putting the responsibility on young boys to use condoms might be desirable from a public health standpoint, since condoms, which Leach recommends until other contraceptive measures can be arranged, do provide some protection against sexually transmitted diseases and they can be obtained without seeing a physician. At the same time, it is potentially problematic to assign the greater responsibility for contraception to boys, who, by Leach's own description, are caught in a period of overwhelming interest in sex, are less motivated toward pregnancy prevention, and get less sexuality education from parents.

But between the abstinent teens and the teens who are proficient with contraception are the majority of young people who become sexually active during the teen years—from 9% at age 12 to 82% at age 19 (Alan Guttmacher Institute, 1994). Spock suggests that sexuality education should be expanded, whereas Rosemond and Dobson question the programs' effectiveness and even suggest that they have been harmful. But research shows that Rosemond's and Dobson's concerns that comprehensive sexuality programs will increase sexual activity is empirically unfounded, though they are often not effective in delaying the onset of sexual intercourse. On the other hand, no school-based abstinence-only program has demonstrated effectiveness either, though church-instigated virginity pledges have been protective for some teens. Dobson's and Rosemond's insistence on abstinence-only education and opposition to comprehensive sexuality education are not supported by the most recent work of the researcher that Rosemond quoted, Douglas Kirby.

Teen pregnancy rates for all women ages 15–19 increased 23% from 1972 to 1990, though pregnancy rates among those in this age group who were actually having sex declined by 19% during those years. Planned Parenthood has been a major provider of education about sexuality and a target for Dobson since the organization facilitates abortions, of which he also disapproves, but both its public Web site (http://www.plannedparenthood.org/BC/abstinence.html) and its packaged sexuality education materials provide extensive lists of reasons why teens may want to remain abstinent. These are not the communications that would be expected from an organization that would promote teen pregnancy because of a need to sustain itself. There are many other trends besides sexuality education influencing both teen pregnancy and abortions, including risks of HIV/AIDS, availability of contraception, and the increasing saturation of media with sexual themes and innuendos (Cope-Farrar & Kunkel, 2002).

SUBSTANCE ABUSE

A phone ringing in the middle of the night can produce a new sense of alarm for parents of adolescents who are out late. Images flash through their minds of their children drinking alcohol or using other drugs, driving drunk, being picked up by police, or worse yet as victims of drug-fueled assaults or arrested for possessing or dealing controlled substances. For some parents, whose family histories have been intertwined with the dramatic, often tragic consequences of abuse of alcohol or hard drugs, the increased independence of their adolescent children brings renewed concern. Even parents who gain their only awareness of teens' drug-related calamities from media accounts, or whose children are not yet adolescents, are likely to be vitally interested in substance abuse prevention. It has become a national priority, as evidenced by antidrug education programs in the schools and public service announcements that emphasize drug refusal skills.

One of the difficulties in identifying parenting practices that cause or prevent use of illicit substances in adolescence is that by high school the use of some substances, particularly alcohol, becomes increasingly normative. By the time that they are high school seniors, over 75% of young people report ever having tried an alcoholic beverage; over 50% report having been drunk in the last year; over 30% report that they have been drunk in the last month (Johnston, O'Malley, Bachman, & Schulenberg, 2004). The high social acceptability and accessibility of alcohol and adolescents' widespread experimentation with it makes prevention difficult (Ellickson, Tucker, Klein, & McGuigan, 2001). In one prospective study of childhood predictors of adolescent drug use, the only significant predictor of alcohol use in grades 9–10 (uncomplicated by smoking or the use of other illicit drugs) was reciprocal positive social behaviors on the playground in grades 2–4 (Hops, Davis, & Lewin, 1999). Thus, by the later high school years, occasional experimentation with alcohol may actually be a signal of greater social connectedness among teens. This is despite the fact that its use is illegal for teenagers in this country and that even brief episodes of abuse can have potentially disastrous consequences for their health and safety. Since most teens try drugs in later adolescence, recent research has increasingly focused on substance use in early adolescence. Use at that point is less normative and particularly problematic because of its association with later substance abuse and other problem outcomes (Ellickson et al., 2001; Hawkins et al., 1997; Jackson, Henriksen, Dickinson, & Levine, 1997).

Research on Substance Abuse Causes

CHILD ATTRIBUTES PREDICTING EARLY EXPERIMENTATION AND ABUSE. Personality attributes and social behaviors, evident as early as the preschool and early elementary years, constitute one major class of predictors of problem drug use. Two long-term studies of adolescents from affluent, well-educated families followed since preschool provide unique evidence of just how early problems can be detected. In the first study, clinical assessments at age 3 and 4 of those children in a community sample who turned out to be users of marijuana at age 14 revealed that girls who later turned out to be users were described as demanding, inconsiderate preschoolers who were already not getting along well with other children. Boys who subsequently became early marijuana users were active, aggressive, risk-taking children who frequently tested the limits of acceptable behavior (Block, Block, & Keyes, 1988). By age 7, children of both sexes who became early users were already showing bodily symptoms of stress and thinking of themselves as "bad" (Shedler & Block, 1990). In the second study (Baumrind, 1991a, 1991b), more problem behavior at preschool had cropped up as early as age 4 in those teens who subsequently became alcohol or drug dependent at age 15.

There is supportive evidence from larger longitudinal studies. In a large cohort followed from birth, 3-year-old boys who were described as impulsive, restless, and distractible were at increased risk for drug dependence by age 21 (Caspi, Moffitt, Newman, & Silva, 1996). Among disadvantaged boys, personality attributes of novelty seeking and low harm avoidance at age 6 predicted early onset of use of cigarette, alcohol, and other drugs (Masse & Tremblay, 1997), and disruptive behavior in kindergarten (e.g., physical aggression, hyperactivity, and oppositional behavior) was pivotal in the development of early substance abuse at age 13 (Dobkin, Tremblay, Masse, & Vitaro, 1995). The common theme running through these studies is behavioral undercontrol, particularly evident in boys, which may have substantial heritability (Chassin et al., 2004; Iacono, Carlson, Taylor, Elkins, & McGue, 1999).

Studies that attempt to predict substance use in later adolescence from attributes in middle childhood and early adolescence provide further evidence of the extent and nature of the risk factors. Wide-ranging academic and social difficulties in grades 2–4, including aggression for boys and withdrawal by girls, predicted more deviant drug use patterns in grades 9 and 10 (Hops et al., 1999). Similarly, Ellickson et al. (2001) found that grade 7 academic problems and delinquency predicted grade 12 alcohol misuse. In their extensive review of research on risk factors, Hawkins, Catalano, and Miller (1992) found that behavior problems evident in school, including hyperactivity, academic failure, and peer rejection, were among the factors that predicted later problem drug use. In summary, it is clear that for many adolescent early users and abusers, drugs are not the root cause of their problems; rather, they serve as a means of self-medication, offering an escape from long-standing difficulties.

PEER SELECTION AND INFLUENCE. The belief underlying antidrug programs, such as D.A.R.E. and "Just say no" media campaigns, is that peers are the ones who encourage drug use. In their review of substance abuse risk factors, Hawkins et al. (1992) identified drug-using peers as among the most important influences on adolescent substance use. Peers often provide access to substances and someone to use drugs with, as well as an audience for counter-conventional behavior. There is substantial evidence that peers, and siblings as well, play an important role in which teens use illicit substances and which teens do not (Dishion, Capaldi, Spracklen, & Li, 1995; Reifman, Barnes, Dintcheff, Farrell, & Uhteg, 1998; Wills, McNamara, Vaccaro, & Hirky, 1996). Not only is the age at which adolescents begin using drugs affected by who their friends are (Ennett & Bauman, 1994); it is also the case that friends influence whether drug use will be occasional or escalate over time (Wills & Cleary, 1999).

But child attributes and family factors, including parenting practices, affect who young people select as peers. Evidence suggests that adolescents choose friends whose smoking and drinking patterns are similar to their own (Fisher & Bauman, 1988; Rowe, Woulbroun, & Gulley, 1994). Substance-using friends are undoubtedly the strongest near-term predictor of problem substance use, but older siblings also can model and encourage smoking and alcohol use, and siblings often share friends (Ary, Tildesley, Hops & Andrews, 1993; Duncan, Duncan & Hops, 1996). Older siblings are a separate risk factor for smoking (Rose, Chassin, Presson, & Sherman, 1999) and for alcohol misuse in grade 12 (Ellickson et al., 2001). Genetically transmitted risk may also be responsible for older and younger siblings' similarity in starting substance use and similar patterns of change in use across the adolescent years (Duncan et al., 1996), though adoptive sibling pairs also show similarity in alcohol use patterns, suggesting that family environment plays a role as well (McGue, Sharma, & Benson, 1996).

Critics have pointed out that the correspondence among peers in drug use may be artificially inflated because in most research, teens report about both themselves and their peers, and there is evidence that teen respondents who are drug users systematically overestimate their friends' use (Bauman & Ennett, 1996; Chassin et al., 2004). When peers are surveyed directly, concordance for drug use is lower, though still positive (Kandel, 1978).

PARENT PRACTICES. One depiction of the pattern of problem drug use is that poor parenting practices create deficits in social skills and self-regulation that lead to rejection by most peers (Dishion et al., 1995). Adolescents then affiliate with deviant peers, which increases their risk for smoking, alcohol abuse, and use of hard drugs (B. B. Brown, Mounts, Lamborn, & Steinberg, 1993; Patterson, DeBaryshe, & Ramsey, 1989). Parents emerge repeatedly as important sources of influence in adolescent substance use. But what is it that parents do that leads children to try, to use, and perhaps to abuse substances?

Parents have been repeatedly enjoined to serve as role models for their children (Simpson, 2001). Parents' own substance use is invariably among the most important predictors in studies that assess it (e.g., Andrews, Hops, Ary, Tildesley, & Harris, 1993; Jackson & Henriksen, 1997; Jackson, Henriksen, & Dickinson, 1999; Scal, Ireland, & Borowsky, 2003; Wills et al., 1996). Parents' drug use provides adolescents with models for behavior and may also reflect a shared genetic susceptibility (Kendler et al., 1999; True et al., 1999). Summarizing evidence from 54 studies, Kandel and Wu (1995) concluded that if parents smoke, their children are more likely to do so as well. Most studies find that parental influence is strongest in those families where both mothers and fathers are reported to smoke (Kandel & Wu, 1995). The gender of parent and child may contribute. Mothers who smoke are more likely to have teenage children, especially girls, who smoke (Chassin, Presson, Todd, Rose, & Sherman, 1998; Griffin, Botvin, Doyle, Diaz, & Epstein, 1999; Kandel & Wu, 1995).

In a review of early research, Glynn (1981) concluded that a parent's use of a substance was the best predictor of his or her adolescent child's use of the same substance, and subsequent research has confirmed that claim. For example, recent longitudinal research has provided compelling evidence of the importance of parents' pattern of drug use (Kaplow, Curran, Dodge, & the Conduct Problems Prevention Research Group, 2002). Many parenting factors were assessed after kindergarten as potential predictors of children's experimentation prior to age 12 with substances other than tobacco: parental warmth, use of physical punishment, use of verbal reasoning, parental school involvement, maternal depression, and parental substance abuse. For a group of children from schools with high rates of conduct problems, parental substance abuse problems reported just after their children were in kindergarten were the single strongest predictor of children's substance experimentation by the sixth grade. It is not clear, though, whether the increased risk is due to genetic transmission of risk, modeling of substance use, or the lower level of supervision that is often provided by substance-using parents. The only other significant parent predictor of substance experimentation by 12-year-olds was less use of verbal reasoning reported by parents (Kaplow et al., 2002).

CULTURAL CONTEXT AND AVAILABILITY. Among suburban youth, more strongly than among inner-city youth, drug use is linked to depression (Way, Stauber, Nakkula, & London, 1994) and to physiological anxiety among girls and worry among boys (Luthar & D'Avanzo, 1999). Poverty is among the factors increasing risk of adult alcohol and drug abuse in adults who were antisocial as children (Robins & Ratcliff, 1979, as cited in Hawkins et al., 1992).

According to the massive Monitoring the Future Study, the National Institute of Drug Abuse-sponsored annual survey of drug use among adolescents, the proportion of high school seniors who have ever sampled an illicit drug (including alcohol) has remained largely stable for the last 5 years and is substantially lower than it was during the 1980s (Johnston et al., 2004). More kinds of drugs are on the contemporary scene, many with brain-damaging and even fatal effects (e.g., ecstasy, Rohypnol, PCP, inhalants); a few young people are using them, and any use is a serious concern. But use levels for marijuana, cocaine, LSD, and amphetamines are low, and their use is stable or declining after major increases in use in the 1980s and major decreases in the early 1990s (Johnston et al., 2002).

Over 75% of high school seniors report that marijuana, cigarettes, and alcohol are "very easy" or "fairly easy" to obtain. Rated availability for hard drugs is lower, at 40%–60% (Johnston et al., 2004). Long-term data are available for marijuana, and stable high percentages of high school seniors have reported for years that it is fairly easy or very easy to get (88% in 1975 and 86% in 2004; Johnston et al., 2004). So there is evidence of a continuing problem rather than cultural decay. These high levels of availability exist despite extensive legal and taxation structures put in place to reduce the availability of drugs that are licit for adults and massive federal efforts to halt commerce in illegal drugs, including harsh sentences for users, harsher sentences for dealers, and efforts to reduce drug smuggling from abroad.

In summary, a large number of risk factors may lead a child to develop early substance use and subsequent abuse. Adolescent drug misusers are more likely to have social and learning problems during their preschool years. There is some evidence that the parenting that they experience during these early years may contribute (Shedler & Block, 1990). Hyperactivity and delinquent behavior are more likely to be observed in later childhood among children who subsequently misuse drugs, suggesting a general risk for deviant behavior. Parents, older siblings, and friends who smoke, drink, or use recreational drugs both model drug use and provide access for young people who are inclined to try drugs. The overwhelming majority of American adolescents find commonly abused drugs, such as alcohol, cigarettes, and marijuana, easy to obtain.

Experts' Identification of Substance Abuse Causes

INDIVIDUAL CHARACTERISTICS. Only Spock and Leach consider psychological attributes of youth that would make them more vulnerable to the attractions of mind-altering drugs. "Dependence and abuse occur most often in youths who are somewhat immature, self-centered, and passive, and who have little sense of direction in life" (Spock & Parker, 1998, p. 635). He describes "depression and other psychiatric problems; low self-esteem, anxiety, and a sense of powerlessness; and the feeling of being unable to control the world" as factors that increase the risk of serious drug abuse (Spock & Parker, 1998, p. 635). Leach also focuses on psychological risk factors: "It is children with the most desperate need to change themselves, or prop themselves up, who seem most likely to adopt a chemical support system which may eventually destroy them" (Leach, 1989b, p. 337).

PEER INFLUENCES. Spock, Dobson, Leach all identify peer influence as an important factor in which teens become involved in substance use. Leach, for example, writes: "Many youngsters drink or take drugs first to be 'one of the gang'" (Leach, 1989b, p. 338). In his book for teens, Dobson recounts a situation that he argues is "the most important reason why drugs are being used by teenagers every day throughout this country" (Dobson, 1989, p. 51):

Suppose you're in a car with four other young people each about sixteen years old. You're driving around at night, looking for fun, when the driver reaches into his pocket and retrieves a bottle with some pills in it. He takes one pill, pops it in his mouth, then hands the bottle to the guy sitting by the door. . . . You are the last one to be handed the bottle, and all four of your friends have taken the pills.

As it is handed to you what are you going to say? You know that those pills are a form of drug and that they are very harmful to the body. You don't want to take them, but you don't want to be laughed at either. . . . So you give in. You pop the pill. What a relief to be one of the boys again!

You'll find that the next time drugs are offered, it'll be a little easier to take them because you've done it before. Then you start getting the habit, and soon you'll be seriously hooked on drugs, all because of conformity. (Dobson, 1989, pp. 50–51)

Rosemond (2001d) recounts two family narratives in which hanging out with bad peers is one step in a downward spiral whose progression is marked by lack of respect for parents, plummeting grades, substance abuse, and early sexual activity. In both cases, hanging out with kids, to use Rosemond's words, "destined to become among the scummiest of the scum of the universe" (Rosemond, 2001d, p. 174) is another signal of negative changes, rather than making a further descent into bad behavior more likely. When describing substance use prevention, Rosemond writes that teens should be taught to think for themselves and resist peer pressure (Rosemond, 2001d, p. 182), a signal that he thinks peers play a role in adolescent substance use.

PARENT USE/ABUSE. Spock acknowledges the role that parents play in their children's drug usage, describing a straightforward modeling process: "In the younger years, children imitate their parents. Many parents have alcohol or drug problems, or too readily turn to drugs to solve problems of all sorts. If children see their parents using drugs such as alcohol and tranquilizers, they may find it easier to justify their own use of drugs" (Spock & Parker, 1998, p. 631). Rosemond also writes briefly and forcefully on the importance of what parents do: "If you smoke pot openly around your child, your child is 99 percent more likely to smoke pot (and probably use other drugs as well). . . . But *you*—the parent reading this book—are not that kind of parent" (Rosemond, 2001d, p. 170).

CULTURAL CONTEXT AND AVAILABILITY. Spock is unique among the experts in tying substance abuse to economic factors: "One important influence leading to this increase might be the economy which offers many youths very little hope for the future" (Spock & Parker, 1998, p. 631). Rosemond writes that concerning drugs and teens, three facts stand out:

1. More teens are experimenting with/using drugs than ever. . . .
2. The age at which the average "experimenter" first experiments is lower than ever, and getting lower all the time. Drug use has been on the rise among sixth, seventh, and eighth graders since the mid-1980s.
3. The drugs with which teens are experimenting are more dangerous than ever, and getting more dangerous all the time. In the 1960s, most drug-using teens limited themselves to smoking marijuana, which made their throats sore before it got them stoned. Today's teen drug-user is likely to not just use pot, but cocaine, LSD, and amphetamines (uppers) as well. (Rosemond, 2001d, p. 178)

According to Rosemond (2001d), "It's easier to get drugs than has ever been the case" (p. 180), and availability is the reason why drug use has been increasing, though he does not explain *why* drugs would be more available than they have been in the past. After commenting that "school-based drug education/prevention programs like D.A.R.E have been a dismal waste of our tax dollars" (Rosemond, 2001d, p. 180), Rosemond writes that "a 'psycho-social' approach such as this might work if low self-esteem were the root cause of the teen drug problem, but it isn't. As I said, it's availability, which means the only way to stop teens from using drugs is to put an end to availability. That would require marshaling the efforts of federal and state government; therefore, drugs are going to continue to be readily available for a long time to come" (Rosemond, 2001d, p. 180).

Research on Prevention

PROTECTIVE EFFECTS OF PARENTING STYLE. Major researchers on parenting styles have repeatedly linked authoritative parenting style to better school performance and social adjustment among high school students (Lamborn, Mounts, Steinberg, & Dornbusch, 1991; Steinberg, Lamborn, Darling, Mounts, & Dornbusch, 1994), though some adolescents elicit more support and verbal reasoning because of their higher levels of compliance and achievement. In preventing substance use in adolescence, however, it is not at all clear that authoritative parenting has a consistent advantage over authoritarian parenting. Baumrind's (1991b) longitudinal research found that both authoritative and directive-authoritarian parenting were associated with roughly comparable low levels of substance use and significantly less alcohol use and illicit drug use than that of teens whose parents were unengaged (called "uninvolved" in most research). Similarly, Lamborn et al. (1991) found that teens' self-reported substance use varied according to the parenting they reported on dimensions of acceptance/involvement and strictness/supervision. Drug use by teens who described their parents as authoritative—high on both dimensions—differed little from those who reported that their parents were authoritarian—high on strictness/supervision only. Once again both authoritarian and authoritative parenting were associated with significantly lower levels of use than parenting that was described by teens as uninvolved or neglectful.

Two recent studies have provided some evidence that the authoritative style may function better in preventing substance misuse. One key attribute of authoritative parenting is use of verbal reasoning and explanations, in contrast to the simple demands for obedience characteristic of authoritarian parenting. When interviewed after their children's kindergarten year, mothers' reports of verbal reasoning with children in response to standard misbehavior vignettes predicted lower likelihood of substance use initiation by age 12 (Kaplow et al., 2002). It might be argued that reasoning does not work as well with children who show the impulsive, demanding, uncooperative behaviors that predict early substance use and abuse, but parent use of verbal reasoning had a preventive role even when child overactivity and social problem-solving skill deficits were included in the logistic regression predicting early substance use. Kindergarten oppositional and delinquent behavior had no additional predictive usefulness (Kaplow et al., 2002). In a shorter term 2-year longitudinal study predominantly made up of 14-, 15-, and 16-year-olds, Herman, Dornbusch, Herron, and Herting (1997) found that less psychological autonomy (e.g., "How often do your parents tell you that their ideas are correct and you should not question them?") predicted more deviant patterns of drug use. The evidence is much stronger, though, that other aspects of parenting provide effective prevention.

PROTECTIVE EFFECTS OF PARENTAL WARMTH AND FAMILY COHESION. Some studies find that parental warmth makes a difference in substance use (Crosnoe, Erickson, & Dornbusch, 2002; Guo, Hill, Hawkins, Catalano, & Abbott, 2002; Lloyd-Richardson, Papandonatos, Kazura, Stanton, & Niaura, 2002; Oxford, Harachi, Catalano, & Abbott, 2000; Wills, Resko, Ainette, & Mendoza, 2004), but this finding is not universal (Kaplow et al., 2002). Shedler and Block (1990) conducted a unique structured observation of mother–child pairs engaged in challenging problem-solving tasks when the children were 5 years old. Frequent marijuana use (once a week or more) at age 18 was preceded by observer-rated hostile, critical, and undersupportive parenting at age 5. This implies that mothers' lack of emotional warmth early may foretell problem drug use, though many teens who were abstainers at 18 received parenting that was hostile and undersupportive. Adolescent-reported family cohesion was related to decreases in alcohol use across 3 years of a longitudinal study, with similar results across ethnic groups, and increases in family conflict were associated with increases in alcohol use (Bray, Adams, Getz, & Baer, 2001).

Family problems in adolescence also predict problem drug use. Current family conflict predicted girls' deviant patterns of drug use in grades 9 and 10 (Hops et al., 1999) and girls' initiation of experimental smoking (van den Bree, Whitmer, & Pickworth, 2004). Teens' increases in inappropriate emotional detachment from parents during middle school predicted increases in their drug use (Bray et al., 2001). In their review, Hawkins et al. (1992) identified parents' behaviors, family management practices, family conflict, and low bonding to the family as risk factors for drug problems in adolescence. Of course, it is important to recognize that rebellious teens with poor impulse control may be difficult for parents to embrace warmly and that lower levels of warmth and family cohesion might be the result of reciprocal effects (Chassin et al., 2004).

PROTECTIVE EFFECTS OF COMMUNICATION. Both authoritative parenting and family cohesiveness involve more parent–teen communication, and general communication (sharing opinions and feelings and parents explaining reasons for decisions) predicts less risk for becoming a monthly drinker, though its protective effect appears to diminish during early adolescence (D. A. Cohen, Richardson, & LaBree, 1994).

Cross-sectional research provides evidence of protective effects of focused communication about smoking. Mothers' discussion of and reported punishment for smoking were associated with less smoking among their adolescent children (Chassin et al., 1998). Third- and fifth-grade children who reported that their parents talked with them about not smoking, who expected that parents would detect their smoking, and who expected negative consequences if they did smoke were less likely to have tried cigarettes. This held true even if one or both of their parents were current smokers (Jackson & Henriksen, 1997). Parents' current smoking habits, though, clearly influence what is communicated to children. In a cross-sectional survey of children in grades 3 through 8, children in homes in which one or both parents smoked reported fewer warnings about smoking risks (Jackson, Henriksen, & Dickinson, 1998). Children in the lowest quartile of reported warnings about smoking showed the greatest intention to smoke when older.

In contrast, there is only mixed evidence from longitudinal research for the efficacy of focused communication about smoking and drinking on preventing subsequent use. Mothers' cautionary statements regarding alcohol to their 11- through 15-year-old children were negatively related to the initiation of alcohol and marijuana use, as confirmed with an air sample at 1-year follow-up (Andrews et al., 1993). However, for boys only, mothers' reports of cautionary statements regarding alcohol were *positively* related to adolescents' starting to smoke, suggesting that teens may react to perceived parental restrictiveness by trying another substance likely to be disapproved. This finding of apparent adolescent backlash, though not unprecedented (Brook, Brook, Gordon, Whiteman, & Cohen, 1990), deserves further study.

Moreover, focused messages do not always make a difference. Mothers' reports of communication about alcohol and smoking when their adolescent children were between 12 and 14 years old did not predict substance use 1 year later (Ennett, Bauman, Foshee, Pemberton, & Hicks, 2001). Mothers' reports of parents' alcohol and tobacco *use* turned out to be an important predictor, however, demonstrating that what parents do is more important than what parents say. Fifth-grade children's reports of parental communication against alcohol use did not predict whether they later reported drinking alcohol as seventh graders, after their parents' alcohol use was statistically controlled (Jackson et al., 1999). In both these studies, there was sufficient substance use to be able to detect effects of other aspects of parenting.

PROTECTIVE EFFECTS OF PARENTAL MONITORING. Though verbal reasoning and parents' warmth have demonstrated preventive roles in some research studies, the key parenting predictor of drug initiation and escalation is parents' management of family life and especially their monitoring—parents' general awareness of where their teens are, what they are doing, and who they are with. In their 2-year longitudinal study, Herman et al. (1997) found that regulation (locus of decision making, monitoring, and household organization), rather than connectedness and the use of noncoercive discipline, was the most potent parenting dimension in predicting substance use. Family management, including monitoring, clarity of rules, and parental positive reinforcement, as reported by adolescents between 12 and 13, predicted abstinence from alcohol between 14 and 15 (Peterson, Hawkins, Abbott, & Catalano, 1994). Monitoring was most important in preventing smoking initiation, and time spent with parents was the most protective factor against becoming a monthly drinker in a longitudinal study that included a large ethnically diverse sample of fifth graders and seventh graders surveyed annually for 4 years and 3 years, respectively (D. A. Cohen et al., 1994).

Bidirectional effects cannot be ruled out in these studies, because teens who allow themselves to be monitored may be at lower risk (Kerr & Stattin, 2000; Stattin & Kerr, 2001). When adolescents ages 13–16 were interviewed annually for 6 years, Time 1 parental support predicted Time 2 receptivity to monitoring, which predicted Time 3 alcohol misuse (Barnes, Reifman, Farrell, Uhteg, & Dintcheff, 1994). More parent monitoring resulted in low initial levels of adolescent alcohol misuse and predicted a slower increase in alcohol misuse through ages 18 to 22 (Barnes, Reifman, Farrell, & Dintcheff, 2000). In a 1-year longitudinal study, parental rules and monitoring had direct negative effects on the likelihood of beginning substance use at ages 11 and 12 and also had an indirect impact on substance initiation via less involvement with antisocial peers (Oxford et al., 2000).

Some research suggests that very frequent monitoring may be no better than routine "checking in," but the absence of parental monitoring is critical in predicting later substance use problems. Children who reported in interviews the least parental monitoring between the ages of 8 and 10 were more likely to initiate drug use early and to use marijuana, cocaine, and inhalant drugs (Chilcoat & Anthony, 1996). Similarly, in another prospective study, if children in grade 5 believed that their parents would not know if they were drinking alcohol, they were 2.6 times more likely to report having drunk alcohol in grade 7 (Jackson et al., 1999). Aside from parental substance use or abuse, which may reflect a genetic vulnerability that children share, monitoring emerges as the strongest parenting behavior predictor of later onset of drug-use behavior in adolescents.

EXPERIMENTATION. Shedler and Block (1990) found that 18-year-old youths who had experimented with marijuana actually had better psychological health than either heavy users of marijuana or abstainers. The authors note that experimenting with marijuana certainly does not improve psychological health (Shedler & Block, 1990), but occasional experimentation requires drug access, and access may be easier for socially integrated teens, who may also have better psychological health. This argues against parents coming down hard on older adolescents for experimenting with this drug, though it frequently has been named as a gateway to hard drug use. In light of the number of older adolescents who try drugs that adults use (Johnston et al., 2004) and research findings that most adults do not show a pattern of alcohol abuse (Johnston et al., 2004) and are socially competent (Hops et al., 1999), there is little evidence that mild experimentation is *in itself* harmful. But this does not take into account the disastrous effects of alcohol binges and drug overdoses and the likelihood of becoming addicted. Parents need to make sure that the risks, even of mere experimentation, are communicated to teens.

ADOLESCENT PROBLEM BEHAVIOR SYNDROME. A small number of parents have teen children with a serious problem: substance abuse to the point of dependency. Research shows that early teenage substance experimentation, which often presages later teenage substance abuse, often has its roots in parenting that is hostile, coercive, and lacking in support. These families experience high levels of conflict and are more likely to have low levels of parent–child involvement. Lack of involvement results in poor parental monitoring, which predicts affiliation with deviant peers who are more likely to use drugs (Amato & Fowler, 2002; Ary, Duncan, Duncan, & Hops, 1999; Dishion et al., 1995; Patterson, DeBaryshe, & Ramsey, 1989). In such situations, it is likely that substance abuse is accompanied by other problems: depression, academic problems, delinquent behaviors, and high-risk sexual activity (Kandel et al., 1997; Wills et al., 1996). Early and multidimensional interventions are called for to attack all the evident problems, but since substance abuse may derive from more fundamental problems, it may be a mistake to focus solely on abstinence as if it would be a cure-all.

THE NATIONAL INSTITUTE OF DRUG ABUSE ON PREVENTING ADOLESCENT SUBSTANCE USE. The National Institute on Drug Abuse (NIDA) has among its goals educating the public about drug abuse and prevention. The family risk factors that it identifies are:

- lack of mutual attachment and nurturing by parents or caregivers;
- ineffective parenting;
- a chaotic home environment;
- lack of a significant relationship with a caring adult; and

- a caregiver who abuses substances, suffers from mental illness, or engages in criminal behavior. (NIDA, 2003, p. 8)

NIDA identifies elements of drug abuse prevention that are family-based, notably, strengthening parenting involvement and communication with children. Parenting that reduces children's drug risk includes praising children for appropriate behavior; rule-setting and enforcement; monitoring children's and teens' activities; and using moderate, consistent discipline that enforces well-defined family rules (Kosterman, Hawkins, Haggerty, Spoth, & Redmond, 2001; NIDA, 2003, p. 3). In addition to parenting and family interventions, the NIDA staff also emphasize school and community prevention efforts.

In their policy statement on the use of tobacco, alcohol and other drugs, the AAP Committee on Substance Abuse argues against even recreational use of drugs, noting that drug use is illegal and is a major cause of injury and death among adolescents (AAP Committee on Substance Abuse, 1998). In the latest edition of the AAP's *Caring for Your Teenager* (Greydanus, 2003), parents are told to prohibit their children from using any drug, including tobacco and alcohol. Their rationale should reaffirm parents' affection and emphasize that drugs are dangerous and illegal. Parents' communications should emphasize the immediate negative consequences of drug use (e.g., smoking causes bad breath and stains teeth), their expense, and their addictive nature; they should teach their teens drug refusal skills. As one component of prevention, parents are cautioned to make sure that they do not inadvertently communicate pro-drug attitudes and model inappropriate drug use.

Experts' Strategies for How Parents Can Prevent Substance Use and Abuse

AUTHORITATIVE VERSUS AUTHORITARIAN PARENTING. As described in chapter 4, none of the experts condone permissive or uninvolved parenting, but clearly some are more authoritative, combining reasonable demands with parental responsiveness, whereas others are more authoritarian, combining demands and expectations for obedience with less responsiveness.

Spock and Rosemond show remarkable differences in the type of parent–child relationship that they believe discourages drug use. For Spock, it is important to form a good relationship with children early: "Friendliness rather than predominantly scolding. Mutual trust. Expecting the best.

Openness in conversations, whether they are day-by-day happenings or serious matters of morality. Mutual respect, politeness, and visible love. When I say 'from the beginning,' I mean from the age of two or three. It is difficult to make up for lost time during adolescence" (Spock & Parker, 1998, p. 630). Spock's aim, rather than strict obedience to parental prohibitions about drugs, is to have children internalize and apply a set of moral standards. "If I were to choose one basic skill to instill in your young child so that he has the strength to avoid drug abuse, it would be good decision-making skills based on a core set of values" (Spock, 1998, pp. 635–636). This contrasts with Rosemond's advice to parents who want to encourage their teens to say no to substance use in adolescence:

> You can limit television watching, make your marriage the number one priority in your family (or, if single, take good care of yourself), say 'no' to your child's requests ten times more than you say 'yes,' help your child, at an early age, learn to occupy and entertain himself, assign him to a regular routine of chores around the home and pay him not a red cent for doing them, teach your child spiritual values, avoid the tendency to micromanage during the teen years, etc., etc. (Rosemond, 2001d, p. 169)

This may be good advice in parts, but it suggests a much more distant relationship between parents and children than the closeness and mutual respect argued for by Spock.

COMMUNICATION. Spock stresses the importance of communication about drugs with preadolescents and adolescents: "Instead of passively waiting for your child to bring up the subject of drugs, you should ask her about it in a nonjudgmental, nonanxious, nonhysterical tone of voice" (Spock, 1998, p. 639). He warns about the risks of silence: "In fact, silence probably increases the likelihood of drug use. What happens is that the child goes to others to talk about this issue, usually friends who may have a very different perspective on the advisability and potential consequences of drug use from yours" (Spock & Parker, 1998, p. 630).

Leach also stresses the importance of communication, with an emphasis on avoiding parental hypocrisy about abstinence:

> Give every child realistic information. That means ensuring that growing children understand both the compulsive nature of habits like drug taking *and* their destructive effects. But it also means discussing

with then the (sad) fact that almost everybody in our society is at least mildly addicted to something which is at least a little damaging to their health. Your child is more likely to take seriously your diatribe against heroin if you are willing to acknowledge that you cannot start the day without coffee. (Leach, 1989b, p. 337)

Good communication also is based on her assumption that parents inevitably are reacting to a society that already is way ahead of them in its power and permissiveness.

Other authors are less resigned yet still practical. In one of his parenting columns, Dobson describes the findings of a large survey of teens and uses the findings to urge parents to talk to their teens about drugs:

> If teen-agers felt that their parents or siblings approved of smoking, they were likely to follow suit. And if there was one person who could convince them not to participate, it was usually a member of their own family. . . . Talk to your sons and daughters when they are young about the dangers of cigarette smoking. . . . Warn them repeatedly about drug abuse and what it can do to the body. Parents can make a difference in avoiding addictive behavior in their children if they take the time to teach them. (1998, p. B2)

Likewise, Rosemond (2001d, p. 182) focuses on the importance of general communication and listening responsively to teens so that they know that parents value their opinions, even if they do not agree.

DEALING WITH EXPERIMENTATION. Given that most adolescents do try smoking or drinking alcohol, and many try even riskier drugs, parents might need guidance in responding. Spock, Leach, and Rosemond counsel against panic and overreaction. Spock addresses the issue this way:

> In fact, a hysterical overreaction to a brief flirtation with drugs may do more harm than good. I'm not saying that experimentation is okay, but I think you should recognize that even the best teens in this day and age are curious and flirt with drugs. If that happens, it's your job to have a dialogue. Bear in mind that very few teens who experiment with drugs go on to have a long-term problem. (Spock & Parker, 1998, p. 635)

Consistent with her advice on adolescent sexuality, when advising parents about teen drug use, Leach cautions them not to force teens to choose between themselves and a peer group: "You may edge her into a position where she keeps peer group activities secret from you" (Leach, 1989b, p. 338). Leach also counsels: "Don't overreact to experiments. She may have to try the glamorous and grown-up habits she sees all around her. A true shock reaction from you is liable to hand her an irresistible weapon in any rebellion which is coming" (Leach, 1989b, p. 338). Dobson demonstrates his concern with drug use by providing an appendix to *The New Dare to Discipline* describing drug use as the beginning of deterioration in personal appearance, schoolwork, and relationships with parents. This appendix includes symptoms of drug abuse, a list of the most commonly abused drugs, and a glossary of street slang for drugs.

Evaluating the Experts on Adolescent Substance Misuse

Those authors who address substance abuse causes are largely accurate but with some telling oversights. Depression is a key precursor and correlate of adolescent substance abuse, as both Spock and Leach describe, but they fail to warn parents of the attributes predicting early use and later abuse: active, disruptive children with risk-taking temperaments and widespread academic problems. Their advice appears to be more geared to parents of occasional users rather than to parents of drug-dependent teens. In their parenting manuals, Rosemond and Dobson do not address personal attributes as risk factors, so they offer no danger signals to parents of children who are at special risk. All the experts recognize the importance of peer influence, which research confirms, so there is no disagreement there. Rosemond's attribution of adolescent drug problems to availability is good common sense but not the whole story. It does not account for the individual attributes that make some young people less at risk than others and the fact that some parenting practices seem to buffer young people from drug-related risks.

Turning to the topic of prevention, Spock's advice to parents to prevent substance abuse by friendliness, openness, and mutual trust and respect should provide some protection—if it leads to more cohesive, communicative parent–child relationships. Alternatively, children and teens with whom such relationships are possible may be simply less at risk for substance abuse. The most important—and surprising—discrepancy between the parenting experts' advice and adolescent substance abuse research is the lack of recognition that parent monitoring plays a significant role in preventing substance use. None of the experts recognize the value of the one general parenting behavior that substance abuse research has validated most often: keeping track of young people through regular monitoring of their whereabouts, friends, and activities. They are not alone in this oversight. Although the importance of monitoring in substance abuse prevention is recognized by the National Institute of Drug Abuse in its research-based publication, it is also overlooked in the American Academy of Pediatrics' latest manual on parenting adolescents.

Perhaps parental monitoring seems too simple, too obvious to merit consideration. Perhaps high-risk teens are just able to effectively prevent monitoring by not reporting their activities to their parents. The research is very good news, however, because monitoring is something that can be done easily and inexpensively. Simple questions such as "Where are you going? When will you be home?" can help provide evidence to teens of parental interest and concern and, according to research, help reduce the risk of early drug use and abuse. It would be naive, however, to assume that monitoring will have a protective effect when parents have been uninvolved for years or when parent–child relationships are intrusive or fractious. The success of monitoring depends on parents who have maintained a reasonable level of involvement with their children and cooperative, mostly honest teens. That is often not true of adolescents for whom substance misuse is just one of several problem behaviors.

Rosemond and Spock are correct on parents' need to avoid use of drugs they disapprove of for teens, given the extensive research of intergenerational transmission of substance use. Dobson's focus on symptoms and drug slang in *The New Dare to Discipline* and his writing about peer influence shows his concern with preventing teen drug use. He emphasizes detection skills for parents, but his writing about prevention gives them little to use besides focused communication about drug risks. Dobson does not differentiate between drug experimentation and abuse, seemingly because of the concern that even drug sampling might lead to abuse. Leach (1989b) seems more resigned to teen drug use and concerned about avoiding parental overreaction. Because of the number of very dangerous drugs developed recently, and the penalties for drug infractions in this country, her advice seems risky for teens. Spock, Dobson, and Leach place more emphasis on focused communication about drugs than does Rosemond, who describes facilitating general communication. On the other hand, the experts provide very useful information to parents on how to handle experimentation. Research has been largely silent on this issue, despite the voluminous literature on treatment of adolescent drug abuse.

Most parents deal with substance experimentation that accelerates during the high school years, and that is the situation that the parenting experts handle most effectively. Of course, even one binge or overdose can have disastrous consequences—fights, drunk driving, criminal acts or victimization, or death. According to the best current data (Johnston et al., 2002), 50% of high school seniors have been drunk in the last year, so parents are right to be concerned.

What are the implications of the research on protective factors? First, most effective, and perhaps most difficult for most parents to implement, is to avoid the use of alcohol, cigarettes, and illegal drugs. Parental abstinence reduces household availability and avoids providing a model that teens can imitate to become adultlike. Parents who are not abstinent should avoid discussing and using even licit drugs in ways that make them attractive to teens. Second, as argued above, monitoring teens' activities and whereabouts can be a simple and effective means of prevention.

Other preventive possibilities are less directly supported by research findings. Family warmth and cohesion appears to exert protective effects in most studies, and there is recent evidence that parental use of reasoning in early childhood may be protective. The evidence for the preventive effectiveness of communication about smoking is stronger than it is for other drugs. Communication about other drug risks is often not effective; at least it does not predict less future substance use. Coaching children and teens on social skills may help by making them less likely to be socially rejected and thus less disposed to join groups that misuse substances. Given the rates of use in the high school years, however, this is far from a sure thing. Indeed, whatever the approach taken, there are no guarantees. Parents will still have reason to worry as their children move into adulthood—beyond their control and perhaps playing with fire.

CHAPTER 7
CONCLUSION

FIVE AUTHORITATIVE SOURCES, five engaging personalities, five powerful communicators, five people who have had exceptional influence over American family life. They have emerged through the mass media and have provided answers about parenting for generations of American parents. Their persistent presence serves as a source of social authority in the public media, and they have put a face on professional expertise that is only remotely accessible to many parents.

Perhaps because of their stature in the media, the quality of their advice is rarely questioned in public. Nor do pediatricians, social workers, teachers, or counselors have the time to scrutinize that advice. This book is one attempt to fill that gap. It has compared the media experts' recommendations with research on topics that are important and problematic for parents and controversial for society. In such a selective review, drawing primarily on their parenting manuals, my goal has been to capture both the substance and the flavor of their advice. Attempting to represent in a brief profile the essential contributions of five major guides to the up-bringing of American children is not intended to produce answers to the major questions of contemporary parents. It cannot and should not supplant the writings of the authors themselves; to fully appreciate their perspectives, their books need to be read, their TV programs watched, their audio tapes listened to, and their Web sites visited. That is time well spent for anyone interested in family life.

The rise of professional expertise about parenting is necessarily a modern phenomenon. By now it seems natural that parents would be guided by professional experts talking about family life, just as people read medical columnists providing general health advice and listen to mechanics' radio shows dealing with car problems. Probably because advice from media parenting experts is widely distributed, and conceptions of good parenting so disparate and yet so fundamental, these authors arouse continuing public interest and intermittent controversy. Furthermore, the experts' divergent opinions are not merely competing constructions of family life in an open and pluralistic marketplace of ideas. Because they reach millions of parents through their media outlets, parenting experts have a greater responsibility than a relative or neighbor who might make suggestions about how to deal with a child's behavior. Because media experts contribute to cultural understandings of parenting, other professionals have a responsibility to take them seriously and to assess their advice.

CRITERIA FOR ASSESSMENT

As knowledge from research and clinical practice has accumulated, it has become increasingly possible to make reasoned judgments about the quality of experts' advice. These judgments draw on standards for critical analysis and ethical conduct and include the following: accuracy, comprehensiveness, avoiding harm, sensitivity to differences, practicality, nurturing children's positive attributes, and improving family life.

The substance of this book has been largely devoted to an examination of the *accuracy* of the experts' advice. Parenting and child development research has been used to test accuracy, and when available, advice has been evaluated against policy statements or best practice standards from committees of professionals. Accuracy about the basic facts of development, particularly age norms, is important because it can help parents decide how they will cope and whether to seek help (McCall, 1987).

Comprehensiveness is a key criterion for evaluation. The experts' guidance should serve as a source of continuity across a variety of topics, something that specialized volumes, each exploring a particular parenting niche, are not likely to do. One key point of evaluation, then, is the extent to which parenting experts cover what parents need to know about the behavior of infants, children, and adolescents.

Once coverage has been established, a tougher, more fundamental question emerges. None of the five experts recommends abuse or neglect of children; they all firmly and repeatedly reject it; but does their advice, however well intentioned, make it more likely? The experts have an obligation to advocate policies that *do no harm* to children. To use an analogy, ethical political leaders never advocate hate crimes, but sometimes their politics and policies make them distinctly more likely to happen. Should not the pronouncements made by family leaders, such as parenting experts, also be child protective in order to minimize the harm that parents do to their children? This is an essential criterion, one that should be met even if coverage is incomplete.

Better parenting advice also recognizes infant and child variability. There are continuing controversies about the relative contributions of genetic factors and parenting practices to development and increasingly strong evidence of interaction between the two (Ge et al., 1996; O'Connor, Deater-Deckard, Fulker, Rutter, & Plomin, 1998). Experts must be *sensitive to differences* embodied in temperamental differences that parents must deal with. But genetic influences expressed in temperament are far from the only factors beyond parents' control. There is accumulating evidence of the impact on children and teens of influences outside the family, notably entertainment media, schools, and peers, that contribute to differences among children and youth. Parental influence is inevitably just one of the strands that are interwoven in development, and the experts' advice should incorporate that reality.

The *practicality* of parenting experts' advice is another criterion for evaluation. Here the experts have a clear advantage over researchers who often are focused on hypothesis testing that has little immediate concern for applicability. The authors' advice on strategies that parents can use to reduce crying and fussiness during early infancy can be put to use immediately. Sometimes the advice is less useful, for example, when recommending child care for infants on the basis of the assumption that parents can find excellent care, when in fact it is often not available (Helburn et al., 1995; NICHD ECCRN, 1997a).

Two final criteria also are important. In addition to the "do no harm" injunction mentioned above, the media experts should provide advice that actively *nurtures children's positive attributes*: their social and emotional competence, their sense of moral values, and their skills for success in school and eventual employment. The experts' advice to parents should help contribute to children's responsible citizenship and their ability to make effective contributions to the society in which they live. Further, their advice should *improve family life* as evidenced by better parent–child communication, more reciprocal affection, and less conflict among family members, while maintaining healthy relationships with those outside the family.

INDIVIDUAL ASSESSMENTS

Spock

Benjamin Spock's advice can be explained neither by looking at the experts who had preceded him, nor by his medical and psychoanalytic training, nor by his married life and the parenting of his own sons. His own description of his mother's blend of progressivist health enthusiasms and strictness to the point of severity makes it clear that she is the source of many of his distinctive emphases (Spock & Morgan, 1989); yet he advocates a kinder, gentler form of strictness than he experienced as a child. Spock is famous for his direct and reassuring tone, including the oft-quoted first line of each edition of *Dr. Spock's Baby and Child Care*: "Trust yourself, you know more than you think you do" (Spock & Parker, 1998, p. 1). One of Dr. Spock's virtues is that he does not expect parents to be perfect. Parents are not given the burden of having to be solely rational, intellectual creatures. Spock recognizes how emotions can influence parenting, both positively and in ways that parents neither expect nor want (Spock & Parker, 1998, pp. 442–445).

Spock is the most comprehensive of the five experts. His advice assumes communicatively fluent parents who work to establish collaborative relationships between themselves and their children. Spock provides effective problem-solving strategies in dealing with problem crying and a straightforward approach to toilet training. Research validates his understanding that discipline begins in the early loving parent–child relationship and that physical punishment is a challenge to that relationship, though not all researchers agree that spanking is in itself harmful. His disciplinary style is clearly authoritative, which has been associated with good outcomes for children (Maccoby & Martin, 1983; Steinberg et al., 1994). Critics of his political positions labeled his parenting advice permissive, and certainly he is less rigid than his early 20th-century predecessors, but that is not an accurate characterization of his advice on discipline or other topics. Critics may have mistaken him as lax because of his stand against physical punishment. His stand is consistent with his reluctance to reduce parenting to the exercise of superior force, but he does not advocate leniency with young children. Spock describes children of permissive parents as "vines without a pole to grow on" (Spock & Parker, 1998, p. 431).

Spock's advice on infant day care provides an example of research that is not informed by the current realities that parents face. He expresses few concerns about early substitute child care provided the care is of high quality, but fails to recognize that there is little high-quality early child care in this country (Dunn & Kontos, 1997; NICHD ECCRN, 2000a). He mentions altering parents' work schedules to minimize the time spent in child care, but the best estimate is that only 25% of parents are able to accomplish that (NICHD ECCRN, 1997c). Given the recent evidence of greater behavior problems on school entry (NICHD ECCRN, 2003b) and elevated stress hormones in children who spend more hours in day care (Watamura et al., 2003), more caution is appropriate.

Spock's denouncement of violence in the media is strongly expressed, and a large body of research, both short-term and long-term, provides evidence for his argument that media violence has negative effects on children. His concern about violence, sexuality, and commercialism in the media are aspects of his general opposition to cultural forces that he believes encourage materialism and sabotage family life, but he correctly recognizes that media are ubiquitous in American households and gives parents advice that has been demonstrated by research to reduce their negative effects. To the extent that Spock's advice about teenage sexuality education can be supported by the current state of research, it, too, appears to be accurate.

It is important to note that a substantial portion of *Dr. Spock's Baby and Child Care* is devoted to physical care. When Spock advocates removing meat and milk products from young children's diets, he is on less solid ground than he is with his advice about behavior. Parents who read and use his book need to know that his dietary recommendations for young children were met with concern in the pediatric community when the seventh edition (Spock & Parker, 1998) was published; that advice should not be followed without consulting with the family's pediatrician (AAP Committee on Nutrition, 1998).

Spock's phenomenally successful book transformed his life, and he revised and updated it until shortly before his death. In addition to attacks from Norman Vincent Peale and Spiro Agnew about his supposed permissiveness, Spock was harshly criticized by Gloria Steinem and other feminists over the years, and he revised his book toward more gender equity in parenting responsibilities. In the latest edition of *Dr. Spock's Baby and Child Care*, the descriptions make it clear that fathers, just as much as mothers, are expected to be active, involved parents.

Spock, even several years after his death, remains the parenting expert who has had the greatest influence on American family life. *Dr. Spock's Baby and Child Care* was a watershed volume, and subsequent parenting publications have inevitably been influenced by it. It remains to be seen whether those who would maintain his legacy by offering advice through his Web site and editing his previous writing can do so successfully.

Brazelton

T. Berry Brazelton is a personable, grandfatherly, multimedia figure and a pediatrician's pediatrician, surrounded by a cluster of residents and researchers at the Child Development Unit that he founded at Children's Hospital Boston. He has been active in professional arenas that are largely invisible to the public: training pediatricians, developing assessment instruments, and building professional and parent training infrastructure. Brazelton has written more than any of the other four experts on the years from birth to age 6. His research studies made critical contributions to the pediatrics of infant crying and toilet training, among other areas, and his books draw upon his research and his 35 years of clinical practice.

Among the five, he is unique in applying evolutionary theory to help parents understand infants' behaviors. He has a strong emphasis on temperament, with separate chapters on different temperament types in *Infants and Mothers* and extensive treatment in his other volumes. He uses narrative engagingly as he describes profiles of different temperaments so that parents can identify their child with one of the descriptions and learn parenting strategies specifically tailored to that particular temperament. He was a pioneer in the concept of anticipatory guidance, which gives parents the ability to look ahead and potentially head off some problems. His insights into what he labels touchpoints—spurts in development when rapid, destabilizing reorganization occurs—are unique among the experts (Brazelton, 1992). His focus is assisting children to acquire the ability to regulate their own behavior, beginning with self-soothing in infancy, and on the internalization of parental moral and social controls.

Brazelton is accurate in attributing much of early infant crying to an immature nervous system. His advice on toilet training and his step-by-step instructions provide advice to parents that he has systematically tested with research, and his technique is effective enough that Spock adopted it. On discipline, his policy of rejecting physical punishment but advocating firm control is safe for parents to administer, because it avoids the risk of punishment escalating into abuse. His recommendation that parents explain to children why they are being disciplined is a teaching tool that helps avoid making parent–child discipline encounters into power struggles. His use of cool-down, time-out periods helps head off problems and minimize disciplinary episodes.

On early child care, his position clearly changed over the years, as research has documented the frequently mediocre or poor care available for infants and toddlers (Helburn et al., 1995; NICHD ECCRN, 1997a) and negative effects of early care as well as some positive ones (NICHD ECCRN, 2002b). His recently expressed position against enrolling infants and toddlers in full-time care, in his advocacy book cowritten with Stanley Greenspan (Brazelton & Greenspan, 2000), is cautious to the point of being alarmist for parents who may have insufficient income to allow one of them to stay at home. As a parenting policy recommendation, it is safe, meeting the "do no harm" criterion, because the long-term effects are not yet known for the quality of child care that large number of parents are actually able to obtain. Some very recently collected findings have suggested that negative effects fade during the early elementary years (NICHD ECCRN, 2004b; Peisner-Feinberg et al., 2001), but caution is still sound policy.

Brazelton's expressed concerns about media violence are supported by extensive research demonstrating its negative effects; his statements that extensive TV viewing of entertainment viewing leads to lowered levels of creativity have received some confirmation, at least for girls (D. R. Anderson, Huston, Schmitt, Linebarger, & Wright, 2001). His ideas about parents watching television with their children are demanding for parents, but when they do so, children watch less television and shows that are of better quality. To briefly summarize, on infant and early child topics he is an unbeatable guide for parents. He writes authoritatively and engagingly on the topics that they need to know about and provides reassurance when it is called for. Is he the best of the best? If children never got any older than 6, arguably so. The problem, however, was identified by a mother who once asked me, "Who do I read after Brazelton?" When their children "age out" of the Brazelton books, parents must then refer to other experts for advice on older children and adolescents.

Dobson

James Dobson's coverage of children's development and relevant parenting strategies is not comprehensive, though he clearly addresses many topics in addition to the parent–child relationships and discipline tactics that he describes in his famous first book, *Dare to Discipline*. He has written books covering topics from infancy to adolescence, as well as one addressed to adolescents. More than any of the other experts, Dobson has come to rely on an army of collaborators and "extenders" to spread his message. The recent publication of a parenting manual written by a panel of experts from his Focus on the Family organization is one instance of this, but so are the monthly magazines that Focus publishes for children, teens, and parents, and the guest speakers on Dobson's radio programs. In recent years, he has become less visible as a parenting expert and more visible as a political activist at the head of Focus on the Family with its massive outreach and fund-raising operations.

Dobson's is a firm, value-based approach to raising children, combining the distinctive religious flavor of his conservative Protestant upbringing with the tools of behavior analysis and modification. Parents are understood to be standing in for God in socializing children to be respectful, responsible, and caring adults. Dobson writes only in passing about babies, seemingly because he is not really interested in infants as infants, but rather in preparing even the smallest children for their adult roles in the family, church, and society. Children should accept parents' rules and respect their standards, but ultimately they should accept God's standards for behavior as expressed in scripture. Dobson's writing on parenting focuses on love and control, which he emphasizes must be in balance. He equates too much love with permissiveness, which most researchers on parenting would not do. Drawing on his background in behavior modification, he instructs parents in the use of preventive controls and token economies so that they will dispense rewards more often than punishments.

Dobson has a concern about children's expression of defiance that is unique among the experts. Defiance is a more important factor in determining punishment than the child's intent to do evil, the actual harm done to other children, or the extent of damage to property. He recommends the use of physical punishment to get compliance. Here Dobson diverges from many parenting researchers and clinicians. Granted, there is evidence that physical punishment can be useful in producing immediate compliance (Gershoff, 2002), but there is also evidence from research on young children that firm parental control is the likely cause of defiance rather than its result (Crockenberg & Litman, 1990). If Dobson is correct that physical punishment, in fact, induces respect for the parent (and by extension, God), then it would be expected that those children who receive the most of it would be the best behaved. However, long-term studies demonstrate that children who have received larger amounts of corporal punishment are in fact worse behaved and show more violent behavior and criminality as adults. After controlling for their early aggressive and antisocial behavior, there is no relationship between parents' punishment practices and children's outcomes, so early corporal punishment does not have any apparent preventive effect (Eron et al., 1991; Farrington, 1995). Moreover, when spanking, Dobson suggests using a switch or a paddle, and the American Academy of Pediatrics Committee on Psychosocial Aspects of Child and Family Health (1998) has come out firmly against the use of objects in physical punishment.

Dobson encourages parents to clamp down on children who are defiant and will not obey. He is concerned with engaged but permissive parents who tolerate out-of-control behavior from their children. In fact, children with the worst behavior problems are not those children who are engaged with parents yet occasionally willful and disobedient, but rather children who have very few positive interactions with their parents and many aversive ones (Patterson, 1982). The parents in these families often have poor household management skills, show low rates of interaction with their children, and engage in nattering and erratic punishment that can be very severe on occasion. They resort to the use of physical punishment because affectional controls do not work, and other forms of discipline are often used ineptly. Escalating to the use of physical punishment in this context does not improve children's behavior, because they have few incentives to try to please their parents (Patterson, 1982). Child defiance is not the central problem in these families; it is lack of parental engagement and effective management.

Evaluating Dobson's disciplinary strategies, it is important not to overlook his emphasis on the bonds of affection between parents and children, which he argues help to motivate compliance. But his concern with establishing control over young children leads him to misread some signs. Infant behavior that he regards as disobedient or manipulative (e.g., following when told not to, intense crying on separation) may in fact be rooted in young children's strong bonds of attachment. Ironically, these affectionate bonds are the ones that form the basis for compliance (Kochanska et al., 2004). His concern about controlling children leads to a one-dimensional classification of children concerning how strong-willed they are, which misses important dimensions of temperament. His advocacy for physical punishment, particularly in response to defiance, comes not from a systematic weighing of effectiveness and drawbacks based on parenting research, nor from his expertise as a school psychologist, but because physical punishment is "scripturally correct"—the rod of correction is endorsed in the Book of Proverbs.

There are several reasons why many parents like Dobson, but certainly one of them is that he gives them permission to spank children when they misbehave. Physical punishment is attractive to many parents because it can be used immediately. The child is spanked, and then, in their minds at least, the punishment incident is over. By contrast, administering time-out inevitably means dealing with the child both immediately and later, because continued attention is often needed to ensure that the child stays in time-out. Other advantages are that time-out can be used even when parents have failed to take preventive steps to avoid problems and when their rapport with the child, for whatever reason, is not good enough to get cooperation. It can be used by parents who sense that their child did something very wrong and are too angry to think of alternatives or lack the verbal skills to explain to the child why he or she is being punished. Unfortunately, when Dobson cites biblical authority for use of physical punishment, recommends spanking with an object, and even writes that children who cry too much about being spanked should be threatened with more of the same, he makes abuse more likely. Although he repeatedly reaffirms his stand against abuse, physical punishment episodes can escalate into abuse, and in fact, that is how most abuse incidents begin (Kadushin & Martin, 1981; Straus, 1994).

Dobson writes with concern on the extent of TV violence and its likely effects, assertions that get solid support from a large base of research. His advocacy for abstinence-only sexuality education has less to do with what works to delay onset of sexual intercourse among teens than with his rejection of sexual activity outside of marriage. Comprehensive sexuality education does not lead to earlier sexual activity (Bennett & Assefi, 2005; Kirby, 2002), contrary to Dobson's assertions. His argument for parents' focused communication on the risks of drug use has not been well supported by research, which suggests that in many instances such communications have little effect. In summary, Dobson's advice centers on issues of control and should help bring about the outcomes that he values in children: immediate compliance in the short term and affection and respect for parents and the social hierarchy in the long term. It is less clear that his techniques foster the development of ethical decision making outside of social conventions.

Leach

Penelope Leach is interesting because she is the best-known British child psychologist who also has been sought out by American parents. Her writing is highly readable and engaging, and her coverage is so extensive that her books are close to encyclopedic. She vividly describes and provides illustrations of infants' and children's most endearing qualities. What makes Leach distinctive is her intense focus on the infant–parent bond and her strategy of communication-rich cooperative parenting. The first enables the second: Establishing a strong infant–parent bond will help make children want to behave; then parents can teach them parents' and society's standards for proper behavior. This understanding of the parenting process colors her advice in its particulars: Babies should never have to "cry it out," and they should not be thoughtlessly plunked in substitute care (Leach's advocacy writing describes day care separations as being similar to bereavements). The parent–infant bond must be as strong as possible so that the child is motivated to please the parent, who can use this strong connection to facilitate the child's mastery of developmental tasks—most importantly, self-control and appropriate internalization of adult standards.

Leach's comment that "worthwhile discipline has to be self-discipline" (1989b, p. 208) and her avoidance of "the deliberate infliction of pain, physical or mental" (Leach, 1994, p. 129) are additional indications of her priorities: She is more concerned with motivating and shaping parent–child cooperation and child mastery, and less with having parents maintain a high degree of control. For the same reasons, she insists that children must always be given reasons for discipline so that they can learn proper behavior. One of her strengths is her ability to get parents to view situations from a child's perspective, as when she explains a child's jealousy about the impending birth of a sibling by comparing it to the feeling a wife might have on learning that her husband was going to marry an additional wife (Leach, 1998, p. 422). She offers parents reasons why children might be misbehaving from the child's perspective.

In some important aspects, Leach's advice is inaccurate. Her advocacy writing about early child care impairing attachment to mothers is not supported by research. She is correct, though, that frequent turnover in caregivers makes many day care situations far from optimal, especially for infants and toddlers. Her advice on toilet training makes the process more rather than less complex. Despite her assertions to the contrary, toddlers can be and are routinely disciplined by parents. Leach believes that time-outs are difficult to implement, but they are an effective and relatively safe form of discipline (M. W. Roberts et al., 1981). Her disciplinary strategies might work best with children of highly communicative parents who are closely attached to them and who have highly communicative and compliant tendencies themselves. But parents of active 3-year-olds with bouts of aggression, poor impulse control, and only average intelligence might find it very difficult to discipline them without causing any mental pain, even if they can avoid physical pain.

The book in which Leach writes about children and adolescents, *Your Growing Child,* is in serious need of updating, not having been revised since 1989. Her coverage of older children and adolescents is not as good as her coverage of infants and younger children. When Leach writes about adolescents, she conveys the impression that parents of teens should be largely resigned to their lack of control and should accept that adolescents' important attachments are now to their peers. Parents must avoid overreacting to experimentation in sexual activity and substance use, rather than actively counseling against such potentially disastrous adventures. More mystifying is her lack of attention to fathers' roles in development. Fathers are in the illustrations in *Your Baby and Child,* but they are rarely mentioned explicitly in the advice given, as they should for their own sakes as well as for their wives' and children's. Of all the authors, she comes the closest to permissiveness, although with children and teens who are bright and basically compliant, there is research evidence that the parenting methods she recommends will promote effective internalization of moral and social standards and close, harmonious family relationships.

Rosemond

Rosemond's advice is distinguished by his parent-centered approach to child rearing, in which children are given a strong sense of paternal authority. Like Dobson, he writes little about infant topics for which specialized knowledge would be required. Parents are told to focus on their marriages first and, if they are single, to take good care of themselves. There is little discussion of the pleasures of sharing recreational activities with children or of the enjoyment that can come from doing household or hobby projects together. He deemphasizes parental nurturance and affection and emphasizes parental assertion of power. The ultimate explanation to be given to children for any parental decision is "because I said so." Sometimes it seems as if he is exhorting his audiences, composed nearly entirely of mothers, to mother more the way that some fathers do: Get the children to understand that you are the boss, tell them what to do and make sure that they do it, and meanwhile keep your distance and live in your adult world. The model would be the type of father who comes home from the office, eats dinner, and reads the paper in the evening while family life happens around him. He rails against child-centered households in which parents, usually mothers, neglect their spouses in favor of the children's needs, wishes, and desires.

His general child management strategy is demonstrated consistently in specific pieces of advice. For example, within the past several years, he has argued that parents should pick the time to begin toilet training (Rosemond, 1998e). It turns out that most parents believe that children should be toilet-trained at an earlier age than when they actually are ready to learn (Stehbens & Silber, 1971), so his strategy heightens the possibility for conflictual interactions and potentially for abuse. Although it has not been specifically disproven, there is no systematic evidence that toilet training can be accomplished by many children in 1 week by using the techniques that Rosemond describes. His advice not to provide children with reasons for parental decisions asserts parental power but does nothing to help children internalize parental standards. Rosemond is in favor of time-outs, which tend to deescalate conflict situations, and his use of physical punishment counts on parents keeping control of themselves even when spanking in anger. Since most abuse episodes begin as physical punishment (Kadushin & Martin, 1981; Straus, 1994), this assumption is risky.

Rosemond's radical shift in position on the use of early child care, like his shift on toilet training, was presented with very little support from research, and there is little, if any, evidence supporting the direct connection he makes between early child care and increases in depression or in attention-deficit/hyperactivity disorders. Similarly, his positions on media are not supported by existing research, as when he argues that it is the process of watching media that is problematic, not the content. In fact, there is substantial evidence that watching media violence causes heightened aggression and that watching educational television is associated with better academic performance. There is research evidence to support his advice to parents concerning adolescent substance-use prevention, but a lingering double standard is evident in his treatment of adolescent sexuality education: Only girls are counseled about their responsibilities in his manual on parenting adolescents. He advocates abstinence-only sexuality education, which has yet to demonstrate its effectiveness.

What is unusual about Rosemond as a parenting expert is that he gives specific advice that so often turns out to be wrong. His *Better Homes* columns were studies in moderation, but over time and across outlets, he has begun increasingly to define himself against other professionals and against societal trends of which he disapproves. On key issues he has changed positions radically in directions away from research findings and toward the sensibilities of a narrower, more conservative audience. Because he lacks the credentials of the other four experts and because of his inaccurate advice and position changes, it might be easy to dismiss Rosemond, but that would be a mistake. He strikes a responsive chord in large numbers of parents, and many buy his books. He also reaches many parents each week through his newspaper and magazine columns and his Web site. He is a force to be reckoned with, and family professionals need to be aware of his positions when working with parents.

Common Ground and Distinctive Messages

Parenting might seem to involve a fixed set of problems and widely tested solutions, yet the experts' philosophies and particular strategies for parenting differ remarkably. So when their writings converge, it is worth paying attention, because it reveals something important about them and about the culture as well. One important area of convergence is their concerns about the lack of support in contemporary society for families. They depict families as besieged by forces in the larger culture that are not healthy for children or their parents. For families with infants and young children, they lament that the pressure of parents' employment is pulling families apart and leaving children in care that is suboptimal. On this topic Spock, Leach, Brazelton, Dobson, and Rosemond have each written impassioned arguments.

They are all against permissiveness, and their recommendations share an insistence on discipline that is firm and responsive to the child's behavior. In this they are backed up by extensive research (e.g., Baumrind, 1991a, 1991b) that demonstrates that permissive parenting does not optimize development. The experts who take a stand against the use of physical punishment may be perceived by some as lax, as if only parents who use physical punishment can be considered strict. This is particularly ironic because as noted earlier, those parents in community studies who use physical punishment, particularly with older children, are likely to be lax and erratic in discipline and then find themselves using physical punishment in an attempt to regain control (Patterson, 1982; Stoolmiller et al., 1997). But all the experts, whatever their position on physical punishment, share a commitment to well-socialized, respectful, socially competent children. One of the subtexts of all the experts' books may be to give mothers (and fathers) some backbone against children who repeatedly test the limits of parental authority.

All five experts are concerned about children's heavy use of electronic media, and largely the same aspects of media elicit their complaints: the violence, the sexuality, the commercialism. Children's actual viewing time and parent practices are more extensively researched and better documented on this topic than on others, and there is a discouragingly wide gap between the experts' advice and what parents actually do. Of course, the experts do not agree about limiting viewing hours (Leach dissents, arguing that limits make television more valuable), but those that limit suggest an hour or two a day at the most. This definitely is a call for change, as the average American child is watching more than 3 hours a day (Nielsen Media Research, 1998; Rideout et al., 2005). The experts agree that parents should control TV content, and there is evidence that they are correct: When parents do what the experts advise, the quality of children's viewing is higher (Rideout et al., 2005; St. Peters et al., 1991). Unfortunately, a recent survey found that barely 50% of families reported using the TV rating system to restrict the TV content that their children watched (Kaiser Family Foundation, 2001a). Thus, there is a substantial gap between what most experts advise and what parents actually practice, even when the experts are in consensus on a topic.

In summary, the five authors, each in their own way, are all family advocates who strengthen parents against their own children's unreasonable demands and against the temptations of a broader culture that they perceive to be either neutral or unfriendly to families. The parenting experts are superior communicators who have refined their messages to reach a mass audience. Each has a personality that is attractive enough that people are drawn to their messages, and each has a passion or at least a commitment to the positions that they espouse. In reviewing the accuracy of their advice, it is clear that on some topics the advice given by one or more of them is quite discrepant from that suggested by research and policy statements. So they are not authorities by virtue of their ratio of correct to incorrect advice, or that is certainly not the only operative criterion. Nor can research and clinical evidence always carry the day when there is very little evidence on some researchable questions that are important for parents. What is the best method for toilet training? Which disciplinary method leads to the longer interval before recurrence of the infraction? These are basic questions that have yet to be addressed with the intensity and careful methods that their importance dictates.

In many fields, disagreement among experts would lead to the conclusion that the knowledge base is uncertain and that none of the potential sources of advice is trustworthy, and in this instance, that would be a mistake. As will be discussed, these discrepancies are not the result of random errors but instead are intentional and systematic and conveyed through powerful persuasive strategies.

THE EXPERTS' PERSUASIVE TECHNIQUES

How do parenting experts' messages build an audience such that parents return to them again and again? One of the themes that resonates through the authors' writing is reassurance. This may be one aspect of building rapport with readers, much as practicing pediatricians and psychologists must build rapport with patients in order to begin treatment. With some clearly identified exceptions, parents are told repeatedly that the behavioral crisis at hand, whatever it might be, will pass in time. They are reminded in a number of contexts that not all episodes of child distress and misbehavior are signs of their own incompetence. They are advised that some difficult-to-deal-with behaviors are in fact signs of healthy development. It seems evident that the expert understands that parents are trying to do the best job they can and that there are many things that parents do not have to worry about. The appeals to common sense may be one aspect of the message of reassurance. Spock, Dobson, and Rosemond—experts whose positions are otherwise very different—all feature common sense in their book titles, chapter titles, and articles. Common sense implies good judgment that is not dependent on specialized knowledge. Most parents *know* that they lack specialized training in child psychology or pediatrics, and while they may doubt their own judgment, they know it is something they can develop. Thus, affirmation of common sense can both guide and comfort the reader.

Narrative is a powerful tool that the experts use to persuade their audience. When Brazelton writes, an active temperamental style in infancy turns into an ongoing narrative of life in a household in which a rambunctious baby has spilled cereal, pulled the books out of bookshelves, and generally kept parents off balance. The vivid narrative is interspersed with advice on how to manage a baby with this temperament. Sometimes stories are used to interject humor, as when anecdotes are inserted from the lives of children and grandchildren. Sometimes the narratives are more extended, and their purpose is clearly to serve as cautionary tales for parents. Dobson describes a defiant, disobedient 13-year-old, who as a 2-year-old spat in his mother's face when she put him in his crib. She did not punish him for it, and the mother "never had the upper hand with her child after that night!" (Dobson, 1992, p. 28). Rosemond's and Dobson's writings about adolescence are frequently illustrated with stories of good children gone wrong. Sometimes the parents are too timid to intervene decisively, in which case bad behavior goes to worse. Sometimes parents intervene decisively, switching them to another school or selling their car, and the downward spiral is arrested and family harmony is regained. These narrative "case histories" may be more persuasive to readers than theoretical or statistical information that is more difficult to understand (McCall, 1987).

Perhaps most compelling among the persuasive strategies that bring readers back time after time is the hope the authors provide of a more gratifying family life, a family-centered idealism. Regardless of the particular parenting strategies advocated, they appeal to parents' sense that there could be a better way of being a family, and they remind parents of a core sense of values that should inform parenting. This idealism is contrasted with the harsh reality of an uncaring world. The family is valued but also set apart. Parenting experts guide parents through a hostile culture that is perceived to devalue spiritual and moral values in general and family life in particular. Given that parenting has self-sacrificial qualities (who would choose to get up at 2:30 AM as parents of infants routinely do?), the invocation of idealism may resonate with parents and help them see their efforts as part of a higher calling. Consider, for example, the title of one of Spock's books, *A Better World for Our Children*. As he writes there, "I believe that spiritual values and idealism—within or without organized religion—are as real and as powerful as the physical and intellectual attributes of human being. I believe that we can give our children standards to live by and keep them from cynically accepting amorality and immorality" (Spock, 1994, p. 101). For Dobson, these standards have a specifically religious origin: "The best source of guidance for parents can be found in the wisdom of the Judeo-Christian ethic, which originated with the Creator and was then handed down generation by generation from the time of Christ. This is what my mother, my grandmother, and my great-grandmother understood almost intuitively" (Dobson, 1992, p. 16). Brazelton and Leach invoke a vision of family life that is closer to the ideal when they compare the situation that currently exists for families with what should be available in relatively wealthy portions of the world like the United States and the United Kingdom. Readers are reminded that in this culture, children and families are not as much of a priority as they should be.

Inevitably, much of the advice that the parenting experts have given over the years was not established by their training in pediatrics or psychology. Of course, those who were practicing got feedback from families about whether their suggestions worked. But especially during the years when the five authors were doing most of their writing, parenting research and professional policy statements provided only bare outlines that might help them in addressing parents' concerns. There were few generally established facts about young children, and the authors were inevitably filling in the blanks among them. How they filled them in their books on parenting is highly revealing of their perspectives and their appeal to parents.

The experts' values are revealed not only by what they profess but also by what they oppose. Consider Spock's concern about teaching children values: "If we give them no spiritual values to live by, they are wide open to the materialism pounded in by television programs, music videos and other commercial hucksterism" (Spock, 1994, p. 151). Dobson appeals to parents by writing against those whom he believes have replaced biblically based values in parenting. Among the varied list of offenders, such as Sigmund Freud, Benjamin Spock, educator A. S. Neill, sex therapist Dr. Ruth Westheimer, and talk show hosts Phil Donahue and Oprah Winfrey (Dobson, 1992), are people who have made few public pronouncements on parenting. What they did do, though, was address topics in family life (or education) from perspectives that were largely secular or did not emphasize good behavior and respect for authority. Rosemond's foils are mental health professionals, who are "bandits. Con artists" (Rosemond, 2001b, p. xvi) capable of perpetrating cover-ups on the public (see chapter 3). This may have appeal for parents who are uncomfortable with what they have heard about Freud and Spock and who are distrustful of the specialized knowledge of therapists and caseworkers.

A related appeal invokes nostalgia. Rosemond makes frequent references to the way that grandma used to parent; Dobson frequently reminds readers of time-honored values in discipline. At times this nostalgia slides into themes of social decay and apocalyptic rhetoric that have been prevalent in Dobson's writing throughout his career and more frequent in Rosemond's recent books and newspaper columns. Spock reminisces that when he was a boy, values for children were set by clergy, parents, and teachers, but complains that today many children and teens are getting their standards primarily from movies and television and that programming is produced with little sense of responsibility (Spock, 1994, pp. 97–98). The exception here is Leach, who regards such nostalgic themes as based on a largely fictional understanding of family life in the past, a theme that has been articulated by others as well (e.g., Coontz, 1992).

PARENTING ADVICE IN CONTEXT: MARKETING STRATEGIES AND NEWSWORTHINESS

The experts' values are often revealed more in their advocacy writing than in their parenting manuals, though Spock and Dobson thunder about cultural immorality in all their books. The others are seemingly more calculating, often taking more centrist positions in their manuals and general audience publications than they do in newspaper columns and advocacy books. For years Rosemond wrote the general parenting columns for *Better Homes and Gardens* and politics were never mentioned. During that same period, his newspaper columns became increasingly politicized so that eventually whole columns were devoted to the prospect of a Children's Rights Amendment (Rosemond, 1995c, p. 3E) or his perception that "helping professionals" were leading "America's parents into a blind alley" (Rosemond, 1994d, p. 3E).

Brazelton's and Leach's advocacy books and public statements occasionally contrast sharply with what they write in their parenting manuals. Presumably their advocacy writings represent their genuine beliefs. This raises the question of how large a gap is defensible between the manuals and the advocacy writings. For instance, Leach writes with some enthusiasm in her parenting manual about substitute care (see chapter 4), in marked contrast to her advocacy book, *Children First* (1994), in which she argues forcefully against it. If she truly believes that it is bad for infants and toddlers, that view should certainly be expressed in the most recent edition of *Your Baby and Child* (1998), which reaches a wide audience of parents. Similarly, Brazelton, in his book with Greenspan (2000), recommends against parents placing infants or toddlers in child care 30 or more hours a week (with the qualification "if they have reasonable options" [p. 48]). But in a subsequently printed edition of *Touchpoints*, Brazelton's parenting manual, which lists the book coauthored with Greenspan among the authors' other titles, the cautionary advice about early child care is omitted, although the edition is updated in other ways. It may be the case that in their manuals, though not in their advocacy writings, Brazelton and Leach are reluctant to appear judgmental about substitute care because they know it is frequently used. In light of their concerns about early substitute care, it seems appropriate for Brazelton and Leach to revise their parenting manuals to tell parents to stay home if they have the opportunity to do so (reasonable options in Brazelton's language), just as they do in their advocacy books and interviews. Raising children is challenging enough without having to consider how advice might be shaped by marketing considerations.

Professionals in medicine or the behavioral sciences who want to publish their research are familiar with the judgments of peer review. There is careful evaluation whether their research procedures are adequate to address the question at hand and whether their judgments and interpretations are supported by their findings. Any claims beyond the most cautious interpretations of findings are assailed vigorously by reviewers and editors. Clinicians are similarly well acquainted with review and oversight as patients or clients seek second opinions and health insurers set treatment guidelines. By contrast, interpretations of research or advice given in a newspaper column or on a Web site are rarely scrutinized by professionals other than the writer and are protected as self-expression under the First Amendment to the Constitution. This "double standard" in documentation has been bemoaned in the scientific community (e.g., Garn, 1979) and sets the stage for important ethical issues. For instance, is it unethical to publish advice in public media that might lead to bad outcomes for some children?

It is not the case that scrutiny of the content of books and newspaper columns is absent, but rather that a different set of standards is applied in public media. As McCall (1987) dryly noted, "Persuasion and rules of evidence are different" (p. 1210). Media outlets are businesses, and some types of information sell better than others. The solidity of the evidence base does not seem to make much difference; editors consider whether information is news (McCall, 1987). News often challenges existing thought and typical ways of doing things (Gans, 1980; C. H. Weiss, 1985). For instance, common beliefs about effective parenting are revealed as being myths, and changes are recommended. Controversy draws readership and so does celebrity. So book authors and columnists, even those who write on parenting, have an incentive to revise their positions, to take positions contrary to conventional wisdom and to create controversy by attacking other professionals. As noted by Donna Bryant of the University of North Carolina–Chapel Hill, who compares John Rosemond to Rush Limbaugh, a focus on "divisive hot buttons" may be part of Rosemond's strategy because "it's good for business" (Sheehan, 1999, p. A23).

Some of Rosemond's apparent attempts to generate controversy are relatively transparent, for example, when he pronounces in a column that there is no such thing as a glass ceiling on women's achievement (Rosemond, 1994f), or supports Newt Gingrich's idea of giving welfare mothers the option of putting their children in "orphanages" (Rosemond, 1995b), but because they are overtly political statements that any individual might weigh in on, they can be easily evaluated by readers. Parents can take or leave that opinion, and it will not necessarily make any difference in how they treat their children. But when he writes in a column that children can be toilet trained in a week (Rosemond, 1998d), or denies that ADHD has a biological basis and attributes it to a "dysfunctional parenting philosophy" (Rosemond, 2003a, p. E9), or tells parents that attachment disorder is "psychobabble" (Rosemond, 2003b, p. C1), he might create problems for families. He is writing on a topic for which he would be expected to have privileged professional knowledge and to rely on evidence, and in fact his use of evidence is selective, and in some cases relevant evidence that contradicts his position is simply ignored.

As noted in previous chapters, Rosemond changes his positions independent of changes in research and clinical evidence. If his advice does not meet standards of evidence, he surely meets editors' and publishers' standards for interest and readability. There is some irony in the fact that because he lacks a doctorate in psychology he cannot legally conduct counseling or psychotherapy with clinical populations without being supervised by a doctoral-level psychologist in his home state of North Carolina, but he can and does speak and write on counseling and therapeutic topics to large audiences around the country. The reprimand and consent order issued by the North Carolina Psychology Board (Sheehan, 1999) would be enough to dry up referrals for most practicing psychologists, but they received very little attention in the press, where his columns continue to appear on a regular basis. Rosemond continues to give parenting advice to large live, newspaper, and Web audiences who are seemingly unaware of these disciplinary actions. In fact, in his most recent general parenting manual, Rosemond (2001b) chooses to excoriate the Board and the mental health professions and to tout his self-consciously unconventional positions. When parents read an article by a media expert, they assume that they are getting advice that is based on the current state of knowledge in the profession, screened for error and overstatement. In fact, what they are getting when they read Rosemond is advice that doubles as a salvo in a culture war.

It is not surprising that there would be different opinions on parenting. It is surprising that the experts could give such diverse advice while invoking the authority of science and the professions. This is a challenge for the behavioral sciences. There is a need for better dissemination of the considerable body of behavioral science findings so that media and market forces have little or no influence and evidence-based successful practices have greater influence in the public conversation about parenting as they have in treatment (DeAngelis, 2005). The experts are potentially part of the solution as communicators of research and clinical findings, but when their advice is wildly discrepant from those findings, and they increase the audience for their advice by creating controversy, it is a sign of a weakness in the behavioral sciences and the social service professions. Until the research is communicated more effectively, public discussion of parenting is still one in which values are believed to be more important than empirical findings and practice.

POLITICS AND PARENTING

The parenting manuals, supplemental books, tapes, and Web sites are marketed and bought under the assumption that they will help parents socialize their children. But far more important is the role that the experts' manuals play in socializing parents. Certainly, parents learn specific helpful tips for managing children on the basis of professional know-how, but more important they learn the experts' ways of thinking about children, and they absorb cultural expectations about good parenting and good behavior in children. It is also the case that parents are more likely to select experts who they find to be congenial; reading their books strengthens their beliefs and further socializes them in directions to which they are already inclined.

The experts' books discuss a vast range of topics, from infant nutrition to children's art projects to teenage social cliques. In each case, the many observations and opinions are held together by a political philosophy. Consider Spock's, Brazelton's, and Leach's extensive, careful descriptions of infants and young children. Whatever the topic, the focus is on the individual autonomy that is characteristic of progressive liberalism. Parents are thought to be, or taught to be, rational and responsible decision makers.

They should use their own good judgment rather than relying on others. Thus, the focus of the experts is on giving parents the knowledge of the child's development that they need to make their own decisions.

For children the focus is on internalization of moral principles so that they can make their own reasoned judgments. Parenting is supposed to aid the development of children's ability to function autonomously in moral decision making. They recommend giving children age-appropriate reasons when they are disciplined, so that they can internalize the moral standards that parents are trying to teach. The long-term goal is to teach children to be good when the parent is not around, to function independently as moral individuals. This idea may seem unobjectionable, but it is not without contradictions, especially when applied to family life. For society to sustain itself and for individuals to thrive, children need to not only grow up and out of families but back into them and into other forms of connection and interdependency. Liberalism, however, tends to focus relatively little on such customary relationships as the family (Plamenatz, 1973–1974).

For progressive liberals such as Spock, Brazelton, and Leach, society has certain obligations. It should not trample individual rights, and it should not let powerful social forces (e.g., the market economy or ethnic or religious prejudices) crush individuals. Societies have a responsibility to protect the vulnerable, those at the margins, young children among them (Plamenatz, 1973–1974). A characteristic liberal approach is to recognize that most mothers of young children are working outside the home, to investigate the current quality of substitute care and find that it is not good, and to call for better government support and regulation of the quality of care for young children. Thus, Spock advocates for better child care and recommends better federal funding to help bring it about. Similarly, Brazelton argues against welfare reform, arguing that it would be a special hardship for mothers with young children (Healy, 1998). These are stock examples of a progressive liberal response to social problems.

By contrast, consider Dobson's concern about "manipulative" crying by babies less than a year old. Recall his insistence that the family is the only appropriate context for sexuality education and his rejection of any public instruction in contraception. Likewise, consider Rosemond's insistence that parents not reason with a child in disciplinary situations. These positions held by these two very different individuals are unrelated to research and clinical knowledge, but they are linked together by an underlying set of beliefs and a consistent way of approaching problems in the family, in the community, and in the larger society.

As described in the introductory chapter, James Dobson has a clear sense of being on a mission from God. He apparently has total confidence, reinforced by daily prayer, that he is a pipeline for God's views, and as Dobson expresses them, God's views are those of the conservative Protestant. Through most of his career, Rosemond has written in a more secular vein, but of late he has begun to claim that he, too, is conveying the word of God: "There is nothing I have ever said that does not have root in His Word" (Rosemond, 2001b, p. xiii). The mission of the social conservative is to reestablish the preeminence of traditional, hierarchically organized social institutions, especially the family and the church (Vierhaus, 1973–1974). Babies who, according to Dobson's analysis, cry in order to control their parents must be left to cry it out; otherwise the natural hierarchy of the family, with mother over children and father over all, will be disturbed. Physical punishment is not only approved of in the Book of Proverbs; it also helps children remember that they are under the control of powerful adults who ultimately must answer to God. Dobson does not care if abstinence-based sexuality education has not clearly demonstrated its effectiveness, because in his view, any sexual activity outside of marriage is explicitly disapproved of in the Bible and is a threat to the sanctity of the family as well. Tests of statistical significance are simply not relevant in this context.

Similarly, Rosemond's refusal to give children reasons when they are disciplined, and his insistence that the ultimate reason for any disciplinary decision is always "because I said so," reinforces the natural hierarchy of the family and avoids making disciplinary episodes anything like a conversation between equals. His decision that early child care can best be done at home by a parent reasserts the family's importance. Toilet training must not be tied to the child's level of maturation (even if that would make it a lot easier) because doing so is "child-centered parenting" and violates the natural hierarchy of the family. Only parents should decide when their child should be trained (Rosemond, 1998e).

Conservatives value organic institutions that precede the state, such as the family and the church (Vierhaus, 1973–1974). Thus, biblical content that can be interpreted as providing instruction in parenting is carefully attended to, as are church traditions regarding young children's proper behavior. Otherwise, decisions about how to parent should come from within the family. Knowledge from secular sources, including professionals with specialized expertise, is clearly secondary, especially when it challenges traditional authority. Thus, Dobson describes behavior scientists as "observing and documenting subtle understandings that have been evident in the Scriptures for thousands of years" (Dobson, 1987, p. 26).

Just as liberalism applied to family life has its weaknesses and contradictions, there is an internal contradiction in being a conservative parenting expert. Sometimes Rosemond acknowledges this, reminding parents that he has no specialized knowledge to contribute: "As the reader will see, I am basically restating what our ancestors took for granted concerning family life, and the parent–child relationship in particular. I am relegitimizing their attitudes, their beliefs, their values, and their practices" (Rosemond, 1995a, p. 2). Yet when parents purchase one of Rosemond's books, they are accepting a professional expert's advice rather than learning traditions at home or in the community. They are not relying on knowledge handed down from their parents and grandparents, other family members, or people from their faith tradition.

It is important to consider the writings of James Dobson and John Rosemond (and Beverly LaHaye, Gary and Ann Marie Ezzo, and other conservative writers and speakers about the family) in the broader context of conservative thought generally. They and others are voices of a worldwide movement that is certainly not unique to this country. Many, perhaps most, societies have individuals and groups within them that reject social change in favor of unchanging, eternal truths. Such individuals are deeply concerned about immorality and share a belief in a God-fearing past that is superior to the present (Arnett, 2000; Marty & Appleby, 1993). They often share a sense of being besieged by the modern world, as when Rosemond describes himself as holding "psychologically incorrect" views and states that the world would be a better place if "all mental-health professionals, the good and the bad, were suddenly to disappear" (Rosemond, 2001b, p. xvi). Such strong words must strike a chord. The popularity of Rosemond, Dobson, and other conservatives, whose most characteristic positions are at times wrong or even dangerously wrong, is a clear sign of the attraction of their themes, not least the call to traditional values.

The two positions just described, simplifications of the liberal-to-conservative continuum among commentators on family life, illustrate how different parents are going to be persuaded by different messages. Even so, while specific pieces of advice may contradict each other, the authors' broader persuasive appeals are not necessarily incompatible. In some of his writings, Spock evinces just as much nostalgia for the old days of clear authority as Dobson does, and many of us believe in both individuality *and* community. And, of course, parents may read one expert on one topic, then switch to another if the author's viewpoint is not congenial or the topic they are interested in is not addressed. But the five authors should be understood as a part of an ongoing public dialogue between fundamentalists and progressives. That dialogue permeates their advice, even advice concerning infants, and extends far beyond child development and family life to the broader social arena, not just in this country but in many countries around the world. Consumers may or may not understand this when they buy a parenting video for a friend who is pregnant or look for a book by familiar name because their 18-month-old will not sleep through the night. Parents know they are getting advice and are happy to have it, but they may not understand all that comes with it. To be best served, they need both the experts and a context for evaluating and applying their advice.

MOVING FORWARD

What is the next step in parenting advice? These five authors have established themselves as public figures, and they have made invaluable contributions to the contemporary culture of family life. They and others like them are often more important sources of information than family sources and local advice (Fuligni & Brooks-Gunn, 2002). However compelling and authoritative they are as individuals, they are individuals and will eventually pass from the public scene. New media parenting experts could emerge, and undoubtedly will, and there may be a further fracturing and specialization of advice. An increasingly common alternative to opening a well-worn parenting manual is a Web search on toilet training, or on imaginary friends, or on whatever the urgent question is right at the moment. Which of the answers obtained would be authoritative and could be trusted? Given the wide disparities and position changes observed among these five best-known authorities and the observation that no single author achieved total accuracy and comprehensive coverage, the answer is probably none of them. Is this an indication that there is no behavioral knowledge applicable to parenting and family life, that there are no better or worse answers about what works with children? That is clearly not the case either, but it leads to a possible next step in linking parents with the best knowledge that the researchers and the clinicians can provide.

Within the past few years, the American Academy of Pediatrics has published a large number of policy statements, many of which have addressed parenting topics. The committee of selected pediatricians who write them make recommendations that all pediatricians are instructed to pass along to parents. The AAP publishes policy statements in its journal, *Pediatrics*, and on its Web site, and they can have a remarkable effect. Consider the case of infant sleeping position. In 1992, the Academy recommended that infants be placed on their backs to sleep. In the 8 years following, the frequency of babies sleeping on their stomachs decreased from over 70% to less than 20% of infants in this country. More importantly, this one change, this one new piece of advice to parents, was associated with over a 40% decrease in deaths from Sudden Infant Death Syndrome (Daley, 2004; Moon, Gingras, & Erwin, 2002).

The AAP, by establishing a Web presence for its policy statements, has initiated a new public advocacy role. In addition, accreditation organizations, other professional groups, and even individual researchers have begun identifying their own sets of standards that can help parents make the best decisions regarding their children. Discussion and further development of joint evidence-based practice or best practice recommendations that would be widely publicized is a logical next step. Is it possible to do this for parenting practices? The AAP's statement on discipline (AAP Committee on Psychosocial Aspects of Child and Family Health, 1998) illustrates a case in which it has already been done.

Assembling other such best practice statements would undoubtedly provoke controversy: It is not clear how many such statements could be generated, and it is not clear that a consensus could ever be achieved on some topics. But even the controversies that might attend such discussions would be useful, if only because they would bring together researchers, clinicians, journalists, and parents themselves for renewed dialogue about parenting. Such discussions could help to identify gaps in the available knowledge and generate research designed to address those gaps. There will always be tension between any set of best practice guidelines and the individual decisions that parents must make in the context of their own attributes and those of their children, families, and communities. Parents will and should ultimately make their own decisions, but where there is consensus about best practices based on research and clinical evidence, parents would be able to evaluate their own actions in that context.

One of the many ironies of parenting is that parents seem to get it figured out only after the children have grown up. Even this is an illusion, as parents of "second families" could attest, but it is an illusion that reveals our predicament as parents: wanting to get it right, sure that there is a right way, and yet never knowing enough. This may be unavoidable for individuals, but perhaps societies can do better. As a society—and particularly as one with the blessings of a scientific establishment, an active dialogue about religious and ethical values, and a free press—we have the opportunity to communicate, study, argue, and learn how to raise children well. The popular authorities on parenting are important voices in this process, but they should not be the only voices. Too much is at stake.

REFERENCES

Abelman, Robert. (1995). Gifted, LD, and gifted/LD children's understanding of temporal sequencing on television. *Journal of Broadcasting & Electronic Media, 39,* 297–312.

Abelson, R. P. (1985). A variance explanation paradox: When a little is a lot. *Psychological Bulletin, 97,* 129–133.

Achenbach, T. (1991). *Manual for the Child Behavior Checklist/4-18 and 1991 profile.* Burlington, VT: Author.

Ahnert, L., Gunnar, M. R., Lamb, M. E., & Barthel, M. (2004). Transition to child care: Associations with infant–mother attachment, infant negative emotion, and cortisol elevations. *Child Development, 75,* 639–650.

Ahnert, L., Rickert, H., & Lamb, M. E. (2000). Shared caregiving: Comparisons between home and child-care settings. *Developmental Psychology, 36,* 339–351.

Ainsworth, M.D.S., & Bell, S. M. (1969). Some contemporary patterns of mother-infant interaction in the feeding situation. In A. Ambrose (Ed.), *Stimulation in early infancy* (pp. 133–170). New York: Academic Press.

Ainsworth, M. S., Blehar, M. C., Waters, E., & Wall, S. (1978). *Patterns of attachment: A psychological study of the Strange Situation.* Hillsdale, NJ: Erlbaum.

Alan Guttmacher Institute. (1994). *Sex and America's teenagers.* New York: Author.

Alvarez, M. (2004). Caregiving and early infant crying in a Danish community. *Journal of Developmental & Behavioral Pediatrics, 25,* 91–98.

Amato, P. R., & Fowler, F. (2002). Parenting practices, child adjustment, and family diversity. *Journal of Marriage and the Family, 64,* 703–716.

Ambrose, A. (1969). Contribution to discussion. In A. Ambrose (Ed.), *Stimulation in early infancy* (pp. 103–104). New York: Academic Press.

American Academy of Pediatrics. (2003). Report of the task force on the family. *Pediatrics, 111,* 1541–1571.

American Academy of Pediatrics. (2004). About AAP. Retrieved September 23, 2004, from http://www.aap.org/about.html.

American Academy of Pediatrics Committee on Nutrition. (1998). *Pediatric nutrition handbook* (4th ed., R. Kleinman, Ed.). Elk Grove Village, IL: American Academy of Pediatrics.

American Academy of Pediatrics Committee on Psychosocial Aspects of Child and Family Health. (1998). Guidance for effective discipline. *Pediatrics, 101,* 723–728.

American Academy of Pediatrics Committee on Psychosocial Aspects of Children's Health and Committee on Adolescence. (2001b). Sexuality education for children and adolescents. *Pediatrics, 108,* 498–502.

American Academy of Pediatrics Committee on Public Education. (1999). Media education. *Pediatrics, 104,* 341–343.

American Academy of Pediatrics Committee on Public Education. (2001a). Children, adolescents, and television. *Pediatrics, 107,* 423–426.

American Academy of Pediatrics Committee on Substance Abuse. (1998). Tobacco, alcohol, and other drugs: The role of the pediatrician in prevention and management of substance abuse. *Pediatrics, 101,* 125–128.

American Psychological Association. (2004). *About APA.* Retrieved September 23, 2004, from http://www.apa.org/about.

American Public Health Association and American Academy of Pediatrics. (1992). *Caring for our children. National health and safety performance standards: Guidelines for out-of-home child care programs.* Elk Grove Village, IL: Author.

Anderson, C. A. (2004). An update on the effects of playing video games. *Journal of Adolescence, 27,* 113–122.

Anderson, C. A., Berkowitz, L., Donnerstein, E., Huesmann, L. R., Johnson, J. D., Linz, D., et al. (2003). The influence of media violence on youth. *Psychological Science in the Public Interest, 4,* 81–110.

Anderson, C. A., & Bushman, B. J. (2001). Effects of violent video games on aggressive behavior, aggressive cognition, aggressive affect, physiological arousal, and prosocial behavior: A meta-analytic review of the scientific literature. *Psychological Science, 12,* 353–359.

Anderson, C. A., & Bushman, B. J. (2002). The effects of media violence on society. *Science, 295,* 2377–2379.

Anderson, D. R., Huston, A. C., Schmitt, K. L., Linebarger, D. L., & Wright, J. C. (2001). Early childhood television viewing and adolescent behavior: The recontact study. *Monographs of the Society for Research in Child Development, 66*(1, Serial No. 264).

Anderson, D. R., Levin, S. R., & Lorch, E. P. (1977). The effects of TV program pacing on the behavior of preschool children. *AV Communication Review, 25,* 159–166.

Anderson, K. E., Lytton, H., & Romney, D. M. (1986). Mothers' interactions with normal and conduct-disordered boys: Who affects whom? *Developmental Psychology, 22,* 604–609.

Andison, F. S. (1977). TV violence and viewer aggression: A cumulation of study results: 1956–1976. *Public Opinion Quarterly, 41,* 314–331.

Andrews, J. A., Hops, H., Ary, D. V., Tildesley, E., & Harris, J. (1993). Parental influence on early adolescent substance use: Specific and nonspecific effects. *Journal of Early Adolescence, 13,* 285–310.

Arend, R., Gove, F. L., & Sroufe, L. A. (1979). Continuity of individual adaptation from infancy to kindergarten: A predictive study of ego-resiliency and curiosity in preschoolers. *Child Development, 50,* 950–959.

Arnett, J. J. (2002). The psychology of globalization. *American Psychologist, 57,* 774–783.

Arsenio, W. F. (2004). Commentary: The stability of young children's physical aggression: Relations with child care, gender, and aggression subtypes. *Monographs of the Society for Research on Child Development, 69* (4, Serial No. 278), 130–143.

Ary, D. V., Duncan, T. E., Duncan, S. C., & Hops, H. (1999). Adolescent problem behavior: The influence of parents and peers. *Behaviour Research and Therapy, 37,* 217–230.

Ary, D. V., Tildesley, E., Hops, H., & Andrews, J. (1993). The influence of parent, sibling, and peer modeling and attitudes on adolescent use of alcohol. *International Journal of the Addictions, 28,* 853–880.

Azrin, N. H., & Foxx, R. M. (1974). *Toilet training in less than a day.* New York: Simon & Schuster.

Azrin, N. H., & Holz, W. C. (1966). Punishment. In W. K. Honig (Ed.), *Operant behavior: Areas of research and application* (pp. 380–447). New York: Appleton-Century-Crofts.

Ball, S. J., & Bogatz, G. A. (1970). *The first year of Sesame Street: An evaluation.* Princeton, NJ: Educational Testing Service.

Barkley, R. A., Cook, E. H., Dulcan, M., Campbell, S., Prior, M., Atkins, M., et al. (2002). Consensus statement on ADHD. *European Child & Adolescent Psychiatry, 11,* 96–98.

Barlow, D. H. (2004). Psychological treatments. *American Psychologist, 59,* 869–878.

Barnas, M. V., & Cummings, E. M. (1994). Caregiver stability and toddlers' attachment-related behavior towards caregivers in day care. *Infant Behavior & Development, 17,* 141–147.

Barnes, G. M., Reifman, A. S., Farrell, M. P., & Dintcheff, B. A. (2000). The effects of parenting on the development of adolescent alcohol misuse: A six-wave latent growth model. *Journal of Marriage and the Family, 62,* 175–186.

Barnes, G. M., Reifman, A. S., Farrell, M. P., Uhteg, L., & Dintcheff, B. A. (1994). Longitudinal effects of parenting on alcohol misuse among adolescents. *Alcoholism: Clinical and Experimental Research, 18,* 507.

Barr, R. G. (1990). The normal crying curve: What do we really know? *Developmental Medicine and Child Neurology, 32,* 356–362.

Barr, R. G. (1996). Colic. In W. A. Walker, P. R. Durie, J. R. Hamilton, J. A. Walker-Smith, & J. B. Watkins (Eds.), *Pediatric gastrointestinal disease: Pathophysiology, diagnosis, and management* (pp. 241–250). St. Louis, MO: Mosby.

Barr, R. G. (1998). Crying in the first year of life: Good news in the midst of distress. *Child: Care, Health, and Development, 24,* 425–439.

Barr, R. G. (2000). Excessive crying. In A. J. Sameroff & M. Lewis (Eds.), *Handbook of developmental psychopathology* (2nd ed., pp. 327–350). New York: Plenum Press.

Barr, R. G. (2001). "Colic" is something infants do, rather than a condition they "have": A developmental approach to crying phenomena, patterns, pacification and (patho)genesis. In R. G. Barr, I. St. James-Roberts, & M. R. Keefe (Eds.), *New evidence on unexplained early infant crying: Its origins, nature, and management* (pp. 87–104). Calverton, NY: Johnson & Johnson Pediatric Institute.

Barr, R. G., Konner, M., Bakeman, R., & Adamson, L. (1991). Crying in !Kung San infants: A test of the cultural specificity hypothesis. *Developmental Medicine and Child Neurology, 33,* 601–610.

Barr, R. G., McMullen, S. J., Spiess, H., Leduc, D. G., Yarenko, J., Barfield, R., et al. (1991). Carrying as colic "therapy": A randomized controlled trial. *Pediatrics, 87,* 623–630.

Bates, J. E., Marvinney, D., Kelly, T., Dodge, K. A., Bennett, D. S., & Pettit, G. S. (1994). Child care history and kindergarten adjustment. *Developmental Psychology, 30,* 690–700.

Bates, J. E., Pettit, G. S., Dodge, K. A., & Ridge, B. (1998). Interaction of temperamental resistance to control and restrictive parenting in the development of externalizing behavior. *Developmental Psychology, 34,* 982–995.

Bauman, K. E., & Ennett, S. T. (1996). On the importance of peer influence for adolescent drug use: Commonly neglected considerations. *Addiction, 91,* 185–198.

Baumrind, D. (1971). Current patterns of parental authority. *Developmental Psychology Monographs, 4*(1, Pt. 2).

Baumrind, D. (1991a). Effective parenting during the early adolescent transition. In P. A. Cowan & E. M. Hetherington (Eds.), *Family transitions* (pp. 111–163). Hillsdale, NJ: Erlbaum.

Baumrind, D. (1991b). The influence of parenting style on adolescent competence and substance use. *Journal of Early Adolescence, 11,* 56–95.

Baumrind, D. (1996). The discipline controversy revisited. *Family Relations: Journal of Applied Family and Child Studies, 45,* 405–414.

Baumrind, D., & Black, A. (1967). Socialization practices associated with dimensions of competence in preschool boys and girls. *Child Development, 38,* 291–327.

Baumrind, D., Larzelere, R. E., & Cowan, P. A. (2002). Ordinary physical punishment: Is it harmful? Comment on Gershoff (2002). *Psychological Bulletin, 128,* 580–589.

Bayley, N. (1969). *Bayley Scales of Infant Development.* New York: Psychological Corporation.

Bearman, P. S., & Bruckner, H. (2001). Promising the future: Virginity pledges and the transition to first intercourse. *American Journal of Sociology, 106,* 859–912.

Bell, R. Q. (1968). A reinterpretation of the direction of effects in studies of socialization. *Psychological Review, 75,* 81–95.

Bell, S. M., & Ainsworth, M.D.S. (1972). Infant crying and maternal responsiveness. *Child Development, 55*, 718–728.

Belsky, J. (2001). Emanuel Miller Lecture: Developmental risks (still) associated with early child care. *Journal of Child Psychology and Psychiatry, 42*, 845–859.

Belsky, J., Rosenberger, K., & Crnic, K. (1995). The origins of attachment security: Classical and contextual determinants. In S. Goldberg, R. Muir, & J. Kerr (Eds.), *Attachment theory: Social, developmental, and clinical perspectives* (pp. 153–402). Hillsdale, NJ: Analytic Press.

Belsky, J., Woodworth, S., & Crnic, K. (1996). Trouble in the second year: Three questions about family interaction. *Child Development, 67*, 556–578.

Benda, B. B., & DiBlasio, F. A. (1991). Comparison of four theories of adolescent sexual exploration. *Deviant Behavior, 12*, 235–257.

Bennett, S. E., & Assefi, N. P. (2005). School-based teenage pregnancy prevention programs: A systematic review of randomized controlled trials. *Journal of Adolescent Health, 36*, 72–81.

Berk, L. B., & Friman, P. C. (1990). Epidemiological aspects of toilet training. *Clinical Pediatrics, 29*, 278–282.

Berkowitz, L. (1988). Frustrations, appraisals, and aversively stimulated aggression. *Aggressive Behavior, 47*, 165–181.

Bertholf, R. L., & Goodison, S. (2004). Television viewing and attention deficits in children. *Pediatrics, 114*, 511–512.

Bethell, C., Peck, C., & Schor, E. (2001). Assessing health system provision of well-child care: The Promoting Healthy Development Survey. *Pediatrics, 107*, 1084–1094.

Bickham, D. S., Wright, J. C., & Huston, A. C. (2001). Attention, comprehension, and the educational influences of television. In D. G. Singer & J. L. Singer (Eds.), *Handbook of children and the media* (pp. 101–120). Thousand Oaks, CA: Sage.

Blakeslee, S. (2005, March 8). Colicky baby? Read this before calling an exorcist. *The New York Times*, p. 6F.

Block, J., Block, J. H., & Keyes, S. (1988). Longitudinally foretelling drug usage in adolescence: Early childhood personality and environmental precursors. *Child Development, 59*, 336–355.

Blum, N. J., Taubman, B., & Nemeth, N. (2003). Relationship between age at initiation of toilet training and duration of training: A prospective study. *Pediatrics, 111*, 810–814.

Blum, N. J., Taubman, B., & Nemeth, N. (2004). During toilet training, constipation occurs before stool toileting refusal. *Pediatrics, 113*, e520–e522.

Blum, N. J., Taubman, B., & Osborne, M. L. (1997). Behavioral characteristics of children with stool toileting refusal. *Pediatrics, 99*, 50–53.

Bolotin, S. (1999, February 14). The disciples of discipline. *The New York Times Magazine*, 32–37.

Booth, C. L., Clarke-Stewart, K. A., Vandell, D. L., McCartney, K., & Owen, M. T. (2002). Child-care usage and mother–infant "quality time." *Journal of Marriage and the Family, 64*, 16–26.

Booth, C. L., & Kelly, J. F. (1998). Child-care characteristics of infants with and without special needs: Comparisons and concerns. *Early Childhood Research Quarterly, 13,* 603–621.

Bowlby, J. (1969). *Attachment and loss: Vol. 1. Attachment* (2nd ed.). New York: Basic Books.

Bray, J. H., Adams, G. J., Getz, J. G., & Baer, P. E. (2001). Developmental, family, and ethnic influences on adolescent alcohol usage: A growth curve approach. *Journal of Family Psychology, 15,* 301–314.

Brazelton, T. B. (1962a). A child-oriented approach to toilet training. *Pediatrics, 29,* 121–128.

Brazelton, T. B. (1962b). Crying in infancy. *Pediatrics, 29,* 579–588.

Brazelton, T. B. (1983). *Infants and mothers: Differences in development* (Rev. ed.). New York: Dell.

Brazelton, T. B. (1984). *To listen to a child: Understanding the normal problems of growing up.* Reading, MA: Addison-Wesley.

Brazelton, T. B. (1985). *Working and caring.* Reading, MA: Addison-Wesley.

Brazelton, T. B. (1990). Crying and colic. *Infant Mental Health Journal, 11,* 349–356.

Brazelton, T. B. (1992). *Touchpoints: Your child's emotional and behavioral development.* Reading, MA: Addison-Wesley.

Brazelton, T. B. (1999). *Going to the doctor.* Cambridge, MA: Perseus Publishing.

Brazelton, T. B. (2001, March 22). Working parents need day-care options. *The Albany Times Union,* p. D2.

Brazelton, T. B., Christophersen, E. R., Frauman, A. C., Gorski, P. A., Poole, J. M., Stadtler, A. C., & Wright, C. L. (1999). Instruction, timeliness, and medical influences affecting toilet training. *Pediatrics, 103,* 1353–1358.

Brazelton, T. B., & Cramer, B. G. (1990). *The earliest relationship: Parents, infants, and the drama of early attachment.* Reading, MA: Addison-Wesley.

Brazelton, T. B., & Greenspan, S. I. (2000). *The irreducible needs of children.* Cambridge, MA: Perseus Publishing.

Brazelton, T. B., & Sparrow, J. D. (2001). *Touchpoints three to six: Your child's emotional and behavioral development.* Cambridge, MA: Perseus Publishing.

Brazelton, T. B., & Sparrow, J. D. (2003a). *Calming your fussy baby the Brazelton way.* Cambridge, MA: Perseus Publishing.

Brazelton, T. B., & Sparrow, J. D. (2003b). *Discipline: The Brazelton way.* Cambridge, MA: Perseus Publishing.

Brazelton, T. Berry. (1993). In J. Graham (Ed.), *Current Biography Yearbook* (pp. 88–92). New York: H. W. Wilson Company.

Brazelton Institute. (2004). *T. Berry Brazelton, M.D.* Retrieved September 28, 2004, from http://www.brazelton-institute.com/berrybio.html.

Brody, G. H., Stoneman, Z., & Flor, D. (1996). Parental religiosity, family processes, and youth competence in rural, two-parent African American families. *Developmental Psychology, 32,* 696–706.

Brody, J. (1998, June 30). Feeding children off the Spock menu. *The New York Times,* p. F7.

Brook, J. S., Brook, D. W., Gordon, A. S., Whiteman, M., & Cohen, P. (1990). Stability of personality during adolescence and its relationship to stage of drug use. *Genetic, Social, and General Psychology Monographs, 116,* 111–267.

Brown, B. B., Mounts, N., Lamborn, S. D., & Steinberg, L. (1993). Parenting practices and peer group affiliation in adolescence. *Child Development, 64,* 467–482.

Brown, J. D., Childers, K. W., & Bauman, K. E. (1990). The influence of new media and family structure on young adolescents' television and radio use. *Communication Research, 17,* 65–82.

Brown, J. D., & Newcomer, S. F. (1991). Television viewing and adolescents' sexual behavior. *Journal of Homosexuality, 21,* 77–91.

Bryant, J., & Rockwell, S. C. (1994). Effects of massive exposure to sexually oriented prime-time television programming on adolescents' moral judgment. In D. Zillmann, J. Bryant, & A. C. Huston (Eds.), *Media, children, and the family: Social scientific, psychodynamic, and clinical perspectives* (pp. 183–195). Hillsdale, NJ: Erlbaum.

Burchinal, M., Howes, C., & Kontos, S. (2002). Structural predictors of child care quality in child care homes. *Early Childhood Research Quarterly, 17,* 87–105.

Burchinal, M., & Nelson, L. (2000). Family selection and child care experiences: Implications for studies of child outcomes. *Early Childhood Research Quarterly, 15,* 385–411.

Burchinal, M. R., Peisner-Feinberg, E., Pianta, B., & Howes, C. (2002). Development of academic skills from preschool through second grade: Family and classroom predictors of developmental trajectories. *Journal of School Psychology, 40,* 415–436.

Bushman, B. J., & Anderson, C. A. (2001). Media violence and the American public: Scientific facts versus media misinformation. *American Psychologist, 56,* 477–489.

Bushman, B. J., & Cantor, J. (2003). Media ratings for violence and sex. *American Psychologist, 58,* 130–141.

Bushman, B. J., & Huesmann, L. R. (2001). Effects of televised violence on aggression. In D. G. Singer & J. L. Singer (Eds.), *Handbook of children and the media* (pp. 223–254). Thousand Oaks, CA: Sage.

Byrne, J. M., & Horowitz, F. D. (1981). Rocking as a soothing intervention: The influence of direction and type of movement. *Infant Behavior & Development, 4,* 207–218.

Campos, R. G. (1989). Soothing pain-elicited distress in infants with swaddling and pacifiers. *Child Development, 60,* 781–792.

Campos, R. G. (1994). Rocking and pacifiers: Two comforting interventions for heelstick pain. *Research in Nursing and Health, 17,* 321–331.

Cantor, J., & Mares, M.-L. (2001). Effects of television on child and family emotional well-being. In B. Jennings & J. A. Jennings (Eds.), *Television and the American family* (2nd ed.) (pp. 317–332). Mahwah, NJ: Erlbaum.

Carey, W. B. (1968). Maternal anxiety and infantile colic: Is there a relationship? *Clinical Pediatrics, 7,* 590–595.

Caspi, A. (2000). The child is father of the man: Personality continuities from child-hood to adulthood. *Journal of Personality and Social Psychology, 78,* 158–172.

Caspi, A., Moffitt, T., Newman, D., & Silva, P. (1996). Behavioral observations at age 3 predict adult psychiatric disorders. *Archives of General Psychiatry, 53,* 1033–1039.

Cassidy, J., & Berlin, L. J. (1994). The insecure/ambivalent pattern of attachment: Theory and research. *Child Development, 65,* 971–981.

Chamberlain, P., & Patterson, G. R. (1995). Discipline and child compliance in par-enting. In M. H. Bornstein (Ed.), *Handbook of parenting: Vol. 4. Applied and practical parenting* (pp. 205–225). Mahwah, NJ: Erlbaum.

Chao, R. K. (1994). Beyond parental control and authoritarian parenting style: Un-derstanding Chinese parenting through the cultural notion of training. *Child Development, 65,* 1111–1119.

Chassin, L., Hussong, A., Barrera, M., Molina, B., Trim, R., & Ritter, J. (2004). Adolescent substance use. In R. M. Lerner & L. Steinberg (Eds.), *Handbook of adolescent psychology* (2nd ed., pp. 665–696). Hoboken, NJ: Wiley.

Chassin, L., Presson, C. C., Todd, M., Rose, J. S., & Sherman, S. J. (1998). Mater-nal socialization of adolescent smoking: The intergenerational transmission of parenting and smoking. *Developmental Psychology, 34,* 1189–1201.

Cheng, T. L., Brenner, R. A., Wright, J. L., Sachs, H. C., Moyer, P., & Rao, M. R. (2004). Children's violent television viewing: Are parents monitoring? *Pediatrics, 114,* 94–99.

Chilcoat, H. D., & Anthony, J. C. (1996). Impact of parent monitoring on initiation of drug use through late childhood. *Journal of the American Academy of Child & Adolescent Psychiatry, 35,* 91–100.

Christakis, D. A., Zimmerman, F. J., DiGiuseppe, D. L., & McCarty, C. A. (2004). Early television exposure and subsequent attentional problems in children. *Pediatrics, 113,* 708–713.

Christophersen, E. R. (2003). The case for evidence-based toilet training. *Archives of Pediatric and Adolescent Medicine, 157,* 1153–1154.

Christophersen, E. R., & Rapoff, M. R. (1992). Toileting problems in children. In C. E. Walker & M. C. Roberts (Eds.), *Handbook of clinical child psychology* (pp. 399–411). New York: Wiley.

Clark, R., Hyde, J. S., Essex, M. J., & Klein, M. H. (1997). Length of maternity leave and quality of mother–infant interactions. *Child Development, 68,* 364–383.

Clarke-Stewart, K. A. (1988). Parents' effects on children's development: A decade of progress? *Journal of Applied Developmental Psychology, 9,* 41–84.

Clarke-Stewart, K. A. (1989). Infant day care: Maligned or malignant? *American Psychologist, 44,* 266–273.

Clarke-Stewart, K. A. (1998). Historical shifts and underlying themes in ideas about rearing young children in the United States: Where have we been? Where are we going? *Early Development and Parenting, 7,* 101–117.

Clarke-Stewart, K. A., & Allhusen, V. D. (2002). Nonparental caregiving. In M. H. Bornstein (Ed.), *Handbook of parenting: Vol. 3. Being and becoming a parent* (pp. 215–252). Mahwah, NJ: Erlbaum.

Clarke-Stewart, K. A., Gruber, C. P., & Fitzgerald, L. M. (1994). *Children at home and in day care.* Hillsdale, NJ: Erlbaum.

Clarke-Stewart, K. A., Vandell, D. L., Burchinal, M., O'Brien, M., & McCartney, K. (2002). Do regulable features of child-care homes affect children's development? *Early Childhood Research Quarterly, 17,* 52–86.

Cline, V. B., Croft, R. G., & Courrier, S. (1973). Desensitization of children to television violence. *Journal of Personality and Social Psychology, 27,* 360–365.

Cohen, D. A., Richardson, J., & LaBree, L. (1994). Parenting behaviors and the onset of smoking and alcohol use: A longitudinal study. *Pediatrics, 94,* 368–375.

Cohen, J. (1988). *Statistical power for the behavioral sciences* (2nd ed.). Hillsdale, NJ: Erlbaum.

Collins, R. L., Elliott, M. N., Berry, S. H., Kanouse, D. E., Kunkel, D., Hunter, S. B., et al. (2004). Watching sex on television predicts adolescent initiation of sexual behavior. *Pediatrics, 114,* e280–e289.

Collins, W. A., Maccoby, E. E., Steinberg, L., Hetherington, E. M., & Bornstein, M. H. (2000). Contemporary research on parenting: The case for nature and nurture. *American Psychologist, 55,* 218–232.

Collins, W. A., Sobol, B. L., & Westby, S. (1981). Effects of adult commentary on children's comprehension and inferences about a televised aggressive portrayal. *Child Development, 52,* 158–163.

Comstock, G. (1991). *Television and the American child.* San Diego, CA: Academic Press.

Comstock, G., & Scharrer, E. (1999). *Television: What's on, who's watching, and what it means.* San Diego, CA: Academic Press.

Cook, T. D., Appleton, H., Conner, R. F., Shaffer, A., Tamkin, G., & Weber, S. (1975). *Sesame Street revisited.* New York: Russell Sage Foundation.

Coontz, S. (1992). The way we never were: American families and the nostalgia trap. New York: Basic Books.

Cope-Farrar, K. M., & Kunkel, D. (2002). Sexual messages in teens' favorite prime-time television programs. In J. D. Brown, J. R. Steele, & K. Walsh-Childers (Eds.), *Sexual teens, sexual media: Investigating media's influence on adolescent sexuality* (pp. 59–78). Mahwah, NJ: Erlbaum.

Corteen, R. S., & Williams, T. M. (1986). Television and reading skills. In T. M. Williams (Ed.), *The impact of television: A natural experiment in three communities* (pp. 39–86). Orlando, FL: Academic Press.

Cowan, P. A., & Cowan, C. P. (2002). What an intervention design reveals about how parents affect their children's academic achievement and social competence. In J. Borkowski, S. Landesman-Ramey, & M. Bristol (Eds.), *Parenting and the child's world: Multiple influences on intellectual and social–emotional development* (pp. 75–97). Hillsdale, NJ: Erlbaum.

Cowan, P. A., Cowan, C. P., & Kerig, P. K. (1993). Mothers, fathers, sons, and daughters: Gender differences in family formation and parenting style. In P. A. Cowan, D. Field, D. A. Hansen, A. Skolnick, & G. E. Swanson (Eds.),

Family, self, and society: Toward a new agenda for family research (pp. 165–195). Hillsdale, NJ: Erlbaum.

Coyle, K. K., Kirby, D. B., Marin, B. V., Gomez, C. A., & Gregorich, S. E. (2004). Draw the line/respect the line: A randomized trial of a middle school intervention to reduce sexual risk behaviors. *American Journal of Public Health, 94*, 843–851.

Crockenberg, S., & Litman, C. (1990). Autonomy as competence in 2-year-olds: Maternal correlates of child defiance, compliance, and self-assertion. *Developmental Psychology, 26*, 961–971.

Crosnoe, R., Erickson, K. G., & Dornbusch, S. M. (2002). Protective functions of family relationships and school factors on the deviant behavior of adolescent boys and girls: Reducing the impact of risky friendships. *Youth & Society, 33*, 515–544.

Cryer, D., Hurwitz, S., & Wolery, M. (2000). Continuity of caregiver for infants and toddlers in center-based child care: Report on a survey of center practices. *Early Childhood Research Quarterly, 15*, 497–514.

Daley, K. C. (2004). Update on sudden infant death syndrome. *Current Opinion in Pediatrics, 16*, 227–232.

Davis, E. C., & Friel, L. V. (2001). Adolescent sexuality: Disentangling the effects of family structure and family context. *Journal of Marriage and the Family, 63*, 669–681.

Davison, W. P. (1983). The third-person effect in communication. *Public Opinion Quarterly, 47*, 1–15.

Day, R., Peterson, G. W., & McCracken, C. (1998). Predicting spanking of younger and older children by mothers and fathers. *Journal of Marriage and the Family, 60*, 79–94.

DeAngelis, T. (2005, March). Shaping evidence-based practice. *Monitor on Psychology, 36*, 26–31.

Deater-Deckard, K., & Dodge, K. A. (1997). Externalizing behavior problems and discipline revisited: Nonlinear effects and variation by culture, context, and gender. *Psychological Inquiry, 8*, 161–175.

Deater-Deckard, K., Fulker, D. W., & Plomin, R. (1999). A genetic study of the family environment in the transition in early adolescence. *Journal of Child Psychology and Psychiatry, 40*, 769–775.

Dennis, W. (1973). *Children of the creche.* New York: Appleton-Century-Crofts.

Desmond, R. J., Singer, J. L., & Singer, D. G. (1990). Family mediation: Parental communication patterns and the influences of television on children. In J. Bryant (Ed.), *Television and the American family* (pp. 293–309). Hillsdale, NJ: Erlbaum.

Dettling, A. C., Gunnar, M. R., & Donzella, B. (1999). Cortisol levels of young children in full-day childcare centers: Relations with age and temperament. *Psychoneuroendocrinology, 24*, 519–536.

Deutsch, F. M., Ruble, D. N., Fleming, A., Brooks-Gunn, J., & Stangor, C. S. (1988). Information seeking and maternal self-definition during the transition to motherhood. *Journal of Personality and Social Psychology, 5*, 420–431.

Dishion, T.J., Capaldi, D., & Spracklen, K.M. (1995). Peer ecology of male adolescent drug use. *Development and Psychopathology, 7,* 803–824.

Dishion, T.J., Kavanagh, K., Schneiger, A., Nelson, S., & Kaufman, N.K. (2002). Preventing early adolescent substance use: A family-centered strategy for the public middle school. *Prevention Science, 3,* 191–201.

Dix, T. (1991). The affective organization of parenting: Adaptive and maladaptive processes. *Psychological Bulletin, 110,* 3–25.

Dix, T., Ruble, D., & Zambarano, R.J. (1989). Mothers' implicit theories of discipline: Child effects, parent effects, and the attribution process. *Child Development, 60,* 1373–1391.

Dobkin, P.L., Tremblay, R.E., Masse, L.C., & Vitaro, F. (1995). Individual and peer characteristics in predicting boys' early onset of substance abuse: A seven-year longitudinal study. *Child Development, 66,* 1198–1214.

Dobson, J. (1970). *Dare to discipline.* Wheaton, IL: Tyndale House Publishers.

Dobson, J. (1982). *Dr. Dobson answers your questions about raising children.* Wheaton, IL: Tyndale House Publishers.

Dobson, J. (1987). *Parenting isn't for cowards.* Dallas, TX: Word Publishing.

Dobson, J. (1989). *Preparing for adolescence.* Wheaton, IL: Tyndale House Publishers.

Dobson, J. (1992). *The new dare to discipline.* Wheaton, IL: Tyndale House Publishers.

Dobson, J. (1997, July 29). Debate goes on over moms in the home. *South Bend Tribune,* p. D3.

Dobson, J. (1998, June 13). Children's behavior linked to family members. *Chattanooga Free Press,* p. B2.

Dobson, J., & Bauer, G.L. (1990). *Children at risk.* Dallas, TX: Word Publishing.

Dobson, James. (1998). In D. Jones & J.D. Jorgenson (Eds.), *Contemporary authors: A bio-bibliographical guide to current writers in fiction, nonfiction, poetry, journalism, drama, motion pictures, television, and other fields* (Vol. 68, pp. 131–132). Detroit, MI: Gale Group.

Dorr, A., Kovaric, P., & Doubleday, C. (1989). Parent–child coviewing of television. *Journal of Broadcasting & Electronic Media, 33,* 35–51.

Dorr, A., Rabin, B.E., & Irlen, S. (2002). Parenting in a multimedia society. In M.H. Bornstein (Ed.), *Handbook of parenting: Vol. 5. Practical issues in parenting* (2nd ed., pp. 349–373). Mahwah, NJ: Erlbaum.

Drabman, R.S., & Thomas, M.H. (1974a). Does media violence increase children's toleration of real-life aggression? *Developmental Psychology, 10,* 418–421.

Drabman, R.S., & Thomas, M.H. (1974b). Exposure to filmed violence and children's tolerance of real life aggression. *Personality and Social Psychology Bulletin, 1,* 198–199.

Drabman, R.S., & Thomas, M.H. (1976). Does watching violence on television cause apathy? *Pediatrics, 57,* 329–331.

Duncan, T.E., Duncan, S.C., & Hops, H. (1996). The role of parents and older siblings in predicting adolescent substance use: Modeling development via structural equation latent growth methodology. *Journal of Family Psychology, 10,* 158–172.

Duncan, T. E., Duncan, S. C., Strycker, L. A., Li, F., & Alpert, A. (1999). *An introduction to latent variable growth curve modeling: Concepts, issues, and applications.* Mahwah, NJ: Erlbaum.

Dunn, L., & Kontos, S. (1997). What have we learned about developmentally appropriate practice: Research in review. *Young Children, 52,* 4–13.

Dunnewind, S. (2003, January 25). Mixed messages: Parenting advice books all promise to turn anyone into the perfect parent but since experts rarely agree on the "correct" way to raise kids, finding a good guide can be a gamble. *The Seattle Times,* p. E0.

Ellickson, P. L., Tucker, J. S., Klein, D. J., & McGuigan, K. A. (2001). Prospective risk factors for alcohol misuse in late adolescence. *Journal of Studies on Alcohol, 62,* 773–782.

Ellison, C. G., Bartkowski, J. P., & Segal, M. L. (1996). Conservative Protestantism and the parental use of corporal punishment. *Social Forces, 74,* 1003–1028.

Ennett, S. T., & Bauman, K. E. (1994). The contribution of influence and selection to adolescent peer group homogeneity: The case of adolescent cigarette smoking. *Journal of Personality and Social Psychology, 67,* 653–663.

Ennett, S. T., Bauman, K. E., Foshee, V. A., Pemberton, M., & Hicks, K. A. (2001). Parent–child communication about adolescent tobacco and alcohol use: What do parents say and does it affect youth behavior? *Journal of Marriage and the Family, 63,* 48–62.

Erlanger, H. S. (1974). Social class and corporal punishment in childrearing: A reassessment. *American Sociological Review, 39,* 68–85.

Eron, L. D., Huesmann, L. R., Lefkowitz, M. M., & Walder, L. O. (1972). Does television violence cause aggression? *American Psychologist, 27,* 253–263.

Eron, L. D., Huesmann, L. R., & Zelli, A. (1991). The role of parental variables in the learning of aggression. In D. J. Pepler & K. H. Rubin (Eds.), *The development and treatment of childhood aggression* (pp. 169–188). Hillsdale, NJ: Erlbaum.

Ezzo, G., & Bucknam, R. (2001). *On becoming babywise: I.* Louisiana, MO: Parent-Wise Solutions.

Farkas, S., Johnson, J., & Duffett, A. (2002). *A lot easier said than done: Parents talk about raising children in today's America.* New York: Public Agenda.

Farrar, K., Kunkel, D., Biely, E., Eyal, K., Fandrich, R., Donnerstein, E., et al. (2003). Sexual messages during prime-time programming. *Sexuality and Culture, 7,* 7–37.

Farrington, D. P. (1995). The twelfth Jack Tizard Memorial Lecture: The development of offending and antisocial behaviour from childhood: Key findings from the Cambridge Study in Delinquent Development. *Journal of Child Psychology and Psychiatry, 36,* 929–964.

Feldman, S. S., & Brown, N. (1993). Family influences on adolescent male sexuality: The mediational role of self-restraint. *Social Development, 2,* 15–35.

Fetler, M. (1984). Television viewing and school achievement. *Journal of Communication, 34,* 104–118.

Fisch, S. M., Truglio, R. T., & Cole, C. F. (1999). The impact of Sesame Street on preschool children: A review and synthesis of 30 years' research. *Media Psychology, 1,* 165–190.

Fish, M., Stifter, C. A., & Belsky, J. (1991). Conditions of continuity and discontinuity in infant negative emotionality: Newborn to five months. *Child Development, 62,* 1525–1537.

Fisher, L. A., & Bauman, K. E. (1988). Influence and selection in the friend–adolescent relationship: Findings from studies of adolescent smoking and drinking. *Journal of Applied Social Psychology, 18,* 289–314.

Fisichelli, V., Karelitz, S., Fisichelli, R., & Cooper, J. (1974). The course of induced crying activity in the first year of life. *Pediatric Research, 8,* 921–928.

Fletcher, A. C., Steinberg, L., & Williams-Wheeler, M. (2004). Parental influences on adolescent problem behavior: Revisiting Stattin and Kerr. *Child Development, 75,* 781–796.

Focus on the Family. (2000). *Welcome to Focus on the Family.* Retrieved September 16, 1999, from http://www.family.org/welcome/aboutfof/A0000111.html.

Focus on the Family. (2004a). *Dr. James Dobson.* Retrieved November 29, 2004, from http://www.family.org/welcome/bios/a0022947.cfm.

Focus on the Family. (2004b). *Financial reports.* Retrieved November 29, 2004, from http://www.family.org/welcome/aboutfof/A0028626.cfm.

Forgatch, M. S., & DeGarmo, D. S. (1999). Parenting through change: An effective prevention program for single mothers. *Journal of Consulting and Clinical Psychology, 67,* 711–724.

Forrest, J. D., & Singh, S. (1990). The sexual and reproductive behavior of American women, 1982–1988. *Family Planning Perspectives, 22,* 206–214.

Forste, R., & Haas, D. W. (2002). The transition of adolescent males to first sexual intercourse: Anticipated or delayed? *Perspectives on Sexual and Reproductive Health, 34,* 184–190. Retrieved November 26, 2002, from http://www.guttmacher.org/pubs/journals/3418402.html.

Fox, N. A., & Polak, C. P. (2001). The possible contribution of temperament to understanding the origins and consequences of persistent and excessive crying. In R. G. Barr, I. St. James-Roberts, & M. R. Keefe (Eds.), *New evidence on unexplained early infant crying: Its origins, nature, and management* (pp. 25–41). Calverton, NY: Johnson & Johnson Pediatric Institute.

Frederick, H. V. (1998, June 8). Bringing up baby. *Publishers Weekly, 245,* 30.

Fuligni, A. S., & Brooks-Gunn, J. (2002). Meeting the challenges of new parenthood: Responsibilities, advice, and perceptions. In N. Halfon, K. T. McLearn, & M. A. Schuster (Eds.), *Child rearing in America* (pp. 83–116). Cambridge, England: Cambridge University Press.

Fulker, D. W., De Fries, J. C., & Plomin, R. (1988, December 22–29). Genetic influence on general mental ability increases between infancy and middle childhood. *Nature, 336,* 767–769.

Fuller, B., Holloway, S. D., & Liang, X. (1996). Family selection of child-care centers: The influence of household support, ethnicity, and parenting practices. *Child Development, 67,* 3320–3337.

Funk, J. B., Buchman, D. D., Jenks, J., & Bechtoldt, H. (2003). Playing violent video games, desensitization, and moral evaluation in children. *Applied Developmental Psychology, 24,* 413–436.

Furstenberg, F., Jr., Eccles, J., Elder, G., Jr., Cook, T., & Sameroff, A. (1997). *Managing to make it.* Chicago: University of Chicago Press.

Gable, S., & Cole, K. (2000). Parents' childcare arrangements and their ecological correlates. *Early Education and Development, 11,* 549–572.

Gans, H. J. (1980). *Deciding what's news.* New York: Vintage.

Garn, S. M. (1979). Social science research ethics [Letter to the editor]. *Science, 206,* 1022.

Ge, X., Conger, R. D., Cadoret, R. J., Neiderhiser, J. M., Yates, W., Troughton, E., & Stewart, M. A. (1996). The developmental interface between nature and nurture: A mutual influence model of child antisocial behavior and parent behavior. *Developmental Psychology, 32,* 574–589.

Gecas, V., & Nye, F. I. (1974). Sex and class differences in parent–child interaction: A test of Kohn's hypothesis. *Journal of Marriage and the Family, 36,* 742–749.

Gentile, D. A., Lynch, P. J., Linder, J. R., & Walsh, D. A. (2004). The effects of violent video game habits on adolescent hostility, aggressive behaviors, and school performance. *Journal of Adolescence, 27,* 5–22.

Gershoff, E. (2002). Corporal punishment by parents and associated child behaviors and experiences: A meta-analytic and theoretical review. *Psychological Bulletin, 128,* 539–579.

Gerson, M. J. (1998, May 4). A righteous indignation: James Dobson—psychologist, radio host, family-values crusader—is set to topple the political establishment. *U.S. News & World Report, 124,* 20–29.

Giles-Sims, J., Straus, M. A., & Sugarman, D. B. (1995). Child, maternal, and family characteristics associated with spanking. *Family Relations, 44,* 170–176.

Glynn, T. J. (1981). From family to peer: A review of transitions of influence among drug-using youth. *Journal of Youth and Adolescence, 10,* 363–383.

Goode, E. (1999, January 12). Two experts do battle over potty training. *The New York Times,* p. A1.

Goode, E. (2000, February 23). Sharp rise found in psychiatric drugs for the very young. *The New York Times,* p. A1.

Goodnow, J. J. (1995). Parents' knowledge and expectations. In M. H. Bornstein (Ed.), *Handbook of parenting: Vol. 3. Status and social conditions of parenting* (pp. 305–332). Mahwah, NJ: Erlbaum.

Gormally, S. (2001). Clinical clues to organic etiology in infants with colic. In R. G. Barr, I. St. James-Roberts, & M. R. Keefe (Eds.), *New evidence on unexplained early infant crying: Its origins, nature, and management* (pp. 133–148). Calverton, NY: Johnson & Johnson Pediatric Institute.

Graziano, A. M., Hamblen, J. L., & Plante, W. A. (1996). Subabusive violence in child rearing in middle-class American families. *Pediatrics, 98,* 845.

Greenberg, B. S., Linsangan, R., & Soderman, A. (1993). Adolescents' reaction to television sex. In B. S. Greenberg, J. D. Brown, & N. L. Buerkel-Rothfuss

(Eds.), *Media, sex, and the adolescent* (pp. 196–224). Cresskill, NJ: Hampton Press.

Greenberg, M. T., Speltz, M. L., & DeKlyen, M. (1993). The role of attachment in the early development of disruptive behavior problems. *Development and Psychopathology, 5,* 191–213.

Greenwald, A. G. (1975). Consequences of prejudice against the null hypothesis. *Psychological Bulletin, 82,* 1–20.

Greenwald, R. L., Bank, L., Reid, J. B., & Knutson, J. F. (1997). A discipline-mediated model of excessively punitive parenting. *Aggressive Behavior, 23,* 259–280.

Greydanus, D. E. (Ed.). (2003). *Caring for your teenager: The complete and authoritative guide.* New York: Bantam Books.

Griffin, K. W., Botvin, G. J., Doyle, M. M., Diaz, T., & Epstein, J. A. (1999). A six-year follow-up study of determinants of heavy cigarette smoking among of high-school seniors. *Journal of Behavioral Medicine, 22,* 271–284.

Grusec, J., & Lytton, H. (1988). *Social development: History, theory, and research.* New York: Springer-Verlag.

Gunnar, M. R., & Donzella, B. (2002). Social regulation of the cortisol levels in early human development. *Psychoneuroendocrinology, 27,* 199–220.

Gunnoe, M. L., & Mariner, C. L. (1997). Toward a developmental–contextual model of the effects of parental spanking on children's aggression. *Archives of Pediatrics & Adolescent Medicine, 151,* 768–775.

Guo, J., Hill, K. G., Hawkins, J. D., Catalano, R. F., & Abbott, R. D. (2002). A developmental analysis of sociodemographic, family, and peer effects on adolescent illicit drug initiation. *Journal of the American Academy of Child & Adolescent Psychiatry, 41,* 838–845.

Gustafson, G. E., & Harris, K. L. (1990). Women's responses to young infants' cries. *Developmental Psychology, 26,* 144–152.

Harrison, L. F., & Williams, T. M. (1986). Television and cognitive development. In T. M. Williams (Ed.), *The impact of television: A natural experiment in three communities* (pp. 87–142). Orlando, FL: Academic Press.

Hawkins, J. D., Catalano, R. F., & Miller, J. Y. (1992). Risk and protective factors for alcohol and other drug problems in adolescence and early adulthood: Implications for substance abuse prevention. *Psychological Bulletin, 112,* 64–105.

Hawkins, J. D., Graham, J. W., Maguin, E., Abbott, R., Hill, K. G., & Catalano, R. F. (1997). Exploring the effects of age alcohol use initiation and psychosocial risk factors on subsequent alcohol misuse. *Journal of Studies on Alcohol, 58,* 280–290.

Healy, M. A. (1998, April 5). Los Angeles Times interview: T. Berry Brazelton: Explaining the needs of children to parents—and lawmakers. *Los Angeles Times,* p. M3.

Hearold, S. (1986). A synthesis of 1,043 effects of television on social behavior. In G. Comstock (Ed.), *Public communication and behavior* (Vol. 1, pp. 65–133). Orlando, FL: Academic Press.

Helburn, S., Culkin, M. L., Howes, C., Bryant, D., Clifford, R., & Kagan, S. L. (1995). *Cost, quality, and child outcomes in child care centers, public report* (2nd ed.). Denver: University of Colorado at Denver, Economics Department.

Herman, M. R., Dornbusch, S. M., Herron, M. C., & Herting, J. R. (1997). The influence of family regulation, connection, and psychological autonomy on six measures of adolescent functioning. *Journal of Adolescent Research, 12,* 34–67.

Hofschire, L. J., & Greenberg, B. S. (2002). Media's impact on adolescents' body dissatisfaction. In J. D. Brown, J. R. Steele, & K. Walsh-Childers (Eds.), *Sexual teens, sexual media: Investigating media's influence on adolescent sexuality* (pp. 125–149). Mahwah, NJ: Erlbaum.

Hogan, M. J. (2001). Parents and other adults: Models and monitors of healthy media habits. In D. G. Singer & J. L. Singer (Eds.), *Handbook of children and the media* (pp. 663–680). Thousand Oaks, CA: Sage.

Hogben, M. (1998). Factors moderating the effect of televised aggression on viewer behavior. *Communication Research, 25,* 220–247.

Holden, G. W. (1983). Avoiding conflict: Mothers as tacticians in the supermarket. *Child Development, 54,* 233–240.

Holden, G. W. (1997). *Parents and the dynamics of child rearing.* Boulder, CO: Westview Press.

Holden, G. W., Coleman, S. M., & Schmidt, K. L. (1995). Why 3-year-old children get spanked: Parent and child determinants as reported by college-educated mothers. *Merrill-Palmer Quarterly, 41,* 431–452.

Holden, G. W., & Edwards, J. (1989). Parental attitudes toward child rearing: Instruments, issues, and implications. *Psychological Bulletin, 106,* 29–58.

Holden, G. W., & Miller, P. C. (1997, April). *Cognitive versus emotional spanking: Alignments between child-rearing cognitions, emotions, and reported behavior.* Paper presented at the meeting of the Society for Research in Child Development, Washington, DC.

Holden, G. W., & Miller, P. C. (1999). Enduring and different: A meta-analysis of the similarity in parents' child-rearing. *Psychological Bulletin, 125,* 223–254.

Holt, K. (2004, February 23). *Just in the niche of time.* Retrieved November 29, 2004, from http://www.publishersweekly.com/article/CA385475.html.

Holt, L. (1914). *The care and feeding of children.* New York: Appleton.

Hops, H., Davis, B., & Lewin, L. M. (1999). The development of alcohol and other substance use: A gender study of family and peer context. *Journal of Studies on Alcohol, 13* (Vol. Suppl. 13), 22–31.

Hornik, R. C. (1978). Television access and the slowing of cognitive growth. *American Educational Research Journal, 15,* 1–15.

Howe, A. C., & Walker, C. E. (1992). Behavioral management of toilet training, enuresis, and encopresis. *Pediatric Clinics of North America, 39,* 413–432.

Howes, C. (1990). Can the age of entry into child care and the quality of child care predict adjustment in kindergarten? *Developmental Psychology, 26,* 292–303.

Howes, C. (1997). Children's experiences in center-based child care as a function of teacher background and adult:child ratio. *Merrill-Palmer Quarterly, 43,* 404–425.

Howes, C. (2000). Social–emotional classroom climate in child care, child–teacher relationships and children's second grade peer relations. *Social Development, 9,* 191–204.

Howes, C., & Hamilton, C. E. (1993). The changing experience of child care: Changes in teachers and in teacher–child relationships and children's social competence with peers. *Early Childhood Research Quarterly, 8,* 15–32.

Howes, C., Phillips, D. A., & Whitebook, M. (1992). Thresholds of quality: Implications for the social development of children in center-based child care. *Child Development, 63,* 449–460.

Hubbard, F.O.A., & van IJzendoorn, M. H. (1991). Does maternal responsiveness increase infant crying?: Replication of the Baltimore study. In R. van der Veer, M. H. van IJzendoorn, & J. Valsiner (Eds.), *Reconstructing the mind: Replicability in research on human development.* Norwood, NJ: Ablex Publishing Corporation.

Huebner, A.J., & Howell, L. W. (2003). Examining the relationship between adolescent sexual risk-taking and perceptions of monitoring, communication, and parenting styles. *Journal of Adolescent Health, 33,* 71–78.

Huesmann, L. R. (1997). No simple relation. *Psychological Inquiry, 8,* 200–204.

Huesmann, L. R., & Eron, L. D. (1986a). The development of aggression in American children as a consequence of television violence viewing. In L. R. Huesmann & L. D. Eron (Eds.), *Television and the aggressive child: A cross-national comparison* (pp. 45–80). Hillsdale, NJ: Erlbaum.

Huesmann, L. R., & Eron, L. D. (1986b). *Television and the aggressive child: A cross-national comparison.* Hillsdale, NJ: Erlbaum.

Huesmann, L. R., Eron, L. D., Klein, R., Brice, P., & Fischer, P. (1983). Mitigating the imitation of aggressive behaviors by changing children's attitudes about media violence. *Journal of Personality and Social Psychology, 44,* 899–910.

Huesmann, L. R., Eron, L. D., Lefkowitz, M. M., & Walder, L. O. (1984). Stability of aggression over time and generations. *Developmental Psychology, 20,* 1120–1134.

Huesmann, L. R., & Miller, L. S. (1994). Long-term effects of repeated exposure to media violence in childhood. In L. R. Huesmann (Ed.), *Aggressive behavior: Current perspectives* (pp. 153–186). New York: Plenum Press.

Huesmann, L. R., Moise-Titus, J., Podolski, C., & Eron, L. D. (2003). Longitudinal relations between children's exposure to TV violence and their aggressive and violent behavior in young adulthood: 1977–1992. *Developmental Psychology, 39,* 201–221.

Hughes, R., & Durio, H. F. (1983). Patterns of childcare information seeking by families. *Family Relations, 32,* 203–212.

Hulbert, A. (2003). *Raising America: Experts, parents, and a century of advice about children.* New York: Knopf.

Hunziker, U. A., & Barr, R. G. (1986). Increased carrying reduces infant crying: A randomized control trial. *Pediatrics, 77,* 641–648.

Huston, A. C., & Wright, J. C. (1998). Mass media and children's development. In W. Damon, I. E. Sigel, & K. A. Renninger (Eds.), *Handbook of child psychology: Vol. 4. Child psychology in practice* (pp. 999–1058). New York: Wiley.

Huston, A. C., Wright, J. C., Marquis, J., & Green, S. B. (1999). How young children spend their time: Television and other activities. *Developmental Psychology, 35,* 912–925.

Iacono, W. G., Carlson, S. R., Taylor, J., Elkins, I. J., & McGue, M. (1999). Behavioral disinhibition and the development of substance-use disorders: Findings from the Minnesota Twin Family Study. *Development and Psychopathology, 11,* 869–900.

Information & Knowledge for Optimal Health Project. (2004). *Best practices. INFO project, Johns Hopkins University.* Retrieved November 13, 2004, from http://www.infoforhealth.org/practices.shtml.

Irwin, A. R., & Gross, A. M. (1995). Cognitive tempo, violent video games, and aggressive behavior in young boys. *Journal of Family Violence, 10,* 337–350.

Isabella, R. (1993). Origins of attachment: Maternal interactive behavior across the first year. *Child Development, 64,* 605–621.

Isabella, R., Ward, M. J., & Belsky, J. (1985). Convergence of multiple sources of information on infant individuality: Neonatal behavior, infant behavior, and temperament reports. *Infant Behavior & Development, 8,* 283–291.

Jackson, C., & Henriksen, L. (1997). Do as I say: Parent smoking, antismoking socialization, and smoking onset among children. *Addictive Behaviors, 22,* 107–114.

Jackson, C., Henriksen, L., & Dickinson, D. (1998). A longitudinal study predicting patterns of cigarette smoking in late childhood. *Health Education & Behavior, 25,* 436–447.

Jackson, C., Henriksen, L., & Dickinson, D. (1999). Alcohol-specific socialization, parenting behaviors and alcohol use by children. *Journal of Studies on Alcohol, 60,* 362–367.

Jackson, C., Henriksen, L., Dickinson, D., & Levine, D. W. (1997). The early use of alcohol and tobacco: Its relation to children's competence and parents' behavior. *American Journal of Public Health, 87,* 359–364.

Johnson, J. G., Cohen, P., Smailes, E. M., Kasen, S., & Brook, J. S. (2002, March 29). Television viewing and aggressive behavior during adolescence and adulthood. *Science, 295,* 2468–2471.

Johnston, L. D., O'Malley, P. M., Bachman, J. G., & Schulenberg, J. E. (2004, December 21). *Monitoring the Future Study.* Retrieved February 7, 2005, from University of Michigan News and Information Services Web site: www.monitoringthefuture.org.

Joint statement on the impact of entertainment violence on children: Congressional Public Health Summit. (2000, July 26). Retrieved September 9, 2002, from http://www.aap.org/advocacy/releases/jstmtevc.htm.

Jordan, A. (2004). The role of media in children's development: An ecological perspective. *Journal of Developmental & Behavioral Pediatrics, 25,* 196–206.

Kadushin A., & Martin, J. A. (1981). *Child abuse: An interactional event.* New York: Columbia University Press.

Kagan, J., Snidman, N., Zentner, M., & Peterson, E. (1999). Infant temperament and anxious symptoms in school age children. *Development and Psychopathology, 11,* 209–224.

Kaiser Family Foundation. (1996). *The Family Hour focus groups: Children's responses to sexual content on TV.* Menlo Park, CA: Author.

Kaiser Family Foundation. (2001a). *Parents and the V-chip 2001: How parents feel about TV, the TV ratings system, and the V-chip.* Menlo Park, CA: Author.

Kaiser Family Foundation. (2001b). *Sex on TV2: Executive summary.* Menlo Park, CA: Author.

Kaiser Family Foundation. (2002). *Teens, sex and TV.* Menlo Park, CA: Author.

Kanabar, D., Randhawa, M., & Clayton, P. (2001). Improvement of symptoms in infant colic following reduction of lactose load with lactase. *Journal of Human Nutrition and Dietetics, 14,* 359–363.

Kandel, D. B. (1978). Convergences in prospective longitudinal surveys of drug use in normal populations. In D. B. Kandel (Ed.), *Longitudinal research on drug use: Empirical findings and methodological issues* (pp. 3–40). New York: Wiley.

Kandel, D. B., Johnson, J. G., Bird, H. R., Canino, G., Goodman, S. H., & Lahey, B. B., et al. (1997). Psychiatric disorders associated with substance use among children and adolescents: Findings from the Methods for the Epidemiology of Child and Adolescent Mental Disorders (MECA) Study. *Journal of Abnormal Child Psychology, 25,* 121–132.

Kandel, D. B., & Wu, P. (1995). The contributions of mothers and fathers to the intergenerational transmission of cigarette smoking in adolescence. *Journal of Research on Adolescence, 5,* 225–252.

Kaplow, J. B., Curran, P. J., Dodge, K. A., & the Conduct Problems Prevention Research Group. (2002). Child, parent, and peer predictors of early-onset substance use: A multisite longitudinal study. *Journal of Abnormal Child Psychology, 30,* 199–216.

Keefe, M. R. (2001). The REST regimen: A conceptual approach to managing unexplained early infant irritability. In R. G. Barr, I. St. James-Roberts, & M. R. Keefe (Eds.), *New evidence on unexplained early infant crying: Its origins, nature, and management* (pp. 229–244). Calverton, NY: Johnson & Johnson Pediatric Institute.

Kelly, K. (2000, October 30). Child docs to parents: Stay home and save your kids. *U.S. News & World Report, 129,* 65.

Kendler, K. S., Neale, M. C., Sullivan, P., Corey, L. A., Gardner, C. O., & Prescott, C. A. (1999). A population-based twin study in women of smoking initiation and nicotine dependence. *Psychological Medicine, 29,* 299–308.

Kennedy, M. (1997, February). Should you spank and nine other really tough questions. *Ladies' Home Journal,* 84–88.

Kerr, M., & Stattin, H. (2000). What parents know, how they know it, and several forms of adolescent adjustment: Further support for a reinterpretation of monitoring. *Developmental Psychology, 36,* 366–380.

Kinkead, G. (1994, April 10). Spock, Brazelton and now . . . Penelope Leach. *The New York Times Magazine,* 33–35.

Kirby, D. (2002). Effective approaches to reducing adolescent unprotected sex, pregnancy, and childbearing. *Journal of Sex Research, 39,* 51–57.

Kirby, D., Baumler, E., Coyle, K. K., Basen-Engquist, K., Parcel, G. S., Harrist, R., & Banspach, S. W. (2004). The "Safer Choices" intervention: Its impact on the sexual behaviors of different subgroups of high school students. *Journal of Adolescent Health, 35,* 442–452.

Kirkpatrick, D. D. (2005, January 1). Evangelical leader threatens to use his political muscle against some Democrats. *The New York Times,* p. A10.

Kirsch, S. J. (1998). Seeing the world through Mortal Kombat-colored glasses. *Childhood, 5,* 177–184.

Klackenberg, G. (1971). Expectations and reality concerning toilet training. *Acta Paediatrica Scandinavia, 224*(Suppl.), 85–127.

Kochanska, G. (1995). Children's temperament, mothers, discipline, and security of attachment: Multiple pathways to emerging internalization. *Child Development, 66,* 597–615.

Kochanska, G. (1997). Mutually responsive orientation between mothers and their young children: Implications for early socialization. *Child Development, 68,* 94–112.

Kochanska, G., Aksan, N., Knaak, A., & Rhines, H. M. (2004). Maternal parenting and children's conscience: Early security as moderator. *Child Development, 75,* 1229–1242.

Kochanska, G., Padavich, D. L., & Koenig, A. L. (1996). Children's narratives about hypothetical moral dilemmas and objective measures of their conscience: Mutual relations and socialization antecedents. *Child Development, 67,* 1420–1436.

Komaya, M., & Bowyer, J. (2000). College-educated mothers' ideas about television and their active mediation of viewing by three- to five-year-old children: Japan and the U.S.A. *Journal of Broadcasting & Electronic Media, 44,* 349–363.

Kontos, S., Howes, C., Shinn, M., & Galinsky, E. (1995). *Quality in family child care and relative care.* New York: Teachers College Press.

Kosterman, R., Hawkin, J. D., Haggerty, K. P., Spoth, R., & Redmond, C. (2001). Preparing for the drug-free years: Session-specific effects of a universal parent-training intervention with rural families. *Journal of Drug Education, 31,* 47–68.

Krcmar, M. (1996). Family communication patterns, discourse behavior, and child television viewing. *Human Communication Research, 23,* 251–277.

Krugman, R. D. (1983–1985). Fatal child abuse: Analysis of 24 cases. *Pediatrician, 12,* 68–72.

Kuczynski, L. (1984). Socialization goals and mother–child interaction: Strategies for long-term and short-term compliance. *Developmental Psychology, 20,* 1061–1073.

Kuczynski, L., Kochanska, G., Radke-Yarrow, M., & Girnius-Brown, O. (1987). A developmental interpretation of young children's noncompliance. *Developmental Psychology, 23,* 799–806.

Kunkel, D., Cope, K. M., Farinola, W. J., Biely, E., Rollin, E., & Donnerstein, E. (1999). *Sex on TV: Content and context. A biennial report to the Kaiser Family Foundation.* Menlo Park, CA: Kaiser Family Foundation.

Laird, R. D., Pettit, G. S., Bates, J. E., & Dodge, K. E. (2003). Parents' monitoring-relevant knowledge and adolescents' delinquent behavior: Evidence of cor-related developmental changes and reciprocal influences. *Child Development, 74,* 752–768.

Lally, J. R., Griffin, A., Fenichel, E., Segal, M., Szanton, E., & Weissbourd, B. (2003). *Caring for infants and toddlers in groups: Developmentally appropriate practice.* Washington, DC: Zero to Three.

Lamb, M. E. (1998). Nonparental child care: Context, quality, correlates, and con-sequences. In W. Damon, I. E. Sigel, & K. A. Renninger (Eds.), *Handbook of child psychology: Vol. 4. Child psychology in practice* (pp. 73–133). New York: Wiley.

Lamborn, S. D., Mounts, N. S., Steinberg, L., & Dornbusch, S. M. (1991). Patterns of competence and adjustment among adolescents from authoritative, au-thoritarian, indulgent, and neglectful families. *Child Development, 62,* 1049–1065.

Lammers, C., Ireland, M., Resnick, M., & Blum, R. (2000). Influences on adoles-cents' decision to postpone onset of sexual intercourse: A survival analysis of virginity among youth age 13 to 18 years. *Journal of Adolescent Health, 26,* 42–48.

Langfitt, F. (2004, November 20). Dobson: Now that election day is over, the Chris-tian leader is rallying support for 'moral' Supreme Court appointees. *The Baltimore Sun,* p. 1A.

Lansford, J. E., Deater-Deckard, K., Dodge, K. A., Bates, J. E., & Pettit, G. S. (2004). Ethnic difference in the link between physical discipline and later adolescent externalizing behaviors. *Journal of Child Psychology & Psychiatry, 45,* 801–812.

Largo, R. H., & Stutzle, W. (1977). Longitudinal study of bowel and bladder con-trol by day and at night in the first six years of life. *Developmental Medicine and Child Neurology, 19,* 598–606.

Larzelere, R. E. (1996). A review of the outcomes of parental use of nonabusive or customary physical punishment. *Pediatrics, 98,* 824–828.

Larzelere, R. E. (2003, April). *A meta-analysis comparing the effect sizes and correlates of corporal punishment with alternative disciplinary tactics.* Paper presented at the So-ciety for Research in Child Development meeting, Tampa, FL.

Larzelere, R. E., Kuhn, B. R., & Johnson, B. (2004). The intervention selection bias: An underrecognized confound in intervention research. *Psychological Bulletin, 130,* 289–303.

Larzelere, R. E., Sather, P. R., Schneider, W. N., Larson, D. B., & Pike, P. L. (1998).

Punishment enhances reasoning's effectiveness as a disciplinary response to toddlers. *Journal of Marriage and the Family, 60,* 388–403.

Larzelere, R. E., Schneider, W. N., Larson, D. B., & Pike, P. L. (1996). The effects of discipline responses in delaying toddler misbehavior recurrences. *Child & Family Behavior Therapy, 18,* 35–57.

Leach, P. (1989a). *Your baby and child: From birth to age five* (2nd ed.). New York: Alfred A. Knopf.

Leach, P. (1989b). *Your growing child: From babyhood through adolescence.* New York: Alfred A. Knopf.

Leach, P. (1994). *Children first: What our society must do—and is not doing—for our children today.* New York: Alfred A. Knopf.

Leach, P. (1997). Anna Freud Centenary Lecture: Attachment: Facing the professional demands of today's research findings. *Journal of Child Psychotherapy, 23,* 5–23.

Leach, P. (1998). *Your baby and child: From birth to age five* (3rd ed.). New York: Alfred A. Knopf.

Leach, Penelope. (1994). In S. M. Trosky (Ed.), *Contemporary authors: A bio-bibliographic guide to current writers in fiction, nonfiction, poetry, journalism, drama, motion pictures, television, and other fields* (Vol. 44, pp. 267–268). Detroit, MI: Gale Group.

Lee, C. L., & Bates, J. E. (1985). Mother–child interaction at age two years and perceived difficult temperament. *Child Development, 56,* 1314–1325.

Leslie, L. A., Ettenson, R., & Cumsille, P. (2000). Selecting a childcare center: What really matters to parents? *Child Care and Youth Forum, 29,* 29–35.

Lester, B. M. (1985). There's more to crying than meets the ear. In B. M. Lester & C.F.Z. Boukydis (Eds.), *Infant crying: Theoretical and research perspectives* (pp. 1–27). New York: Plenum Press.

Levine, M. D. (1975). Children with encopresis: A descriptive analysis. *Pediatrics, 56,* 412–416.

Light, R. J., & Pillemer, D. B. (1984). *Summing up: The science of reviewing research.* Cambridge, MA: Harvard University Press.

Lin, C. A., & Atkin, D. J. (1989). Parental mediation and rulemaking for adolescent use of television and VCRs. *Journal of Broadcasting & Electronic Media, 33,* 53–67.

Lloyd-Richardson, E. E., Papandonatos, G., Kazura, A., Stanton, C., & Niaura, R. (2002). Differentiating stages of smoking intensity among adolescents: Stage-specific psychological and social influences. *Journal of Consulting and Clinical Psychology, 70,* 998–1009.

Loeber, R., & Stouthamer-Loeber, M. (1986). Family factors as correlates and predictors of juvenile conduct problems and delinquency. In M. Tonry & N. Morris (Eds.), *Crime and justice: An annual review of research* (Vol. 7, pp. 29–149). Chicago: University of Chicago Press.

Loehlin, J. C. (1992). *Genes and environment in personality development.* Newbury Park, CA: Sage.

Londerville, S., & Main, M. (1981). Security of attachment, compliance, and maternal training methods in the second year of life. *Developmental Psychology, 17,* 289–299.

Longmore, M. A., Manning, W. D., & Giordano, P. C. (2001). Preadolescent parenting strategies and teens' dating and sexual initiation: A longitudinal analysis. *Journal of Marriage and the Family, 63,* 322–335.

Love, J. M., Harrison, L., Sagi-Schwartz, A., van IJzendoorn, M. H., Ross, C., Ungerer, J. A., et al. (2003). Child care quality matters: How conclusions may vary with context. *Child Development, 74,* 1021–1033.

Lucassen, P.L.B.J., Assendelft, W.J.J., Gubbels, J. W., van Eijk, J.T.M., van Geldrop, W.J., & Knuistingh Neven, A. (1998). Effectiveness of treatment for infantile colic: Systematic review. *British Medical Journal, 316,* 1563–1568.

Luster, T., & Small, S. A. (1994). Factors associated with sexual risk-taking behaviors among adolescents. *Journal of Marriage and the Family, 56,* 622–632.

Luthar, S. S., & D'Avanzo, K. (1999). Contextual factors in substance use: A study of suburban and inner-city adolescents. *Development and Psychopathology, 11,* 845–867.

Luxem, M., & Christophersen, E. (1994). Behavioral toilet training in early childhood: Research, practice, and implications. *Developmental and Behavioral Pediatrics, 15,* 370–378.

Lytton, H. (1977). Correlates of compliance and the rudiments of conscience in 2-year-old boys. *Canadian Journal of Behavioral Sciences, 9,* 242–251.

Lytton, H. (1980). *Parent–child interaction: The socialization process observed in twin and singleton families.* New York: Plenum Press.

Lytton, H. (1994). Replication and meta-analysis: The story of a meta-analysis of parents' socialization practices. In R. van der Veer, M. H. van IJzendoorn, & J. Valsiner (Eds.), *Reconstructing the mind: Replicability in research on human development* (pp. 117–149). Norwood, NJ: Ablex Publishing Corporation.

Lytton, H. (1997). Physical punishment is a problem, whether conduct disorder is endogenous or not. *Psychological Inquiry, 8,* 211–214.

Lytton, H., & Zwirner, W. (1975). Compliance and its controlling stimuli observed in a natural setting. *Developmental Psychology, 11,* 769–779.

Maccoby, E. E. (2000). Parenting and its effects on children: On reading and misreading behavior genetics. *Annual Review of Psychology, 51,* 1–27.

Maccoby, E. E., & Lewis, C. C. (2003). Less day care or different day care? *Child Development, 74,* 1069–1075.

Maccoby, E. E., & Martin, J. (1983). Socialization in the context of the family: Parent-child interaction. In P. H. Mussen (Series Ed.) & E. M. Hetherington (Vol. Ed.), *Handbook of child psychology: Vol. 4. Socialization, personality, and social development* (4th ed., pp. 1–101). New York: Wiley.

MacKeith, R., Meadow, R., & Turner, R. K. (1975). How children become dry. *Clinics in Developmental Medicine, 48,* 3–32.

Madsen, C. H., Hoffman, M., Thomas, D. R., Koropsat, E., & Madsen, D. K. (1969). Comparisons of toilet training procedures. In D. M. Gelfand (Ed.), *Social learning in childhood* (pp. 104–112). Belmont, CA: Brooks/Cole.

Maier, T. (1998). *Dr. Spock: An American life*. New York: Basic Books.

Malamuth, N. M., & Impett, E. A. (2001). Research on sex in the media: What do we know about effects on children and adolescents? In D. G. Singer & J. L. Singer (Eds.), *Handbook of children and the media* (pp. 269–287). Thousand Oaks, CA: Sage.

Martin, G., & Pear, J. (1999). *Behavior modification: What it is and how to do it* (6th ed.). Upper Saddle River, NJ: Prentice-Hall.

Martin, J. A., King, D. R., Maccoby, E. E., & Jacklin, C. N. (1984). Secular trends and individual differences in toilet-training progress. *Journal of Pediatric Psychology, 9,* 457–467.

Marty, M. E., & Appleby, R. S. (Eds.). (1993). *Fundamentalisms and society: Reclaiming the sciences, the family, and education.* Chicago: University of Chicago Press.

Masse, L. C., & Tremblay, R. E. (1997). Behavior of boys in kindergarten and the onset of substance use during adolescence. *Archives of General Psychiatry, 54,* 62–68.

Matson, J. L. (1975). Some practical considerations for using the Foxx and Azrin rapid methods of toilet training. *Psychological Reports, 37,* 350.

Matson, J. L., & Ollendick, T. H. (1977). Issues in toilet training normal children. *Behavior Therapy, 8,* 549–553.

McCall, R. B. (1987). The media, society, and child developmental research. In J. D. Osofsky (Ed.), *Handbook of infant development* (2nd ed., pp. 1199–1255). New York: Wiley-Interscience.

McCord, J. (1997). On discipline. *Psychological Inquiry, 8,* 215–217.

McGue, M., Sharma, A., & Benson, P. L. (1996). Parent and sibling influences on adolescent alcohol use and misuse: Evidence from a U.S. adoption cohort. *Journal of Studies on Alcohol, 57,* 8–18.

McHale, S. M., Crouter, A. C., McGuire, S. A., & Updegraff, K. A. (1995). Congruence between mothers' and fathers' differential treatment of siblings: Links with family relations and children's well-being. *Child Development, 66,* 116–128.

McKenzie, S. A. (1991). Troublesome crying in infants: The effect of advice to reduce stimulation. *Archives of Disease in Childhood, 66,* 1416–1420.

McKim, M. K., Cramer, K. M., Stuart, B., & O'Connor, D. L. (1999). Infant care decisions and attachment security: The Canadian transition to child care study. *Canadian Journal of Behavioural Science, 31,* 92–106.

McLoyd, V. C. (1990). The impact of economic hardship on Black families and children: Psychological distress, parenting, and socioemotional development. *Child Development, 61,* 311–346.

McLoyd, V. C., & Smith, J. (2002). Physical discipline and behavior problems in African American, European American, and Hispanic children: Emotional support as a moderator. *Journal of Marriage and the Family, 64,* 40–53.

McNeely, C., Shew, M. L., Beuhring, T., Sieving, R., Miller, B. C., & Blum, R. M. (2002). Mothers' influence on the timing of first sex among 14- and 15-year-olds. *Journal of Adolescent Health, 31,* 256–265.

Mehmet-Radji, O. (2004). Early television exposure and subsequent attentional problems in children. *Child: Care, Health and Development, 30,* 559–560.

Mesibov, G. B., Schroeder, C. S., & Wesson, L. (1977). Parental concerns about their children. *Journal of Pediatric Psychology, 2,* 13–17.

Messaris, P., & Sarett, C. (1981). On the consequences of television-related parent–child interaction. *Human Communication Research, 7,* 226–244.

Miller, A. R., Barr, R. G., & Eaton, W. O. (1993). Crying and motor behavior of six-week-old infants and postpartum maternal mood. *Pediatrics, 92,* 551–558.

Miller, B. C. (2002). Family influences on adolescent sexual and contraceptive behavior. *Journal of Sex Research, 39,* 22–26.

Miller, B. C., Benson, B., & Galbraith, K. A. (2001). Family relationships and adolescent pregnancy risk: A research synthesis. *Developmental Review, 21,* 1–38.

Moberg, D. P., & Piper, D. L. (1998). The Healthy for Life Project: Sexual risk behavior outcomes. *AIDS Education and Prevention, 10,* 138–148.

Mohr, P. (1979). Parental guidance of children's viewing of evening television programs. *Journal of Broadcasting, 23,* 213–219.

Molitor, F., & Hirsch, K. W. (1994). Children's toleration of real-life aggression after exposure to media violence: A replication of the Drabman and Thomas studies. *Child Study Journal, 24,* 191–207.

Moon, R. Y., Gingras, J. L., & Erwin, R. (2002). Physician beliefs and practices regarding SIDS and SIDS risk reduction. *Clinical Pediatrics, 41,* 391–395.

Murray, L., & Cooper, P. (2001). The impact of irritable infant behavior on maternal mental state: A longitudinal study and a treatment trial. In R. G. Barr, I. St. James-Roberts, & M. R. Keefe (Eds.), *New evidence on unexplained early infant crying: Its origins, nature, and management* (pp. 149–164). Calverton, NY: Johnson & Johnson Pediatric Institute.

Nathanson, A. I. (1999). Identifying and explaining the relationship between parental mediation and children's aggression. *Communication Research, 26,* 124–143.

National Association for the Education of Young Children. (1991). *Accreditation criteria and procedures of the National Academy of Early Childhood Programs.* Washington, DC: Author.

National Center for Education Statistics. (1996). *Statistics in brief: Child care and early education program participation of infants, toddlers, and preschoolers* (Publication no. NCES 95-824). Washington, DC: Author.

National Institute on Drug Abuse. (2003). *Preventing drug use among children and adolescents: A research-based guide* (2nd ed.). [Brochure]. Washington, DC: National Institutes of Health.

National Institutes of Health. (2004). *NIH consensus development program.* Retrieved November 30, 2004, from http://consensus.nih.gov/.

National Television Violence Study (Vol. 1). (1996). Thousand Oaks, CA: Sage.

National Television Violence Study (Vol. 2). (1997). Studio City, CA: Mediascope.

National Television Violence Study (Vol. 3). (1998). Santa Barbara: University of California, Center for Communication and Social Policy.

NICHD Early Child Care Research Network. (1996). Characteristics of infant child care: Factors contributing to positive caregiving. *Early Childhood Research Quarterly, 11,* 269–306.

NICHD Early Child Care Research Network. (1997a). Child care in the first year of life. *Merrill-Palmer Quarterly, 43,* 340–360.

NICHD Early Child Care Research Network. (1997b). The effects of infant child care on infant–mother attachment security: Results of the NICHD study of early child care. *Child Development, 68,* 860–879.

NICHD Early Child Care Research Network. (1997c). Familial factors associated with the characteristics of nonmaternal care for infants. *Journal of Marriage and the Family, 59,* 389–408.

NICHD Early Child Care Research Network. (1998a). Early child care and self-control, compliance, and problem behavior at twenty-four and thirty-six months. *Child Development, 69,* 1145–1170.

NICHD Early Child Care Research Network. (1998b). Relations between family predictors and child outcomes: Are they weaker for children in child care? *Developmental Psychology, 34,* 1119–1128.

NICHD Early Child Care Research Network. (1999). Child care and mother–child interaction in the first three years of life. *Developmental Psychology, 35,* 1399–1413.

NICHD Early Child Care Research Network. (2000a). Characteristics and quality of child care for toddlers and preschoolers. *Applied Developmental Science, 4,* 116–135.

NICHD Early Child Care Research Network. (2000b). The relation of child care to cognitive and language development. *Child Development, 71,* 958–978.

NICHD Early Child Care Research Network. (2001a). Child care and common communicable illnesses. *Archives of Pediatric & Adolescent Medicine, 155,* 481–488.

NICHD Early Child Care Research Network. (2001b). Child-care and family predictors of preschool attachment and stability from infancy. *Developmental Psychology, 37,* 847–862.

NICHD Early Child Care Research Network. (2001c, April). *Early child care and children's development prior to school entry.* Paper presented at the meeting of the Society for Research in Child Development, Minneapolis, MN.

NICHD Early Child Care Research Network. (2001d, April). *Type of care and children's development at 54 months.* Paper presented at the meeting of the Society for Research in Child Development, Minneapolis, MN.

NICHD Early Child Care Research Network. (2002a). Child-care structure → process → outcome: Direct and indirect effects of child-care quality on young children's development. *Psychological Science, 13,* 199–206.

NICHD Early Child Care Research Network. (2002b). Early child care and children's development prior to school entry: Results from the NICHD study of early child care. *American Educational Research Journal, 39,* 133–164.

NICHD Early Child Care Research Network. (2003a). Child care and common communicable illnesses in children aged 37–54 months. *Archives of Pediatric & Adolescent Medicine, 157,* 196–200.

NICHD Early Child Care Research Network. (2003b). Does the amount of time spent in child care predict socio-emotional adjustment during the transition to kindergarten? *Child Development, 74,* 976–1005.

NICHD Early Child Care Research Network. (2003c). Social functioning in first grade: Associations with earlier home and child care predictors and with current classroom experiences. *Child Development, 74,* 1639–1662.

NICHD Early Child Care Research Network. (2004a). Multiple pathways to early academic achievement. *Harvard Educational Review, 74,* 1–29.

NICHD Early Child Care Research Network. (2004b). Trajectories of physical aggression from toddlerhood to middle childhood. *Monographs of the Society for Research in Child Development, 69*(4, Serial No. 278).

NICHD Early Child Care Research Network. (2004c). Type of child care and children's development at 54 months. *Early Childhood Research Quarterly, 19,* 203–230.

Niebuhr, G. (1995, May 30). Advice for parents and for politicians: Religious group speaks to family issues and to the right. *The New York Times,* p. A12.

Nielsen Media Research. (1998). *1998 report on television.* New York: Nielsen Media Research.

North Carolina Psychology Board. (1992, September 22). *Consent order in the matter of: John K. Rosemond, M. S., Respondent.* Boone, NC: Author.

North Carolina Psychology Practice Act, N.C.G.S. 90–270.1 et seq. Retrieved July 1, 2005, from http://www.ncpsychologyboard.org/.

North Carolina State Board of Examiners of Practicing Psychologists. (1988, March 15). *Letter of reprimand to John Rosemond.* Boone, NC: Author.

O'Connor, T. G., Deater-Deckard, K., Fulker, D., Rutter, M., & Plomin, R. (1998). Genotype-environment correlations in late childhood and early adolescence: Antisocial behavioral problems and coercive parenting. *Developmental Psychology, 34,* 970–981.

O'Connor, T. G., Hetherington, E. M., Reiss, D., Hetherington, E. M., & Plomin, R. (1995). A twin-sibling study of observed parent–adolescent interactions. *Child Development, 66,* 812–829.

Ogbu, J. U. (1981). Origins of human competence: A cultural–ecological perspective. *Child Development, 55,* 1912–1925.

Oppel, W. C., Harper, P. A., & Rider, R. V. (1968). The age of attaining bladder control. *Pediatrics, 42,* 614–626.

Oxford, M. L., Harachi, T. W., Catalano, R. F., & Abbott, R. D. (2000). Preadolescent predictors of substance initiation: A test of both the direct and mediated effect of family social control factors on deviant peer associations and substance initiation. *American Journal of Drug and Alcohol Abuse, 27,* 599–616.

Paik, H., & Comstock, G. (1994). The effects of television violence on antisocial behavior: A meta-analysis. *Communication Research, 21,* 516–546.

Papousek, M., & Papousek, H. (1996). Infantile persistent crying, state regulation, and interaction with parents: A systems view. In M. H. Bornstein & J. L. Genevro (Eds.), *Child development and behavioral pediatrics* (pp. 11–33). Hillsdale, NJ: Erlbaum.

Papousek, M., & von Hofacker, N. (1998). Persistent crying in early infancy: A non-trivial condition of risk for the developing mother–infant relationship. *Child: Care, Health and Development, 24,* 395–424.

Parke, R. D. (1969). Effectiveness of punishment as an interaction of intensity, timing, agent nurturance, and cognitive structuring. *Child Development, 40,* 213–235.

Parmelee, A. H., Wenner, W., & Schulz, H. (1964). Infant sleep patterns from birth to 16 weeks of age. *Journal of Pediatrics, 65,* 576–582.

Parpal, M., & Maccoby, E. E. (1985). Maternal responsiveness and subsequent child compliance. *Child Development, 56,* 1326–1334.

Patterson, G. R. (1982). *Coercive family process.* Eugene, OR: Castalia.

Patterson, G. R. (1986). Performance models for antisocial boys. *American Psychologist, 41,* 432–444.

Patterson, G. R., DeBaryshe, B. D., & Ramsey, E. (1989). A developmental perspective on antisocial behavior. *American Psychologist, 44,* 329–335.

Patterson, G. R., & Fisher, P. A. (2002). Recent developments in our understanding of parenting: Bidirectional effects, causal models, and the search for parsimony. In M. H. Bornstein (Ed.), *Handbook of parenting: Vol. 5. Practical issues in parenting* (2nd ed., pp. 59–88). Mahwah, NJ: Erlbaum.

Pederson, F. A., Huffman, L. C., del Carmen, R., & Bryan, Y. E. (1996). Prenatal maternal reactivity to infant cries predicts postnatal perceptions of infant temperament and marriage appraisal. *Child Development, 67,* 2541–2552.

Peisner-Feinberg, E. S., Burchinal, M. R., & Clifford, R. M. (2001). The relation of preschool child-care quality to children's cognitive and social developmental trajectories through second grade. *Child Development, 72,* 1534–1553.

Peterson, J. L., Moore, K. A., & Furstenberg, F. F. (1991). Television viewing and early initiation of sexual intercourse: Is there a link? *Journal of Homosexuality, 21,* 93–118.

Peterson, P. L., Hawkins, J. D., Abbott, R. D., & Catalano, R. F. (1994). Disentangling the effects of parental drinking, family management, and parental alcohol norms on current drinking by Black and White adolescents. *Journal of Research on Adolescence, 4,* 203–227.

Pettit, G. S., Bates, J., & Dodge, K. A. (1993). Family interaction patterns and children's conduct problems at home and school: A longitudinal perspective. *School Psychology Review, 22,* 403–420.

Pettit, G. S., Clawson, M. A., Dodge, K. A., & Bates, J. E. (1996). Stability and change in peer-rejected status: The role of child behavior, parenting, and family ecology. *Merrill-Palmer Quarterly, 42,* 267–294.

Pfiffner, L. J., & O'Leary, S. G. (1989). Effects of maternal discipline and nurturance on toddler's behavior and affect. *Journal of Abnormal Child Psychology, 17,* 527–540.

Plamenatz, J. (1973–1974). Liberalism. In P. P. Wiener (Ed.), *Dictionary of the history of ideas*. New York: Charles Scribner's Sons.

Plomin, R. (1994). *Genetics and experience: The interplay between nature and nurture*. Thousand Oaks, CA: Sage.

Polce-Lynch, M., Myers, B. J., Kliewer, W., & Kilmartin, C. (2001). Adolescent self-esteem and gender: Exploring relations to sexual harassment, body image, media influence, and emotional expression. *Journal of Youth and Adolescence, 30*, 225–244.

Power, T. G., & Chapieski, M. L. (1986). Childrearing and impulse control in toddlers: A naturalistic investigation. *Developmental Psychology, 22*, 271–275.

Pratt, C. (Executive Producer). (2004, February 15). *Face the nation* [Television broadcast]. New York: CBS News.

Prechtl, H.F.R. (1984). Continuity and change in early neural development. In H.F.R. Prechtl (Ed.), *Continuity of neural functions from prenatal to postnatal life* (pp. 1–15). Oxford, England: Blackwell.

Raikes, H. (1993). Relationship duration in infant care: Time with high-ability teacher and infant–teacher attachment. *Early Childhood Research Quarterly, 8*, 309–325.

Ramey, C. T., & Ramey, S. L. (1999b). *Right from birth: Building your child's foundation for life*. New York: Goddard Press.

Ramey, S. L., & Ramey, C. T. (1999a). *Going to school: How to help your child succeed*. New York: Goddard Press.

Rautava, P., Lehtonen, L., Helenius, H., & Sillanpaa, M. (1995). Infantile colic: Child and family three years later. *Pediatrics, 96*, 43–47.

Ream, G. L., & Savin-Williams, R. C. (2005). Reciprocal relationships between adolescent sexual activity and quality of youth–parent interaction. *Journal of Family Psychology, 19*, 171–179.

Reifman, A., Barnes, G. M., Dintcheff, B. A., Farrell, M. P., & Uhteg, L. (1998). Parental and peer influences on the onset of heavier drinking among adolescents. *Journal of Studies on Alcohol, 59*, 311–317.

Rice, M. L., Huston, A. C., Truglio, R., & Wright, J. C. (1990). Words from "Sesame Street": Learning vocabulary while viewing. *Developmental Psychology, 26*, 421–428.

Rideout, V. (2004). *Parents, media and public policy: A Kaiser Family Foundation Survey*. Menlo Park, CA: Kaiser Family Foundation.

Rideout, V., Foehr, U. G., Roberts, D. F., & Brodie, M. (1999). *Kids + media @ the new millennium*. Menlo Park, CA: Kaiser Family Foundation.

Rideout, V., Roberts, D. F., & Foehr, U. G. (2005). *Generation M: Media in the lives of 8–18 year-olds. Executive summary*. Menlo Park, CA: Kaiser Family Foundation.

Rideout, V., Vandewater, E. A., & Wartella, E. A. (2003). *Zero to six: Electronic media in the lives of infants, toddlers, and preschoolers. A Kaiser Family Foundation Report*. Retrieved January 30, 2005, from http://www.kff.org/entmedia/3378.cfm.

Ritchie, D., Price, V., & Roberts, D. F. (1987). Television, reading, and reading achievement: A reappraisal. *Communication Research, 14*, 292–315.

Roberts, K. E., & Schoellkopf, J. A. (1951). Eating, sleeping, and elimination practices of group of two-and-one-half-year-old children. *Journal of Diseases of Children, 82,* 137.

Roberts, M. W., Hatzenbuehler, L. C., & Bean, A. W. (1981). The effects of differential attention and timeout on child noncompliance. *Behavior Therapy, 12,* 93–99.

Roberts, M. W., & Powers, S. W. (1990). Adjusting chair timeout enforcement procedures for oppositional children. *Behavior Therapy, 21,* 257–271.

Robinson, T. N., Wilde, M. L., Navracruz, L. C., Haydel, K. F., & Varady, A. (2001). Effects of reducing children's television and video game use on aggressive behavior. *Archives of Pediatrics & Adolescent Medicine, 155,* 17–23.

Robson, W.L.M., & Leung, A.K.C. (1991). Advising parents on toilet training. *American Family Physician, 44,* 1263–1266.

Rodgers, K. B. (1999). Parenting processes related to sexual risk-taking behaviors of adolescent males and females. *Journal of Marriage and the Family, 61,* 99–109.

Roggman, L. A., Langlois, J. H., Hubbs-Tait, L., & Rieser-Danner, L. A. (1994). Infant day-care, attachment, and the "file-drawer problem." *Child Development, 65,* 1429–1443.

Rohner, R. P., Bourque, S. L., & Elordi, C. A. (1996). Children's perceptions of corporal punishment, caretaker acceptance, and psychological adjustment in a poor, biracial southern community. *Journal of Marriage and the Family, 58,* 842–852.

Rose, J. S., Chassin, L., Presson, C. C., & Sherman, S. J. (1999). Peer influences on adolescent cigarette smoking: A prospective sibling analysis. *Merrill-Palmer Quarterly, 45,* 62–84.

Rosemond, J. K. (1989). *John Rosemond's six-point plan for raising happy, healthy children.* Kansas City, MO: Andrews and McMeel.

Rosemond, J. K. (1990). *Parent power! A common sense approach to parenting in the '90s and beyond.* Kansas City, MO: Andrews and McMeel.

Rosemond, J. K. (1991, June 2). Workshops and seminar teach discipline, but not love. *The Charlotte Observer,* p. 4E.

Rosemond, J. K. (1992a, March 11). For parents only. *The Houston Chronicle,* p. 2.

Rosemond, J. K. (1992b, December 4). In early years, home care wins out over day care. *The Miami Herald,* p. 2E.

Rosemond, J. K. (1992c, August 28). More questions on spanking: Is it abuse? Should law change? *The Charlotte Observer,* p. 2E.

Rosemond, J. K. (1992d, August 21). A self-interview on spanking children. *The Miami Herald,* p. 2E.

Rosemond, J. K. (1993a, August 15). Kids don't need a lot of attention. *The Des Moines Register,* p. 3E.

Rosemond, J. K. (1993b). *Making the "terrible" twos terrific!* Kansas City, MO: Andrews and McMeel.

Rosemond, J. K. (1993c, December 5). Old-fashioned ideas worked. *The Des Moines Register,* p. 3E.

Rosemond, J. K. (1993d, July 2). Once again, listen up: Caring for a child at home is better than day care. *The Charlotte Observer,* p. 2E.

Rosemond, J. K. (1993e, May 7). Problem isn't boredom, it's that kids are spoiled. *The Miami Herald,* p. 3E.

Rosemond, J. K. (1993f, December 26). Show 9-year-old "game" is over. *The Des Moines Register,* p. 3E.

Rosemond, J. K. (1994a, November 13). An ADD child in his family. *The Des Moines Register,* p. 3E.

Rosemond, J. K. (1994b, November 6). Children more "sophisticated." *The Des Moines Register,* p. 3E.

Rosemond, J. K. (1994c, January 23). How to handle toilet problem. *The Des Moines Register,* p. 5E.

Rosemond, J. K. (1994d, April 3). Playing without a set of rules. *The Des Moines Register,* p. 3E.

Rosemond, J. K. (1994e). *To spank or not to spank: A parents' handbook.* Kansas City, MO: Andrews and McMeel.

Rosemond, J. K. (1994f, October 2). Women, cut the whining: There's no glass ceiling. *The Miami Herald,* p. 3E.

Rosemond, J. K. (1995a). *A family of value.* Kansas City, MO: Andrews and McMeel.

Rosemond, J. K. (1995b, January 15). Gingrich's plan for "orphanages." *The Des Moines Register,* p. 3E.

Rosemond, J. K. (1995c, February 26). Support grows for kids' rights. *The Des Moines Register,* p. 3E.

Rosemond, J. K. (1996, February 25). "Three strikes" and he's out of fun and games. *The Des Moines Register,* p. 3E.

Rosemond, J. K. (1997a, October 21). Potty training needs touch of dry humor. *The Charlotte Observer,* p. 6A.

Rosemond, J. K. (1997b, October 14). Wait-till-ready toilet training is all wet. *The Charlotte Observer,* p. 7A.

Rosemond, J. K. (1998a, December 18). Despite the debate, toilet training a child is best done by age 2. *The Miami Herald,* p. 2E.

Rosemond, J. K. (1998b, April 6). The downside of day care. *Pittsburgh Post-Gazette,* p. C3.

Rosemond, J. K. (1998c, September 15). Early toilet training calls for voices of experience. *The Charlotte Observer,* p. 3E.

Rosemond, J. K. (1998d, September 1). Here's naked truth on $75 potty training. *The Charlotte Observer,* p. 3E.

Rosemond, J. K. (1998e, August 25). It's parents' responsibility to decide on potty training. *The Charlotte Observer,* p. 3E.

Rosemond, J. K. (1999a, May 18). Disposable training pants are not worth it. *The Charlotte Observer,* p. 6E.

Rosemond, J. K. (1999b, March 9). Dispose of ideas on late toilet training. *The Charlotte Observer,* p. 3E.

Rosemond, J. K. (1999c, April). Living with children: Raising responsible adults. *Iowa Parent and Family Magazine,* 5.

Rosemond, J. K. (2000, January 28). Toilet training works best at 18–24 months. *The Cincinnati Enquirer,* p. E03.

Rosemond, J. K. (2001a, September 8). Discipline and the prize patrol. *The San Diego Union-Tribune,* p. E10.

Rosemond, J. K. (2001b). *New parent power!* Kansas City, MO: Andrews and McMeel.

Rosemond, J. K. (2001c, May 26). Sorry! Day-care study makes sense. *The San Diego Union-Tribune,* p. E10.

Rosemond, J. K. (2001d). *Teen-proofing: Fostering responsible decision making in your teenager.* Kansas City, MO: Andrews and McMeel.

Rosemond, J. K. (2003a, May 17). ADHD? Sure but it's not organic. *The San Diego Union-Tribune,* p. E9.

Rosemond, J. K. (2003b, November 27). It's OK to discipline adopted child. *The Annapolis Capital,* p. C1.

Rosenthal, R. (1978). Combining results of independent studies. *Psychological Bulletin, 85,* 185–193.

Rothbaum, F., & Weisz, J. R. (1994). Parental caregiving and child externalizing behavior in non-clinical samples: A meta-analysis. *Psychological Bulletin, 116,* 55–74.

Rowe, D. C. (1994). *The limits of family influence: Genes, experience, and behavior.* New York: Guilford Press.

Rowe, D. C., Vazsonyi, A. T., & Flannery, D. J. (1994). No more than skin deep: Ethnic and racial similarity in developmental process. *Psychological Review, 101,* 396–413.

Rowe, D. C., Woulbroun, E. J., & Gulley, B. L. (1994). Peers and friends as non-shared environmental influences. In E. M. Hetherington, D. Reiss, & R. Plomin (Eds.), *Separate social worlds of siblings: The impact of nonshared environment on development* (pp. 159–173). Hillsdale, NJ: Erlbaum.

Runco, M. A., & Pezdek, K. (1984). The effect of television and radio on children's creativity. *Human Communication Research, 11,* 109–120.

Scal, P., Ireland, M., & Borowsky, I. W. (2003). Smoking among American adolescents: A risk and protective factor analysis. *Journal of Community Health, 28,* 79–97.

Scarr, S. (1992). Developmental theories for the 1990's: Development and individual differences. *Child Development, 63,* 1–19.

Scarr, S., & McCartney, K. (1983). How people make their own environments: A theory of genotype-environment effects. *Child Development, 54,* 424–435.

Schneider, W. J., Cavell, T. V., & Hughes, J. N. (2003). A sense of containment: Potential moderator of the relation between parenting practices and children's externalizing behaviors. *Development and Psychopathology, 15,* 95–117.

Schor, E. L. (Ed.). (1999). *Caring for your school-age child: Ages 5 to 12.* New York: Bantam Books.

Schum, T. R., McAuliffe, T. L., Simms, M. D., Walter, J. A., Lewis, M., & Pupp, R. (2001). Factors associated with toilet training in the 1990s. *Ambulatory Pediatrics, 2,* 79–86.

Schuster, M. A., Duan, N., Regalado, M., & Klein, D. J. (2000). Anticipatory guidance: What information do parents receive? What information do they want? *Archives of Pediatrics & Adolescent Medicine, 151,* 1191–1198.

Schwartz, C. A., & Turner, R. L. (1994). *Encyclopedia of associations: Vol. 1* (29th ed.). Detroit, MI: Gale Research.

Sears, R. R., Maccoby, E. E., & Levin, H. (1957). *Patterns of child rearing.* Evanston, IL: Row, Peterson, & Company.

Sears, W., & Sears, M. (2003). *The baby book: Everything you need to know about your baby—from birth to age two* (2nd ed.). New York: Little, Brown.

Seim, H. C. (1989). Toilet training in first children. *Journal of Family Practice, 29,* 633–636.

Shedler, J., & Block, J. (1990). Adolescent drug use and psychological health: A longitudinal inquiry. *American Psychologist, 45,* 612–630.

Sheehan, R. (1999, April 11). Parenting: Was Dr. Spock wrong? *The Raleigh News and Observer,* p. A23.

Shelov, S. P. (Ed.). (1998). *Caring for your baby and child: Birth to age 5.* New York: Bantam Books.

Sherry, J. L. (2001). The effects of violent video games on aggression: A meta-analysis. *Human Communication Research, 27,* 409–431.

Showers, G. C., & Cantor, V. (1985). Social cognition: A look at motivated strategies. *Annual Review of Psychology, 36,* 275–305.

Silvern, S. B., & Williamson, P. A. (1987). The effects of video game play on young children's aggression, fantasy, and prosocial behavior. *Journal of Applied Developmental Psychology, 8,* 453–462.

Simpson, A. R. (1997). *The role of the mass media in parenting education.* Boston: Harvard School of Public Health, Center for Health Communication. Retrieved December 29, 2003, from http://www.hsph.harvard.edu/chc/parenting/massmedia.html.

Simpson, A. R. (2001). *Raising teens: A synthesis of research and a foundation for action.* Boston: Harvard School of Public Health, Center for Health Communication. Retrieved January 31, 2005, from http://www.hsph.harvard.edu/chc/parenting/raising.html.

Slater, M. D. (2003). Alienation, aggression, and sensation seeking as predictors of adolescent use of violent film, computer, and website content. *Journal of Communication, 53,* 105–121.

Smith, A. M., & O'Leary, S. G. (1995). Attributions and arousal as predictors of maternal discipline. *Cognitive Therapy and Research, 19,* 459–471.

Sniderman, A. D. (1999). Clinical trials, consensus conferences, and clinical practice. *The Lancet, 354,* 327.

Snyder, J., & Patterson, G. R. (1995). Individual differences in social aggression: A test of a reinforcement model of socialization in the natural environment. *Behavior Therapy, 26,* 371–391.

Spencer, J.A.D., Moran, D.J., Lee, A., & Talbert, D. (1990). White noise and sleep induction. *Archives of Disease in Childhood, 65,* 135–137.

Spitz, R.A. (1946). Anaclitic depression. *Psychoanalytic Study of the Child, 2,* 313–342.

Spock, B. (1946). *Pocket book of baby and child care.* New York: Pocket Books.

Spock, B. (1970). *A teenager's guide to life and love.* New York: Simon & Schuster.

Spock, B. (1994). *A better world for our children: Rebuilding American family values.* Bethesda, MD: National Press Books.

Spock, B., & Morgan, M. (1989). *Spock on Spock.* New York: Pantheon Books.

Spock, B., & Needlman, R. (2004). *Dr. Spock's baby and child care* (8th ed.). New York: Pocket Books.

Spock, B., & Parker, S.J. (1998). *Dr. Spock's baby and child care* (7th ed.). New York: Pocket Books.

Spock, B., & Rothenberg, M.B. (1992). *Dr. Spock's baby and child care* (6th ed.). New York: Pocket Books.

St. James-Roberts, I. (1993a). Explanations of persistent infant crying. In I. St. James-Roberts, G. Harris, & D. Messer (Eds.), *Infant crying, feeding, and sleeping: Development, problems, and treatments* (pp. 26–46). London: Harvester Wheatsheaf.

St. James-Roberts, I. (1993b). Infant crying: Normal development and persistent crying. In I. St. James-Roberts, G. Harris, & D. Messer (Eds.), *Infant crying, feeding, and sleeping: Development, problems, and treatments* (pp. 7–25). London: Harvester Wheatsheaf.

St. James-Roberts, I. (2001a). Infant crying and its impact on parents. In R.G. Barr, I. St. James-Roberts, & M.R. Keefe (Eds.), *New evidence on unexplained early infant crying: Its origins, nature, and management* (pp. 5–24). Calverton, NY: Johnson & Johnson Pediatric Institute.

St. James-Roberts, I. (2001b). Summary: What do we know? What are the implications of the findings for practitioners? What do we need to know? In R.G. Barr, I. St. James-Roberts, & M.R. Keefe (Eds.), *New evidence on unexplained early infant crying: Its origins, nature, and management* (pp. 327–333). Calverton, NY: Johnson & Johnson Pediatric Institute.

St. James-Roberts, I., Conroy, S., & Wilsher, K. (1995). Clinical, developmental, and social aspects of infant crying and colic. *Early Development and Parenting, 4,* 177–189.

St. James-Roberts, I., & Halil, T. (1991). Infant crying patterns in the first year: Normal community and clinical findings. *Journal of Child Psychology and Psychiatry, 32,* 951–968.

St. James-Roberts, I., Hurry, J., Bowyer, J., & Barr, R.G. (1995). Supplementary carrying compared with advice to increase responsive parenting as interventions to prevent persistent infant crying. *Pediatrics, 95,* 381–388.

St. Peters, M., Fitch, M., Huston, A.C., Wright, J.C., & Eakins, D.J. (1991). Television and families: What do young children watch with their parents? *Child Development, 62,* 1409–1423.

Stadtler, A. C., Gorski, P. A., & Brazelton, T. B. (1999). Toilet training methods, clinical interventions, and recommendations. *Pediatrics, 103,* 1359–1368.

Stafford, T. (1988, April 28). His father's son. *Christianity Today, 20,* 16–22.

Stattin, H., & Kerr, M. (2001). Parental monitoring: A reinterpretation. *Child Development, 71,* 1072–1075.

Stehbens, J. A., & Silber, D. L. (1971). Parental expectations in toilet training. *Pediatrics, 48,* 451–454.

Steinberg, L. (1996). *Why school reform has failed and what parents need to do.* New York: Simon & Schuster.

Steinberg, L. (2004). *The ten basic principles of good parenting.* New York: Simon & Schuster.

Steinberg, L., Lamborn, S. D., Darling, N., Mounts, N. S., & Dornbusch, S. M. (1994). Over-time changes in adjustment and competence among adolescents from authoritative, authoritarian, indulgent, and neglectful families. *Child Development, 65,* 754–770.

Steinfels, P. (1990, June 5). No church, no ministry, no pulpit, he is called religious right's star. *The New York Times,* p. A22.

Stenhouse, G. (1988). Toilet training in children. *New Zealand Medical Journal, 101,* 150–151.

Stephens, J. A., & Silber, D. L. (1974). Parental expectations vs. outcome in toilet training. *Pediatrics, 54,* 493–495.

Stickler, G. B., Salter, M., Broughton, D. D., & Alario, A. (1991). Parents' worries about children compared to actual risks. *Clinical Pediatrics, 30,* 522–528.

Stifter, C. A., & Braungart, J. (1992). Infant colic: A transient condition with no apparent effects. *Journal of Applied Developmental Psychology, 13,* 447–462.

Stoolmiller, M., Patterson, G. R., & Snyder, J. (1997). Parental discipline and child antisocial behavior: A contingency-based theory and some methodological refinements. *Psychological Inquiry, 8,* 223–229.

Stranger, J. D. (1997). *Television in the home 1997: The second annual survey of parents and children.* Philadephia, PA: Annenberg Public Policy Center.

Strassberg, Z., Dodge, K. A., Pettit, G. S., & Bates, J. E. (1994). Spanking in the home and children's subsequent aggression toward kindergarten peers. *Development and Psychopathology, 6,* 445–461.

Straus, M. A. (1994). *Beating the devil out of them: Corporal punishment in American families.* New York: Lexington.

Straus, M. A., & Stewart, J. H. (1999). Corporal punishment by American parents: National data on prevalence, chronicity, severity, and duration, in relation to child and family characteristics. *Clinical Child and Family Psychology Review, 2,* 55–70.

Taubman, B. (1988). Parental counseling compared with elimination of cow's milk or soy milk protein for the treatment of infant colic syndrome: A randomized trial. *Pediatrics, 81,* 756–761.

Taubman, B. (1997). Toilet training and toilet refusal for stool only: A prospective study. *Pediatrics, 99,* 54–58.

Thomas, A., Chess, S., & Birch, H. G. (1968). *Temperament and behavior disorders in children.* New York: New York University Press.

Thomas, M. H., & Drabman, R. S. (1975). Toleration of real life aggression as a function of exposure to televised violence and age of subject. *Merrill-Palmer Quarterly, 21,* 227–232.

Tower, R. B., Singer, D. G., Singer, J. L., & Biggs, A. (1979). Differential effects of television programming on preschoolers' cognition, imagination, and social play. *American Journal of Orthopsychiatry, 49,* 265–281.

Tremblay, R. E., Masse, L. C., Pagani, L., & Vitaro, F. (1996). From childhood physical aggression to adolescent maladjustment. In R. DeV. Peters & R. J. McMahon (Eds.), *Preventing childhood disorders, substance, abuse, and delinquency* (pp. 268–298). Thousand Oaks, CA: Sage.

True, W. R., Xian, H., Scherrer, J. F., Madden, P. A., Bucholz, K. K., Heath, A., et al. (1999). Common genetic vulnerability for nicotine and alcohol dependence in men. *Archives of General Psychiatry, 56,* 655–661.

U.S. Census Bureau. (1998). *Statistical abstract of the United States: 1998* (118th ed.). Washington, DC: Author.

Valkenburg, P. M. (2001). Television and the child's developing imagination. In D. G. Singer & J. L. Singer (Eds.), *Handbook of children and the media* (pp. 121–134). Thousand Oaks, CA: Sage.

van den Bree, M.B.M., Whitmer, M. D., & Pickworth, W. B. (2004). Predictors of smoking development in a population-based sample of adolescents: A prospective study. *Journal of Adolescent Health, 35,* 172–181.

van IJzendoorn, M. H., Goldberg, S., Kroonenberg, P. M., & Frenkel, O.J. (1992). The relative effects of maternal and child problems on the quality of attachment: A meta-analysis of attachment in clinical samples. *Child Development, 63,* 840–858.

Vandell, D. L., & Corasaniti, M. A. (1990a). Child care and the family: Complex contributors to child development. *New Directions for Child Development, 49,* 23–37.

Vandell, D. L., & Corasaniti, M. A. (1990b). Variations in early child care: Do they predict subsequent social, emotional, and cognitive differences? *Early Childhood Research Quarterly, 5,* 555–572.

Vandell, D. L., Dadisman, K., & Gallagher, K. (2000). Another look at the elephant: Child care in the nineties. In R. D. Taylor & M. C. Wang (Eds.), *Resilience across contexts: Family, work, culture, and community* (pp. 91–120). Mahwah, NJ: Erlbaum.

Vierhaus, R. (1973–1974). Conservatism. In P. P. Wiener (Ed.), *Dictionary of the history of ideas.* New York: Charles Scribner's Sons.

Vuchinich, S., Bank, L., & Patterson, G. R. (1992). Parenting, peers, and the stability of antisocial behavior in preadolescent boys. *Developmental Psychology, 28,* 510–521.

Walsh, D., Goldman, I. S., & Brown, R. (1996). *A Physician's guide to media violence.* Chicago: American Medical Association.

Watamura, S. E., Donzella, B., Alwin, J., & Gunnar, M. (2003). Morning to afternoon increases in cortisol concentrations for infants and toddlers at child care: Age differences and behavioral correlates. *Child Development, 74,* 1006–1020.

Watamura, S. E., Sebanc, A. M., & Gunnar, M. R. (2002). Rising cortisol at child-care: Relations with nap, rest, and temperament. *Developmental Psychobiology, 40,* 33–42.

Watkins, B., Calvert, S., Huston-Stein, A., & Wright, J. C. (1980). Children's recall of television material: Effects of presentation mode and adult labeling. *Developmental Psychology, 16,* 672–674.

Watson, J. B. (1928). *Psychological care of the infant and child.* New York: Norton.

Way, N., Stauber, H. Y., Nakkula, M. J., & London, P. (1994). Depression and substance use in two divergent high school cultures: A quantitative and qualitative analysis. *Journal of Youth and Adolescence, 23,* 331–357.

Weiss, B., Dodge, K. A., Bates, J. E., & Pettit, G. S. (1992). Some consequences of early harsh discipline: Child aggression and a maladaptive social information processing style. *Child Development, 63,* 1321–1335.

Weiss, C. H. (1985, March/April). Media report card for social science. *Society, 22,* 39–47.

Wells, K. B. (1999). Treatment research at the crossroads: The scientific interface of clinical trials and effectiveness research. *American Journal of Psychiatry, 156,* 5–10.

Werner, E. E., & Smith, R. S. (1992). *Overcoming the odds: High risk children from birth to adulthood.* Ithaca, NY: Cornell University Press.

Wessel, M. A., Cobb, J. C., Jackson, E. B., Harris, G. S., & Detwiler, A. C. (1954). Paroxysmal fussing in infancy, sometimes called "colic." *Pediatrics, 14,* 421–435.

Whitbeck, L. B., Conger, R. D., & Kao, M. (1993). The influence of parental support, depressed affect, and peers on the sexual behaviors of adolescent girls. *Journal of Family Issues, 14,* 261–278.

Whitbeck, L. B., Hoyt, D., Miller, M., & Kao, M. (1992). Parental support, depressed affect, and sexual experience among adolescents. *Youth & Society, 24,* 166–177.

Whitbeck, L. B., Yoder, K. A., Hoyt, D. R., & Conger, R. D. (1999). Early adolescent sexual activity: A developmental study. *Journal of Marriage and the Family, 61,* 934–946.

White, B. P., Gunnar, M. R., Larson, M. C., Donzella, B., & Barr, R. G. (2000). Behavioral and physiological responsivity, sleep, and patterns of daily cortisol production in infants with and without colic. *Child Development, 71,* 862–877.

Wilkie, C. F., & Ames, E. W. (1986). The relationship of infant crying to parental stress in the transition to parenthood. *Journal of Marriage and the Family, 48,* 545–550.

Williams, P. A., Haertel, E. H., Walberg, H. J., & Haertel, G. D. (1982). The impact of leisure-time television on school learning: A research synthesis. *American Educational Research Journal, 19,* 19–50.

Wills, T. A., & Cleary, S. D. (1999). Peer and adolescent substance use among 6th–9th graders: Latent growth analyses of influence versus selection mechanisms. *Health Psychology, 18,* 453–463.

Wills, T. A., Gibbons, F. X., Gerrard, M., Murry, V. M., & Brody, G. H. (2003). Family communication and religiosity related to substance use and sexual behavior in early adolescence: A test for pathways through self-control and protoype perceptions. *Psychology of Addictive Behaviors, 17,* 312–323.

Wills, T. A., McNamara, G., Vaccaro, D., & Hirky, A. E. (1996). Escalated substance use: A longitudinal grouping analysis from early to middle adolescence. *Journal of Abnormal Psychology, 105,* 166–180.

Wills, T. A., Resko, J. A., Ainette, M. G., & Mendoza, D. (2004). Smoking onset in adolescence: A person-centered analysis with time-varying predictors. *Health Psychology, 23,* 158–167.

Wilson, B. J., Smith, S. L., Potter, W. J., Kunkel, D., Linz, D., Colvin, C. M., et al. (2002). Violence in children's television programming: Assessing the risks. *Journal of Communication, 52,* 5–35.

Wolff, P. H. (1969). The natural history of crying and other vocalizations in early infancy. In B. M. Foss (Ed.), *Determinants of infant behavior* (Vol. 4, pp. 89–109). New York: Barnes & Noble.

Wolke, D. (1993). The treatment of problem crying behavior. In I. St. James-Roberts, G. Harris, & D. Messer (Eds.), *Infant crying, feeding, and sleeping: Development, problems, and treatments* (pp. 47–79). London: Harvester Wheatsheaf.

Wolke, D., Gray, P., & Meyer, R. (1994). Excessive infant crying: A controlled study of mothers helping mothers. *Pediatrics, 94,* 322–332.

Wood, W., Wong, F. Y., & Chachere, J. G. (1991). Effects of media violence on viewers' aggression in unconstrained social interaction. *Psychological Bulletin, 109,* 371–383.

Woodard, E. H., & Gridina, N. (2000). *Media in the home 2000: Fifth annual survey of parents and children.* Retrieved October 24, 2002, from the University of Pennsylvania, Annenberg Public Policy Center Web site: http://www.appcpen.org/mediainhome/survey7.pdf.

Young, K. T. (1990). American conceptions of infant development from 1955 to 1984: What the experts are telling parents. *Child Development, 61,* 17–28.

Young, K. T., Davis, K., Schoen, C., & Parker, S. (1998). Listening to parents: A national survey of parents with young children. *Archives of Pediatric & Adolescent Medicine, 152,* 255–262.

Zeskind, P. S., Sale, J., Maio, M. L., Huntington, L., & Weiseman, J. R. (1985). Adult perceptions of pain and hunger cries: A synchrony of arousal. *Child Development, 56,* 549–554.

Zill, N. (2001). Does *Sesame Street* enhance school readiness? Evidence from a national survey of children. In S. M. Fisch & R. T. Truglio (Eds.), *"G" is for growing* (pp. 115–130). Mahwah, NJ: Erlbaum.

INDEX

About the Author

JANE L. RANKIN has taught and conducted research in developmental psychology for twenty-five years. A former Professor of Psychology and Chair of the Psychology Department at Drake University, she is now Associate Dean for Research in the School of Communication at Northwestern University. Much of her research has focused on stereotyping, self-consciousness, and memory in children, adolescents, and older adults. She is the mother of two college-age children.